Brokers, Voters, and Clientelism

Brokers, Voters, and Clientelism addresses major questions in ~~~~~~~~~
is it acceptable for parties to try to win elections by promising to make certain groups of people better off, but unacceptable – and illegal – to pay people for their votes? Why do parties often lavish benefits on loyal voters, whose support they can count on anyway, rather than on responsive swing voters? Why are vote buying and machine politics common in today's developing democracies but a thing of the past in most of today's advanced democracies? This book develops a theory of broker-mediated distribution to answer these questions, testing the theory with research from four developing democracies, and reviews a rich secondary literature on countries in all world regions. The authors deploy normative theory to evaluate whether clientelism, pork-barrel politics, and other nonprogrammatic distributive strategies can be justified on the grounds that they promote efficiency, redistribution, or voter participation.

Susan C. Stokes is John S. Saden Professor of Political Science at Yale University and Director of the Yale Program on Democracy. She is a member of the American Academy of Arts and Sciences, a past vice president of the American Political Science Association (APSA), and a past president of APSA's Comparative Politics Section. Her books and articles explore democratization and how democracy works in developing countries. Her research has been supported by grants and fellowships from the National Science Foundation, the Guggenheim Memorial Foundation, the Russell Sage Foundation, the American Philosophical Society, the MacArthur Foundation, and Fulbright programs.

Thad Dunning is Professor of Political Science at Yale University. He studies comparative politics, political economy, and methodology. His first book, *Crude Democracy: Natural Resource Wealth and Political Regimes* (Cambridge University Press, 2008), won the Best Book Award from the Comparative Democratization Section of APSA and the Gaddis Smith Prize for the best first book on an international topic by a member of the Yale faculty. Dunning has also written on a range of methodological topics; his second book, *Natural Experiments in the Social Sciences: A Design-Based Approach* (Cambridge University Press, 2012), develops a framework for the discovery, analysis, and evaluation of strong research designs.

Marcelo Nazareno is Professor of Political Science at the National University of Córdoba and Professor of Methodology and Public Policy at the Catholic University of Córdoba. He holds a PhD in social science as well as advanced degrees in public administration and in history. He has been a visiting researcher at Yale University and the University of Chicago. His publications, in journals such as *Desarrollo Económico* and the *Latin American Research Review*, touch on the themes of the left in Latin America, clientelism and distributive politics, and fiscal federalism.

Valeria Brusco holds a master's degree in international relations and is completing her doctoral dissertation at the National University of San Martín in Buenos Aires. She is interested in how organizational agents, whether in political parties or in nongovernmental organizations, deal with poverty, and she has published articles on this topic as well as on competitive clientelism. She teaches at the National University of Córdoba and at the Catholic University of Córdoba, Argentina. Brusco has also held a staff post in the municipal government of the city of Córdoba, is active in party politics in Argentina, and helps lead a sports organization for underprivileged youth.

Cambridge Studies in Comparative Politics

General Editor

Margaret Levi   *University of Washington, Seattle*

Assistant General Editors

Kathleen Thelen   *Massachusetts Institute of Technology*
Erik Wibbels   *Duke University*

Associate Editors

Robert H. Bates   *Harvard University*
Gary Cox   *Stanford University*
Stephen Hanson   *The College of William and Mary*
Torben Iversen   *Harvard University*
Stathis Kalyvas   *Yale University*
Peter Lange   *Duke University*
Helen Milner   *Princeton University*
Frances Rosenbluth   *Yale University*
Susan Stokes   *Yale University*

Other Books in the Series

Continued after the Index

Brokers, Voters, and Clientelism

The Puzzle of Distributive Politics

SUSAN C. STOKES
Yale University

THAD DUNNING
Yale University

MARCELO NAZARENO
Universidad Nacional de Córdoba

VALERIA BRUSCO
Universidad Nacional de Córdoba

CAMBRIDGE
UNIVERSITY PRESS

CAMBRIDGE
UNIVERSITY PRESS

32 Avenue of the Americas, New York, NY 10013-2473, USA

Cambridge University Press is part of the University of Cambridge.

It furthers the University's mission by disseminating knowledge in the pursuit of education, learning, and research at the highest international levels of excellence.

www.cambridge.org
Information on this title: www.cambridge.org/9781107660397

© Susan C. Stokes, Thad Dunning, Marcelo Nazareno, and Valeria Brusco 2013

First published 2013

Printed in the United States of America

A catalog record for this publication is available from the British Library.

Library of Congress Cataloging in Publication data
Stokes, Susan Carol.
Brokers, voters, and clientelism : the puzzle of distributive politics / Susan C. Stokes, Yale University, Thad Dunning, Yale University, Marcelo Nazareno, National University of Córdoba, Argentina, Valeria Brusco, National University of Córdoba, Argentina.
    pages cm. – (Cambridge studies in comparative politics)
Includes bibliographical references and index.
ISBN 978-1-107-04220-9 (hardback) – ISBN 978-1-107-66039-7 (pbk.)
1. Political planning – Economic aspects. 2. Politics, Practical – Economic aspects. 3. Political science – Economic aspects. 4. Finance, Public – Political aspects. 5. Economic policy – Political aspects. 6. Political ethics. I. Title.
JF1525.P6S76 2013
324–dc23   2013007954

Cambridge University Press has no responsibility for the persistence or accuracy of URLs for external or third-party Internet Web sites referred to in this publication and does not guarantee that any content on such Web sites is, or will remain, accurate or appropriate.

Sue: My deep appreciation goes to my sons, Sam, David, and Andy, whose curiosity about the world is inspiring, and to Steve Pincus, wonderful scholar and wonderful husband.

Thad: I give my heartfelt thanks to my family, and especially my partner Jennifer, for the humor, kindness, and patience on which I so rely.

Marcelo: I wish to express special gratitude to Laura and to our children, Santiago, Diego, Lautaro, and Lucía, for their patience and support during these years.

Valeria: I wish to thank Mateo y Lucía, my kids, because they walked (and traveled) with me.

Contents

List of Tables

List of Figures

Preface and Acknowledgments

When Sue Stokes first met Valeria Brusco and Marcelo Nazareno, at an academic conference in Buenos Aires, Valeria's newborn baby, Lucía, slept quietly in a carrier by her mother's side. Thad Dunning, as yet unknown to the rest of us, was just beginning graduate school.

Now Lucía Allende Brusco is a strapping teenager. She is learning Italian and likes jazz dance and boys. Thad is a tenured professor. In other words, it took us a long time to write this book.

Many things delay the completion of academic books. Classes must be taught, programs administered, other research projects attended to, children raised. But there are additional reasons for the delayed completion of this particular book.

More so than is usually the case, we were repeatedly stumped by evidence that did not fit received theories – or even common sense. The book is about distributive politics. The received theories usually predict that parties and governments will spend scarce resources on responsive voters. And these responsive voters will be fence-sitters, people who might otherwise not turn out or vote for the party responsible for the distribution but who could be swayed by a favor or a program. Yet over and over again, the evidence seemed to tell us that not fence-sitters but firm party loyalists were the primary beneficiaries of the distributive game.

Because we believed in the received theories, we discarded them only reluctantly. Like good Kuhnians, a few anomalies did not shift our paradigm. But eventually the weight of the anomalies was too much. Constructing an alternative theory was only one of the tasks we faced. Our new theory suggested new questions and new observational implications. Many parties can be decomposed into leaders and low-level operatives or brokers. If brokers play the distributive game by different rules than do their leaders, allocations of resources should come out differently when brokers are in control and when leaders are in control. (They do.) If brokers are imperfect agents of party leaders, anti-machine reform movements, when they break out, may be driven as much by party leaders as by non-partisan reformers. (In several countries, they have been.) And if brokers are imperfect agents, it should be the case that they impose agency losses on parties and parties should devise elaborate techniques to monitor the brokers and minimize these losses. (We offer evidence that both are true.)

If our theoretical deconstruction, reconstruction, and testing took time, this was not for lack of help from many people. A large international network of scholars has been at work on topics directly related to our own, and we have benefited enormously from their research, insights, and criticisms. This network includes Herbert Kitschelt, Beatriz Magaloni, Alberto Diaz-Cayeros, Federico Estévez, María Victoria Murillo, Ernesto Calvo, Luis Fernando Medina, Frederick Schaffer, Allen Hicken, James Robinson, Rebecca Weitz-Shapiro, Philip Keefer, Norma Álvarez, Yolanda Urquiza, Simeon Nichter, Germán Lodola, Dominika Koter, Nicholas Van de Walle, Kanchan Chandra, Steven Wilkinson, Carles Boix, Steve Levitsky, Kasper Lippert-Rasmussen, Arnoldo Rosenfeld, Eddie Camp, and Mariela Szwarcberg. The manuscript went through no fewer than three book conferences, probably a record. The first was at Nuffield College, Oxford, where Iaian McLean, Jörgen Weibull, Peyton Young, and Avinash Dixit discussed it. The second was at the Juan March Institute in Madrid and involved José María Maravall, Ignacio Sánchez-Cuenca, Nasos Roussias, Jan Teorrell, Miriam Golden, Alberto Diaz-Cayeros, Susan Hyde, Alberto Simpser, Ken Greene, and David Rueda. Finally, a University of Washington–Cambridge University Press "Seattle Seminar" included Margaret Levi, Dan Posner, Gary Cox, Brad Epperly, Adam Forman, Barry Pump, and Carolina Johnson.

Other scholars commented on all or parts of the manuscript: Alejandro Bonvecchi, Catalina Shmulovitz, Germán Lodola, Ana María Mustapic, Carlos Gervasoni, Ernesto Calvo, Marcelo Cavarozzi, Noam Lupu, Jim Alt, Giovanni Capoccia, and Avia Pasternak. We have received invaluable advice from several Yale colleagues: David Mayhew, John Roemer, Steven Wilkinson, Ian Shapiro, Don Green, Ellen Lust, Susan Hyde, Luis Schiumerini, Peter Swenson, Alex Debs, and Libby Wood, and – through the Yale Program on Democracy – from Ana De la O, Tariq Thachil, Sigrun Kahl, Adria Lawrence, Hélène Landemore, Marcelo Leiras, César Zucco, Liz Carlson, and Kristin McKie. Our collaboration with Edwin Camp at Yale – who is himself doing path-breaking research on broker-mediated distribution and the logic of clientelist distribution – has been highly rewarding, and he has provided many insightful comments and contributions along the way.

For their work on our voter surveys in Argentina, we are grateful to Mario Riordá and to Gustavo Córdoba of Consultores en Políticas Públicas. We had a terrific set of research assistants, including William Hennessy, Maricel López, Marcos Meyer, Damián Aldama, Laura Valdemarca, Lucas Lázaro, Jeremías Vanoli, Lis Tous, Lucía Nieva, Dolores Najera, Pablo Soffietti, Selva Vázquez, Silvana Oliveira, Valeria Vázquez, Lisandro Podio, Carolina Caeiro,

Ignacio César, Victoria Paniagua, Ignacio Puente, Luis Cecchi, Federico Fuchs, Andrea Flores, Jorge Pyke, Gabriella Albrecht, Eveli Wellbach, Marcela Octacio, Andrea Zadorozne, María Elena Martin, Hilario Moreno, and Gloria Trocello. Victoria Paniagua helped facilitate our interviews with Argentine politicians at the national, provincial, and municipal levels. We are also grateful to Joel Middleton and Edwin Camp for writing a Stata routine to implement the bootstrap procedure described in Appendix A.

We are grateful to many colleagues and collaborators who facilitated our research in Venezuela. The data collection documented in Appendix C was greatly facilitated by the able research assistance of Giuseppe Rionero and Stefania Vitale; our voter survey was implemented by the survey firm DATOS under the direction of Odaliz Salcedo. We organized a conference at Yale in 2007, "The Popular Sectors and the State in Chávez's Venezuela," at which we received helpful comments from Sujatha Fernandes, Kirk Hawkins, Margarita López Maya, Daniel Ortega, Francisco Rodríguez, and Jason Seawright. Francisco Rodríguez generously helped us to navigate the Maisanta data we use in Chapter 2. We are also grateful to Carlos Ocariz and Mariana Giménez de Ocariz and especially Carlos Lagorio for facilitating some of our field research in Venezuela, and we thank Dorothy Kronick, Francisco Monaldi, Richard Obuchi, and Michael Penfold for sharing their many insights over the years.

For their assistance with the India surveys, we thank Bhartendu Trivedi and his survey team at MORSEL, who implemented our surveys in Bihar and Rajasthan, and Padmavathi B. S. and her researchers from Bangalore University, who implemented our survey in Karnataka. For their many helpful suggestions and comments on our research in India, we thank Abhijit Banerjee, David Blakeslee, Kanchan Chandra, Simon Chauchard, Miriam Golden, Rajeev Gowda, Don Green, Macartan Humphreys, Lakshmi Iyer, Francesca Jensenius, Trevor Johnston, Evan Lieberman, Drew Linzer, Jim Manor, SS Meenakshisundaram, Brian Min, Vipin Narang, Vijayendra Rao, Prerna Singh, Sandeep Shastri, Pavithra Suryanarayan, Ashutosh Varshney, Steven Wilkinson, Adam Ziegfeld, and especially Jennifer Bussell. Seminar participants at IIM-Bangalore, Dartmouth, Essex, the London School of Economics, Michigan, Oxford, Princeton, Yale, UCLA, and the Harvard-MIT-Brown Seminar on South Asian Politics generously commented on the research from which we draw in Chapters 2 and 4.

Gary Cox and Allen Hicken reviewed the manuscript for Cambridge University Press and offered many helpful suggestions. We are grateful to both of them for their careful reviews. We also thank our editor, Lew Bateman, and the Cambridge Studies in Comparative Politics series editor, Margaret Levi, for their patience and encouragement. Our thanks as well to Shaun Vigil of Cambridge University Press and to Adrian Pereira of Aptara, Inc. for overseeing the editing and production processes.

We are grateful to a number of institutions for their support. The Whitney and Betty MacMillan Center for International and Area Studies at Yale has been very generous. We are indebted to the MacMillan Center's director, Ian

Shapiro, both intellectually and institutionally. We are also grateful to Yale's Institute for Social and Policy Studies and its directors, Don Green and Jacob Hacker, for their support. The research was also supported by a National Science Foundation research grant (SES-0241958). We presented our work at Yale's Comparative Politics Workshop and received excellent suggestions from participants, including our discussant Erdem Aytac. Thad Dunning visited at the University of Texas at Austin during a research leave in which he worked on this book and was grateful for interactions with Kurt Weyland, Wendy Hunter, Ken Greene, Zach Elkins, Jason Brownlee, Raul Madrid, Dan Brinks, Peter Ward, and Victoria Rodriguez. Sue Stokes received a fellowship from the John Simon Guggenheim Memorial Foundation in support of this research. She also spent a year as a Visiting Fellow at Nuffield College, Oxford. Oxford colleagues David Butler, Nancy Bermeo, Ray Duch, Desmond King, Diego Gambetta, David Miller, Meg Meyer, David Rueda, Pablo Beremendi, Giovanni Capoccia, and David Soskice provided a stimulating and welcoming environment.

PART I

MODALITIES OF DISTRIBUTIVE POLITICS

1

Between Clients and Citizens: Puzzles and Concepts in the Study of Distributive Politics

Markets distribute goods. The drive to earn and to consume moves steel from Anshan to Minnesota, nannies from Brixton to Hampstead, and credit from Wall Street to Athens. Indeed, the movement of steel, nannies, and credit is in a sense what markets – for goods, services, and finance – *are*.

Politics also distributes goods. Government programs channel cash, jobs, credit, and myriad other resources to citizens; elected officials mete out benefits to favored constituencies; and political parties distribute everything from leaflets to liquor in search of votes. And taxes and transfers redistribute income.

The political distribution of goods is more controversial than is their distribution through markets. We expect markets to move valued resources across space and populations. But while few would object to all forms of political distribution, nearly all would object to some forms of it. In any democracy there is broad agreement (though not consensus) that political authority rightly transfers resources across generations by using tax proceeds to fund the education of children or protect of the elderly from penury. Agreement about redistribution through social welfare programs and insurance against social risk is also broad, though far from universal. However, other kinds of political distribution and redistribution – contracts that go to politically connected private firms, for instance, or cash payments in return for votes – are broadly reviled. Indeed, although some forms of political distribution are unquestioningly accepted, others are punishable with prison terms.

Political authorities make choices about distribution. When these authorities' hold on office depends on their winning elections, their choices become bound up with political strategies. And the modes of strategic distribution vary widely. For a sense of this variation, consider some examples.

Progresa/Oportunidades, **Mexico.** A federal antipoverty program in Mexico, *Progresa* (later called *Oportunidades*), distributes cash to 2.5 million

3

families. As De la O explains, "The resources of the program and the formula to allocate them are described in detail in the federal budget, which is proposed by the president but approved in the Chamber of Deputies."[1] Cash goes to mothers in families whose household income is in the bottom two deciles of the national distribution and who keep their children in school and take them for medical checkups. An agency of the federal government administers *Progresa/Oportunidades*. Beneficiaries have bank accounts, linked to ATM-style cards, into which the funds are deposited. Compliance with legal criteria of distribution is audited through random-sample surveys and is high: the criteria for inclusion closely match the profile of beneficiaries.[2]

Emergency Food Aid, Argentina. A municipal social worker in a provincial town in Argentina receives, one by one, townspeople lined up outside her office door. They are seeking to be placed on a list of beneficiaries for an emergency food program. The social worker's desk is replete with photographs of Juan Domingo Perón and Evita Perón, founders of the mayor's party. The mayor's office repeatedly intervenes to check the list, modifying it in ways that will generate votes. Weitz-Shapiro, who interviewed the social worker and studied the program, found partisan intervention to modify recipient lists of beneficiaries in 85 of the 127 municipalities she studied.[3]

La Efectiva, **Mexico.** As part of his 2011 campaign for the governorship of the State of Mexico, the Institutional Revolutionary Party (PRI) candidate, Eruviel Ávila, signed voters up at campaign events for another ATM-style card, this one called "*La Efectiva*," The Effective One. If he won, Ávila promised, card holders would receive payments that could be used toward two out of a long list of promised statewide programs, including health care and food support for women; educational, sports, and cultural scholarships; old-age pensions; home improvement projects; and agricultural subsidies. The campaign distributed more than 2 million cards. The effort elicited personal appeals from residents, some posted on Ávila's website. "Denise," for instance, wrote, "Good afternoon, Eruviel! I'm a high school student and I wish to ask your help to get a scholarship. I have an excellent grade point average..."[4]

Housing Improvement Program, Singapore. The government of Singapore invested heavily in improvements and maintenance of housing and openly used the program as a tool to reward constituencies who voted for the ruling party (People's Action Party [PAP]) and punish those who voted for the opposition. As Tam reported, in 1985 the National Development Minister, Teh Cheang Wan, explained in a news conference that "we must look after PAP

---

[1] De la O 2012, p. 39.

[2] See especially De la O 2012. See also Fiszbein and Schady 2009.

[3] Weitz-Shapiro 2011.

[4] See *La Jornada*, 26 September 2011. The campaign's URL is http://eruviel.com/mi-blog/piensa-en-grande-con-la-efectiva.

constituencies first because the majority of the people supported us." When an opposition Member of Parliament inquired about the treatment of residents who voted for the PAP but who lived in opposition constituencies, "Teh replied 'It is regrettable, but it can't be helped.'"[5]

The examples display stark differences. In *Progresa/Oportunidades*, the criteria of distribution are public and the public criteria are binding. In the Argentine emergency food program, by contrast, local authorities and operatives subverted formal rules of distribution with hidden ones that promoted their electoral objectives. Both *La Efectiva* and the Singapore housing improvement program openly linked access to public benefits to electoral support. In the Mexican setting, this linkage made the strategy scandalous and subject to litigation.[6] In Singapore, an authoritarian state, the linkage was not passively accepted – hence the challenging questions from journalists and opposition politicians – but it seemed unsurprising. Another striking difference is that *Progresa* goes out of its way to depersonalize distribution, replacing campaign workers and party operatives with bureaucrats; *La Efectiva* and the Argentine program involved face-to-face contact and direct party involvement.

Other instances like the second two are easy to find, and not just in Latin America or in the developing world. Although *Progresa*-like distributive strategies are more common in wealthier than in poorer countries, in later pages we cite well-researched distributive programs in wealthy democracies – places such as Sweden, Australia, and the United States – that look more like *La Efectiva* than *Progresa*.

Contemporary advanced democracies were once riddled with electoral exchanges in line with the Argentine and second Mexican examples. A seasoned American political boss, looking back on his career heading New York's Tammany machine, mused:

If there's a fire on Ninth, Tenth, or Eleventh Avenue, for example, any hour of the day or night, I'm usually there with some of my election district captains as soon as the fire-engines. If a family is burned out... I just get quarters for them, buy clothes for them if their clothes were burned up, and fix them up till they get things runnin' again. It's philanthropy, but it's politics, too – mighty good politics. Who can tell how many votes one of these fires bring [sic] me? The poor are the most grateful people in the world.[7]

---

[5] Tam 2008, p. 17.

[6] The tactic, with its apparent linkage of public benefits to electoral support, was controversial and drew formalized complaints from competing parties. Mexico's Federal Electoral Tribunal ultimately decided against these claims on the grounds that there was insufficient evidence that any particular person's vote was bought. See, e.g., SUP-JIN-359/2012, Tribunal Electoral del Poder Judicial de la Federación.

[7] Riordan 1994 [1905], *Plunkitt of Tammany Hall*, p. 6.

tions in the nineteenth century, in turn, featured agents whose job
urchase votes. One explained:

Retaining fees of two guineas or more were sometimes paid as a preliminary earnest of
the candidate's good will. "I asked for their votes," said one canvasser, "but you might
as well ask for their lives, unless you had money to give them."[8]

 This book is about <u>distributive practices that politicians use to try to win
and retain</u> office. We examine especially closely the strategies of clientelism,
machine politics, and patronage, all of them nonprogrammatic distributive
strategies – a term we define in the next section. Understanding how the strategies of distributive politics differ from one another, how they work, and why
they change helps shed light on basic questions that have preoccupied scholars
for decades. Consider a society that undergoes a transition such that voters
who used to trade their votes for cash, poverty relief, or help in obtaining a
job now offer their votes to parties that promise, and deliver, public policies
of which they approve. Most – ourselves included – would consider this a shift
from a less to a more democratic polity. Our study sheds light, then, on processes of democratization and democratic consolidation. What's more, parties
responsive to people who trade their votes distribute favors and largess to individuals, whereas parties attentive to voters who value programmatic appeals
have incentives to construct welfare-oriented public programs. The story of the
demise of clientelism and machine politics is, in this sense, the prehistory of the
welfare state.

1.1 CONCEPTUALIZING MODES OF DISTRIBUTION

Many conceptual distinctions can be drawn among distributive strategies. We
might distinguish programs generating public goods from ones targeting individuals.[9] Public goods may benefit all contributors, or they may subsidize
public expenditures of narrower geographic constituencies.[10] Benefits may be
irreversible (bridges) or reversible (public employment).[11] Parties make long-
term and slow-moving investments in basic programs but campaign, on the
margin, offering "tactical distributions."[12] Incumbents alone may control benefits exclusively (political monopoly) or they may be controlled by opponents
who are economic monopolists.[13]

These are all real differences and have been shown to entail distinct political dynamics. Our scheme is distinctive in that we develop it with one eye
on the empirical world and another on normative democratic concerns. We

[8] Seymour 1970 [1915], p. 394.
[9] See, e.g., Lizzeri and Persico 2004.
[10] This is the definition of *pork-barrel politics* offered by Aldrich 1995.
[11] Robinson and Torvik 2005.
[12] Dixit and Londregan 1996.
[13] Medina and Stokes 2007.

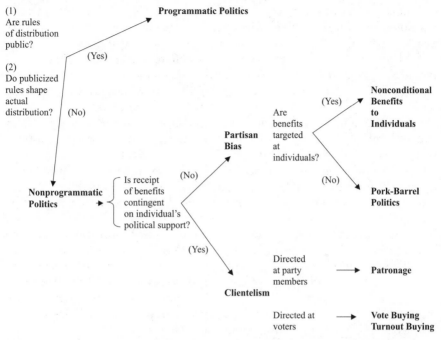

FIGURE 1.1. A Conceptual Scheme of Distributive Politics.

focus on two distinctions. One is between what we call *programmatic* versus *nonprogrammatic* distribution. The other is between unconditional benefits and conditional exchanges. We turn to the programmatic/nonprogrammatic distinction first; it is depicted as the top left branch in Figure 1.1.

1.1.1 Programmatic Distribution

For a distributive strategy to be programmatic, in our usage, two things must be true. First, the criteria of distribution must be public. Often, though not always, a public discussion precedes the crafting of distributive policies and their implementation. Even when *ex ante* public debates are absent – when distributive policies, for instance, are the product of internal governmental discussions or bureaucratic processes – the criteria of distribution are available for public discussion.

Second, the public, formal criteria of distribution must actually shape the distribution of the resources in question. Hence, for a scheme to be programmatic, the criteria that guide distribution must:

1. Be formalized and public, and
2. Shape actual distribution of benefits or resources.

Scholars who study distinct modes of distributive politics often have in mind that some forms are legitimate, whereas others are not. These scholars may not develop explicitly why it is that pork-barrel politics or partisan distributions of social benefits is wrong, but these practices seem to at least fail a "smell test." In our conceptual reflection, we examined the distinctions that scholars made, but could think of legitimate-seeming versions of the strategies to which these scholars had attached illegitimate-sounding labels. *Pork-barrel politics* is an example. If it simply means using tax receipts from a broader constituency to finance local public goods in a smaller constituency, then the concept of pork would have to include the expenditure of national public resources to build schools or bridges in particular regions or localities. If some such spending is illegitimate, then this must be for reasons other than that an intergovernmental transfer is involved. The concept of an "earmark," a term of derision to describe certain kinds of legislation in the United States, presents the same dilemma. Not all bridges are "bridges to nowhere" – there must be something about the process determining how resources are spent that makes some legitimate and others illegitimate.[14] Not just the scholarly literature but also public discussions of earmarks in the United States often struggle to make sense of the difference.

After reviewing many studies about distributive politics, the common element in those that seemed particularly unlikely to pass the smell test was the absence of public criteria of distribution or the failure of official criteria to bite when it came to deciding who would benefit. Our publicity criterion, though inductively arrived at, nevertheless dovetails with normative theories of just distribution that invoke the importance of publicity as a first principle, a point we take up in greater depth in the final chapter. It also fits nicely with definitions of legal and illegal spending, or promises of spending, by office holders and office seekers.

After all, the conceptual distinction between programmatic and nonprogrammatic distribution is not merely academic. All democracies have laws against vote trafficking. In places where these laws are enforced, judges have to draw lines between the legal deployment of resources by ambitious office seekers and the illegal purchase of votes. When they do, publicity comes into play.

As an example, the U.S. Supreme Court in 1982 found that promises of material benefits made openly in campaigns and aimed at broad categories of citizens did not constitute vote trafficking and hence were legal. The Court wrote:

We have never insisted that the franchise be exercised without taint of individual benefit; indeed, our tradition of political pluralism is partly predicated on the expectation that voters will pursue their individual good through the political process, and that the summation of these individual pursuits will further the collective welfare. *So long as the*

---

[14] The debate over federal spending for bridges in Alaska became a salient issue during the 2008 presidential campaign in the United States.

hoped-for personal benefit is to be achieved through the normal processes of government, and not through some private arrangement, it has always been, and remains, a reputable basis upon which to cast one's ballot.[15]

This had not been a private, secret offer, the Court reasoned; rather it was "made openly, subject to the comment and criticism of his political opponent and to the scrutiny of the voters."[16]

Yet perhaps the idea that much distributive politics is filtered through public deliberations and constrained by formal rules is quixotic. Was the Court correct, with regard to the United States or any other democracy, that programmatic politics – open, public offers of material benefits, subject to debate – constitutes the *"normal* process of government"? Indeed, there is substantial evidence that the Court's theory – and what we are calling programmatic politics – is an accurate depiction of distributive politics in many democracies. Mexico's *Progresa* program is an example and one that suggests that open and binding rules can constrain distribution in developing democracies as well as wealthy ones.

Notice, however, a selection bias in the literature. Evidence of bias in the distribution of public resources is noteworthy, whereas reports of programmatic distribution have a dog-bites-man quality. Therefore the academic literature offers much more evidence of the former than the latter. Still, scholarly accounts of partisan bias in the allocation of public programs often contrast this bias with what is considered normal and proper in the national setting under consideration.

In Western Europe, patterns of public spending typically shift when the partisan identity of governments changes. Even when governments are constrained by international markets and institutions, such as the European Union, scholars identify predictable partisan differences in spending priorities.[17] In the United States as well, where the ideological distance between the major parties was for decades less pronounced than between left and right parties in Western Europe, spending priorities reflect the ideological differences between the parties and the contrasting interests of their constituencies.[18] Contrasting priorities are forecast in campaign statements and party platforms and echoed in legislative debates. And campaign spending by political parties is severed from public spending and focused on persuasive communications rather than gifts or treats. Bickers and Stein show that changes in party control of the U.S. Congress induced changes in broad categories of spending – categories, what's more, that corresponded to broad ideological differences between the parties.[19] Their study supports the

[15] Brown v. Hartlage p. 456 of U.S. 57, emphasis added.
[16] Brown v. Hartlage p. 456 of U.S. 57.
[17] See, for instance, Boix 1998, Garrett 2001, or Hibbs 1987.
[18] However, the Campaign Manifestos Project finds substantial ideological and programmatic differences between the platforms of the Democratic and Republican Parties in the United States; see Klingerman et al. 1994.
[19] Bickers and Stein 2000.

court's claim that the "normal process of government" in the United States is public, predictable – in short, programmatic.

Along similar lines, Levitt and Snyder wrote about the pre-1994 U.S. Congress that the

Democratic majority seems unable to target extraordinary amounts of money to specific districts, or to quickly alter the geographic distribution of expenditures. It appears that parties in the U.S. can, given enough time, target *types* of voters, but they cannot easily target individual districts.[20]

In other countries as well, distributive politics is often, perhaps even "normally," programmatic.

1.1.2 Nonprogrammatic Distribution

Nonprogrammatic distributive strategies – beginning at the lower branch of Figure 1.1 – are ones that violate either of the two criteria outlined earlier. Either there are no public criteria of distribution or the public criteria are subverted by private, usually partisan ones.

We began with glimpses of nonprogrammatic distribution in Mexico (the "La Efectiva" campaign) and Argentina. But in advanced democracies as well, distributive schemes sometimes lack public criteria of distribution. To give some examples, in Australia, in the weeks leading up to the 1990 and 1993 elections, the ruling Labour Party allocated constituency grants to build sports stadiums. The parliamentary opposition denounced partisan bias in the program, and eventually there was an investigation by the Auditor-General. The bias was later confirmed by Denmark, whose study suggests that this instance contrasted with normative expectations and normal distributive politics in Australia.[21] The Department of Environment, Sport, and Territories claimed that "community need" was a leading criterion of distribution. However, "no departmental measures or estimations of community need were publicly released."[22]

Sweden is a country that mainly practices programmatic politics. Papakostas notes the absence of a Swedish-language equivalent to the term *clientelism*; when Swedish journalists refer to clientelism "in other countries, they usually have to add that this is a practice where politicians exchange favors for political support."[23] Teorrell investigated Swedish electoral practices in the eighteenth through twentieth centuries and found not a single incident of vote buying.[24] Still, distributive strategies in Sweden have occasionally strayed from the programmatic. In the run-up to a national election in 1998, swing municipalities – ones with large numbers of voters who were indifferent between the

---

[20] Levitt and Snyder 1995 p. 961. Emphasis in the original.
[21] Denmark 2000.
[22] Denmark 2000, p. 901.
[23] Papakostas 2001, p. 33.
[24] Teorrell 2011.

parties – received more, and more generous, environmental grants than did municipalities populated by more partisan voters.[25] The authors noted that "the preparation" of proposals "as well as the final [funding] decisions" were "made by the incumbent government and there [was] no explicit formula describing how the grants should be distributed."[26] They described this experience as unusual; the grants were not related to the "efficiency and equity goals otherwise typically attached to intergovernmental grants."[27]

Notwithstanding the evidence of much programmatic politics in the United States cited earlier, that country as well offers many instances of nonprogrammatic distribution. U.S. presidents can help channel public spending toward the districts of electorally vulnerable members of Congress.[28] The American Congress's use of "earmarks" is another example of hidden criteria of distribution.[29]

The second criterion for programmatic distribution is also not infrequently violated, whether in advanced or developing democracies. Here political actors craft formal, public rules for distribution. But in practice these rules are set aside in favor of more electorally convenient criteria. In such cases, there is no effort to work special treatment into the language of legislation. Instead political actors in control of distribution ignore what legislation or bureaucratic practice call for and channel benefits to groups, regions, or even individuals who would not receive them, or who would be given a lower priority, if official criteria were followed. To offer one example, formalized criteria governed spending on transportation infrastructure in Spain in the 1980s and 1990s. Yet in practice, funds were allocated in such a way as to benefit favored regions with electorally vulnerable incumbents.[30]

Our programmatic/nonprogrammatic distinction, as we noted earlier, crosscuts distinctions drawn by other scholars. A common distinction is based on

---

[25] Dahlberg and Johansson 2002.

[26] Dahlberg and Johansson 2002, p. 27

[27] Dahlberg and Johansson 2002, p. 27.

[28] Berry et al. 2010.

[29] Earmarks are highly particular rules that members of Congress enter into legislation in a quiet, secretive manner. Technically they are public – they are a formalized part of the legislation – but legislators hope that they will remain opaque to the broader public. When they are made public, they are seen as ludicrous and, sometimes, scandalous. Consider the case of a majority leader of the U.S. Senate who wanted to channel benefits to specific hospitals in his state without appearing to do so. In 2009 he inserted an amendment into health care reform legislation that would extend grants to "certain hospitals" that been designated as cancer centers "on July 27, 1978, February 17, 1998, June 13, 2000" (*New York Times*, "Health Bill Could Hold Reward for 4 Cancer Centers," September 22, 2009, p. 20). Dixit and Londregan (1998, p. 163) cited similar examples from the U.S. Tax Reform Act of 1986, such as special "transitional rules" for "a convention center with respect to which a convention tax was upheld by a state supreme court on February 8, 1985" (the Miami Convention Center), and one for "a binding contract entered into on October 20, 1984, for the purchase of six semisubmersible drilling units (a drilling project for Alabamas Sonat Company)."

[30] Castells and Solé-Ollé 2005.

the kinds of goods given out: public, club, targeted, and the like. Not infrequently, the key distinction that others have made is between collective benefits or public goods versus individual or targeted benefits. Hence Lizzeri and Persico equate "clientelism and patronage (pork-barrel politics)" with "redistribution (ad hominem benefits)"; this they contrast with "a public good with diffuse benefits."[31] Shefter distinguished between "divisible benefits – patronage of various sorts" and "collective benefits or appeals to collective interests."[32] It is certainly helpful in many contexts to distinguish between collective and individual benefits. However, programmatic and nonprogrammatic distribution, as we define them, cross-cut this distinction. Distributive programs aimed at individuals may follow public criteria that determine actual distribution. If so, targeting individuals still constitutes programmatic politics, in our usage. By the same token, local public goods may be channeled to responsive localities according to rules that are hidden from public view, or public rules may be ignored in how such resources are divided. In this case, public goods are nonprogrammatic. Many would call this pork-barrel politics, as we do later. The term *pork* connotes a departure from fairness and good government that is not easily reconciled with Lizzeri and Persico's view of public-goods distributions as antithetical to clientelism.

Modes of Nonprogrammatic Distribution

Nonconditional partisan bias. The second branch of Figure 1.1 identifies a basic distinction among forms of nonprogrammatic politics. In some settings, politically discriminatory distributions generate good will among recipients who may, as a consequence, be more likely to support the benefactor candidate or party. However, recipients who defect and vote for a different party suffer no individual punishment. Consider a person from a pivotal constituency who gains access to an antipoverty program, in effect jumping the queue ahead of more needy people in other districts. We define this as a situation of *nonconditional individual benefits*. If the program targets collectivities, such as geographic constituencies, we call this *pork-barrel politics*. Nonconditional individual benefits and pork can add votes for the benefactor to the extent that the largess boosts voter good will toward the candidate and party.[33]

From the perspective of normative democratic theory, the main difficulty raised by nonconditional individual benefits and pork is the departure from publicity. We return to this point in the final chapter.

---

[31] Lizzeri and Persico 2004, p. 708, 713.

[32] Shefter 1977, p. 88.

[33] Different polities and legal systems draw the lines between vote buying, nonconditional (nonprogrammatic) benefits to individuals, and harmless campaign practices in different places; these definitions also change in individual settings over time. A campaign or election-day event in which any person who cares to show up can receive food, drink, and entertainment are contisidered innocuous practices in some settings but treating in others.

Clientelism. In other settings, the party offers material benefits only on the condition that the recipient returns the favor with a vote or other forms of political support.[34] The voter suffers a punishment (or reasonably fears that he or she will suffer one) should he or she defect from the implicit bargain of a benefit for a vote; not (just) good will, but fear of punishment, turns distributive largess into votes. We call nonprogrammatic distribution combined with conditionality *clientelism*.

The importance of conditionality and *quid-pro-quo* understandings to our conceptual scheme again conforms to legal theory. In the U.S. Supreme Court decision cited earlier, it was important to the Court that the candidate's offer "was to extend beyond those voters who cast their ballots for [him], to all tax-payers and citizens." His offer "scarcely contemplated a particularized acceptance or a *quid-pro-quo* arrangement."[35]

Quid pro quo exchanges of cash, alcohol, or building materials (to name just a few items) in return for a vote raise normative red flags. These exchanges seem to violate the free action or autonomy of voters. Even if we accept that voters are never fully autonomous and always come under the influence of some other actor – parents, co-workers, "opinion makers," or party leaders – still the image of the voter being held to account for his or her choice is disquieting. Perhaps this is because an implicit threat to cut the voter off from future benefits as a direct consequence of his or her voting choices moves uncomfortably close to coercion. Political philosophers, and undoubtedly most lay citizens, would deem coercion of the vote antithetical to democracy.[36] Or perhaps vote trafficking has nefarious social side effects or negative externalities, whatever its effects on vote sellers. Consider that, in a narrow material sense, nothing is at stake in an individual's vote: it is unlikely to change the outcome of the election, and if benefits come by way of programmatic distribution, a vote will not influence the probability that the person who yields it will receive benefits. Therefore, offers of benefits in direct exchange for votes hold the power to trump other considerations in voters' choices. In such a setting, individual benefits with conditionality – clientelism – would be especially toxic. They can blunt elections as instruments for holding governments to account and for communicating the distribution of voters' preferences.[37] We return to these questions in the final chapter.

Patronage Versus Vote and Turnout Buying. Figure 1.1 further develops distinctions among types of clientelism. Political machines orient some of their

---

[34] Our distinction at the first branch of Figure 1.1, between public and binding rules and non-public or nonbinding ones, is novel. The distinction between conditional and unconditional exchanges – the second branch – is more common in the literature; see especially Kitschelt and Wilkinson 2007, p. 10.

[35] Brown v. Hartlage p. 465 of U.S. 58.

[36] See, e.g., Mansbridge 2010.

[37] See Karlan 1994 on the socially desirable features of elections and how they can be undone by vote trafficking.

ogrammatic largess toward their own party members. Typically, the benefit they offer is public employment, though other resources may also flow to party operatives. The term *patronage* is colloquially used to refer to intra-party flows of benefits, and we adopt that usage here. At the bottom right side of Figure 1.1, the *voter* (not the party operative) is the object of party largess. Political machines may treat or bribe to persuade people to vote for them; we call this *vote buying*. Or they treat or bribe to get voters to the polls; following Nichter, we call this *turnout buying*.[38] In later chapters, we discuss contingent payments designed to elicit other kinds of political support, such as attendance at rallies.

Constituency Service. Machines don't just offer voters largess in the run-up to elections. They also help constituents to solve problems, interceding on their behalf to obtain resources from higher levels of the state, contacting officials to deal with emergencies, and the like. They are "personal problem-solving networks."[39] Machine operatives usually insist that they offer such assistance without regard for the electoral sympathies or identities of the supplicant; the only criterion for spending time and effort on behalf of constituents is their need. When this is true, their actions call to mind what in the United States is called *constituency service*. Fenno has shown that U.S. members of Congress generally do render constituency service indiscriminately to all comers. The criteria of distribution are district residence and need.[40] We show that clientelist machine operatives do not merely perform constituency service in this sense; instead, they typically use other criteria, such as a voter's electoral responsiveness and willingness to join local organizations, when deciding how to deploy their scarce resources.

We do not locate constituency service in Figure 1.1. It is like programmatic distribution in that it offers assistance to voters independent of their responsiveness, but it is not "programmatic" in the sense of constituting a particular initiative signaled by campaign pronouncements or by party ideology. Yet it is clearly an electoral strategy. By generating good will among constituents who receive assistance, and by allowing the politician to build a reputation for fairness and competence, constituency service is probably an effective tactic. Constituency service as it is practiced today in the United States contains echoes of machine politics of old. But many of the functions of the machine have been taken over by governmental bureaucracies, and rarely would an individual constituent be denied access to a social program because he or she has proved to be electorally unresponsive – as is the case of clientelism.

We illustrate in Table 1.1 the potential for our conceptual scheme to translate into codings of the practices studied by particular scholars. It presents

---

[38] Nichter 2008. Parties may also treat or bribe to keep voters away from the polls, as discussed by Cox and Kousser 1981. We don't find this strategy, which we call *abstention buying*, to be a particularly prevalent strategy and therefore don't discuss it extensively. However, we return to the normative implications of abstention buying in the final chapter.

[39] Auyero 2001. On modes of problem solving in Latin America, see Collier and Handlin 2009.

[40] Fenno 1978.

TABLE 1.1. *Studies of Nonprogrammatic Distributive Politics, Coded by Type*

Country	Author, Publication Year	Time Period	Program	Type of Nonprogrammatic Strategy
United States	Wright 1974	1933–1940	New Deal federal spending in states	Nonconditional benefits and vote buying
United States	Levitt and Snyder 1995	1984–1990	Federal spending in congressional districts	Nonconditional benefits and pork
United States	Herron and Theodus 2004	1999–2000	State assembly to districts (Illinois)	Nonconditional benefits and pork
United States	Ansolabehere and Snyder 2006	1957–1997	State governments to counties	Benefits and pork
United States	Chen 2008	2004	Federal emergency aid in Florida	Nonconditional benefits
United States	Berry et al. 2010	1984–2007	Federal spending in Congressional districts	Nonconditional benefits and pork
Sweden	Dahlberg and Johansson 2002	1998	Environmental grants to municipalities	Pork
Sweden	Johansson 2003	1981–1995	Central government spending in municipalities	Nonconditional benefits and pork
Canada	Crampton 2004	Mid-1990s	Job creation fund	Nonconditional benefits
Canada	Miligan and Smart 2005	1988–2001	Regional development grants	Non conditional benefits and pork
Australia	Worthington and Dollery 1998	1981–1982, 1991–1992	Commonwealth grants to states	Pork
Austalia	Denemark 2000	Early 1990s	Sports stadiums	Pork
Italy	Golden and Picci 2008	1953–1994	Infrastructure	Pork
Italy	Chubb 1982	1950s–1970s	Multiple types	Patronage and vote buying

TABLE 1.1 (*continued*)

Country	Author, Publication Year	Time Period	Program	Type of Nonprogrammatic Strategy
Spain	Castells and Solé-Ollé 2005	Late 1980s–early 1990s	National infrastructure spending in regions	Pork
Portugal	Veiga and Pinho 2007	1979–2002	Municipal grants	Pork
Lebanon	Corstange 2012	2009	Cash, food, jobs, etc.	Vote buying
Japan	Curtis 1971	1950s–1960s	Cash and small gifts	Vote buying
Japan	Scheiner 2007	1990s	Public works	Pork
South Korea	Kwon 2005	1988–1997	National/ministerial spending in regions	Pork and vote buying
India	Chandra 2004	1990s–2000s	Public employment	Patronage
India	Rodden and Wilkinson 2004	1957–2003	National spending in states	Pork and vote buying
India	Cole 2009	1992–1999	Agricultural credits to states	Pork and vote buying
India	Khemani 2007	1972–1995	Fiscal transfers to states	Pork and vote buying
India	Vaishnav and Sircar 2010	1977–2007	School buildings	Pork
Taiwan	Wang and Kurzman 2007	1993	Minor gifts (cigarettes, tea)	Vote buying
Philippines	Schaffer 2007	2001	Cash, small gifts	Vote buying
Thailand	Hicken 2007	1970s–2000	Cash, small gifts	Vote buying
Mexico	Bruhn 1996	Early 1990s	PRONASOL funds center to states	Pork and vote buying
Mexico	Hiskey 1999	Early 1990s	PRONASOL funds to municipalities	Pork vote buying
Mexico	Magaloni 2006	1990s	PRONASOL funds to municipalities	Pork and vote buying

Country	Source	Date	Policy	Type
Mexico	Magaloni, Diaz-Cayeros, and Estevez 2007	1990s	PRONASOL funds to municipalities	Pork and vote buying
Mexico	Molinar and Weldon 1994	Early 1990s	PRONASOL funds center to states	Pork vote buying
Brazil	Ames 2001	Early posttransition	Central government to municipalities	Pork and vote buying
Brazil	Rodden and Arretche 2003	1991–2000	Center transfers to states	Pork and vote buying
Peru	Schady 2000	1991–1995	Antipoverty, development funds from center to counties	Nonconditional benefits and pork
Venezuela	Hawkins 2010	2005	Targeted "mission" benefits to municipalities	Nonconditional benefits and pork
Argentina	Calvo and Murillo 2004	1987–2000	Fiscal transfers from center to provinces	Patronage, pork, and vote buying
Argentina	Lodola 2005	1995–1999	Workfare transfers to municipalities	Vote buying
Argentina	Gordin 2006	1983–2003	Fiscal and housing transfers to provinces	Vote buying and pork
Argentina	Weitz-Shapiro 2006	1995–2001	Workfare transfers to municipalities	Vote buying
Argentina	Nazareno, Stokes, and Brusco 2006	1995–1999	Workfare transfers to municipalities	Vote buying
Sub-Saharan Africa	Van de Walle 2003	1990s	Municipal and village building programs	Pork
Kenya	Barkan and Chege 1989	Early 1980s	Decentralization of public spending	Pork
Benin	Wantchekon	1990s	Local public goods	Pork
Benin and Senegal	Koter 2013	1950s, 2006–2007	Public goods, individual favors	Vote buying and pork

of a large number of case studies of distributive politics, in all
es that are non-programmatic. We have excluded from the table
h we lack sufficient information to code them. For instance, was
the politicized transfer of funding to Ghana's District Assemblies a case of
nonconditional individual benefits or of clientelism? Banful's study indicates
nonprogrammatic distribution, but without more information about the structure of parties and their interactions with voters, we hesitate to push the coding
further.[41] Still, it should be clear that many instances of distributive politics
can be readily coded according to our scheme.

To summarize, a first question our study poses is, "How can we best distinguish among various forms of distributive politics?" Our answer is that the
key distinctions are between ones that follow public, binding rules and those
that do not and between strategies that attempt to influence voters and others
that attempt to hold them more sharply to account.

1.2 BASIC QUESTIONS ABOUT DISTRIBUTIVE POLITICS

Despite the very large number of excellent studies of clientelism and distributive
politics, still some basic questions remain unanswered. Much progress has been
made. However, core aspects of the topic remain poorly understood, which is
what motivates us to write this book. In particular, we are dissatisfied with
answers – including those we have offered in our own earlier contributions –
to three basic questions.

1. How does nonprogrammatic politics, and especially clientelism, work?
2. What causes shifts away from clientelism and toward other, non–broker-
   mediated distributive strategies?
3. Which kinds of distributive politics are consistent with the norms of
   democracy, which are inconsistent, and why?

1.2.1 How Does Clientelism Work?

Despite a spike in academic studies and a good deal of attention in the policy
world, we still lack an understanding of some facts about clientelism. One
basic question that any reasonable theory should be able to answer is, "What
types of voters tend to enter into vote-trafficking arrangements?" As the next
chapter makes clear, our received theories fail at this basic task. The collective
theoretical wisdom does a bad job explaining empirical regularities regarding
the effect of *partisanship* on vote selling. It does a better job explaining the
impact of *income* on vote selling: poor people are more likely to sell their
votes. However, we don't have consistent explanations for *why* this is true.

A major contribution we hope to make with this book is to build a theory of
clientelism that does a better job explaining what until now have been empirical

---

[41] Banful 2010.

anomalies or incomplete explanations. The theory that we build in Chapter 3 begins with a series of observations about the informational requirements of clientelism. As a prelude to that more thoroughgoing discussion, we outline some of these observations now.

Under clientelism, parties distribute benefits to individuals and attempt to hold them accountable for their votes. The information required to carry off these rather remarkable tasks is substantial. Parties must know which voters and families need what kinds of help; a bag of rice for Juanita won't be helpful if what she really needs is medication for a sick child. (This problem would be ameliorated if parties bought votes with cash. They sometimes do so, but trading in cash facilitates brokers pocketing the benefits.) Parties also need to know who is likely to turn out without much additional prodding, who will vote for them come hell or high water, who will *not* vote for them come hell or high water, and who is on the fence. This information, what's more, may change over time: whether Juanita's child is still ill; whether Sanjay now has a job; whether Philip used to support the party but thinks it has performed badly in the last term. Monitoring the vote also requires parties to gather substantial information about the decentralized actions of individual voters. Both the delivery and the holding-voters-to-account sides of machine politics are demanding on the party as an information-gathering and -processing mechanism. This is true under public voting, all the more so once the ballot becomes secret.

To deal with these information demands, machines hire armies of intermediaries or brokers. The brokers go by a variety of names. They are *cabos electorais* (canvassers) in Brazil; *gestores* (facilitators) or *caciques* (political boss) in Mexico; fixers and *dalal* (middlemen) in India; *hua khanaen* (vote canvassers) in Thailand; *anggota tim sukses* (success team members) in Indonesia; and *porteurs de voix* (vote carriers), *relais électoraux* (electoral relays), or *vecteurs* (vectors) in Senegal. They were precinct captains in the United States and party agents in Great Britain. Of particular value are people who live in the same neighborhood as the set of voters for whose actions they are responsible. It's much easier for a neighborhood insider to know whose children are ill, who turned out in the last election and who stayed home, whether a voter turned against the party, or who seems to have defected and voted for an opponent, despite having benefitted from party largesse.

Brokers solve many information problems for machines. But they create problems as well. They are agents of the party whose actions cannot be exhaustively observed or perfectly monitored by the party. Did support collapse in a given neighborhood because the opponent did a good job poaching or because the party's broker sold the rice and kept the cash for himself? Did the broker work hard for the primary candidate, or was he secretly pushing for another candidate? Did he direct party resources toward responsive voters, or did he expend them on his cronies, who can help him boost his own career? Was the candidate a hard sell in that neighborhood, or was the broker inept?

These kinds of questions plague machine leaders. We find such doubts – the sense that one's operatives in the neighborhoods, towns, and boroughs may be "parasites" and "traitors"[42] – to be omnipresent, festering in the minds of party leaders from nineteenth-century Britain, to Gilded Age America, to contemporary Argentina or India. Their omnipresence suggests that they are structural, growing out of the very needs of parties to build organizations that insinuate themselves into the lives and networks of voters.

These observations about the informational and organizational settings of machine politics are at the center of our study. They help us to build a broker-mediated model of clientelism that solves persistent puzzles and explains enduring empirical anomalies.

In sum, our answer to the question, "How does vote buying work?" will turn on the role of the political broker. Although many studies of machine politics have noted the centrality of brokers, most have not sufficiently internalized the logic of broker-mediated distribution. Our micro-theory aims to expose the agency issues that characterize this relationship and develop a theoretical understanding of the ways in which clientelism thus brings both costs and benefits to party leaders.

1.2.2 The Macro-Logic of Transitions From Clientelism

In some countries, distributive politics has shifted over time from vote buying and other nonprogrammatic forms to programmatic politics. Why did this change occur?

By posing this question, we do not mean to suggest that a shift from non-programmatic to programmatic distribution is inevitable around the world. Still, in the United States, the George Washington Plunkitts have been displaced by less personalized, more bureaucratic organizations, and few victims of fires or natural disasters, even in the working-class neighborhoods of New York, Chicago, or other erstwhile machine cities, expect to receive aid from party bosses or ward-heelers. In the same way, the modern-day British Labour, Liberal-Democrat, or Conservative parties would have little use for the vote-buying party agents on whom they used to rely. In other countries, clientelism and vote buying have declined but not disappeared. Gone are the days when Italy's Christian Democratic party sent "pasta trucks" through the popular quarters of Naples or Palermo, in search of votes.[43] However, the Italian parliament in 2004 saw reason to pass legislation barring the introduction of cells phones into the voting booth. Voters were reported to be using the cameras in their phones to photograph their ballots, thus verifying that they had complied with implicit vote-buying contracts.

---

[42] As explained in Chapter 8, party leaders in Britain and the United States saw their electoral agents and brokers in these and other unflattering ways.
[43] See Chubb 1981.

What explains such transitions, complete or partial? Simple answers, such as economic growth and modernization, tell only part of the story.

Just as it helps explain the internal micro-dynamics of clientelism, so the broker-mediated model helps makes sense of the macro-dynamics of machine demise. Because leaders both rely on but suffer under their electoral agents, we should not be surprised that these same leaders play a role in cutting out the group of brokers when conditions are ripe. Grasping the imperfect agency relations between party leaders and their brokers helps us understand the macro-logic of transitions between clientelism and programmatic politics. As our analysis of the micro-logic of vote buying suggests, clientelism brings both costs – in the form of rent-seeking and inefficient targeting by brokers – as well as benefits to party leaders. Understanding the sources of these costs and benefits is thus crucial for understanding the emergence and persistence of clientelism. As our investigation of historical as well as contemporary cases suggests, party leaders often chafe at the inefficiency of their brokers. Transitions from clientelism have often involved leaders from different parties colluding against the entire class of brokers.

Structural forces such as economic growth and modernization influence the relative returns to clientelism, compared with other distributive strategies, and thus affect the incentives of leaders to subvert their machines. Social changes in the electorate induced by industrialization or economic development shape the terms of exchange between party leaders and brokers, as well as between brokers and voters. Population growth and urbanization make it harder for brokers to discern individual voters' electoral choices. Investments in party machines tend to bring constant returns: in light of the intensity and frequency of relations required between brokers and their clients, as the electorate grows, parties need to hire many more brokers. The political machine does not "scale" as well as more programmatic forms of political communication. The latter, in contrast, can involve heavy start-up costs but low fixed costs, leading to increasing returns to scale; when the costs to leaders of communicating directly with voters (i.e., without brokers) decline, the returns to programmatic strategies increase.

In sum, our answer to the question, "What causes shifts between clientelism and other forms of nonprogrammatic or programmatic distribution?" emphasizes macro or structural changes that enhance or erode the efficiency of brokers. When industrialization enlarges electorates, shifts the weight of electorates from poor to middle-class voters, and makes individual voters' actions harder to discern, the inefficiencies of the electoral agent will weigh all the more heavily on party leaders, tempting them to do away with their own machines. When party leaders undertake policies that enlarge the number of poor voters while also spurning their traditional constituencies, brokers will appear less wasteful and inefficient to leaders. The broker-mediated theory, then, helps unravel puzzles of clientelism, both as a steady state and as a strategy that rises and falls in distinct settings.

1.2.3 Distributive Politics and Normative Democratic Theory

We hope to help solve some puzzles in normative considerations of distributive politics. Earlier we framed the question as, "Where does one draw the line between acceptable and unacceptable forms of distributive politics?" By now it should be clear that not one line alone but several will need to be drawn. Most normative theorists of democracy would probably agree with the U.S. Supreme Court's stance that a line should be drawn between public commitments and offers (which are legal and acceptable) and private, hidden side deals (which are not). However, even among practices that flout public, binding rules, some undercut democratic norms more than others. We have suggested, for instance, that democracy is less severely undermined when distributive strategies *influence* rather than *coerce* voters and hence that clientelism is more toxic than is unconditional partisan bias.

Figure 1.1 opens additional questions, as well. One of them is whether the practice of turnout buying should be subjected to as much opprobrium as is vote buying. Legal standards suggest that the answer may be no. Parties' transporting or hauling voters to the polls is often legal, whereas paying them for their votes is not. That payments to voters are selective incentives to vote, and that the elimination of payments is often followed by a drop in turnout, is one of the justifications that is sometimes offered for vote buying; or at least this is considered a countervailing good that can mitigate the bad. This defense of private payments to voters raises questions, however, about the meaning of participation when it is purchased, a question we return to in the final chapter.

In addition to the participation justification of clientelism, others include that it is redistributive and that it is efficient. We take all three up in the final chapter.

1.3 WHY STUDY CLIENTELISM?

The forgoing discussion will, we hope, help answer this question. Nonprogrammatic distributive politics in general, and clientelism in particular, are puzzling phenomena. In the next chapter we see that political machines fail to give out goods in the way that theorists have long predicted, giving too much to the wrong kinds of voters. Partisan bias, clientelism, and patronage sometimes disappear from places where they have long been endemic and reassert themselves in places where they have never been prevalent. And if political philosophers and lay observers think nonprogrammatic distributions tarnish democracy, why don't programmatic distributions of material benefits do so as well? In short, there are puzzles to solve. Sheer curiosity, we hope, will carry the reader into the following chapters.

Another reason why we – and many other scholars of the developing world – have taken up the problem of clientelism and distributive politics is

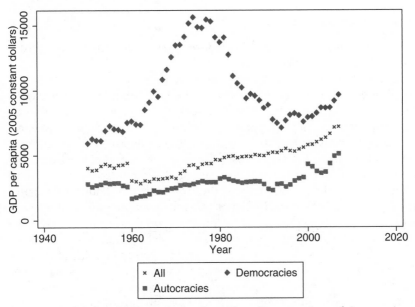

FIGURE 1.2. Median GDP per Capita Over Time: Democracies and Autocracies.

that it is widespread. The third wave of democratization brought into the club of democratic nations a set of countries that found themselves at considerably lower levels of economic development than the elite club of older democracies; hence, as a group, democracies became poorer. Figure 1.2 demonstrates this trend. The median gross domestic product per capita among all democracies peaked in the late 1970s, then declined sharply through the 1980s and mid-1990s, when most Latin American and European Communist countries democratized. The trend was reversed in the late 1990s, but by 2007 the median per capita gross domestic product (GDP) of democratic countries remained 50 percent lower than it had been at its peak. The downward movement in average per capita GDP among democracies is due to the growth in the number of democracies in the world.[44]

A simple reason why clientelism, patronage, and other modes of nonprogrammatic politics have become important topics in the scholarly and policy communities is that there is an elective affinity between it and poverty; the birth of many new, poor democracies make it more prevalent. Yet we also see signs of the decline of clientelism, or at least major challenges to it, challenges epitomized by the *Progresa/Oportunidades* program mentioned at the outset.

---

[44] Figure 1.2 uses Penn World Tables 6.3 and the Cheibub et al (2009) extension of the Przeworksi et al. (2000) regime codings to code democracies and autocracies from 1950–2007.

1.4 STRUCTURE OF THE BOOK

In addition to this Part I – which introduced our conceptual scheme of distributive politics – the book that follows is divided into three more parts, each corresponding to one of the questions raised earlier.

Part II addresses the crucial question of how distributive politics works. Chapter 2, "The Gap between Theory and Fact," uses original micro-level evidence from four developing-world democracies – Argentina, India, Mexico, and Venezuela – to underscore the lack of fit between positive political-economy models and real-world patterns. Most positive theories treat clientelist parties as single unitary actors, and they predict that *swing* or indifferent voters will be the chief targets of distributive largess. But this prediction finds little support in the cases we study. We then attempt to explain this empirical anomaly in three ways: by assuming that voter types (loyal voters, swing voters) are a by-product of distributive largess (*endogenous loyalty*); by assuming that largess is aimed at mobilizing voters to turn out, rather than persuading them to change their vote (*turnout buying*); and by positing that what appears in the data to be payments to loyal voters are actually payments to low-level brokers, whose task is to generate support among voters (*subcontracting*). Only this last alternative steps away from the assumption of clientelist machines as single unitary actors. None of the three effectively resolves the tension between theory and facts.

Chapter 3, "A Theory of Broker-Mediated Distribution," attempts to close this gap. We analyze a formal model that builds on the basic idea that brokers – ground-level intermediaries between the party and voters – are imperfect agents of their parties. This model makes sense of empirical regularities that were anomalous from the perspective of earlier theories, such as the channeling of largess toward loyalists who were also committed non-abstainers. The broker-mediated theory generates a prediction more in line with the evidence: that political machines target loyal voters, even ones who are in no danger of abstaining, though without completely ignoring swing voters.

Having developed a theory with the "right" predictions, at least regarding the effect of voters' ideological or partisan type on their chances of receiving party largess, much of the rest of the book further tests this theory. It does so by offering evidence in support of the theory's basic assumptions, its claims and predictions, and its additional observable implications. Chapter 4, "Testing the Broker-Mediated Theory," focuses on key assumptions of the broker-mediated model. These include that brokers are interested in extracting rents from their parties *and* in having their party win elections. We also show evidence that brokers are able to threaten party leaders with a withdrawal of blocks of voters whom they control. In addition, we show that party leaders, unable to observe directly either the types of particular voters or the effectiveness and efforts of brokers, use brokers to monitor and sanction voters and use party activity and electoral outcomes to try to monitor brokers. The evidence in Chapter 4 comes from a number of sources, including a unique survey of a probability sample of 800 party brokers in Argentina. Our efforts to draw samples of brokers in four regions in Argentina – despite the non-e any obvious sampling frame – and our use of several survey experim us to circumvent inferential difficulties that other kinds of studies fi ˌuently encounter.

Chapter 5, "A Disjunction between Leaders' and Brokers' Strategies?," begins with the observation that if our theory is right, distributive politics should favor swing *districts* but loyal *individuals*. To test this observable implication, we again draw on original data sources as well as on studies of distribution from parties and central governments to regions, provinces, and localities from all major regions of the world, including the United States and Canada, Western European countries, Asia, Africa, and Latin America.

Chapter 6 explores our theory's implications for the relationship between poverty and clientelism. A near-universal assumption in scholarly, policy, and lay discussions is that vote buying is basically a strategy aimed at low-income voters. Cross-national survey data support this assumption. So does our individual-level evidence from four developing-world democracies. There is less consensus about *why* the poor are most likely to sell their votes. Our model in Chapter 3 assumes diminishing marginal utility of income, an assumption we share with several other theories of machine politics. This assumption implies that the higher a voter's endowment or prepolitical income, the more a party will have to pay the voter to overcome any disutility endured from voting against his or her preferred type. With limited and fixed budgets, machines start with poor voters and are decreasingly likely to target voters as one advances up the income distribution. Another explanation focuses on the risk aversion that is also implied by diminishing marginal utility of income. Here it is not the limited budget of the party but the unwillingness of the voter to accept an uncertain future reward, promised by a programmatic politician, instead of a steady flow of concrete benefits. We test diminishing-utility-of-income versus risky-programs explanations with original survey data.

Part III of the book shifts from contemporaneous to over-time dynamics of distributive politics. In Chapter 7, "Party Leaders Against the Machine," we build on the broker-oriented theory and develop formally some predictions about the macro-historical conditions that might encourage, or discourage, clientelism and vote buying. Chapter 8, "What Killed Vote Buying in Britain and the United States?," offers evidence relevant to the broker-mediated and macro-theories. It poses and offers answers to two historical questions. In nineteenth-century Britain and the United States, vote buying was a central feature of elections. Why did it subsequently basically disappear in both countries, displaced by more programmatic approaches to winning elections? And why, despite the similarities in this basic scenario of decline, did clientelism and machine politics persist longer in the United States than in Britain?

Our historical exploration offers much additional evidence of agency problems in the relation of party leaders and brokers. That these problems are in such clear evidence in contexts historically and geographically remote from those in relation to which we developed the theory underscores that these problems arise out of the incentives and information asymmetries that these two sets of actors face.

The final section and chapter consider nonprogrammatic politics through the lens of normative theories of distributive justice. Normative considerations are clarified by the sharper picture of distributive politics which, we hope, will emerge from these pages. Chapter 9 poses the question, "What's Wrong with Vote Buying?" (and other forms of nonprogrammatic distribution). Can it be justified on efficiency grounds? On redistributive grounds? On participation grounds? How does it measure up to theories of distributive justice? The answer to the last question – not very well – is no surprise. Yet there are nuances, depending on what kind of nonprogrammatic strategies we have in mind. It matters, we contend, whether the practice in question is pork-barrel politics – targeting groups or localities – versus the targeting of individuals, whether the goal is to change people's votes or to boost turnout, whether goodies are given out to get supporters to the polls or to keep opponents at home, and whether the recipients of largess are party loyalists, swing voters, or opposition supporters.

1.5 A COMMENT ON RESEARCH METHODS

To probe the questions that animate this study, we use tools of theory, both positive and normative. Our empirical research, in turn, makes use of a multi-layered mix of strategies.[45] Drawing inferences about the quantities we study is challenging. In Chapter 2, for example, we assess the effects of voters' partisan loyalty or ideological orientation on their receipt of benefits; yet, there are few ready natural experiments with as-if random variation in partisan loyalty.[46] Our approach depends on triangulation of evidence from many sources. We have conducted sample surveys of voters in Argentina, Venezuela, and India, and use publicly available individual data from Mexico, to make inferences about the kinds of voters whom political machines target. Our Venezuelan survey was designed to fill the gaps in an enormous database of Venezuelan voters that the Chávez government created. Although other social scientists have studied the Venezuelan government's database, we are the first to be able to add crucial additional information, for example, about voters' income levels, by matching voters sampled for our own survey to the records in the government's database. We draw on original experimental research reflecting party and voting behavior in India. We have conducted open-ended qualitative interviews with party leaders, brokers, and voters in Argentina, Venezuela, and

---

[45] See the Appendixes, as well as discussions in the chapters, for more details about our data sources.

[46] Dunning 2012.

India. We are also able to draw on a vast and rigorous secondary literature and offer what we believe to be the broadest empirical review of ecological studies of distributive politics yet produced. And we have dug deeply into secondary historical materials to make arguments about the demise of at least some forms of nondistributive politics in several of today's advanced democracies. Thus we test different aspects of our theories using different research designs and unique datasets on voters, brokers, and leaders, combined with qualitative fieldwork. Each strategy on its own has some limitations, but together we believe they make a compelling case for the arguments we advance.

One empirical strategy that we make only cursory use of is large-N cross-national research. One reason has to do with the nature of our dependent variables. Like corruption, many forms of nonprogrammatic distribution are illegal, immoral (by local standards), or both, and no ready cross-national measures are available. That these practices are not socially desirable creates potential bias in the single-country measures and survey results that we do use. A promising approach, but one that is just getting off the ground as of this writing, is to gauge levels of vote buying through list experiments.[47] Even so, these studies tend to produce one-off measures of the level of vote buying at a single point in time. And the very anonymity they offer respondents then reduces the amount of individual-level information that they provide.[48] Beyond the intentional obfuscation by the actors involved, another obstacle to gathering valid cross-national measures is that context matters for the coding of our dependent variable. For this reason, another promising recent approach to the cross-national study of clientelism and other modes of party-voter linkages is elite surveys, in particular those carried out by Kitschelt and his coauthors.[49] As the next chapter makes clear, public spending may be programmatic or not, depending on the political context in which it is carried out and on how faithfully it reflects formalized rules. These are questions that scholars have addressed in particular national contexts, and a great deal can be learned by comparing the results of myriad country-level studies. But the importance of context makes simple large-N statistical comparisons treacherous. For these reasons, the few scholarly efforts to gather cross-national measures of clientelism, pork, or vote buying have not been particularly successful.

---

[47] See, e.g., Corstange 2010, Gonzalez-Ocantos et al. 2011.

[48] Some analysts have attempted to extend list-item techniques to allow inclusion of individual-level data (see Corstange 2008), though these rely rather heavily on the assumptions of regression models for individual-level responses.

[49] See Kitschelt 2011.

PART II

THE MICRO-LOGIC OF CLIENTELISM

2

Gaps Between Theory and Fact

> "The groups that are densely represented at the center [of the ideological spectrum] will be the beneficiaries of redistributive politics. [Groups at the extremes] will not partake in this benefit: they will be written off by one party and taken for granted by the other."[1]

> "A broker will give goods to swing voters to attract more people; voters who prefer the party are already on his side."[2]

The first quote expresses a theoretical finding about partisan attachments and distributive politics. The second one expresses the same idea, this time voiced by a low-level operative in an Argentine political party. What has become the dominant view among theorists is the same as this practitioner's rule of thumb: a party will not waste its resources on loyal supporters (or on die-hard enemies), but instead spend on swing voters. The reason is that parties will use largesse to *change* people's votes; swing voters, with no prior commitment to one party or another, will be uniquely responsive.[3]

The intuition behind the theory and rule of thumb is straightforward. However, as we show in this chapter, it is not supported by the facts. Reality stubbornly resists conforming to our theories. In a range of developing-world democracies, swing voters receive too few benefits, whereas loyal voters – those

---

[1] Dixit and Londregan 1996, p. 1143.

[2] 2009 interview with broker in Buenos Aires. This interview was part of a survey of Argentine political brokers (see Appendix A) that we carried out in conjunction with Edwin Camp and Mariela Szwarcberg.

[3] So powerful is the intuition behind this rule that Kitschelt and Wilkinson build it into their definition of clientelism. Giving a benefit to a voter is an instance of clientelism if, *inter alia*, "it is all but certain that the local voters would switch sides to other parties" in the absence of the benefit (Kitschelt and Wilkinson 2007, p. 14).

whose strong preference for the party should make them unresponsive – receive too many.

Whereas in the previous chapter we distinguished conceptually between forms of distributive politics, here we begin by briefly reviewing positive theories of how distributive politics work – in particular, the types of voters that parties and candidates tend to favor when they hand out benefits. We then use evidence from public opinion surveys, government databases, and survey experiments to show that clientelist distribution does not give priority to swing voters. This is true in four distinct developing democracies for which we have individual-level data: Argentina, Venezuela, Mexico, and India. We then try to explain this anomaly by testing the *endogenous loyalty, turnout buying,* and *subcontracting* explanations mentioned in Chapter 1. Yet, none of these explanations fully accounts for the anomaly. To be clear, some swing or marginal voters do receive benefits. But from the perspective of received theory, the overriding conclusion is that too many loyal voters receiving party largess.

The failure of received theories to account for who gets what in the distributive game in developing democracies forces us to re-think the theory, a task we take up in Chapter 3.

2.1 THEORIES OF DISTRIBUTIVE POLITICS

2.1.1 The Swing-Voter Logic

Parties with limited budgets will distribute rewards to some voters but exclude others. What types of voters do they target? To answer this question, the scholarly literature has focused on one dimension along which voters vary: their ideological or partisan proximity to the machine and to its opponents. The groundwork for what has become the dominant view was laid out in a probabilistic voting model by Lindbeck and Weibull.[4] When two parties compete by offering distributive rewards to voters, both will focus their efforts on swing, or ideologically indifferent, voters.[5] To reward voters who are ideologically proximate to the party or ideologically distant from it is to waste resources.

A simple formalism helps communicate the conventional wisdom. We can think of a voter as deriving utility from casting a vote for a party and from receiving a material payment from a party. We use σ to denote a dimension of partisanship on which each voter can be located, with mean of zero (see Figure 2.1). Parties also have locations on this dimension. The partisan or ideological location of a given voter i is denoted by σ^i, and the location of party P is σ^P. We think of these positions of parties and voters as fixed and independent of targeted material payments, at least in the short run. Their positions may reflect preferences about policies – for example, how large should the

---

[4] Lindbeck and Weibull 1987.
[5] Lindbeck and Weibull used the term "marginal" voters.

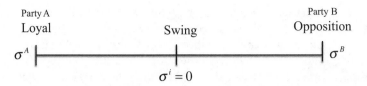

FIGURE 2.1. A Dimension of Partisanship.

government be? – or they may reflect ethnic or religious attachments between parties and leaders. Although it may be the case that partisan or ideological location is related in the long run to material payments (a question we take up below), in the "spot market" of vote buying, it makes sense to distinguish between the partisan or ideological utility of voting for a party or candidate and the benefit from receiving a material payment from a party.

Assume a system in which two parties compete, Party A and Party B. Their positions can be depicted as σ^A and σ^B. A negative value of σ^i indicates a voter's preference for party A, a positive one a preference for party B. Hence a loyal supporter of Party A – a person with a negative σ value – maximizes his or her partisan or ideological utility from voting by casting a ballot for Party A and will experience disutility from voting for Party B. Indifferent voters, those with $\sigma^i = 0$, receive equal utility for voting for A and B. We call them *swing voters*.[6]

We use b^i to denote the utility a voter derives from receiving a discrete benefit from a party. Assume for simplicity that a voter can receive either nothing or a benefit of standardized value, so $b^i \in \{0, b\}$.

The voter's utility takes the following functional form:

$$U^i(b^i, \sigma^i, \sigma^P) = -(\sigma^i - \sigma^P)^2 + b^i$$

The quadratic-loss term implies that a voter's utility rises as the distance between his or her position on σ and that of the party he or she votes for decreases; independently, the voter enjoys receiving a distributive reward.

Theorists have shown that under certain assumptions, parties will focus their distributive largess – b – on swing voters. Groups of voters known to be heavily populated with swing voters will receive more rewards.[7]

The swing-voter theoretical result holds when no party can deliver benefits with particular efficiency to any group of voters. It also holds when this assumption is relaxed and one party can deliver benefits to a group of "core constituents" with relatively little "leakage"[8] or lower administrative costs.[9]

---

[6] Technically, because σ is continuous, the set of voters with $\sigma^i = 0$ has measure zero; to be more precise, we might define swing voters as those in an open interval around $\sigma^i = 0$, or use limits.
[7] Lindbeck and Weibull 1987, Dixit and Londregan 1996.
[8] Dixit and Londregan.
[9] Lindbeck and Weibull.

Efficiency of delivery alters which groups get how much, but it does not basically undermine the logic of swing voters' receiving more benefits.

The reason is that theorists such as Lindbeck and Weibull, and Dixit and Londregan, envision efficiency of delivery as separate from partisanship. For Dixit and Londregan, parties that can deliver benefits efficiently to a given group of voters are ones that are closely intertwined with the group's social networks: "A party's core constituencies need not prefer its issue positions. It is the party's advantage over its competitors at swaying voters in a group with offers of particularistic benefits that makes the group core."[10] The degree of efficiency of distribution – the "leakiness of the bucket" – in Dixit and Londregan's machine/core-voter case is a dimension that is independent of a group's ideology.

We can formalize the idea of efficiency of delivery as a distinct dimension from partisanship or ideology. Following Dixit and Londregan, think of $\theta^{i,P}$ as the leakiness or dead-weight loss associated with the delivery of benefits from party P to voter i; $\theta^{i,P} \in (0,1)$. Consider a voter i who belongs to a group with close ties to Party P. In this case, $\theta^{i,P}$ may be close to zero, a fact that increases the voter's chances of receiving a benefit, whatever his or her ideological orientation or partisanship. Hence we might posit that the probability that voter i receives a benefit b from party P is

$$P^i(b^{i,P} = b|\sigma^i, \theta^{i,P}) = \Phi[-\theta^{i,P}(\sigma^i)^2],$$

where Φ is some probability density function that is symmetric around zero. The probability of a voter receiving a benefit from a given party increases as σ^i approaches zero and, separately, as $\theta^{i,P}$ approaches zero.

To underscore the distinction Dixit and Londregan make between the dimensions of ideology and of efficiency of distribution, we introduce the following terminology. Voters who are proximate to a party in ideological or partisan terms we call *loyalists*.[11] Voters who are network-proximate to a party we call *core constituents*.[12]

An important early paper by Cox and McCubbins apparently represents a sharp departure from the swing-voter logic.[13] Their model leads to parties' preferentially favoring core supporters over swing groups. Cox and McCubbins conceived of groups of voters as falling into three types: core, swing, and opposition. The authors left ascriptive traits of candidates (and voters) and ideological inclinations outside of the model, so these types are not identical to loyal, swing, and opposition voters as they line up on the σ dimension in Figure 2.1. Instead, Cox and McCubbins's conception of core and swing groups

---

[10] Dixit and Londregan 1996, p. 1134.

[11] These are voters for whom $-(\sigma^i - \sigma^P)^2$ approaches zero.

[12] These are voters for whom θ^{iP} approaches zero. Note that $-(\sigma^i - \sigma^P)^2$ may then be large or small; the probability of receiving a benefit is maximized at either $\sigma^i = 0$ or at $\theta^{iP} = 0$.

[13] Cox and McCubbins 1986.

is behavioral: "support groups are those who have consistently supported" a candidate "in the past and to whom he looks for support in the future..." whereas "swing groups are those who have been neither consistently supportive nor consistently hostile."[14]

In deciding which groups it should target, a party takes into account not just their relative responsiveness but the degree of variability of their responsiveness. Cox and McCubbins make assumptions about the responsiveness of distinct groups to distributive largess. Opposition groups are unresponsive and hence will be written off. Turning to core and swing groups, Cox and McCubbins posited that although swing voters may be the most responsive, core support-ers are the most predictable: "candidates are generally less uncertain about the electoral responses of support groups than they are about the electoral responses of swing groups," and hence "risk-averse candidates should invest relatively more in their support groups (thus increasing stability)..."[15] With echoes of other theorists' ideas about administrative proximity and efficiency of delivery to core groups, here core voters are better known to their party, their responsiveness to rewards more predictable.

To accept this version of why distributive parties focus on core (but note, not necessarily ideologically like-minded) voters, one must be prepared to accept that core supporters' *responsiveness to rewards* is less variable than that of swing votes. This is quite different from core voters being predictable in their *vote choices*.[16] One must also accept that candidates would be willing to sac-rifice *vote share* in favor of greater *stability* of electoral coalitions.

Common to the models of distributive politics that we have been discussing is that they resolve commitment problems by fiat. Parties that offer people rewards before the election do not renege afterwards, and voters are implicitly assumed not to turn their backs on machines in the privacy of the voting booth. This shortcoming is addressed in a paper by Stokes.[17] She models distributive politics as an iterated game of prisoner's dilemma. A machine offers a voter a reward in return for his vote. The voter cares about the ideological position of the party and about the reward. The embeddedness of machines in the networks of voters allows them to draw inferences about how voters voted and hence to circumvent, at least in part, the secrecy of the ballot. Even without perfect information about voters' electoral choices, machines can use this embedded-ness to credibly threaten to retaliate against defectors by withdrawing rewards in the future.

Hence, whereas embeddedness increases distributive efficiency in Dixit and Londregan's model and reduces uncertainty in Cox and McCubbins's, in Stokes's model, embeddedness allows machines to monitor voters' choices and to credibly threaten to punish defectors.

[14] Cox and McCubbins 1986, p. 376.
[15] Cox and McCubbins 1986, pp. 377–378.
[16] Uncertainty about responsiveness is not directly modeled by Cox and McCubbins.
[17] Stokes 2005.

Stokes's theoretical conclusions are in some ways similar to Lindbeck and Weibull's and Dixit and Londregan's. From the viewpoint of Party A in Figure 2.1, all voters to the left of the swing voter – all for whom $\sigma^i < 0$ – can be "taken for granted."[18] But rather than "writing off" all voters to the right of the swing voter, there is a set of voters – Stokes calls them the "weakly opposed" – whose disutility for voting for Party A can be compensated with the reward b^i. They, along with swing voters, are the predicted targets of machine largess.

To summarize, the main thrust of theories of distributive politics is that swing voters, or ones who are weakly opposed to the party machine, are its main targets. Voters who make up a party's core constituents also benefit; not their partisanship but their network proximity or reliability brings them to the party's attention. Even among core constituents, the implicit prediction is that strong partisans can be taken for granted, whereas indifferent or mildly opposed voters will get special attention from party machines.

2.1.2 Testing Swing-Voter Theories

To test the swing-voter prediction, we turn to individual-level evidence from several sources, including our original survey data from contemporary Argentina, Venezuela, and India, and from publicly available surveys of individual voters from Mexico.[19] These countries vary in many important ways, such as in their levels of economic development, presidential versus parliamentary systems of government, colonial heritage, age of democracy, and degrees of federalism. But they are all settings in which parties exchange targeted material benefits for votes and political support. The consistency of the effect of voters' ideological or partisan type on their probability of receiving machine largesse across these settings – and the inconsistency of these effects with theoretical predictions – underscore the need for rethinking the theory.

Argentina
Argentina's 1983 return to democracy revived a party system dominated by the Peronist (PJ) and Radical (UCR) parties, the two leading parties during Argentina's democratic interludes since the 1940s.[20] Our first survey, conducted in December 2001–January 2002, captured this highly competitive two-party system. Two Radical-led presidential administrations ended in disasters;

---

[18] Here we consider a "machine party" with resources to distribute; this machine need not fear that voters with $\sigma^i < 0$ will be poached by party B.

[19] We have reason in subsequent chapters to revisit the actions of distributive parties as they make more aggregate-level choices – whether to favor one or another district, province, or city. However, we follow the observation of Cox (2007) that distribution among districts or other aggregate units is not necessarily pertinent to the question of what kind of voters are being targeted. Benefits sent to swing districts might be meted out within these districts to the parties' most ardent supporters, or largesse spent on districts that are "loyal" at the aggregate level might go to undecided or swing voters within those districts.

[20] PJ stands for Partido Justicialista, UCR for Unión Cívica Radical.

TABLE 2.1. *Primary Survey Data: Sample and Sources*

Country and Year of Survey	Sample	Source for Details
Argentina 2001–2002	480 adults in each of 4 provinces	Appendix B and Brusco et al. 2004
Argentina 2003	500 adults in each of 4 provinces	Appendix B
Argentina 2009	600 adults in each of 2 provinces	Appendix B and Lupu 2011
Argentina 2009–2010	200 brokers in each of 4 provinces	Appendix A and Camp 2012
Venezuela 2009–2010	2,000 adults in 8 largest cities partially merged with Maisanta database	Appendix C
Mexico 2000	National sample of approximately 2,400 adults across 4 waves	http://web.mit.edu/ polisci/facutly/ C.Lawson.html
India 2009–2012	6,977 adults in the states of Karnataka, Bihar, and Rajasthan	Appendix E Dunning and Nilekani 2013

the first disaster, under Raúl Alfonsin (1983–1989), was economic, the second, under Fernando de la Rúa (1999–2002), economic and political. Our post–De la Rúa surveys, carried out in 2003 and 2009, coincided with a changed party system. The Radical Party struggled nationally and in many provinces and localities. The Peronist Party was dominant over other parties but was also riven by factions; the party competed against a debilitated Radical Party and against other parties, some to its left and some to its right. Across the full period, our surveys detected vote buying and reliance on political parties for access to state resources, jobs, and other valued goods. Beginning in 2009, we also conducted a survey of low-level party operatives or brokers, which we discuss later.[21]

Table 2.1 provides information about our Argentine voter surveys as well as other surveys that we analyze from Venezuela, Mexico, and India (see also Appendixes A through D for more detailed information). The 2001–2002, 2003, and 2009 Argentina voter surveys were each probability samples of distinct voters from several Argentine provinces; they were not a panel. The 2003 survey filtered out higher-income people from the sampling frame. In all three Argentine voter surveys, we asked similar questions designed to detect exchanges of benefits for votes.

---

[21] Our research here is informed by excellent studies of clientelism and distributive politics in Argentina, including Auyero 2001, Calvo and Murillo 2004, Camp 2012, Levitsky 2003, Lodola 2005, Szwarcberg 2009, Weitz-Shapiro 2011, and others.

The 2001 survey asked questions that referred to national legislative and provincial elections that had taken place two months earlier. We asked respondents whether, during the campaign, political operatives or candidates had given out goods in their neighborhood. Eight hundred thirty-nine people – 44 percent of the sample of 1,920 – said they had. We asked what had been given out. The most common item mentioned was food, but also mentioned were clothing, mattresses, medicine, milk, corrugated metal, construction materials, blankets, hangers, utility bill payments, money, eyeglasses, chickens, trees, and magnets. One hundred forty-one people – 7 percent of the sample – acknowledged receiving goods themselves.

When asked which party distributed goods, the most frequent answer was the Peronists (418 respondents); 48 individuals reported that the Radical party was the one giving out goods; and another 7 percent of the sample – 138 people – responded "Peronists and Radicals" to this open-ended question. Of those who reported having received something, close to 70 percent reported that it was the Peronist Party that was doing the distributing, as against 10 percent for the Radicals. The remaining 20 percent mentioned minor parties or groupings.

Given the preponderance of the Peronist Party in vote buying – a survey result utterly in line with the considerable recent literature on Peronism and distributive politics in Argentina – it is instructive to explore the opinions that those who received goods held of that party. These views, in a nutshell, are positive. Recipients of campaign distributions are more closely aligned with Peronism than the swing-voter prediction leads us to expect.

People who received goods generally held more favorable opinions of the Peronist Party than did those who did not. Figure 2.2 captures differences in opinions of the Peronist Party among people who did, and did not, receive campaign benefits. Each bar shows the proportional difference between the percentage holding a given opinion – from "very good" to "very bad" – depending on whether or not the respondent received a gift. For instance, about 8.2 percent of people who received rewards thought the party was very good, but only about 2.6 percent of those who did not receive them held this opinion – a proportional difference of (8.2–2.6)/2.6 or around 2.15 (or 215 percent). At the other extreme, a considerably lower proportion of those who received a gift than those who did not considered the party "very bad" – 11 percent versus 32 percent, a proportional difference of −0.66 or −66 percent. Later in this chapter, we consider the possibility that gift recipients might view the machine more positively simply because they have received gifts – that gifts cause loyalty rather than loyalty attracting gifts. However, we conclude that this alternative explanation cannot readily account for our evidence. Here, we simply document the fact that voters with good opinions of the party are more likely to have received gifts.

In our 2003 survey as well, we asked whether goods were given out in the respondent's neighborhood and whether the respondent received anything. The reference in this question was to the April 2003 national election. Thirty percent

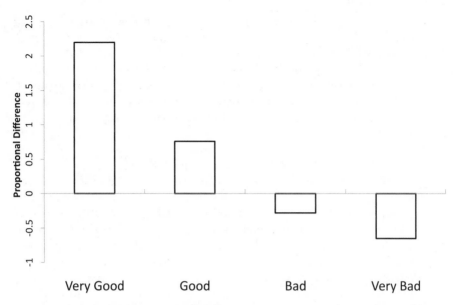

FIGURE 2.2. Argentina: Proportional Difference Between Reward Recipients and Non-recipients in Percentages Holding "Very Good," "Good," "Bad," and "Very Bad" Opinions of the Peronists. *Source:* 2001–2002 Argentina survey, N = 1,776.

of the sample reported that a party gave things out in their neighborhood (589 people out of a sample of 2,000); just under 7 percent (135 individuals) reported personally having received something. Among those who could name the party distributing goods in their neighborhood, by far the most frequently mentioned party was, again, the Peronists: 74 percent (166/224) said the Peronists gave things out, as against 15 percent who said the Radical party did.[22]

It therefore again makes sense to compare opinions of the Peronists among those who did and who did not receive campaign handouts. Recall that, if the swing voter proposition is right, we expect machines not to target their loyal supporters with campaign handouts. In the Argentine setting, Peronist supporters should receive goods at lower rates than non-Peronists, if at all.

But the data go against this expectation. For example, we asked whether the person identified with any political party (and then followed up with those who answer yes with the question, "which party?"). Whereas about 5.5 percent of the non-Peronists received goods, about 8.5 percent of Peronists did. Some

---

[22] As in the 2001 survey, this was an open-ended question, and some people mentioned more than one party. Including all mentions of the Peronists raises the percentage to 79 percent (176 people); including all mentions of the Radicals raises the percentage to 19 percent (43 people).

swing or weakly opposed voters did receive some benefits, but the mix of recipients is heterogeneous; and, contra the theory, a larger proportion of loyalists received benefits than swing voters.

Like the 2001–2002 and 2003 surveys, our 2009 survey offers evidence that, contra Lindbeck and Weibull, Dixit and Londregan, and Stokes, loyal, not swing, voters received most campaign gifts. Here we solicited more fine-grained opinions of parties, from zero (dislikes the party greatly) to 10 (likes the party greatly). The results were roughly the same as in 2001–2002: more than twice the percentage of those who had highly favorable views of the Peronists than those who were indifferent toward it received campaign gifts.

The 2009 survey also asked respondents a more abstract question about whether a hypothetical broker would distribute benefits "like bags of food, mattresses, or subsidies" to a voter who "preferred the broker's party" or to one who was indifferent between competing parties. Here again, 60 percent of respondents said goods would go to the voter who preferred the party, 40 percent to other sorts of voters. Hence a majority anticipated goods going to the party loyalists; a minority (though not a small one) appeared to agree with distributive theorists in expecting goods to go to indifferent people.

Yet perhaps these results are misleading. Partisanship aside, we expect machines to target poor people, a point we develop in detail later in this book. Peronist affinities are more common among the ranks of the Argentine poor. Hence it is possible that the higher than expected representation of Peronists among the recipients of campaign gifts is an artifact of Peronists on average having lower incomes. To explore this possibility, we inspect the relative frequencies of campaign gift recipients among Peronists and non-Peronists, this time restricting ourselves to low-income respondents.

The results are not very different. About 7 percent of poor non-Peronists received goods, as compared with nearly 11 percent of poor Peronist supporters (i.e., those who responded "Peronist" when we asked the party with which they identify).

The discussion thus far has focused on vote buying before elections. Much the same story emerges when we turn our attention to the distribution of government benefits through social programs, of which there were several in Argentina during this period. Our 2003 survey asked whether the respondent received a "subsidy" (as benefits from social programs are known colloquially). Restricting ourselves again to low-income respondents, 36 percent of the non-Peronist poor received support, compared with 46 percent of the Peronist poor, implying that being a Peronist is associated with an increased likelihood of receiving a benefit of 10 percentage points. Not all government programs use income as an official criterion of distribution, and it is certainly not the only criterion. Still, that the spigots were opened wider for the Peronist poor than for the non-Peronist poor suggests a manipulation of public programs. However, the key point is that the political manipulation here – the departure from programmatic distribution – favors not swing voters but loyalists.

The reader might worry that social norms would make many people reluctant to acknowledge receiving "gifts" during political campaigns. Our questions about social programs go some distance toward avoiding this problem – receiving them is a priori more acceptable than receiving campaign gifts such as food, building materials, or chickens. Still, social desirability problems are worrisome. In a different Latin American setting, González-Ocantos, Kiewiet de Jonge, Meléndez, Osorio, and Nickerson used an innovative list experiment to study the problem of social acceptability and clientelism.[23] Their study found that 24 percent of Nicaraguans surveyed had in fact received a campaign gift, whereas, when asked directly, taking a gift was acknowledged by a mere 2.5 percent.

To counter social desirability bias, in 2009 we devised a survey experiment. In this survey, as in the earlier two, we asked respondents whether they had received goods from candidates or party operatives in the prior campaign, this time referring to recent national mid-term elections. However, here we randomly assigned respondents to one of four versions of the question. Each subsequent treatment provides what were designed to be increasingly acceptable justifications for accepting a campaign gift. The wordings are reproduced here:

Treatment 1 During the recent electoral campaign, did you receive a handout (*ayuda*) or benefit from a candidate or political operative?

Treatment 2 In Argentina it is perfectly legal for a voter to receive benefits from candidates or party operatives during electoral campaigns.[24] During the recent electoral campaign, did a candidate or political operative give you a handout or benefit?

Treatment 3 In a democracy, voters expect to receive benefits from candidates and political operatives during campaigns. During the recent electoral campaign, did a candidate or political operative give you a handout or benefit?

Treatment 4 In a democracy, voters expect to receive benefits from candidates and political operatives during campaigns, and in Argentina it is perfectly legal for a voter to receive benefits from candidates or party operatives during electoral campaigns. During the recent electoral campaign, did a candidate or political operative give you a handout or benefit?

Five percent of our sample overall answered yes to these questions. The percentage answering yes rose monotonically across the experimental conditions. At the extremes, just under 4 percent answered yes to the question as posed in the first treatment, in which there was no priming to increase the social acceptability of taking a campaign gift; just over 6 percent answered yes to the question in the fourth treatment, which doubly primed respondents to see receiving a gift as socially acceptable. The differences in responses were not

[23] González-Ocantos, Kiewiet de Jonge, Meléndez, Osorio, and Nickerson, 2011.
[24] Indeed, by Argentine law, it is illegal for parties to treat voters but not for voters to receive treats.

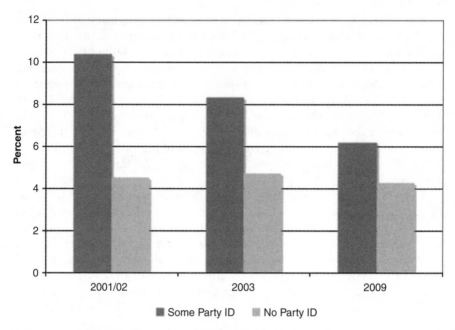

FIGURE 2.3. Argentina: Percentage of Respondents Receiving Campaign Gifts by Some or No Party Affiliation. *Source:* Voter Surveys, N = 5,014.

statistically significant, however, so our experimental conditions do not appear to increase the social acceptability of reporting vote buying.

Again, the swing voter prediction was contradicted. The probability of a positive answer rose slightly among Peronist supporters. Probit analysis shows a small positive effect of holding a Peronist identity on the probability of reporting that one received a campaign gift, though the coefficient estimate loses significance when controls for income are introduced. However, recall that the theoretical prediction that we are testing is that Peronists would be *less* likely to receive goodies than would swing voters; the prediction, again, is in tension with real-world practice.

Up until now we have been treating non-Peronists as though they were swing voters and treating Peronists as loyalists to Argentina's machine party. But another way to think about swing voters is that rather than being people who are indifferent toward the machine, they are people with no party affiliation at all. By this interpretation, did swing voters attract more gifts?

The answer is no. Recall that in all three Argentine voter surveys, we asked whether the person identified with any political party and which one. As Figure 2.3 shows, fewer non-identifiers received gifts consistently across the three surveys: in 2001, less than half the percentage, in 2003 half the percentage, and in 2009 50 percent fewer. The same holds true of beneficiaries of social programs. Seventy-three percent of party identifiers reported having received a state subsidy, compared with 62 percent among people with no party identification. The gap of more than 10 percentage points again goes against the swing-voter prediction.

In sum, our survey research in Argentina, conducted over nearly a decade, offers little support for the theoretical conclusion that swing voters are the primary recipients of distributive largess – either social programs or campaign gifts. Loyal supporters receive too much of the machine's resources, swing voters too little.

Venezuela

Our original research in Venezuela also affords opportunities to test swing-voter predictions. Two political parties dominated Venezuelan politics between 1958 and the start of the 1990s: Democratic Action (Acción Democrática, AD), and COPEI. AD favored more redistributive policies and had strong links with organized labor; COPEI was Christian Democratic in origin and more conservative in policy orientation. Both parties were factionalized, and both competed with a mix of programmatic appeals, patronage, and clientelism.[25] In 1998, Hugo Chávez, a left-leaning former military officer, was elected president. Electoral support for AD and COPEI collapsed; never again has either attracted large numbers of votes.

By several measures, clientelism remained an important feature of electoral politics in Venezuela under Chávez.[26] Surveys from 2004 onward register about 10–12 percent of voters reporting that they received benefits in exchange for their votes.[27]

These surveys are an indication that vote buying did not come to a halt under Chávez, who also deployed programmatic distributive benefits and ample rhetorical efforts to stay ahead of the opposition. Electoral support for Chávez in 1998 came from a diffuse group of voters, in class terms, and the new president was elected with a substantial mandate and very high initial approval ratings. But in the early 2000s, with low world oil prices and mixed success in helping poor Venezuelans, Chávez's popularity sank. The Venezuelan polity became polarized between pro-Chávez supporters and the opposition, a polarization that strongly crystallized in 2002 and 2003. A failed coup attempt in April 2002 was accompanied by violent confrontations in the streets of Caracas between pro- and anti-Chávez groups. At the end of 2002 and beginning of 2003, Chávez also faced a nearly three-month general strike that was

---

[25] See Coppedge 1994.

[26] See, e.g., Hawkins 2010, Ortega and Penfold 2008.

[27] In LAPOP's 2010 survey, 11.6 percent of Venezuelan respondents answered yes to the question, Did a political party offer you a material benefit in exchange for your vote? Latinobarometer surveys in 2005 found 12 percent of Venezuelans reporting having received a gift in exchange for their votes. However, our own survey in 2007 found less than 3 percent of respondents saying they had received such a benefit. We describe our survey in detail in Appendix C.

concentrated in the oil sector. In the wake of the strike, the president's popularity was at an all-time low (see Appendix C).

In response, in 2004 the Venezuelan government ratcheted up its distribution of targeted material rewards. The political pressure for spending came from the opposition's drive to remove Chávez from office through a recall referendum, whereas the economic opportunity came from the spike in oil prices after the United States' invasion of Iraq. The dramatic rise in social spending in the run-up to the recall elections of 2004 allows us to evaluate the impact of partisanship, as perceived by the government, on its distribution of benefits. As we explain later in more depth, this case also helps to some extent to avoid problems of reverse causation, with prior giving inducing "loyalty" rather than partisan loyalty inducing giving, because both *chavismo* – partisan loyalty to the President – and the social programs were quite new.

Drawing on a government database and a follow-up survey, we were able to study the distribution of targeted social programs conditional on the partisan orientations of voters. During the campaign against the recall election in 2004, the government compiled information from two separate recall petitions signed against Chávez and against certain opposition deputies. This "Maisanta" database, which we describe in detail in Appendix C, contained data on the ideological orientation and turnout histories of more than 12 million individuals, the universe of registered voters who as of July 10, 2004, were eligible to vote in the August 15th referendum.[28] The data were then distributed to local party activists in the form of a software program with a user-friendly interface. Individual records were searchable either by name or address or by "*cédula*," a unique national identification number comparable in power to a Social Security Number in the United States but used much more widely by Venezuelans in daily life (e.g., to sign credit card bills in restaurants).[29]

As the screenshot of the software depicted in Figure 2.4 shows, a successful hit in the database returns an individual's address, location of his or her voting center, and his or her access to government-sponsored social programs at the time of Maisanta's construction.[30] Each record also reports whether the voter signed a recall petition against Chávez (people who did are coded in the government's dataset as "opposition" voters), signed a recall petition against opposition deputies (coded as "patriots"), or did not sign any recall petition.[31] For instance, the individual shown in the screenshot in Figure 2.4 did not sign any recall petition (as indicated by the phrase "did not sign against the President" in the shaded box; in Spanish, "*No firmó contra el Presidente*"). The

---

[28] To be exact, the Maisanta database contains 12,394,109 entries, corresponding to individual Venezuelan voters.

[29] In Appendix C, we discuss further details about the construction, dissemination, and use of the Maisanta dataset. For other studies that use the Maisanta database, see Dunning and Stokes 2007, Hsieh et al. 2011, and Albertus 2010.

[30] We have blacked out the individual's name in the "Apellidos y Nombre" box in Figure 2.4.

[31] We only found a few instances of individuals who signed recall petitions both against Chávez and against opposition deputies, so these can be considered mutually exclusive categories.

FIGURE 2.4. Venezuela: Screenshot of Maisanta Software Interface.

bottom left of the user interface also recorded whether this voter was viewed as an "abstainer" – *absencionista* – a measure we discuss further later. Thus, using this software, local militants could learn voters' partisan or ideological tendency, past turnout/abstention history, and the extent of participation in social programs at the time of the recall campaign (as measured by the Misión Ribas and Vuelvan Caras boxes at the bottom left of Figure 2.4). At the time Maisanta was developed, however, the Mission social programs were in their infancy (see Appendix C).[32]

One piece of information that the database did not include was individuals' incomes. Because low incomes are expected to correlate both with support for Chávez and with eligibility for social assistance, a failure to take income into account could bias results. Nor does the database record participation in a variety of new social programs, *Misiones*, that were rolled out starting in 2003 and 2004.[33] We therefore supplemented the Maisanta database with additional original research. In 2007, we administered a survey to a probability sample of 2,000 adults in the eight largest Venezuelan cities, gathering information about individuals' receipt of benefits during and after the recall

---

[32] Readers may note this particular individual was born in 1905 – as indicated by the box labeled "Fecha Nac," which stands for "*fecha de nacimiento*" or "date of birth."

[33] Note that participation in two social programs as of 2004 – the "Misión Ribas" and "Vuelvan Caras" – is noted in boxes at the bottom left of Figure 2.4. However, participation in many other programs, such as the Misión Robinson discussed later, as well as a panoply of other social Missions, is not recorded in Maisanta; moreover, even for Misión Ribas and Vuelvan Caras, participation greatly expanded after the construction of Maisanta.

campaign, social program participation, and other variables.[34] To be able to link respondents to the information about them in the Maisanta database, we also solicited their unique personal identifiers.[35] Our analysis here focuses on people's participation, during and after the recall election, in two targeted social programs: an adult literacy program called *Misión Robinson* and a high-school equivalency program called *Misión Ribas*. Both provide scholarships to participants. Payments under the Ribas Mission come in the form of "grants" (of 180,000 Venezuelan *bolivares* a month as of 2004, or about US$85 at official exchange rates) and "incentives" (of 200,000 *bolivares*, or about US$94). Our field research suggests that scholarships were not closely tied to attendance in the program or to scholastic achievement; instead they served mainly as cash transfers to recipients.

Whether we focus on people's attitudes toward the government as they reported them in our survey or on their posture vis-a-vis the government as registered in the Maisanta database, the results offer little support for swing-voter theories. Figure 2.5 displays the distribution of beneficiaries of targeted programs by the respondent's self-reported party preference. Those who prefer parties from the ruling coalition received benefits at a higher rate than those who said they preferred no party (the "swing" voters); swing voters in turn received more benefits than did opposition supporters. The same trend is visible in Figure 2.6, which uses the Maisanta databases's coding of individuals by political orientation. Here again, pro-Chávez petitioners (those who signed petitions against opposition deputies) received most benefits, swing voters received less, and those who signed petitions against the president received least of all.[36]

---

[34] See Appendix C. In this analysis, we do not use the information on benefit receipt contained in the Maisanta database itself, which was current as of the end of 2003 and therefore does not likely reflect targeting based on the information on political affiliation contained in Maisanta; moreover, participation in these programs was just beginning at this time as the programs were new. Rather, information on the dependent variable is drawn from our ex-post surveys of a probability sample of citizens.

[35] We were able to obtain valid *cédula* numbers and merge them with the Maisanta database for about one-quarter of respondents. The data are probably not missing at random: respondents whom we were able to merge with Maisanta are, on average, slightly older, poorer, and less educated, and they are somewhat more likely to work in the public sector and identify with a party in the governing coalition. However, although statistically significant, the differences are relatively small: for instance, those who gave us valid IDs are only about 6 percentage points more likely to identify with a party in the governing coalition. See Appendix C for fuller discussion of the data and possible threats to valid causal inference.

[36] However, the sample size drops considerably, from N = 1,849 in Figure 2.5 based on self-reports of partisan affiliation to N = 492 based on recorded preference in Maisanta; this drop is due to failure to merge about three quarters of our sample with the Maisanta database (see previous note). Although the missingness is not strongly related to observable variables such as age, gender, and self-reported income, it could clearly introduce some bias, e.g., if tendency to report a valid *cédula* to survey interviewers is related to political affiliation or benefit receipt. The fact that results are very similar in Figures 2.5 and 2.6 may give some confidence that missing data do not excessively distort our results.

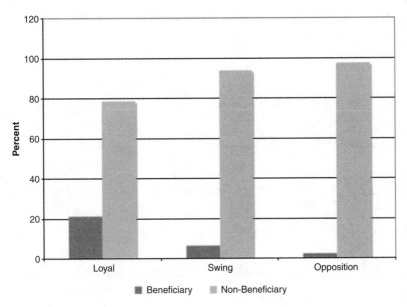

FIGURE 2.5. Venezuela: *Misiones* Beneficiaries by Self-Reported Party Preference. *Source:* Survey Data, N = 1,849.

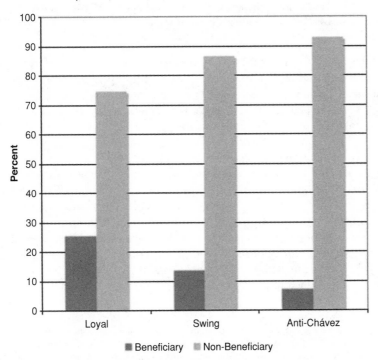

FIGURE 2.6. Venezuela: *Misiones* Beneficiaries by Preference Recorded in *Maisanta*. *Source:* Maisanta Database and Survey Data, N = 492.

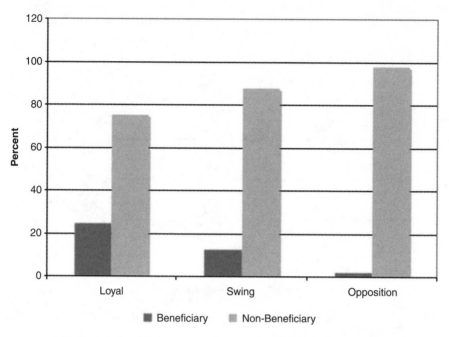

FIGURE 2.7. Venezuela: *Misiones* Beneficiaries by Self-Reported Party Preference, Poorest 20 Percent of Respondents. *Source:* Survey Data, N = 377.

Yet, as in Argentina, we must ask, Is the ruling party's apparent preference for its own partisans actually a spurious effect of these people having low incomes and hence being more eligible for targeted benefits?

The answer seems to be no. The distribution of support conditional on party preference among the bottom 20 percent of the income distribution reveals a strong bias toward loyalists, a weaker trend toward swing voters, and very few rewards going to opposition voters (see Figure 2.7).

Multivariate analysis yields similar results.[37] In Table 2.2, we present results from nearest-neighbor matching, using the matching algorithm of Abadie et al.[38] In the first row, each loyal voter – that is, each voter who signed a recall petition against an opposition deputy – is compared with a control voter who did not sign a recall petition (a swing voter) or a voter who signed a recall petition against Chávez (an opposition voter); the comparison voter in the control group is matched as closely as possible with the "treated" voter with respect to gender, age, education level, whether the respondent is a public-sector

---

[37] In Appendix C, we present a more complete description of the threats to inference in this case.
[38] Abadie et al. 2004. Here, the weighting matrix for the distance metric is the inverse variance. Individual matches in the control group may be used more than once (matching with replacement).

TABLE 2.2. *Targeting of Loyal Voters in Venezuela (Nearest-Neighbor Matching)*

	Sample Average Treatment Effect
Loyal voters	14.3%
(vs. swing and opposition voters)	(4.6%)
Swing voters	7.3%
(vs. opposition voters)	4.1%

The first row of the table shows the estimated effect of having signed against Chávez on the probability of receiving a targeted benefit through participation in Misión Ribas or Robinson (expressed as a percentage). The second row shows the estimated effect of not having signed any recall petition, relative to signing a petition against Chávez, on the same probabililty. Nearest-neighbor matching on gender, age, education, whether the respondent is a public-worker, and a full set of dummy variables for the voting center at which the respondent votes. For the first row, N = 483; for the second row, N = 354.

worker, and geographic place of residence.[39] The matching variables are all discrete, so in principle exact matching is possible; in practice, however, it is usually impossible to find an untreated observation that exactly matches each treated observation on all of these measured covariates.

As the first row of Table 2.2 shows, loyal voters have a markedly larger probability of participating in a targeted social program than do swing or opposition voters. Indeed, the estimated average treatment effect (the difference between average participation by treated and control respondents) is 0.143, or 14.3 percentage points. Because the probability of participating in one of the targeted social programs is 11.3 percent among matched swing and opposition voters, the estimated effect implies an increase of nearly 127 percent in the probability of participation in the targeted program.[40] Results are qualitatively similar (but the sample size is smaller) if respondents are also matched on self-reported income, rather than on level of education.

The second row of Table 2.2 compares swing voters (those who neither signed recall petitions against the government or against the opposition) to opposition voters (those who signed against Chávez); loyal voters, those who signed against opposition deputies, are dropped. Again, we matched swing voters to opposition voters of the same gender, age, education level, public-sector occupation, and geographic location of their polling place. The evidence also shows an effect of political variables, though not as large as for the loyal voters: the probability that swing voters participate in a targeted program is

[39] We use the voting center at which the respondent votes as our measure of geography.

[40] Note that the unconditional (unadjusted) probability of participating in a targeted program, among loyal voters, is 0.254; the unconditional probability among all swing and opposition voters is 0.113. Thus the difference of 0.141 between these groups is only negligibly different from the estimate obtained after matching. With an estimated standard error of 0.046, the estimated average treatment effect is also highly statistically significant.

0.073 points greater than the probability that an opposition voter does so. (With an estimated standard error of 0.041, the estimate is significant at the 0.1 level.) Being a swing voter increases the estimated probability of receiving government support by around 74 percent, relative to opposition voters.[41]

There are some nontrivial possible limitations on the validity of causal inferences in this setting, which we discuss more fully in Appendix C: for instance, problems related to missing national ID data or the possibility of confounding from unobserved variables – which is why we turn later to research designs in other contexts that help us to surmount some of these difficulties. Yet, the evidence from Venezuela, as from Argentina, is strongly suggestive: it points toward loyal voters being favored in the distributive game more than swing voters and swing voters being targeted more than opposition voters.

Mexico

During more than 70 years of uninterrupted rule, Mexico's Party of the Institutionalized Revolution (*Partido Revolucionario Institucional*, PRI) traded public resources for political compliance and support. We begin with evidence that loyal supporters of the PRI benefited from PRI largess at higher rates than did the indifferent or the undecided. Our evidence comes from just one election period and one form of clientelism; later in the book we turn to more variegated evidence about clientelist strategies in Mexico.[42] With the individual evidence at hand, we shall see that, in Mexico as in Argentina and Venezuela, substantial resources flowed to voters who already appeared to be strong PRI supporters. To be sure, some indifferent and even strongly opposed voters were targeted during the electoral campaign, a fact consistent with brokers' sending benefits to an ideologically heterogeneous group. Still, the evidence points toward the ruling party heavily targeting loyal supporters.

To study the impact of a person's partisan orientation on her likelihood of attracting benefits from the PRI, we draw on the Mexico 2000 Panel Study. Investigators interviewed around 2,400 people across four waves, before and just after the watershed national elections of 2000.[43] Later in this chapter we

---

[41] As discussed in connection with Table 2.7 later, we reach a similar conclusion from estimation of logistic regression models: the predicted probability of benefit receipt among loyal certain voters is at least twice the predicted probability of benefit for receipt of any other combination of partisan orientation and turnout propensity, setting other variables at their empirical means (or medians).

[42] There is a rich literature on clientelism and distributive politics in Mexico, from which we draw. See, e.g., Magaloni 2006, Magaloni et al. 2007, Greene 2007, Molinar and Weldon 1994, Hiskey 1999, Bruhn 1996.

[43] Respondents were sampled and interviewed in a first wave; a subset was selected randomly and reinterviewed in a second wave; the respondents left out of the second wave were interviewed in a third wave; and all respondents were sought for interviews for a fourth wave. This four-wave panel study took place before the 2000 election; another survey took place after the election with a different randomly drawn cross-section of respondents. See Mexico 2000 Panel Study, "Explanation of the Data", at http://web.mit.edu/polisci/faculty/C.Lawson.html.

exploit the panel structure of the data to test the hypothesis that PRI benefits turned recipients into "loyalists."

We study the relationship between a voter's partisan orientation and his or her receipt of a campaign gift from the PRI. As Cornelius has noted, the level of campaign vote buying detected in the survey was modest by Mexican standards.[44] Not surprisingly, the then-incumbent and long-ruling PRI was consistently reported to be the party doing most of the vote buying. Survey respondents were asked whether they were PRI, National Action Party (*Partido de Acción Nacional*, PAN), or Revolutionary Democratic Party (*Partido Revolucionario Democrático*, PRD) supporters, or whether they supported no party. In the Mexican context at the time, it makes sense to consider PAN and PRD supporters to be "opposition voters," those located toward the one end of the σ dimension in Figure 2.1.[45] The PAN was the most serious competitor to the PRI and indeed defeated the ruling party in the 2000 election. PRD supporters were also strongly in opposition; although the party was headed by a former PRI leader, it was opposed to the PRI on the dimensions both of democratization and of economic policy.[46] Those claiming no party affiliation can be conceived of as swing voters.

Three waves of the survey included the question, "In the last few weeks, have you received gifts or assistance from a party?" A yes response was followed by the question, "Which party?" The PRI was far and away the party most frequently cited as giving out benefits in campaigns, and PRI supporters were consistently the largest group receiving them. Those claiming no party support consistently were the second-most feted group, followed by supporters of the PAN and the PRD. Figure 2.8 illustrates this pattern. It cross-tabulates those who said they received a gift in one of the three waves when this question was asked with voter's self-declared partisan affinity. Fifty percent of those receiving campaign benefits reported that they were PRI supporters. Twenty-eight percent were undecided. Opposition voters, those supporting the PAN or PRD, represented 12 and 6 percent of beneficiaries, respectively.

Hence in Mexico, as in the other two Latin American countries, greater proportions of loyal than swing voters were favored in machine politics, defying most theoretical predictions.

India

We can also appeal to evidence from another context in which vote buying is rife: contemporary India. India is a developing-country democracy with much

---

[44] See Cornelius in Domínguez and Lawson 2004. The question read, "In recent weeks, have you received gifts or assistance from some political party?" We focus on the PRI because it is the party most often mentioned as having given a gift. One hundred sixty-four people, less than 7 percent of the sample, reported receiving a campaign gift at some point over the waves of surveys.

[45] Obviously, the PAN and PRD differ historically on a number of ideological dimensions; here we are emphasizing partisan affinities, relative to the PRI.

[46] See Collier 1992.

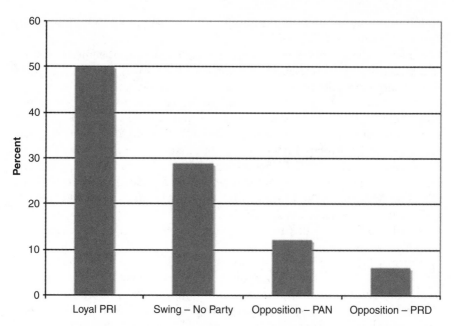

FIGURE 2.8. Mexico: Campaign Distribution by Partisanship. *Source:* Mexico 2000 Survey Data, N = 114.

nonprogrammatic distributive politics – a "patronage democracy," in Chandra's phrase – and one in which inter-party competition is intense.[47] Much distributive politics in India is clientelistic: parties make quid-pro-quo exchanges with voters, demanding the latters' participation and their votes. The importance of "vote banks" to Indian parties, and the use of targeted inducements around elections to motivate particular kinds of voters to turn out and vote for parties, has been noted at least since Independence.[48]

Dunning and Nilekani gathered survey data from villagers and from the members and presidents of village councils (called *gram panchayats*), as well as from local bureaucrats in the Indian states of Karnataka, Rajasthan, and Bihar.[49] They asked questions about the receipt of jobs and other benefits by villagers, the functioning and priorities of councils, and fiscal data on spending allocations. Village councils are significant conduits for central and state government funds, and many of the benefits that are allocated by village councils, such as housing, employment, and receipt of individual welfare schemes, are individually targeted goods. Dunning and Nilekani's fieldwork, along with evidence from previous studies, suggests that council members, and especially the

---

[47] Chandra 2004. See also Wilkinson 2007, Krishna 2003, Ziegfeld 2012, Cole 2009, Khemani 2007, and Rodden and Wilkinson 2004.

[48] Srinivas 1955.

[49] Dunning 2010, Dunning and Nilekani 2013. See Appendix D.

council president, can exercise substantial discretion and influence in selecting the beneficiaries of such schemes.[50]

Although Dunning and Nilekani found very weak distributive effects of other factors that might explain targeting – in particular, the presence of electoral quotas for marginalized castes and tribes – they show that party affiliation is strongly and significantly related to the allocation of benefits.[51] Their surveys asked citizens and council presidents to state to which political party they belonged; a follow-up question asked citizens (including those who professed no party membership) to which party they felt closest.[52] We used responses to these questions to code two indicator variables. The first is equal to one if the respondent shares the political party of the village council president and zero otherwise; the second is equal to one if the respondent feels closest to the party of the council president and zero otherwise.[53]

Citizens in Karnataka who share the political party of the council president are nearly 13 percentage points more likely than others in the state to have received a job or benefit from the council in the previous year, a difference that is highly statistically significant (Table 2.3, first row). Among citizens from marginalized groups (Scheduled Castes and Scheduled Tribes), the difference is also nearly 10 percentage points (Table 2.3, second row). In separate analyses, we also found that citizens who share the party of the council president are 13 percentage points more likely than others to say they had received a gift from a political party or candidate before an election, in return for turning out to vote (significant at the 0.001 level).[54] Our findings are similar in other Indian states, including Rajasthan and Bihar (see Appendix D and Dunning and Nilekani 2013).

---

[50] See also Chattopadhyay and Duflo 2004 or Besley et al. 2008 for evidence that the identity of the council president affects policy and distributive targeting.

[51] Dunning 2010 and Dunning and Nilekani 2013 used a regression-discontinuity design to study the effects of caste-based quotas for council presidencies. The null effect of caste-based quotas in part appears to be a function of the patterns of party competition these authors uncovered; see Dunning and Nilekani 2013 and also Chapter 5 for details.

[52] Parties play an important role in village councils, even though council elections are supposed to be party-free in Karnataka, and candidates are banned from running on party symbols. Our surveys, which were based on probability samples within villages, show that citizens and members themselves have substantial knowledge of the party affiliation of council members. An estimated 81.8 percent of citizens can identify the political party of the council president, whereas 87.7 percent know the party of the candidate for whom they voted in the most recent elections. Party membership is also widespread among voters: 73.3 percent of citizens report membership in a political party, whereas 78.8 percent of party members reported voting for their party's candidate in the most recent elections. When council members were asked to list the party affiliations of all other members of their councils, the great majority were able to do so without difficulty. See Chapter 5 for further discussion.

[53] Citizens who did not report a party affiliation or a party to which they feel closest were dropped. However, results are similar if we include these respondents among those who do not share the party affiliation of (or who do not feel closest to) the party of the council president.

[54] The relevant survey question read: "Have you ever received a gift from a political party or political candidate before an election to induce you to turn out to vote on election day?"

TABLE 2.3. *Party Membership and Receipt of Benefits in India (Percentage of Citizens Who Received a Job or Benefit from Village Council)*

	Group 1: Yes (A)	Group 2: No (B)	Difference of Percentages (A-B)	*p* Value
Respondent is member of council president's party (all respondents)	54.9 (3.1)	42.7 (1.9)	12.2 (3.6)	0.001**
Respondent is member of council president's party (SC/ST respondents)	57.5 (4.4)	47.7 (2.7)	9.8 (5.2)	0.06*
Respondent feels closest to president's party (all respondents)	47.9 (2.5)	44.5 (2.1)	3.3 (3.3)	0.31

This table reports evidence from the Indian state of Karnataka (Appendix D). The first and second columns report the percentage of citizens who reported receiving a job or benefit from the village council in the previous year. The third column gives the difference of these percentages, and the fourth column gives the two-sided *p* value for the difference. Standard errors are in parentheses. In the first and third rows, which report parameter estimates for the whole survey universe, sampling weights are used to correct for the oversampling of SC and ST respondents (see Appendix D for description of the sampling design). * $p < 0.1$, ** $p < 0.001$.

We return later to a discussion of possible reciprocal effects behind this finding. But the evidence thus far is at odds with swing-voter theory and in line with our evidence from Argentina, Venezuela, and Mexico. The patterns uncovered also suggest that our theoretically anomalous findings are not confined to clientelism in Latin America, or to presidential systems, or to new or frequently interrupted democracies. In India's relatively stable, old, and parliamentary patronage democracy, voters who are already the most sympathetic with the party – the party's members or affiliates – are disproportionately likely to receive benefits when their co-partisan is the executive of the highest local office.

2.2 EXPLAINING THE ANOMALY: IS "LOYALTY" ENDOGENOUS?

Perhaps the apparent priority that machines give loyal supporters is a case of reverse causation. Rather than their ideological support of the machine causing voters to receive gifts and subsidies, gifts and subsidies may cause people to support the machine.

It is worth noting from the outset that there are two versions of this problem. One is a matter of measurement error. When we ask survey respondents whether they have received a gift or social benefits from a party and elicit their feelings about that party, we want to know their opinions of the party independent of – prior to – their receipt of a personalized benefit. However, it is certainly possible that in answering this question, respondents take the benefits they receive into account. Their answers may be telling us, "taking into consideration the individual rewards the Peronist party (e.g.,) provides me, I support it," and not "independent of rewards I receive from it, I support the Peronist party." The problem would be one of measurement error to the degree that people have predistribution party affinities that are independent of their experience of receiving gifts, but our questions are eliciting responses that take into account distributions.

Evidence that simple measurement error is not the whole story comes from our 2009 Argentine voter survey. Recall that in this survey we described a hypothetical scenario of a broker choosing to bestow a benefit on one of two neighbors. In fact, we posed four different types of neighbors to our respondents (to be elaborated later), but all involved one hypothetical neighbor who "preferred the party of the broker," with no reference to past distributions. The respondent would have to read a good deal into the question were he or she to interpret it as describing a voter who is "loyal" because he has received a stream of benefits in the past. As mentioned, 60 percent of respondents reported that campaign goodies or subsidies would go to the voter who "preferred the party" of the broker, and 40 percent to a voter who is "indifferent among the parties" competing.

A deeper endogeneity problem would arise if voters' type – whether they are loyalists, swing voters, or opposition voters – is merely a function of whether they receive particularistic gifts. That is, it might be that people's party "affinities" are entirely a function of their distributive relationship with the party.

Returning to the formalization offered earlier, recall that we specified voters' utility from supporting a party as a function of their proximity to the party they vote for and from any targeted benefit they receive:

$$U^i(b^i, \sigma^i, \sigma^P) = -(\sigma^i - \sigma^P)^2 + b^i. \tag{2.1}$$

Now consider that a voters' partisanship, his or her σ location at any given time, is a function of party largesse in the past. Partisanship means feeling good about a party, but good feelings have to be reinforced periodically by gifts or access to social programs. In this case, we might depict the voter's utility as in the following two equations:

$$U^{i,t}(b^{i,t}, \sigma^{i,t}, \sigma^P) = -(\sigma^{i,t} - \sigma^P)^2 + b^{i,t} \tag{2.2}$$

and

$$-(\sigma^{i,t} - \sigma^P)^2 = f(b^{i,t-1}). \tag{2.3}$$

Now a benefit in the last election reduces a voter's σ distance from the benefactor party; his or her resulting greater proximity to the party in the current election increases his or her likelihood of voting for it. The benefit that the voter receives in this election isn't so much an inducement to vote for the

an investment in his or her remaining close to the party and hence
it the next election.

ore radical departure from conventional theories would do away
with the σ dimension entirely, so that electoral choices are a function of bribes,
nothing more and nothing less:

$$U^i(b^i) = b^i. \tag{2.4}$$

Whether equations (2.1), (2.4), or the system of equations (2.2) and (2.3)
come closest to reality is an empirical question. Yet it seems to us unlikely that
parties in most settings draw on no enduring links to voters that go beyond
mere bribes. Materials presented later in this book, such as the attitude of some
British voters in the nineteenth century, may approximate this situation; these
voters would offer their vote to "Mr Most:" whoever offered them the most
money, access to poor relief, or ale. Certainly among today's new democracies,
there are some systems that feature little-institutionalized parties and much
volatility in electoral outcomes. Yet we also know that campaigns draw on
enduring traits of the electorate, ones that vary little from one election to
the next, in building electoral coalitions. These include ethnic bonds, religious
communalism, ideological like-mindedness, and regional pride. These collective
identities are themselves shaped by the strategic actions of political parties and
other actors. Yet one need not fall back on a naive primordialism to view such
electorally relevant identities as, in many settings, fixed aspects of voters in the
lead-up to any particular electoral contest.

In the remainder of this section, we draw on evidence from the developing
democracies discussed earlier to test the proposition that the people whom we
are calling *loyal* voters and who receive – from the standpoint of most theories –
too many benefits from their parties are actually merely people whose ongoing
loyalty is reliant on past benefits.

2.2.1 Probing for Endogenous Loyalty in Argentina

A question we address in the Argentine context is whether the die-hard loyalist,
a person who keeps voting for the party in the absence of rewards, is a conceptual category without actual voters to populate it. Some of our Argentine
research contradicts this possibility. To test the loyal-voters-as-an-empty-set
hypothesis in the Argentine context, we queried party brokers about their
strategies and about voters' likely responses. Beginning in 2009, we conducted
a survey of a probability sample of brokers in four provinces: Buenos Aires,
Córdoba, San Luis, and Misiones.[55] The brokers survey included the following
questions:

Imagine a person who always turns out to vote and prefers the candidate whom you
support. Of every 10 people in your neighborhood, how many are like this? (Figure 2.9,
Panel 1)

[55] See Appendix A for a description of the sampling design.

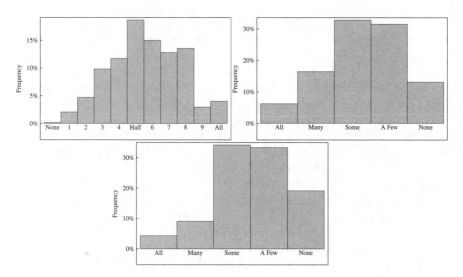

FIGURE 2.9. Argentine Brokers' Perceptions of the Frequency of Certain Loyal Voters, N = 773, 779, 753.

And thinking about voters of this type – ones who always turn out to vote and who prefer the candidate whom you support – how many have received benefits from the party in the past? (Figure 2.9, Panel 2)

And thinking about voters of this type – ones who always turn out to vote and who prefer the candidate whom you support – how many do you think would change their preferences if they never again received benefits? (Figure 2.9 Panel 3)

As the top-left panel of Figure 2.9 shows, the modal answer to the first question about the percentage of certain/loyal voters is "half."[56] Almost no brokers said "none," whereas about 67 percent of brokers estimated the frequency of certain/loyal voters in their neighborhoods at "half" or more. Only about 23 percent of respondents said that "all" or "many" of such voters – who always turn out to vote and prefer the candidate of the broker – had received benefits from the party in the past (top-right panel of Figure 2.9). Moreover, only about 13 percent of brokers said that "all" or "many" of these voters would change their party preferences if they never again received benefits, whereas fully 52 percent said "few" or "none" (bottom panel of Figure 2.9). Even considering that brokers will plausibly exaggerate (in their own minds, and to interviewers) the breadth of their support and its being rooted in something other than material rewards, still the category of the loyalist who would remain supportive of the party even absent rewards was, in their eyes, far from empty.

[56] Many of the areas we surveyed, such as those in the Conurbano in Buenos Aires, or in Misiones province in San Luis, are indeed strongholds of the parties whose brokers we interviewed, so such answers are not on their face self-delusional.

Another strategy we deploy in the Argentine context to test the endogenous-loyalty hypothesis is to develop instruments for party loyalty that are not themselves plausibly caused by a person's receiving targeted benefits. Several of our Argentine surveys discerned positive correlations between the respondent's partisanship and that of his or her parents. In the 2003 and 2009 surveys, we asked whether respondents remembered from their youth what their fathers' and mothers' party identities had been. The correlations between a father's identifying as a Peronist and the respondent's identifying as a Peronist were 0.3 in 2003 and 0.25 in 2009. (Peronist identity was also correlated between the mother and the respondent, but more weakly.) We are able to take advantage of the fact that party identities are in part a product of family socialization, with children picking up their Peronist party identity from their parents, to estimate the effect of the "exogenous" portion of party loyalty on benefit receipt.[57]

It is important to emphasize that our strategy implies that parents' partisan affiliation is not correlated with unobserved determinants of children's benefit receipt. We do condition on some potential confounders, such as children's poverty, yet there might still be correlations with unobservables that would invalidate our instrumental-variables strategy.

We estimate linear probability models, in which the dependent variable is benefit receipt (*Gift*) and the main independent variable of interest is the respondent's partisanship (a dummy variable called *Peronist*); the independent variable is instrumented with a dummy variable for whether the respondent's father was a Peronist (*Father Peronist*). The first two columns of Table 2.4 report results of the instrumental-variables analysis, both for bivariate and multivariate models.[58] The instrumental-variables estimator yielded positive estimated coefficients in both years, though in both cases the standard errors were large; as the table shows, the estimated coefficient on *Peronist* is positive, though small. (Using data from 2009, the coefficient was positive but not

---

[57] Hence we must make an exclusion restriction: we assume that father's party identity does not affect benefit receipt by the respondent through any channel save the respondent's political ideology. An exception to this statement would be in the case of younger respondents, some of whom would still occupy a household with their parents. In these cases, the exogeneity of the respondent's father's partisanship might be called into question. We estimated the same instrumental variable regressions reported previously, excluding respondents who were 25 and younger and 30 and younger. In the 2003 surveys, for both subsamples excluding younger respondents, the coefficient relating a person's instrumented partisanship to their probability of receiving a gift was larger and associated standard errors were smaller than with samples including the full range of ages. In the 2009 survey, the magnitudes of the coefficients were basically insensitive to the age of the samples. Therefore, the conclusion still holds that the association of receipt of benefits with support of the party is unlikely to be an artifact of reverse causation.

[58] We include controls such as income and education in the multivariate models because these variables might be correlated with father's partisan identity as well as gift receipt, which would make the instrument endogenous. Once such variables are added to the model specification, the assumption that father's partisan identity is independent of the error term in our linear probability model is more plausible.

TABLE 2.4. *The Effect of Ideology on Benefit Receipt in Argentina (Instrumental-Variables Regression)*

	(1) gift	(2) gift	(3) gift	(4) gift
Peronist	0.0631	0.0460		
	(1.67)	(1.17)		
Father Peronist			0.0188	0.0140
			(1.67)	(1.17)
Income		−0.0225*		−0.0230*
		(−1.99)		(−2.02)
Age		−0.00112**		−0.00104*
		(−2.77)		(−2.56)
Gender		−0.00199		−0.00243
		(−0.17)		(−0.20)
Education		−0.0131**		−0.0148***
		(−3.10)		(−3.84)
Buenos Aires		−0.0203		−0.0281
		(−1.13)		(−1.65)
Córdoba		0.0765***		0.0733***
		(4.54)		(4.39)
Misiones		−0.0381*		−0.0376*
		(−2.29)		(−2.26)
Constant	0.0419*	0.201***	0.0584***	0.220***
	(2.57)	(4.38)	(7.46)	(5.61)
N	2000	1777	2000	1777

Columns 1 and 2 report bivariate and multivariate linear probability models estimated by instrumental-variables least squares instrumenting *Peronist* with *Father Peronist*. Columns 3 and 4 report reduced-form regressions: linear probability models in which *Gift* is regressed directly on the instrument *Father Peronist*.
t statistics in parentheses.
* $p < 0.05$, ** $p < 0.01$, *** $p < 0.001$.

significant.) The third and fourth columns of Table 2.4 report reduced-form regressions, in which the dependent variable (*Gift*) is regressed directly on the instruments. Here again, the coefficient is imprecisely estimated, but the basic message is the same: there is some evidence for a positive relationship between father's Peronist ideology and receiving a benefit from the Peronists. Because the theoretical expectation is of a *negative* coefficient relating (instrumented) party identity and the probability of a gift, these results weigh against the loyal-voter result being an artifact of past receipt of rewards.

2.2.2 Overtime Shifts in Gift Receipt and Partisanship? Mexico

The panel structure of the Mexico 2000 study affords another opportunity to test the endogenous-loyalty explanation for our anomalous findings. That the same voters' opinions of the PRI and experience of receiving campaign largess

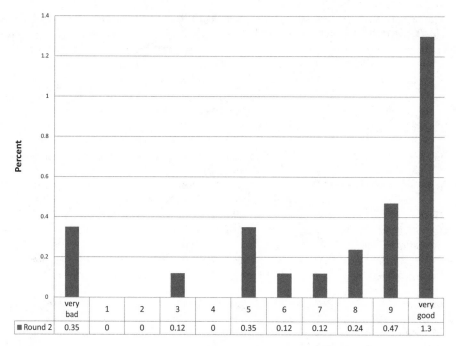

■ Round 2	very bad	1	2	3	4	5	6	7	8	9	very good
	0.35	0	0	0.12	0	0.35	0.12	0.12	0.24	0.47	1.3

FIGURE 2.10. Mexico 2000: Rates of PRI Gift Receipt in Second Wave of Survey by Opinion of PRI in First Wave. *Source:* Mexico 2000 Surveys, N = 849.

were tracked over time allows us to study possible reciprocal effects of receiving benefits on recipients' "loyalty" to the party.

Campaign gift-giving started at a low level in 2000 but accelerated over the course of the campaign. Total rates of gift receipt rose from 3 percent in the second wave to 6.9 percent in the third wave and to 7.4 percent in the fourth wave.

Recall that swing-voter theory would predict that parties target indifferent voters who, as a result, vote for the benefactor party. We saw earlier that this proposition was cross-sectionally false in Mexico, at least in 2000: the ruling party distributed campaign benefits preferentially to people whose contemporaneous opinions of the party were positive.

Adding the temporal dimension reinforces this finding. The first wave of the survey, conducted in February 2000, asked people to rate the parties, including the PRI, from 0 (very bad) to 10 (very good). We classify people who rated the PRI from 0 (very bad) to 3 as opponents (of the PRI), people who rated it from 4 to 6 as indifferent, and those who rated it 7 or above as loyalists. The second wave, conducted two months later, asked whether they had received a gift or assistance from a party or candidate in the previous few weeks.

Figure 2.10 shows the rates of self-reported receipt of a PRI gift in the second-wave survey by the opinions of the PRI that respondents offered in the first wave. The majority of those who reported in the second wave that they received a gift from the PRI had in the first wave held favorable opinions of the party, scoring it 5 or higher.[59] About 40 percent of people who reported having received a gift from the PRI (3 percent of the second wave) had earlier said they thought the PRI was "very good." An ideal data structure would reach further back in time, tracking voters' opinions and receipt of benefits before the year of the election. And keeping in mind the broad range of social programs that scholars have shown to be the currency of nonprogrammatic distribution in Mexico, one would want to track distribution of social programs and over even longer periods. Still, the fact that campaign "gift" receipt started at a low level, according to the Mexico 2000 survey results, and accelerated in subsequent waves reassures us that we are capturing a good deal at least of campaign-season handouts.

Respondents were also asked to identify their partisanship (in addition to asking their opinions of parties). Here too, PRI loyalists – people who identified themselves as PRI supporters in the first round – consistently received the largest number of gifts. This was the case when partisanship and gift receipt were measured simultaneously, as we saw earlier, in the same waves of the survey. The result is not fundamentally different when one studies the correlation of partisanship in an earlier wave with gift receipt in a later one. For instance, Figure 2.11 shows that just under 50 percent of those who received PRI gifts in the third wave had declared themselves as *priistas* in the first wave of the survey. Twenty-eight percent of those receiving gifts were swing voters, 15 percent were PAN opposition supporters, and 3 percent were PRD supporters.

Thus far the evidence for endogenous loyalty in Mexico is not terribly strong. Consider, in addition, that if the endogenous-loyalty hypothesis were a good description of dynamics in Mexico, we might expect the following:

- The PRI targets loyal voters at the outset; the loyalty of these voters is strengthened.
- The loyal voters whom the PRI targets are more likely to vote for the party than they would have been without a campaign gift.

Is this pattern consistent with the Mexican evidence?

As a preliminary point, note that any discussion of the effects of electoral bribery on identities and voting that draws on self-reporting in surveys should be prefaced with several caveats. There are good reasons to believe that some respondents will not answer questions about receiving campaign gifts honestly, potentially biasing our results. Although the Mexico 2000 survey was well-designed and administered, not all respondents were reinterviewed in each successive wave, and one cannot be sure that selection effects were not at work in attrition. We present very simple statistics with little attempt to control for

---

[59] Round 2 selected a random sample of the initial cross-sectional study.

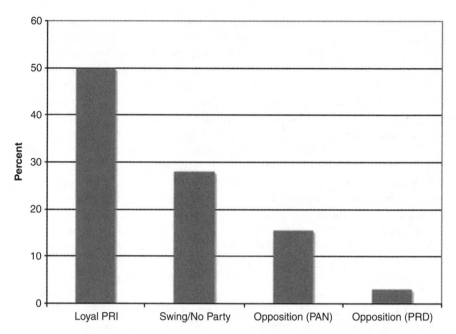

FIGURE 2.11. Mexico: Gift Receipt by Partisan Affect. *Source:* Mexico 2000 Survey Data, N = 64.

confounders; the possibility of unobserved covariates further counsels caution in the interpretation of results.

With these considerations in mind, we first inspect the stability of loyalties for the PRI over the course of the campaign. Out of 2,363 people interviewed in the first wave, 863, or about 37 percent, declared themselves to be PRI supporters. Similar percentages of respondents declared their affinity for the PRI in the second (367/959, or 38 percent) and third (343/976, or 35 percent) waves.[60] Three hundred seventy-seven of the original PRI supporters were reinterviewed in the second wave; 76 percent of them remained PRI supporters. The percentage dropped to 71 percent who remained in support when reinterviewed in the third wave.[61] The picture is one of substantial, though not absolute, stability in party identification over the course of the campaign.

---

[60] We set aside the fourth-wave data, collected after the election. Responses in that wave appear to deflate support for the PRI and votes for its presidential candidate, perhaps a result of a post-election bandwagon effect in favor of the winner, Vicente Fox, and his party, the PAN. For instance, whereas the PRI's presidential candidate, Francisco Labastida, drew 36 percent of the national vote, only 32 percent of those surveyed acknowledged having voted for him. Self-declared support for the PRI also dipped in the fourth survey, in comparison with the first three waves.

[61] The number of PRI supporters in the first wave reinterviewed in the third was 366.

What impact did the receipt of campaign gifts have on the stability of party identities? The answer seems to be a little, but not much. We calculated correlations between affinities with the PRI in earlier waves and in later waves, among those PRI supporters who did or did not receive gifts. The correlations were consistently a bit higher among those who did report receiving a gift. To give a feel for these results, the correlation between PRI identity in waves two and three was 0.71 among those who did not report receiving a gift in the second-wave survey and 0.84 among those who did receive a gift. This was the largest difference we found. At the low end, the correlation between PRI support in waves one and three was 0.59 among those who did not report a gift in either the second or third round and 0.60 among those who did.

One should not overestimate the significance of these correlations. We estimated a probit model of the strongest effect, PRI support in the third wave as a function of declared PRI support and gift receipt in the second wave. The marginal effect of earlier PRI support was large and highly significant, reflecting stability over time in party identities. The marginal effect of gift receipt, by contrast, was small and imprecisely measured, not significantly different from zero.

What about the impact of campaign largess on loyalists' propensity to vote for their party's candidate? Later we look at this question from the standpoint of turnout buying; here we must assume that even those who see themselves as *priistas* might vote for another party, perhaps for retrospective-performance reasons, or reasons connected to candidate quality, or because they valued party rotation and democratization. Certainly, at the outset and across the waves of surveys, some self-described PRI supporters declared intentions to vote for a presidential candidate other than the PRI's Francisco Labastida. Between about 15 and 20 percent of *priistas* consistently said they planned to vote for another candidate. Implicitly, these voters' stances demonstrate a distinction between party identities, which are enduring and may have to do with social images and family socialization, and vote intentions in any given election.[62] But the independent effect of campaign largess in solidifying loyalists as a PRI electoral bloc was small. In probit models, again, coefficients relating prior declarations of PRI identities with late-campaign intentions to vote for Labastida were large and highly statistically significant, whereas coefficients on self-stated receipt of gifts typically had positive signs but were not statistically significant.

That "too many" loyal PRI supporters were the recipients of campaign discretionary spending does not, then, appear to be entirely explained by the party's need to continually invest in the "loyalty" of its core constituents. We saw some small impact of campaign gifts on the stability of PRI identities and on the willingness of PRI supporters to vote for the party's candidate. However, for the most part, the machine's supporters remained supportive, regardless of whether they received campaign largess. And they tended to vote

[62] On theories of party identity, see e.g., Green et al. 2004, Achen 1992, Campbell 1960.

for their party's candidate, gifts or no gifts. The results fall short of revealing endogenous loyalty as the resolution of the anomaly of too much largess going to loyal supporters.

The surveys are also suggestive of an electoral cost imposed when brokers fail to target swing voters, a point to which we return in the next two chapters. When PRI gifts did end up in the hands of swing voters, these voters showed some heightened propensity to vote for the PRI presidential candidate, Labastida. In the first wave of the survey, 782 respondents – 33 percent of the sample – reported no party affiliation. Among nonaffiliated or swing voters, 30 percent of those who reported receiving a PRI gift in some subsequent wave said in the final pre-election survey that they planned to vote for Labastida. Of the swing voters who reported *not* receiving a gift, 22 percent planned at the end to vote for the PRI. Because of attrition of respondents and small numbers of swing voters who received gifts, it would be unwise to make too much of these results.[63] Nevertheless, they are suggestive of some electoral responsiveness to campaign largess among swing voters and therefore that channeling resources to loyalists causes parties to win fewer votes than they could.

2.2.3 New Programs in Venezuela and Party Membership in India

Venezuela's recent history of targeted programs affords another opportunity to test the endogenous-loyalty hypothesis. The targeted Missions programs mentioned earlier were the Chávez government's first efforts to use distributive policies to shore up its support among Venezuelans of modest incomes. If today's apparently "loyal" supporters are simply yesterday's swing voters who are grateful for the distributive largess, we should see the Venezuelan government, at the outset of its efforts at distributive politics, cultivate relatively indifferent voters. But as we saw earlier, this was not the case. The government's programs had as their primary beneficiaries people who were already predisposed in its favor; swing voters, including those who resisted signing pro- or antigovernment petitions, were second in line for benefits.

Turning to India, we reported earlier Dunning and Nilekani's finding that the recipients of targeted benefits in Karnataka, India, were preferentially members of the same party as the president of their village councils. Again, one can debate the direction of causality; perhaps citizens become party members as a result of the incumbent party's distributive largess. What's more, party membership is not randomly assigned, and in principle there could be confounders associated

---

[63] A total of 976 respondents answered both the first-wave question regarding party affiliation and the third-wave one regarding vote intentions. Of these, 72 reported receiving a gift from the PRI over one of the pre-election waves in which this question was asked; 49 of them were partisans and 23 nonpartisans.

TABLE 2.5. *Partisan Ties and Benefit Receipt in India: A Survey Experiment*

	Candidate Is Co-Partisan	Candidate Not Co-Partisan	Difference of Means
Vote intention	5.25	4.78	0.47
(by party membership)	(0.07)	(0.07)	(0.10)
Vote intention	5.07	4.75	0.32
(by party closeness)	(0.05)	(0.05)	(0.07)
Expected benefit receipt	7.73	7.30	0.43
(by party membership)	(0.12)	(0.12)	(0.17)
Expected benefit receipt	7.26	6.82	0.44
(by party closeness)	(0.08)	(0.08)	(0.12)

Source: Dunning and Nilekani 2012. Survey experiment in Rajasthan and Bihar. Probability sample of $N = 1,755$ party members and $N = 3,603$ residents who name a party to which they feel closest, in $N = 314$ village council constituencies. Vote intention is measured on 1–7 scale; expectations of benefit receipt are measured on a 2–14 scale combining two survey questions. Standard errors in parentheses.

both with sharing the party of the council president and receiving benefits from the council. However, returning to Table 2.3, the final row shows that merely feeling closest to the party of the council president is *not* statistically related to benefit receipt. This finding may allay some concerns about reverse causality: after all, if we had found a stronger relationship here, it could well have been that benefit receipt causes citizens to feel close to the council president's party, rather than the other way around. Instead, as we emphasize in Chapter 4, it appears that integration into party networks, through party membership, causes citizens to be rewarded by the party in power with material benefits.

Hence only the most committed partisans are here rewarded with benefits. An "endogenous loyalty" explanation might instead find swing voters being targeted and thus moving into the "weak supporter" category – that is, into the set of voters who lean toward a party but are not party members. Instead, we find in our India evidence that such weakly supportive voters are no more likely to receive benefits than voters who do not feel positively toward the incumbent party.

Moreover, drawing on Dunning and Nilekani, Table 2.5 reports the results of a survey experiment in the states of Bihar and Rajasthan, in which the caste and party affiliation of a hypothetical candidate for village council president was experimentally manipulated.[64] In this context, as discussed earlier, council presidents often play the role of local brokers for party higher-ups, distributing benefits at election time and also throughout the term of the village council (for evidence that the president plays this role, see Dunning and Nilekani 2013).

[64] Dunning and Nilekani 2013.

ey experiment, respondents were randomly assigned to a candidate
d their partisan affiliation (alternately, the party to which they feel
closest, or the party of which they are a member); they were also assigned to a
cross-cutting condition, a candidate from their own caste or a different caste.
Pooling across the caste assignments, then, we have a survey experiment in
which we can cut into the endogeneity and reciprocal causality of survey-based
self-reports of party identification and benefit receipt.

As Table 2.5 shows, respondents were substantially more likely to support –
and to expect to receive benefits from – a candidate from their own party. Thus
loyal voters expect to be rewarded when a local broker from their own party
comes to power. This evidence helps to allay concern about reverse causality,
in which citizens support candidates from whom they have in fact received
benefits, because here candidates' party ID was randomly assigned.

In sum, individual-level data from Argentina, Venezuela, Mexico, and India
yield little evidence that voters' loyalty is an endogenous result of their receiving
party largess. Loyalty attracts largess, rather than largess inducing loyalty. The
anomaly remains.

2.3 EXPLAINING THE ANOMALY: TURNOUT-BUYING?

Theorists of distributive politics sometimes relax the assumption of full turnout.
A modification of the voter's utility from voting for party P would add a cost
term, c:

$$U^i(b^i, \sigma^i, \sigma^P) = -(\sigma^i - \sigma^P)^2 + b^i - c^i$$

Some theorists assume that the cost of voting is the same across all voters
and conclude that parties pay voters not to change their vote but to turn out.
This conclusion would solve the loyal-voter anomaly: if parties deploy targeted
benefits as a way of getting people to the polls, they will focus their payments
on people who are likely to vote for them – their loyal supporters.[65] Others
treat the cost of voting as a trait that varies from voter to voter and hence,
implicitly, as a continuous variable.[66] In this case, largess focuses on a different
kind of swing or "marginal" voter, this time one who is on the fence between
voting and staying away from the polls.[67]

Dunning and Stokes distinguished people for whom the cost of voting is
negligible (even negative) – "Certain Voters" – from those for whom voting
is costly – "Potential Voters."[68] Treating the propensity-to-turnout dimension
as independent of the partisanship (σ) dimension, Dunning and Stokes's key
formal finding is that distributive parties will target Potential Voters who are

---

[65] Nichter 2008.
[66] Lindbeck and Weibull 1987.
[67] This is Lindbeck and Weibull's language.
[68] Dunning and Stokes 2008.

TABLE 2.6. *Electoral Rewards and Two-Dimensional Voter Types*

	Potential Voters	Certain Voters
Loyalists	**Mobilization**	*Persuasion of Loyalists*
Swing Voters	*Mobilization of Swing*	**Persuasion**

loyalists (a strategy they call *mobilization*; see Table 2.6). And they will target Certain Voters who are swing or weakly opposed, a strategy Dunning and Stokes call *persuasion*. The intuition is straightforward: when it comes to voters who always go to the polls, a machine can only gain additional votes by bribing swing voters or opponents; constituents who prefer the party sincerely will vote for it anyway. In turn, the party tries to get out to the polls only voters whom it expects will support it on ideological grounds, whereas it is happy to see its opponents' supporters stay home.

2.3.1 Probing for Turnout Buying in Argentina

Are the loyal Peronists who appear to be receiving too many of the party's goodies actually potential abstainers? It is not obvious that this is the case. In all our Argentine surveys, a larger percentage of non-abstainers than abstainers received campaign gifts.[69] This is true when we restrict the analysis to party loyalists, as Dunning and Stokes's paper suggests we should.[70] The result holds no matter how we define abstainers – whether they are people who abstained just in the past election or who have abstained in at least one election in which they were eligible to vote – and no matter how we define receiving a gift – whether we treat nonresponders as missing data, as gift receivers, or as nonreceivers.

As an example, our 2003 survey revealed that among loyalists, a higher proportion of non-abstainers (10 percent) than abstainers (7 percent) received campaign gifts. Here we mean by "abstainers" people who, by their own recounting, failed to turn out to vote in at least one presidential or gubernatorial election in which they were eligible to do so, since the return to democracy in 1983. (Our use of this nonexacting definition of being an "abstainer" reflects high turnout rates, and behind them compulsory voting laws, in Argentina, discussed in more depth later. In our sample, 52 percent never abstained at all across the elections for which they were eligible.) The theoretical prediction of a correlation between abstention and receiving a reward also fails to find support in people's responses to questions about the receipt of "subsidies," or government programs (as opposed to gifts from candidates during campaigns).

---

[69] Here, we focus on the 2003 surveys; we present data elsewhere for 2001 and 2009.
[70] Dunning and Stokes 2008, see also Gans-Morse et al. 2009.

Here again, a larger percentage of voters than abstainers benefitted from such programs.[71]

But simply comparing abstention rates among those who do and do not receive largess may be misleading. As Nichter points out, in equilibrium those who might abstain receive gifts and, as a consequence, go to the polls.

If machines preferentially target people who they think are in danger of abstaining, they must perceive an underlying propensity to abstain, and they must have some read on the turnout propensities of the individuals whom they target. Beyond the behavioral measures discussed earlier (turnout histories), we also try to discern an underlying propensity to turn out or abstain, and to study its effect on the probability of a person's receiving rewards. Our 2009 surveys asked:

If you found yourself on election day in a situation that made it difficult for you to vote – for instance, if you had a bad cold – how likely would it be that you would vote anyway?

Respondents were asked to score their probability of voting from zero – or very unlikely – to 10 – very likely. Nearly a third of the sample indicated that they would definitely vote even despite significant inconvenience. This result shows the habituation to voting in this country with compulsory voting laws and is consistent with high – though not universal – turnout rates, generally above 70 percent. (This result might also reflect social desirability bias). If turnout buying is the solution to our anomaly, we should find higher rates of vote-selling among people with low propensities to turn out and lower rates among those who are quite sure that they would vote anyway.

In fact we find no significant differences. Indeed, among those who indicated a willingness to vote come hell or high water, we found one of the highest rates of having received campaign handouts (around 6 percent). The correlation between the hypothetical probability of voting despite illness and receiving a campaign gift was small but positive. (Interestingly, if social desirability bias leads some voters to report having never abstained, it is especially striking that these same voters are more likely to say they have received handouts, presumably a socially undesirable action). Moreover, whether the person predicted, in a separate question, that abstention would lead to a sanction with a very low or a very high probability was uncorrelated with receiving a campaign gift.

Another way to deal with potential simultaneity in these results – that receipt of gifts drives people both to turn out to vote and to prefer the party doing the gift-giving – is to make use of the hypothetical question, mentioned earlier,

---

[71] Where the theory predicts more discretionary government spending going to those in danger of abstaining, in our 2003 sample 36 percent of non-abstainers received subsidies, and 30 percent of abstainers.

that we posed in the 2009 Argentina voter survey. The respondent was asked to make a prediction about the effect of voters' types (defined by turnout propensities and party affinities) on the actions of a hypothetical broker. The question wording avoids any suggestion that potential recipients had previous dealings with the broker that might have influenced either participation or affinities.

In each of the four treatment conditions of this survey-experimental question, the initial description of the situation was the same:

Imagine a local party broker during a very competitive election campaign. The party has given the broker resources and has asked him to mobilize voters.

We then posed four differing versions of the remainder of the question to each of one-quarter of our sample, with the versions being assigned at random (our labeling of these versions corresponds to our terminology in Table 2.6):

Loyal Certain vs. Swing Certain There are two neighbors who always turn out to vote of their own accord. One neighbor prefers the broker's party, and the other neighbor is indifferent between the two parties. To which of the neighbors would the broker give the benefit (a bag of food, a mattress, or a subsidy)?

Loyal Potential vs. Swing Potential There are two neighbors, neither of whom always turns out to vote of their own accord. One neighbor prefers the broker's party, and the other neighbor is indifferent between two parties. To which of the neighbors would the broker give the benefit?

Loyal Certain vs. Loyal Potential There are two neighbors, both of whom prefer the broker's party. One is always disposed to vote even if no one takes him to the polls, the other is not disposed to turn out to vote. To which of the neighbors would the broker give the benefit?

Swing Certain vs. Loyal Potential There are two neighbors. One neighbor is indifferent between the two parties' candidates but is always disposed to turn out to vote. The other prefers the broker's party but is not disposed to turn out to vote. To which of the neighbors would the broker give the benefit?

All treatments produced split decisions. In only one did the theoretically predicted strategy prevail over nonpredicted ones: among voters who are not disposed to vote, respondents predicted that loyal voters would be favored over swing voters. Respondents understood intuitively that parties will prefer to buy the participation of loyal supporters over the uncommitted.

In all other ways, the results are substantially at odds with the prevailing theories. Many people predicted rewards going to loyalists, even when these imagined loyalists were not at risk of abstaining. For instance, a majority of voters expected Certain, Loyal voters – those who would vote for the broker's party even absent an inducement – to be preferred over potential, loyal voters, a stance that is nonsensical from the vantage point of the prevailing theories.

2.3.2 Probing for Turnout Buying in Venezuela and Mexico

Venezuela again offers an excellent setting in which to study the impact of voters' propensity to turn out on their receipt of campaign rewards, one that allows us to circumvent to a substantial extent the problem of endogenous turnout. This is because the ruling party's Maisanta database coded all voters as abstainers or participants, giving us a unique window into a distributive party's categorization of voters on the propensity-to-turn-out dimension. And the window was opened at the outset of the government's major boost in distributive outlays.

The Maisanta database, as mentioned, coded individuals by their partisan orientations, reflecting their actions during the recall referendum campaign, as well as their then-current participation in social programs, suggesting that the information in the database would be used in connection with ongoing distribution of benefits. (It is difficult to verify systematically the extent of actual use by brokers, but, as discussed in Appendix C, it is clear that Maisanta's user-friendly interface was intended for this purpose.) The database also recorded whether individuals were "abstainers" (*abstencionistas*), as indicated by the corresponding box on the bottom-left of Figure 2.4; this coding would have been readily available to any local broker or activist with access to the Maisanta interface, which was widely distributed by the Chávez government. Although we have not been able to verify precisely how the dichotomous indicator for "abstainer" was coded by the government – for instance, whether one became an *abstencionista* simply by having failed to vote in any election for which one was eligible or whether another, less demanding criterion was used – the important point is that the measure reveals the government's perception of each voter's turnout propensity. Using the Maisanta software's user-friendly interface, local militants could therefore learn about voters' partisan or ideological tendency, past turnout/abstention history, and extent of participation in social programs at the time of the recall campaign.

Had the post-2003 distributive policies been about "turnout buying" – an effort to get these abstainers to the polls – we would expect to see abstainers receiving scholarships or other targeted benefits at higher-than-average rates. This is not the case. In fact, pooling across partisanship, we find nearly identical percentages (15 percent) of participation in the individually targeted social programs among abstainers and non-abstainers (Figure 2.12).

These unadjusted results also persist in the presence of multivariate strategies. Table 2.7 presents the predicted probabilities, expressed as percentages, of receiving a benefit from a targeted Mission, based on estimation of a logit regression model. Here, covariates include sex, age, education, occupational category, and a dummy for public-sector workers; to calculate the predicted probabilities, covariates are set at their sample means.[72] This multivariate

---

[72] Here, education is used as a (less-noisy) measure of socioeconomic status than self-reported income, but results are qualitatively similar using self-reported income.

TABLE 2.7. *Persuasion vs. Mobilization in Venezuela (Predicted Probabilities, Logistic Regression Analysis with Covariates)*

	Loyal Voters (Signed Against the Opposition)	Swing Voters (Did Not Sign)	Opposition Voters (Signed Against Chávez)
Certain voters	29.8%	12.5%	6.6%
(not *abstencionistas*	[19.8, 39.8]	[7.1, 17.9]	[2.0, 11.1]
Potential voters	13.4%	17.9%	13.6%
(*abstencionistas*)	[0.92, 25.9]	[7.6, 28.3]	[−1.3, 28.4]

Each cell of the table gives predicted probabilities, expressed as percentages, of participation in a targeted Mission (*Misión Ribas* or *Misión Robinson*). Cell entries come from estimating a logistic regression model and setting covariates at their sample means. Covariates include sex, age, education, occupational category, and a dummy for public-sector workers. Ninety-five percent confidence intervals, calculated by the delta method, are in brackets. Political ideology and turnout propensity are as recorded in Maisanta. Respondents are those interviewees whose cédula ID numbers we matched to the Maisanta database. N = 483 (10 dropped due to missing data on covariates).

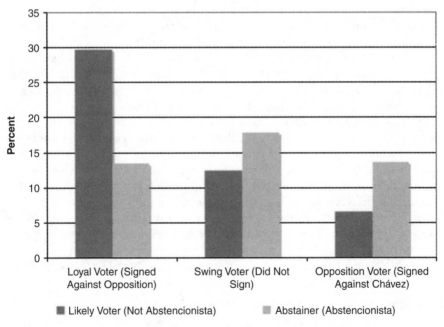

FIGURE 2.12. Venezuela: Percent of Voters, by Loyalty and Turnout Propensity, Participating in *Misiones*. *Source:* Maisanta and Survey Data, N = 483.

analysis is consistent with the unadjusted results displayed in Figure 2.12. In particular, notice that the largest predicted probability of participation in a targeted Mission – of 29.8 percent – is for Certain, Loyal Voters. Indeed, this predicted probability is substantially larger than for either Certain, Swing voters – 12.5 percent – or Potential Loyal voters – 13.4 percent. Although the confidence intervals for each predicted probability are fairly large, this evidence is clearly not consistent with the claim that clientelistic parties would persuade Certain, Swing voters and turn out Potential, Loyal voters. Instead, again, we have more evidence that loyal supporters who are also consistent participants receive more in the way of benefits than conventional theories of distributive politics would suggest.

Finally, the Mexico 2000 panel data also fail to offer much support for the turnout-buying solution of our anomaly. Each wave of the survey asked people the likelihood that they would abstain in the upcoming national election. In all relevant waves, a stated intention to abstain was negatively correlated with receipt of a gift. And a stated intention to abstain in the first wave was also negatively correlated with receipt of a gift in the second or third waves.

We do not mean to suggest that turnout buying is never important or never provides a basis for the targeting of ideologically sympathetic voters. Indeed, the evidence that distributive politics is about buying turnout rather than persuading people to vote for one's own party – rather than a rival – is mixed. In some settings, like the United States, where turnout is low, the prospects of victory are much better for the side that turns out its electoral base (even though persuading independents is also clearly key for voting in many U.S. elections).[73] The logic of turnout buying may also help explain the tendency to target loyal voters suggested by our evidence from India.[74]

In countries such as Argentina, however, with compulsory voting laws and high turnout, machine politics is unlikely to be all about boosting turnout, as our evidence indicates. Thus turnout buying is unlikely to provide a complete explanation for the tendency of parties to target many more loyalists than prevailing theories of distributive politics would predict. What's more, even if distributive politics is sometimes a strategy to turn out loyalists, if some voters are likely to turn out of their own accord, and especially if intense partisans – loyalists – are particularly keen to participate even without being nudged along with a benefit, then it remains puzzling, within the assumptions of the models we have discussed, why loyalists are the preferential targets of distributive politics.

2.4 EXPLAINING THE ANOMALY: SUBCONTRACTING?

We now explore a final resolution to the anomaly: perhaps the loyal supporters whom our surveys detect as receiving many gifts are not simply voters but also

[73] Chen 2009.
[74] We pursue this line of argument in Chapter 4.

campaign workers, activists, or brokers. They might receive benefits as payment for their work in mobilizing voters. The idea, following Camp and co-authors, is that:

core supporters will vote for you anyway, but if taken care of and given some cash or appropriate in-kind transfers, are more likely to be energized and become activists who provide extra services such as holding meetings, going door-to-door before elections, volunteering as observers at polling stations, giving rides to voters who need to get to and back from voting."[75]

This solution shifts toward the analytical disaggregation of parties into leaders and brokers, which we pursue more fully in Chapter 3, though here we simply assume that these brokers' interests are basically in line with those of their parties.

If our loyalist/gift recipients are actually brokers, we would expect them to be especially active in campaigns and party organizations. Were they?

A challenge in answering this question is that many of the campaign activities and settings about which we asked were simultaneously places where one would expect party workers to show up and where voters in attendance might receive, say, bags of food or certificates authorizing them to participate in social programs. For instance, our surveys inquired about attendance at rallies or motorcades featuring candidates, settings in which small benefits were likely to be distributed.

Helpful in this regard was our 2001–2002 Argentine voter survey. As part of a series of questions about respondents' organizational memberships (in, e.g., labor unions, professional associations, parent–teacher associations, sports clubs), we asked whether they belonged to a political party. Only 2.25 percent of the sample said they did, suggesting that our general pattern of results is unlikely to be driven by the experiences of party employees or brokers. And among the small group who described themselves as party members, there was basically no difference in the percentage who said they did or did not receive party benefits or social assistance during the campaign.

We would also expect brokers and activists to be more engaged in politics than plain voters and to talk more frequently about it. Therefore, we can treat interest and engagement in politics as a proxy for a person's working as a party broker. In Argentina, only a slightly smaller percentage of respondents to our 2001–2002 survey who described themselves as "very well informed" about politics received party benefits than those who said they were "uninformed."[76] In Mexico, respondents to the 2000 panel surveys who said they spoke about politics daily or several times per week were no more likely to receive campaign gifts than those who said they rarely or never spoke about politics.

To summarize the argument of this chapter, theories of distributive politics do not square with the evidence. Too many loyal supporters receive benefits,

[75] Camp et al. 2013, p. 9.
[76] The respective percentages are 7 and 9.

too few swing or uncommitted voters. This is the conclusion that emerges from fine-grained evidence from four developing-world democracies. Small modifications of the theory do not eliminate the anomaly. The loyalists on whom largess is visited are not basically loyalists *because* they receive benefits; nor are they generally people who would otherwise stay away from the polls; nor, in all likelihood, are they activists and brokers who will turn around and mobilize swing voters. In view of the tensions between received theories and the evidence, in the next chapter we undertake a more basic reconsideration of the theory.

3

A Theory of Broker-Mediated Distribution

We have seen that many important facts about nonprogrammatic distribution are not easily explained by accumulated theory. In this chapter, we build a theory of distribution that we subject to empirical inquiry in later chapters. Our theoretical model also provides the building blocks for our later analysis of the choice of party leaders between programmatic, nonprogrammatic, and clientelistic modes of distribution – and therefore helps us understand the political incentives that undergird the decline of clientelism in some settings.

The starting point of our theoretical work is the observation that clientelism entails substantial informational challenges for parties (Chapter 1). To distribute benefits in a highly targeted way, guided by political criteria, and to monitor the actions of voters, parties need fine-grained information about voters' preferences and behaviors. To gather this information, they require *brokers*. Brokers are local intermediaries who provide targeted benefits and solve problems for their followers; in exchange, they request followers' participation in political activities such as rallies – and often demand their votes. Thus brokers are engaged in sustained and frequent interactions with voters, observing their individual behavior and gaining knowledge of their inclinations and preferences. Brokers can be distinguished from party leaders, who are typically elected officials at higher levels of government or constitute the upper echelons of a nonelected party hierarchy. As such, unlike brokers, party leaders are not usually involved in sustained face-to-face interactions with a particular set of voters.[1]

---

[1] Note that this definition does not preclude brokers from themselves seeking elected positions; for instance, elected members of municipal councils may maintain territorially based networks and engage in frequent face-to-face interactions with voters. Yet, elected leaders at higher levels of government will often fail to do so, relying instead on affiliations with local brokers to connect them to voters.

s are essential to clientelistic distribution. Indeed, because clientelism quid pro quo exchange – in which benefits are conditioned on votes, and in which at least imperfect monitoring of voters is required to sustain the clientelist bargain – brokers are a sine qua non: it is the brokers who are embedded in dense social networks and who provide the local knowledge that is required for conditioning distribution on voter preferences or behavior.[2] Thus electoral strategies that distribute benefits to particular categories of voters – such as the swing voters who are ideologically indifferent between competing parties – depend on the intermediation of brokers. To the extent that individual voter preferences and behavior of *particular* voters is observable to parties at all, it is only through their brokers. Brokers are therefore of potential electoral value to party leaders.

Yet, brokers have their own interests and objectives that sometimes diverge from the interests of party leaders – which suggests their electoral cost to parties. The innovative work of Camp forcefully conveys this point.[3] Brokers are locally networked and locally powerful individuals who may seek to extract advantages from their influence over the persons that they assist. Thus such leaders may seek to "sell" to leaders of different parties the support of blocks of voters over whom they exert influence. Building large networks of clients is therefore valuable to brokers; they can leverage this local influence to obtain resources from party leaders. Precisely because the composition of these networks – that is, who among a broker's followers is a swing voter and who is a loyal party supporter – is not observable to party leaders, leaders have difficulty inferring the impact of brokers on the electoral prospects of the party. Brokers can take advantage of this informational asymmetry to extract various kinds of rents. Moreover, the inability of party leaders to distinguish between swing voters and true ideological sympathizers of the party, combined with the value to brokers of building large networks, can create incentives for brokers to target relatively "cheap" loyal voters – for whom the ideological disutility of voting for the party or attending one of its rallies is low. In sum, brokers may exploit their informational advantage over party leaders to garner rents in the process of service and benefit delivery, and informational asymmetries may also lead to electorally inefficient targeting, in which too few swing voters are targeted from the perspective of party leaders.

In this chapter, we seek to capture in a simple way how relationships between leaders, brokers, and voters may shape the logic of clientelistic distribution.[4] We begin by developing a formal model in which brokers trade off the benefits of capturing rents against the detrimental impact of rent seeking on their party's probability of victory. The model also includes a pre-electoral game, in

---

[2] Stokes 2005.

[3] Camp 2012.

[4] Although our model is distinctive in its particulars, it shares with others the general feature of positing parties that are internally heterogeneous, including those by Geddes 1991, 1994, Alesina and Spear 1988, May 1973, and Hirschman 1970.

which brokers seek to build networks and sell them to parties in exchange for resources, analyzing the influence of this network-building activity on the types of voters who are targeted for benefits. We use the model to derive comparative-statics predictions about the extent of rent seeking and about the distributive strategies of brokers.

In this model, brokers value both local rents and the probability that their party/candidate wins office; our goal is to analyze what factors lead to greater rent seeking by brokers, as well as the types of voters whom brokers target for purposes of building networks and winning elections. The model produces several results. First, brokers will tend to target poorer voters. Second, when voters value targeted benefits over ideology, the electoral returns to clientelism increase. Third, economic development tends to drive down the electoral returns to clientelism. Fourth, the more brokers care more about winning elections, the sharper their incentives to target swing voters. Finally, the degree of "slack" in electoral outcomes – for instance, the impact that an individual broker has on electoral outcomes – shapes the extent of rent seeking by brokers. The greater a broker's impact, the greater is the opportunity cost of rent seeking by the broker. Many of these factors have implications for the electoral returns to clientelism for party leaders because they influence the incentives of brokers to target electorally valuable swing voters.

3.1 A MODEL OF RENT-SEEKING BROKERS

There are two parties, M and O, with M for machine and O for opposition. Initially, we assume that only party M has resources to distribute in a targeted fashion, and party M will hire a single broker who will distribute resources to voters. This simplification allows us to focus on the agency relationships between leaders, the broker, and voters. Here, one can think of party M as an incumbent machine party that has resources to distribute.

There are K potential brokers in the local district or area in which the parties compete. These may be neighborhood leaders/organizers or simply well-connected local individuals who seek to work in politics on behalf of the party. The potential brokers are indexed by η_k, a parameter we discuss later; without loss of generality, we order the index $k = 1, \ldots, K$ so that $\eta_K > \eta_{K-1} > \cdots > \eta_k > \cdots > \eta_2 > \eta_1$.

Finally, there is also a continuum of voters of mass one, and three groups of voters $j = p, m, r$, for "poor," "middle-class," and "rich." The groups have population proportions α^j, with $\sum_j \alpha^j = 1$; they are endowed with incomes y^p, y^m, and y^r, with $y^r > y^m > y^p$. Thus average income is given by $\sum_j \alpha^j y^j \equiv \bar{y}$.

The timing of the game is as follows:

1. Each broker organizes a network of followers, promising each follower i in group j a benefit of b^{ij} if the voter participates in her network.

2. Leaders in party M observe the size of brokers' networks and decide which broker to hire and then distribute resources to that broker.[5]
3. Elections take place. If party M wins office, the broker distributes resources to voters in his network, extracts any unspent resources as rents, and reaps the continuation value of her party staying in power.

There are various interpretations of the first stage of the game. Brokers may indeed literally compete to be "hired" by their party as a broker by building networks, and we provide some evidence to this effect in later chapters. In other settings, the competition may not be over *inclusion* in the party's organization as a broker; instead, brokers may compete for the quantity of resources obtained by the party; in this case, the "hiring" decision is not dichotomous but continuous. Finally, as we emphasize later, there are extensions of this basic structure in which brokers obtain rents from parties to build their power locally, and this involves recruiting local clients.[6] We remain somewhat agnostic on a theoretical level about the right interpretation to attach to the structure of the game, though later we investigate empirically how brokers do in fact interact with party leaders. Our goal here is to understand how career concerns – the need for brokers to demonstrate competence to party leaders – may shape the distributive strategies of brokers. The model is flexible enough to investigate that question without committing to a specific modality of career advancement for brokers.

Notice too that we assume full commitment to distributive strategies, in that brokers distribute resources at node 3 as promised in node 1. Our justification for this assumption is that brokers and their clients are in fact involved in repeated interactions. Although it would be possible to study this interactive relationship between brokers and voters in an explicit dynamic model, for the sake of simplicity and to focus on the issues of central analytic concern, here we absorb the continuation game into the value R of continuing in office.[7]

Participation in a broker's network carries a material cost for voters, as it obliges the voter to participate in brokers' rallies and similar political activities. Voters only follow a broker if the benefits of doing so outweigh the costs. Let the indicator variable $I(O_{ij}^k) = 1$ if voter i in group j is organized by broker k and 0 otherwise; each voter may participate in the network of only one broker.[8]

---

[5] Because we are focusing here on agency relationships between party leaders and brokers, we model competition between brokers in a single "district" or neighborhood; thus here parties hire just one broker. Elsewhere we consider the problem of allocating resources across multiple neighborhoods or brokers.

[6] See Camp 2012.

[7] See Stokes 2005, who studied a dynamic game between brokers and *voters*.

[8] This assumption is consistent with the behavior of brokers outlined by Auyero 2000 and others, and it also resonates with our fieldwork: brokers organize "their" voters, and exclusivity is maintained by the threat of cutting voters off from benefits should they seek assistance from other brokers.

Thus let voter i in group j be organized by broker k in that district – that is, $I(O_{ij}) = 1$ – if:

$$\kappa H(y^j + \eta_k b^{ij}) - c \geq \kappa H(y^j) + \sigma^{ij}. \qquad (3.1)$$

The left-hand side of this expression captures the material payoff if voter i participates in the network of broker k, net of the material cost c, in terms of time and effort, of participating in the broker's network. Brokers distribute benefits of size b^{ij} to each voter i in group j who participates in their network.[9] Next, the parameter η_k captures the competence of broker k in boosting the utility of network participants by providing them with targeted benefits. The idea here is that brokers differ in their capacity to solve voters' problems; a broker to whom a party leader extends disparate resources (e.g., bags of food, monthly subsidy plans, or building materials) must decide to which neighbors such goods can be most usefully distributed. Thus insertion in social networks and detailed knowledge of the needs of their neighbors allows especially enterprising brokers to target resources most effectively.[10] Some brokers are especially knowledgeable about job-market opportunities for unemployed neighbors or about upcoming food-distribution events; others are less knowledgeable or energetic. Especially competent brokers can thus produce more valued resource output with lower resource input. This "productivity parameter," η_k, is observed by voters but not party leaders. Finally, voters have diminishing marginal utility of total income (so $H'(\cdot) > 0$, $H''(\cdot) < 0$), and κ is a parameter measuring the value that voters place on material benefits, relative to ideology.[11]

In turn, the right-hand side of expression (3.1) gives the material payoff if voters do not participate in the network of broker k – and thus $b^{ij} = 0$, so the material payoff is $\kappa H(y^j)$ – plus the "ideological" (dis)utility of participation in the network. Here, σ^{ij} measures the ideological preference in favor of one party or the other; as in many probabilistic voting models, it is considered a fixed individual-level parameter that captures voters' partisan attachments.[12] The idea here is that ideology may also matter to voters, and it can impose its own cost of participation in a broker's network: for a lifelong Peronist whose parents were also Peronists, participation in the network of a broker for the Peronist party is less costly in ideological terms than it would be for a lifelong

---

[9] Here, b_i and c can both be understood as reduced-form expressions for the stream of costs and benefits associated with participation in the broker's network over time. Note that b_i is indexed by i because different voters can be paid different amounts to participate (in equilibrium, they will be made exactly indifferent between participation and nonparticipation). For simplicity, the material cost c is assumed constant, with individual differences in the cost of participation absorbed in the ideology term.

[10] Auyero 2001.

[11] Also, $H(0)$ is normalized to zero, and H satisfies the classical (Inada) conditions – that is, $\lim_{z \to \infty} H'(z) = 0$ and $\lim_{z \to 0} H'(z) = \infty$.

[12] See Dixit and Londregan 1996, Persson and Tabellini 2000.

Radical.[13] Note also that σ^{ij} captures the degree of attachment to the *party*; although in some settings partisan attachments may reflect underlying policy preferences (such as attitude toward government intervention or self-placement on a left-right scale), this need not be the case. Here, σ^{ij} has mean zero and is distributed uniformly on $[\frac{-1}{2\phi^j}, \frac{1}{2\phi^j}]$, so that negative values of σ^{ij} indicate an ideological preference for the machine party M.

A key point is that although parties know the aggregate distribution of σ^{ij} for each group, only brokers know the value for individual voters within each group. This knowledge reflects the "social embeddedness" of brokers, that is, the fact that they are immersed in dense local networks that give them privileged knowledge of the preferences and behaviors of their neighbors. Voters, in turn, observe the competence η_k of each broker k offering resources: brokers are neighbors who have acquired reputations for their abilities to solve voters' problems. Of course, the key theoretical point here is not that voters or brokers really observe preferences or competence exactly but rather that voters and brokers possess information about each other that allows them to infer capabilities and partisanship, information that is not readily accessible to distant party leaders. Information is transmitted via longstanding social relations in which brokers and voters are enmeshed. Party leaders are not privy to this knowledge; they must use brokers to gain information about individual-level voter preferences and behaviors.

In sum, voters compare the material and ideological benefits and costs of network participation and participate if the benefits outweigh the costs. If they are offered identical benefits by different brokers, voters maximize their expected utility by choosing the most competent broker, which (as we show later) implies that they correctly anticipate the equilibrium choice of the machine party; otherwise, they randomize their choice with equal probability between brokers offering them the same benefit.

What about voting behavior? We assume that non-network participants, as well as those who would prefer party M on ideological grounds ($\sigma^{ij} < 0$), vote sincerely. Thus these voters vote for the machine if

$$0 \geq \sigma^{ij} + \delta. \tag{3.2}$$

On the other hand, opposition voters may be induced to participate in the network of the party M's broker, and vote for party M, if and only if

$$\kappa H(y^j + \eta b^{ij}) - c \geq \kappa H(y^j) + \sigma^{ij} + \delta. \tag{3.3}$$

Here, δ is an aggregate popularity shock in favor of the opposition, party O, distributed uniformly on $[\frac{-1}{2\psi}, \frac{1}{2\psi}]$.[14] Thus a large positive realization of δ helps

---

[13] Note therefore that equation (3.1) can be understood to include two "cost" terms: the material cost in terms of time and effort, c, which does not depend on the partisan orientation of the voter; and the ideological cost, σ^{ij}, which does.

[14] Note the difference between the densities of the aggregate popularity shock δ and the individual preference parameter σ^{ij}: ψ is not indexed by j, while ϕ^j is group-specific.

party O, whereas a large negative δ helps the machine, party M. The density ψ of the random variable δ is a measure of the "slack" in electoral outcomes. Comparing (3.1), (3.2), and (3.3), we note that although the network-participation function is fully known to brokers when they propose their allocations, vote choice is determined by the realization of the random variable δ.

The other parameters in (3.2) and (3.3) are the same as in (3.1); in particular, the parameter σ^{ij}, which measures the ideological disutility of participation in the network of a broker from party M, also measures the disutility of voting for that party. Note that c in (3.3) again measures the cost of network participation.[15] Building on a large literature on clientelism, our assumption here is that inducing a voter who prefers party O on ideological grounds ($\sigma^{ij} > 0$) to vote for party M requires network participation: only through insertion in a broker's network can voters be monitored by brokers. Thus the ongoing relationship between brokers and the voters in their networks makes the clientelist bargain enforceable, particularly in the presence of a secret ballot.[16]

In sum, voters who are organized by the party's broker receive a benefit from the broker and participate in the brokers' network; if (3.3) is satisfied, they also vote for the brokers' party.[17] For voters who are not organized by the party's broker, $b^{ij} = 0$ and $c = 0$, so equation (3.3) reduces to sincere voting as in (3.2) – that is, voters vote for the party that they are closest to on the σ dimension. Notice that just as in the voting participation decision (3.1), voters are made more responsive to transfers if η – the parameter measuring brokers' productivity – and κ – the extent to which voters value money over ideology – are high. We discuss the interpretation of these parameters further later.

A broker who is hired by party M to distribute resources to brokers receives two types of benefits. If the party wins, then she receives an exogenous post-election payoff R. In addition, the broker may extract pecuniary "rents" r by failing to pass on some measure of resources to voters; although some rents may be obtained before an election, we assume that the broker's ability to extract resources also depends on the party retaining office. If a broker k is hired by party M, her expected utility is therefore

$$EU^k = p_M(r + R). \tag{3.4}$$

Here, p_M is the probability that the broker's party wins office. Winning gives the broker access to the continuation value of holding office, R. However, r gives the (endogenous) rents chosen by the broker. For the moment, the value R of post-election resources is left exogenous, though in a dynamic game it

[15] In Chapter 2, we used this notation to indicate the cost of turning out to vote, but here the concept is broader: distributing a benefit to induce voters who prefer party O on ideological grounds to vote for party M depends on organizing voters as part of a network.

[16] See Stokes 2005 for explicit derivation of the conditions under which equilibrium vote buying can be supported in repeated games, e.g., with grim-trigger strategies. Here we abstract from that problem and assume that voters can be induced to support party M if (3.3) holds.

[17] Later, we discuss issues of credibility and examine why it may be incentive compatible for voters to respect the rule in (3.3).

could reflect the per-period equilibrium value of r, given that the broker's party wins the election. If a broker is not hired by party M, her reservation utility is normalized to zero.

Finally, the budget constraint is given by $\Omega = \sum_{j \in \{P,M,R\}} \bar{b}^j + r$, where Ω gives the total resources distributed by party M to its broker, $\bar{b}^j \equiv \alpha^j \int_{I(Q_j)=1} b^{ij} dz$ is the total resources the party's broker distributes to each income group among its organized supporters, and r gives rents extracted by this broker. Ω is left exogenous (for the moment) and is known by the brokers. Thus potential brokers maximize the probability that they will be chosen as party M's broker, times (3.4), subject to the budget constraint.

The solution concept is Nash subgame perfect equilibrium. Thus strategy profiles must form Nash equilibria in the game between brokers, who are competing to be hired by the party. Hiring decisions by party leaders and voting and network-participation decisions by voters must also be Nash, in that there is no profitable deviation from their equilibrium actions, given what other actors are doing.

3.1.1 Analysis

We solve for the equilibria of the game by backwards induction, beginning our analysis at the final node. The analysis of this final stage of the game parallels standard probabilistic voting models.[18]

First, we define the vote shares of each party and hence the probability of victory of party M. Note that a network participant who is induced by the benefit b^{ij} to be indifferent between voting for party M and O is a voter with ideology parameter σ^{ij} such that

$$\sigma^{ij} = \kappa [H(y^j + \eta_k b^{ij}) - H(y^j)] - c - \delta. \tag{3.5}$$

In any election, a true swing voter has ideology parameter σ^{ij} such that the equality in (3.5) holds with $b^{ij} = 0$ and $c = 0$. For such voters, we simply have $\sigma^{ij} = -\delta$. Thus, if the realization of the aggregate popularity shock does not favor either party ($\delta = 0$), a swing voter who does not participate in the broker's network is exactly indifferent between the parties on ideological grounds.[19]

However, such ideologically neutral voters will not in general be the only voters who are just indifferent between voting for the two parties in equilibrium. Indeed, given y^j, σ^{ij}, and a particular realization of δ, some b^{ij} may be chosen such that (3.5) holds exactly for network participants. It is thus helpful to distinguish "true" swing voters, who are indifferent between parties M and O absent network participation, from voters who are just indifferent between the parties, but only conditional on the benefits they receive.

---

[18] See Lindbeck and Weibull 1987, Dixit and Londregan 1996, Persson and Tabellini 2000.

[19] In expectation, of course, $\delta = 0$, justifying our earlier claim that a swing voter is one for whom $\sigma^{ij} = 0$.

The following definition is useful in describing the (expected) vote share of party M:

Definition 1 *The largest value of σ^{ij} such that the equality in (3.5) holds, given some benefit distribution schedule, is defined as σ^{j*}. Then, $b^{j*} > 0$ is the value of b^{ij} such that (3.5) holds with $\sigma^{ij} = \sigma^{j*}$, that is,*

$$\sigma^{j*} = \kappa[H(y^j + \eta_k b^{j*}) - H(y^j)] - c - \delta. \tag{3.6}$$

It is easy to show that given a broker maximizing (3.4) subject to a budget constraint, the following claim then follows:

(1) All voters i in group j for whom $\sigma^{j*} \geq \sigma^{ij}$ vote for party M.

Suppose not: then a broker could have taken resources from a voter with $\sigma^{ij} = \sigma^{J*}$ and distributed it to some opposed voter with ideological location closer to the machine's, whose vote would (in expectation) be cheaper to purchase. Notice that voters with $\sigma^{ij} = -\delta$ are swing voters, in the sense defined earlier. Thus among nonorganized voters, the set who vote for party M prefer it on ideological grounds, that is, $\sigma^{ij} \leq -\delta$. By (3.6), $\sigma^{j*} < -\delta$ as long as $\kappa[H(y^j + \eta_k b^{j*}) - H(y^j)] - c > 0$. Then some set of organized voters prefers party O on ideological grounds (given the realization of the popularity shock) but are given a benefit just large enough to make them indifferent between the parties.

A corollary to this claim is that for all voters who prefer party O on ideological grounds (i.e., for whom $\sigma^{ij} > 0$) yet are paid $b^{ij} > 0$ to vote for party M, b^{ij} is increasing in σ^{ij}, the individual ideological preference for party O. That is, the more the voter prefers party O, the larger is the reward he or she attracts from party M. Another corollary is that if a marginal dollar is given to or taken from group j, it will be given to or taken from the individual i in group j such that $\sigma^{ij} = \sigma^{j*}$.

This discussion allows us to define the vote share of party M in group j as

$$F_j(\sigma^{j*}) = \int_{\frac{-1}{2\phi^j}}^{\sigma^{j*}} \phi^j dz = \frac{1}{2} + \phi^j[\kappa(H(y^j + \eta_k b^{j*}) - H(y^j)) - c - \delta], \tag{3.7}$$

where F_j is the uniform cumulative distribution function of σ^{ij}.[20] The vote share of party M in the electorate as a whole is then

$$\pi^M = \sum_j \alpha^j \left[\frac{1}{2} + \phi^j[\kappa(H(y^j + \eta_k b^{j*}) - H(y^j)) - c - \delta]\right]$$

$$= \frac{1}{2} + \sum_j \alpha^j \phi^j[\kappa(H(y^j + \eta_k b^{j*}) - H(y^j)) - c - \delta]. \tag{3.8}$$

---

[20] Recall that the density ϕ^j over which we are integrating in (3.7) is a constant; thus we can factor out ϕ^j, leaving $\phi^j[\sigma^{j*} - (-\frac{1}{2\phi^j})]$. Plugging in for σ^{j*} and rearranging gives the right-hand side of (3.7).

Note that π^M is a random variable, because δ is a random variable. The probability that party M wins the election is

$$p_M = Pr\left(\pi^M \geq \frac{1}{2}\right) \tag{3.9}$$

$$= Pr\left(\frac{1}{2} + \sum_j \alpha^j \phi^j [\kappa(H(y^j + \eta_k b^{j*}) - H(y^j)) - c - \delta] \geq \frac{1}{2}\right)$$

$$= Pr\left(\frac{\kappa \sum_j \alpha^j \phi^j [(H(y^j + \eta_k b^{j*}) - H(y^j))]}{\phi} - c \geq \delta\right),$$

where $\phi = \sum_j \alpha^j \phi^j$ is the average of ϕ^j across the three groups $j = p, m, r$. Thus, recalling that ψ is the density of the aggregate shock δ, we have

$$p_M = \int_{\frac{-1}{2\psi}}^{\frac{\kappa}{\phi}[\sum_j \alpha^j \phi^j (H(y^j + \eta_k b^{j*}) - H(y^j))] - c} \psi \, dz$$

$$= \frac{1}{2} + \psi\left[\frac{\kappa}{\phi} \sum_j \alpha^j \phi^j (H(y^j + \eta_k b^{j*}) - H(y^j)) - c\right]. \tag{3.10}$$

Below we analyze the optimal decisions of the broker who is hired by party M, who maximizes $p_M(r + R)$ subject to his or her budget constraint. First, however, we continue our analysis of the previous stages of the game.

Now, which broker will the party hire? Recall that parties do not observe η_k for any broker: this information about the broker's competence is private. Party leaders only observe the size of each broker's network, as proxied, for instance, by the number of citizens that brokers can mobilize for party rallies or get to vote in party primaries and other organization-building activities. Moreover, party leaders cannot observe the ideological composition of the network, because only brokers know which local voters support the party for ideological reasons and which do not. This leads to a second claim:

(2) In equilibrium, the most competent broker – that is, the broker with productivity parameter η_K – is hired by party M.

To see the argument for this claim, note first that the broker who compiles the biggest network is hired with probability 1 by the party – as we show later. Consider, then, the strategy of the first broker, the one with with productivity parameter η_1. Inspection of the participation constraint in (3.1) suggests that the voter who can be recruited most cheaply – that is, with minimal expenditure from the total budget Ω – is the voter with ideology parameter $\sigma^{ij} = \frac{-1}{2\phi^j}$, the loyal voter in group j most ideologically in favor of party M. Moreover, it must be the case that $j = p$. This is because poor voters have the highest marginal utility of income, because $y^p < y^m < y^r$, and so poor voters are the most responsive to transfers. If Ω is such that more than one voter can be recruited, given the participation constraint in (3.1), then the "next" voter that the broker with η_1 will recruit has $\sigma^{ip} = \frac{-1}{2\phi^p} + \epsilon$, with $\epsilon > 0$ being arbitrarily small, and so on, until the budget Ω is exhausted. As we discuss later, brokers may reach values of σ^{ip} for which, given (3.1), it is optimal to switch to targeting the most ideologically loyal middle-class voter, that is, the voter with $\sigma^{im} = \frac{-1}{2\phi^m}$, or even loyal rich voters. However, it can never be rational for the broker to leave "gaps" along the distribution of $\sigma^i j$ for any group j, because each voter "counts" the same in terms of building up the network, and voters with smaller σ^{ij} are cheaper to buy.

Now consider the broker with η_2, who is incrementally more efficient or capable than the broker with productivity parameter η_1. This broker can "match" the offer in terms of resources to each of the voters that the broker with η_1 seeks to organize and still have resources left over; because $\eta_2 > \eta_1$, this broker provides resources to voters more efficiently. Indeed, because σ^{ij} is distributed continuously, the second broker can offer sufficient resources to organize the voter with σ^{ij} just ϵ greater than the last voter organized by the broker with η_1. Thus he or she can build a bigger network than the first broker. Just as for the first broker, it can never be rational for the second broker to leave "gaps" along the distribution of $\sigma^i j$ within each group j, because each voter "counts" the same in terms of building up the network. Moreover, note that the first broker has no profitable deviation here, because he or she has already organized all of the cheapest voters, and each voter counts the same in terms of network size.

This logic carries through all the way to the most efficient broker, the one with η_K. In equilibrium, this broker must have a network that is at least as large as that of the broker with η_{K-1}; because there is a continuum of values of σ^{ij}, the probability that these networks will be exactly the same size has measure zero. Because party leaders can infer this is the most productive/competent broker, and productivity is valuable in terms of producing votes for the party, the party hires the broker with the biggest network. Thus, in equilibrium, party leaders hire the broker with η_K, that is, the most efficient/competent broker.[21]

Note that in principle, brokers could pay voters more than enough to satisfy their participation constraint; that is, (3.1) might hold with strict inequality. However, such promises cannot be made by the selected broker in equilibrium,

---

[21] We might appeal here to the "revelation principle" (Myerson 1982), which says that the equilibrium outcome of this process can be characterized as if it arose from a direct truthful mechanism, in which brokers honestly reveal their type to party leaders. The empirical reality seems to involve a more complex game between leaders and brokers, involving substantial monitoring of the quality and quantity of mobilization by brokers.

because at least one broker has an incentive to defect. Consider an extreme case in which all brokers promise all resources to the most ideologically loyal poor voter. Clearly, a broker could profitably deviate by offering these resources instead to an ideologically proximate voter with $\sigma^{ij} = \sigma^{ij} + \epsilon$.

How will brokers organize their networks in the first stage of the game? Brokers compete with each other to be hired by the party, because the reservation utility of not being hired is zero, whereas the expected value of being hired – even if rents are zero – is at least $p_A R$. Thus, with any positive probability that the party wins office, being employed by the party would leave each broker better off. Competition between brokers induces the following result:

(3) The network of the broker hired by party M will consist of the most ideologically loyal voters. These voters may all be poor, though some could be ideologically loyal middle-class or even rich voters.

The cheapest voter to organize is the poor voter with $\sigma^{ij} = \frac{-1}{2\phi^p}$. This voter is the most ideologically sympathetic to party M among poor voters, and poor voters – given diminishing marginal utility of income – are most responsive to transfers. Consider spending one peso on the most ideologically loyal voter among the poor, the middle-class, or the rich: inspection of (3.1) suggests that the participation constraint will be secured at the lowest cost among poor voters. Poor voters with $\sigma^{ij} = \frac{-1}{2\phi^p} + \epsilon$ will similarly be cheap to organize. As discussed previously, however, depending on the shape of H, the extent of inequality, and the size of the budget Ω, it may at some point make sense for brokers to switch to organizing the most ideologically loyal middle-class voter – that is, the voter with $\sigma^{ij} = \frac{-1}{2\phi^m}$ – rather than to organize a poor voter with high σ^{ij}. In principal, the same logic could induce brokers to target ideologically loyal rich voters, for example, those with $\sigma^{ij} = \frac{-1}{2\phi^r}$. Finally, we have:

(4) The broker with the largest network – in equilibrium, the broker with productivity parameter η_K – will have resources left over to extract as rents or for targeting of additional voters. The size of the residual resources will depend on the difference $\eta_K - \eta_{K-1}$.

This claim follows from the observation that there is a continuum of values of σ^{ij}, and from $\eta_K > \eta_{K-1}$. The broker with η_K will always have a larger network, if he or she promises to spend all of Ω organizing support from ideologically loyal voters. This broker can cut his or her spending on organizing such voters to the point where he or she has a network that is ϵ bigger than the network of the broker with η_{K-1}. The resources saved are therefore proportional to $\eta_K - \eta_{K-1}$. These additional resources retained by the broker hired by party M may thus be extracted as rents, or they may be targeted toward additional voters, as per the analysis that follows. In the discussion of comparative statics that follows, we subscript η with K, because the broker with $\eta_k = \eta_K$ is hired in equilibrium.

3.1.2 Comparative Statics

What factors shape how brokers spend resources? For example, when do they tend to prioritize building their networks by targeting cheap loyal voters, boosting the probability of victory by buying swing voters, or reaping private rewards by extracting rents? The analysis in the previous section allows us to develop comparative-statics results that shed light on these questions.

Conditional on being hired by party M, the broker maximizes $p_M(r + R)$ subject to his or her budget constraint. This logic induces a tradeoff for the broker: extracting rents r raises the pecuniary benefit to the broker but also lowers the probability of election. Indeed, differentiating equation (3.4) with respect to r, we have

$$\frac{\partial EU^b}{\partial r} = \frac{\partial p_M}{\partial r}(r + R) + p_M. \tag{3.11}$$

Intuitively, extracting rents instead of spending resources on voters will decrease the probability of election; by differentiating equation (3.10) with respect to r, we have

$$\frac{\partial p_M}{\partial r} = \frac{-\psi \eta_K \kappa}{\phi} \left[\sum_j \alpha^j \phi^j H'(y^j + \eta_K b^{j*}) \right] < 0. \tag{3.12}$$

So, from equation (3.12) and using the fact that $\frac{\partial EU^b}{\partial r} = 0$ at an interior optimum,

$$\frac{-\psi \eta_K \kappa}{\phi} \left[\sum_j \alpha^j \phi^j H'(y^j + \eta_k b^{j*}) \right] (r^* + R) + p_M = 0. \tag{3.13}$$

Thus

$$r^* = \frac{p_M \phi}{\psi \eta_K \kappa \sum_j \alpha^j \phi^j H'(y^j + \eta_K b^{j*})} - R. \tag{3.14}$$

Equation (3.14) already gives us some simple comparative statics predictions regarding the optimal level of rent extraction by the broker, r^*:

1. First, r^* is decreasing in the density of the random variable δ – that is, ψ – and therefore increasing in its variance – that is, $\frac{1}{12\psi^2}$. The interpretation here is that as the variability of electoral outcomes declines, brokers have less scope for extracting rents without sharply driving down the probability of victory. With noisy electoral outcomes, each broker's impact on the probability of winning the election is low, heightening incentives for rent seeking.[22]

---

[22] Readers might note that with large political machines, each broker's impact on the overall probability of victory should be low indeed. Yet by examining electoral returns at low levels

2. Next, r^* is decreasing in κ, the extent to which voters value benefits over ideology. Thus if voters are not responsive to transfers, brokers will tend to extract rents rather than target voters.

3. Third, equilibrium rents are decreasing in the "effectiveness" of the broker. We interpret this η parameter to indicate, inter alia, the broker's capacity to deliver valued benefits to voters and his or her ability to monitor voters' political behavior. The greater is η, the more effectively can the broker turn resources into votes for the party and thus the weaker are the incentives to extract rents, rather than target voters.[23]

4. Fourth, r^* is decreasing in the exogenous returns to winning office, R: as brokers care more about winning elections, they target voters with benefits to a greater extent and extract smaller rents. Greater inter-temporal continuity in the party system or career incentives for brokers may matter here.

5. Next, equilibrium rents are increasing in the average group-specific marginal utility of income. Other things equal, as average income rises, the marginal benefit of a clientelistic transfer falls, making brokers more prone to extract rents. In contrast, when voters are on average poorer, brokers have stronger incentives to target voters. In this way, economic development – the growth of incomes of poor, middle-class, and rich voters – makes clientelism less politically efficient, reducing the yield in votes for a given level of benefits distributed.[24]

6. Finally, r^* is increasing in the probability of victory, so that if elections are more competitive, brokers have stronger incentives on the margin to invest in targeting voters.[25] If clientelism reduces the competitiveness of elections – say, by amplifying the advantage of incumbent office holders who have access to public resources – this result also suggests that it can be self-undermining. As we discuss in Chapter 7, this may shed light on the decline of once-near-monopolistic machines such as the PRI in Mexico or the Christian Democrats in southern Italy.

---

of aggregation and designing other mechanisms to link broker performance to electoral results, parties can give brokers reason to value their individual impact on the probability of winning. We thus assume that brokers value the probability of victory, along with other things. See Camp 2010 for further discussion.

[23] Note that the probability of victory p_M, which is in the numerator of (3.14), is a positive function of parameters such as η_K and κ. However, the negative relationship between $r*$ and η can be verified by substituting equation (3.10) into (3.12) and applying the quotient rule to solve for $\frac{\partial r*}{\partial \eta}$.

[24] This prediction is distinct from one explored later, which is specifically about the number (mass) of poor voters rather than about average income.

[25] Because here we model an incumbent party with resources to distribute, the ex-ante probability of victory absent resource distribution is at least one-half (see Equation 3.10). So, a decrease in the probability of victory implies that elections are becoming more competitive.

What does this model imply about the targeting of different groups of voters? We already saw that in the first stage of the game, when brokers are organizing networks and competing to be hired by the party, they have incentives to target poor voters, who are cheap to organize. How, then, does the broker with productivity parameter η_K, who is hired in equilibrium, allocate resources for vote-buying across different groups? The broker's tradeoff between targeting the rich, the middle class, or the poor – conditional on the total fraction of resources spent on benefits (rather than rents) – is induced only by the effect of targeting on the probability of victory. In equilibrium, the marginal effects on the probability of victory must be equalized across groups; otherwise, the broker could boost the probability of victory by shifting resources from one group to another. Thus

$$\frac{\partial p_A}{\partial b^{p*}} = \frac{\partial p_A}{\partial b^{m*}} = \frac{\partial p_A}{\partial b^{r*}}, \tag{3.15}$$

which implies

$$\alpha^p \phi^p H'(y^p + \eta_k b^{p*}) = \alpha^m \phi^m H'(y^m + \eta_K b^{m*}) = \alpha^r \phi^r H'(y^r + \eta_K b^{r*}). \tag{3.16}$$

This expression leads to several interpretations, at least two of which suggest that the poor should be most heavily targeted for clientelistic benefits.

- All else equal, groups with higher marginal utilities of private income y^j should receive more benefits. That is, holding constant group size α^j and the density of the ideology distribution ϕ^p, we have $H'(y^p + \eta b^{p*}) = H'(y^m + \eta b^{m*}) = H'(y^r + \eta_K b^{r*})$; because $y^p < y^m < y^r$, the poor must receive more benefits than the middle-class, who receive more than the rich, so as to equalize the marginal utilities. This prediction is in line with a wide range of evidence suggesting that the greater marginal utility of income among poorer voters is a central reason why the poor are targeted for clientelist transfers (e.g., Brusco et al.).[26]
- Group size α^j matters: bigger groups will be targeted for benefits more intensively than small groups. If the poor are the most numerous, then group size thus provides another reason they will be targeted with benefits.
- Finally, more ideologically "mobile" groups – those in which there is substantial mass clustered at the critical value σ^{j*} – will be targeted for benefits: for example, if ϕ^p goes up in equation (3.16), then the marginal utility $H'(y^p + \eta b^{p*})$ must go down, and thus b^{p*} must go up. This comparative statics result has ambiguous implications for the targeting of particular

---

[26] Brusco, Dunning, Nazareno, and Stokes 2007. We return to this topic in Chapter 6.

groups, as it depends on the density of the group-specific ideological distributions. If poor voters are less "ideological," in that they are more responsive to transfers at the margin, then this is an additional reason for targeting them rather than middle-class or rich voters.

Several extensions to the model might illuminate additional issues. For example, we have assumed earlier that brokers can readily choose the amount b^{ij} that each voter i in group j is paid. This assumption generates the result that although loyal voters are the cheapest to buy – and the first marginal dollar spent on network building is targeted toward loyal voters – more overall spending may go to voters who are less ideologically sympathetic: a larger benefit must be offered to weakly opposed voters to make them indifferent between the parties.

In reality, a uniform pricing scheme may be more common. Although some kind of benefits may be offered in greater or lesser quantity – for example, two bags of rice instead of one, and more or less attention and effort to delivering services or helping voters access the bureaucracy – other behavioral or technological features of the environment might imply that targeted voters must be offered the same size of benefits. For instance, perhaps all targeted voters are invited to the same neighborhood party. In terms of our model, this implies that b is the same size for all targeted voters (or perhaps b^j is the same size for all members of a particular group).

The implications of such a restriction are interesting. With uniform pricing, σ^* – the highest value of σ^{ij} such that the voter with this ideological preferences is indifferent between voting for parties A and B, given the benefit distribution schedule – will be smaller than in the case of perfect "price discrimination." After all, if all voters who receive a benefit are paid the same amount, then, the benefits going to "inframarginal" voters – those with $\sigma^{ij} < \sigma^*$ – must be greater than in the case where brokers tailor the benefit to the ideological preference parameter of each individual voter. Thus, given a budget constraint, the amount of funds will not be sufficient to buy a weakly opposed voter who might have been won over under perfect price discrimination. This result also implies that clientelism may be less valuable to party leaders when technological or environmental factors restrict the nature of transfers, because they are not as readily able to buy swing and opposed voters.

This discussion points to another larger issue we take up in subsequent chapters: what kinds of greater information and redesign of benchmarks of broker performance might help party leaders to target voters more effectively? To take an extreme case, if brokers' impact on the probability of election were deterministic rather than probabilistic, and were perfectly observed by leaders, the scope for rent seeking by brokers would vanish. Without a seepage of resources through rent seeking, clientelism would be more valuable for party leaders. In subsequent chapters, when we evaluate the factors that seem to encourage and discourage clientelism in distinct national contexts, we look more closely at the mechanisms through which party leaders can monitor brokers' impact on the probability of victory, and at how the technologies available to leaders may shape the political attractiveness of machine politics.

3.2 THE OBJECTIVES OF PARTY LEADERS

Our model is built on the assumption that brokers trade off the probability of electoral victory against other objectives, such as extracting rents or building local power bases. The goal of the model is to examine how various factors shape brokers' optimal tradeoff between these objectives. We provide empirical support for both the assumptions and predictions of the model in subsequent chapters.

If this way of thinking about machine politics is useful, it has substantial implications for leaders' actions as well. Consider the comparative statics results presented in the previous section. Party leaders who are aware of these dynamics may structure machines to sharpen brokers' incentives to target and persuade swing voters. For instance, our results indicate that the greater the impact of individual brokers on the probability of victory, the smaller the equilibrium rents extracted by leaders. To the extent that leaders can take actions that make (disaggregated) electoral returns more responsive to the individual actions of brokers, the scope for rent extraction by brokers becomes more limited.[27]

Indeed, the empirical evidence we examine in subsequent chapters suggests that party leaders do design mechanisms to limit rent seeking and boost their monitoring of the impact of each broker on the party's probability of victory. In Argentina and Venezuela, our research team found that leaders have put in place extensive and sophisticated techniques for monitoring broker performance. In one county (*municipio*) in the Conurbano of Buenos Aires (traditionally a Peronist stronghold where clientelism has flourished), Florencio Varela, an online database that tracks various activities of brokers (*referentes*), is shared by local councilors (*concejales*).[28] In Venezuela, too, the work of local activists is closely coordinated by party authorities of both the incumbent and opposition parties, who create elaborate structures to monitor brokers.[29]

Such structures are typical of parties in which local brokers are engaged in frequent face-to-face contacts with the electorate and use targeted resources to mobilize voters, and they help leaders make electoral results more responsive

---

[27] We have not yet considered another reason brokers may have to target swing voters: it may be easier for brokers to defect to other parties or candidates if their networks are populated by swing voters, and this exit option may allow them to procure more resources from party leaders (see Camp 2012). However, because we assume that party leaders do not observe the ideological composition of brokers' networks, the credibility of the exit option may not in fact be enhanced by organizing more swing voters.

[28] Field notes, Edwin Camp, April 2010.

[29] Dunning and Stokes 2008.

to the action of brokers, thus reducing incentives to extract rents. These hierar-
chical, multilayered structures increase the ability of leaders to monitor brokers
and thus can make clientelism more efficient from the point of view of party
leaders. By the same token, as leaders become less able to monitor brokers, the
political efficiency of clientelism falls.

Still, our model implies that such efforts by party leaders have their limits: even though we analyze the factors that cause rent seeking by brokers to
increase or decrease, the nature of clientelist parties implies some agency loss
no matter what the party structure. Thus our model leads to the expectation
that party leaders will seek other ways to maximize vote share and the probability of victory. One implication is that the strategies of party leaders for
distributing resources across electoral districts – a setting in which they are
relatively unconstrained by the need to accommodate brokers – should differ
from the observed distribution *within* districts, because within districts brokers are doing the distributing. In Chapter 5, we test this idea with data from
Argentina, Venezuela, India, and Mexico and find that resources tend to flow
disproportionately to "swing" (electorally competitive) districts even as they
flow to many loyal individuals within districts.

Finally, notwithstanding the ability of party leaders to sometimes bolster
the efficiency of clientelism, the model also implies that party leaders will
under some circumstances have incentives to turn to other forms of electoral
persuasion: when rent seeking is too great, or brokers target resources too
inefficiently, party leaders may try to subvert the machine altogether. Thus the
model helps lay a foundation for analyzing transitions away from clientelism.
We return to this question in Chapter 7.

3.3 THE IMPLICATIONS OF AGENCY LOSS

The ability of parties to offer clients targeted benefits and to monitor their
compliance with the clientelistic bargain (e.g., their vote choice) requires the
existence of brokers – that is, local intermediaries who "organize" voters into
networks of followers. As Auyero, Stokes, and other authors have made clear,
brokers and voters are involved in a repeated game, in which brokers may
sometimes deliver benefits, in the form of targeted subsidies, access to social
plans, or other forms of political "problem solving" to voters – and voters
reciprocate by not only trading their vote but also, from time to time, participating in rallies, turning out for primary elections, and so on.[30] Clientelism –
the individualized quid pro quo in which benefits are conditioned on political
support – is characterized by the sustained relationships between brokers and
the clients they organize.

How does intermediation through brokers shape the logic of clientelist distribution? Our model suggests that brokers have an incentive to maximize the

---

[30] Auyero 2001, Stokes 2005.

size of their networks, because party leaders recognize that effective brokers can organize larger networks and thus "employ" brokers who have many followers. Of course, party leaders recognize that such networks may contain many voters who would vote for the party absent targeted benefits. However, brokers who can build large networks are valuable because they can also help persuade swing voters. Competent brokers know their neighbors, and they are able to solve their neighbors' problems effectively because they know who needs what. They can therefore convert a given amount of resources into greater benefits for their clients. This kind of "network competence" is important for organizing both ideologically sympathetic and ideologically neutral or even opposed voters – so, in our model, competence helps build networks and also helps convert swing voters and thereby win elections.

However, the inability of leaders to directly observe competence – combined with their lack of knowledge of the ideological/partisan inclinations of particular *individual* voters – leads to one source of agency loss. Leaders look to metrics such as the size of a broker's network to evaluate brokers' mobilizational capacity. That is precisely why it is so important for brokers to take attendance at rallies: this is a readily observed proxy for the broker's effectiveness.[31] This is not to say that other indicators are not also important. Yet mobilization for events other than general elections is also an important proxy for party leaders. How does this lead to agency loss? As our model makes clear, a broker who maximizes the size of his or her network, and who is subject to a budget constraint, would do best to organize loyal voters – those with an ideological preference in favor of party M. This also implies that brokers who care about obtaining greater resources from the party may not primarily do so by boosting their contribution to the party's probability of victory.[32] We do not mean to imply that the size of the network or the number of voters that brokers can mobilize for other political events, including primary elections, is the only source of information that party leaders have about brokers' competence. However, we emphasize that the difficulty of observing broker effort,

---

[31] Szwarcberg 2009, Auyero 2001.

[32] It might be that brokers can threaten to defect from the party, mobilizing "their" voters on behalf of other candidates or parties; we present evidence to the effect that this is an important reality in Argentina. Then, parties might pay brokers to prevent defection, and they might be particularly prone to do so in swing districts, where the defection of a broker would be especially costly from the perspective the party's overall vote or seat share. Yet, why are threats to defect credible – particularly if brokers are mobilizing loyal/core voters, who presumably would pay a much bigger ideological cost if they were mobilized for the opposition party? Such considerations might in principle give brokers an incentive to organize swing or undecided voters, as this would increase the credibility of their threat to exit. However, of course, the information asymmetry we have highlighted implies precisely that party leaders cannot really tell whether brokers are mobilizing swing or core voters. Any convincing explanation for patterns of broker-mediated targeting must presumably illuminate both how brokers' strategies are individually rational for them *and* why party leaders are invested in broker-mediated clientelistic distribution in the first place.

combined with agency problems created by the diverging incentives of party leaders and brokers, make the use of proxies such as the size of each broker's network important.

Another source of agency loss stems from the desire of brokers to extract rents. The reason that brokers are able to extract rents in equilibrium, even though party leaders and brokers anticipate that they will do so, is that electoral outcomes are "noisy." Thus brokers trade off rent extraction against the value of future employment if their party wins the election. Rent seeking can be understood in pecuniary terms – as appropriation by brokers of a portion of the resources that parties transfer to brokers and enjoyment of a private return on these rents. However, although we have not explicitly modeled the problem this way, it may also be that rent extraction provides another explanation for why brokers target loyal voters. After all, rents may help brokers to build local power bases in ways that do not help the party's electoral prospects. In other words, brokers may extract rents to build a network of loyal followers.

Still, brokers *do* also internalize their impact on their party's probability of victory, at least to some extent. After all, access to patronage opportunities and other state resources and benefits are at least in part a function of whether the party supported by a broker wins the election. Moreover, unlike individual voters, brokers can plausibly have a nontrivial impact on the outcome of elections, giving them an incentive to work for the party's victory.

This is precisely why clientelism can be valuable to party leaders. Brokers do have some incentives to target electorally responsive swing voters. And, crucially, party leaders cannot readily know which voters are swing voters, so they must rely on the knowledge of local brokers. In short, clientelism provides parties with one way to target benefits to individual swing voters, albeit in an often inefficient way that can involve substantial agency loss.

Yet it is clearly very challenging for leaders to make causal inferences about the impact of a particular broker on aggregate electoral performance in a given election. They may gain a rough sense, for instance, by scrutinizing the change in vote share in a broker's locality and comparing it to the change in vote share in similar localities.[33] However, it appears to be infeasible for leaders to reward brokers only on the basis of brokers' contributions to electoral outcomes.[34]

Here, then, we have a simple initial explanation for the tendency of brokers to organize loyal voters, an explanation that is consistent with the evidence

---

[33] Later, we provide examples of how parties attempt to do this, in Venezuela, Argentina, and elsewhere.

[34] Smith and Bueno de Mesquita 2011 developed a model in which parties cultivate electoral support by making the distribution of prizes or rewards to groups of voters contingent on the group's electoral support, e.g., as measured by returns at the level of the precinct or polling station. Note that use of this "prize pivotalness" mechanism, if feasible, would allow parties to circumvent brokers altogether. The extent to which clientelist parties can effectively deploy this mechanism is an empirical question; our evidence suggests that in clientelist parties, broker-mediated targeted distribution to individuals is very common.

presented in Chapter 2 about patterns of clientelist distribution at the individual level. Notice that this explanation does not depend on mobilization of turnout in elections, as in Nichter or Dunning and Stokes: brokers who are maximizing the size of their networks have incentives to target loyal voters, even in systems with compulsory voting (e.g., Argentina) or high levels of voluntary turnout.[35] In addition, and consistent with the evidence in Chapter 2, the prediction of our model is that brokers will build ideologically heterogeneous networks. In other words, the "core" consists of loyal and swing (or weakly opposed) voters.

We turn in the next chapter to testing these assumptions and empirical predictions, using our detailed surveys of a probability sample of brokers in Argentina, including several survey experiments, as well as our surveys of voters, qualitative fieldwork with brokers, and secondary data from Argentina, Venezuela, Mexico, and India. Our evidence suggests that brokers are engaged in frequent day-to-day interactions with voters in their networks and think they know their clients' preferences and behaviors well; they seek to build local power bases, often by rewarding "their" voters. Our survey experiments also reveal that brokers are disproportionately likely to reward loyal voters who would turn out to vote even absent a material inducement (that is, Certain Voters, in the terms of Chapter 2), even as they also target swing voters and thus build ideologically heterogenous networks, and they build large organizations by paying brokers to participate in rallies and other political events. Finally, our surveys and other evidence also reveal that brokers engage in substantial rent seeking, diverting resources for their personal benefit.

---

[35] Nichter 2008; Dunning and Stokes 2008.

4

Testing the Theory of Broker-Mediated Distribution

> "'Machines win elections.'"
>
> — Party operative in Petare, Venezuela, 2010.

> "I've been working there for 20 years and I know who is a Peronist and who isn't or who might have an affinity and vote for the Peronists."
>
> — Broker in Córdoba province, Argentina, 2002.

The broker-mediated model of clientelism is cogent as a theory. It also offers a resolution to the "too-favored-loyalist" paradox. But does our theory capture the realities of distributive politics by machines? This chapter offers evidence in favor of our theoretical approach. We rely on a number of sources of evidence. Because our theory focuses squarely on the incentives and behavior of brokers, we appeal first and foremost to our most direct source of data on brokers: our rich probability sample of city councilors and brokers from four Argentine provinces.[1] We supplement the broker survey with other information, including from our open-ended interviews with brokers, conducted outside of the context of the broker survey. We also draw on original data and information from Venezuela and India.[2]

We offer evidence of the following:

1. **Brokers Know "Their" Voters.** Brokers are indeed involved in long-lived interactions with their neighbors and clients, interactions which – in the brokers' view – give them privileged information about the preferences and behaviors of individual voters. They believe that they can observe the political preferences and actions of "their" voters: they know their clients.

---

[1] See Appendix A.

[2] There is a rich secondary literature on clientelism and the role of caciques or intermediaries in Mexico. We don't discuss Mexico in this chapter but do so in Chapter 5.

2. **Networks Tilt Loyal But Include Swing Voters.** Brokers view their networks as partially comprising loyal voters who always turn out to vote and who would not stop supporting their party absent a benefit. However, they also comprising less committed voters. These are in fact heterogeneous networks, and the logic of persuasion of swing voters is not foreign to brokers.

3. **Brokers Extract Rents.** Our respondents offered candid opinions that their fellow brokers are prone to rent extraction. Despite this striking evidence of rent seeking, substantial numbers of brokers say it is difficult for party leaders to take resources away from brokers who pocket party resources, who divert resources in ways that do not contribute to the party's victories, or who fail to exert effective efforts on the party's behalf.

4. **Brokers Want to Win Elections.** Our broker survey and field research provide evidence that brokers *also* care about their parties' winning elections. Their career paths influence these preferences: many began "militating" as young people, drawn to their party by a friend or family member or attracted by a charismatic leader or a compelling vision for change. Many remain with the same party for long careers. Another reason why brokers care about elections is that election outcomes have an impact on their careers within their parties, even if party leaders cannot fully condition rewards on brokers' campaign effort. When a party loses power, brokers lose access to jobs and resources. These mixed objectives – the desire to extract rents and the desire for their party to win – impose trade-offs on brokers.

5. **Leaders Try to Monitor Brokers and Brokers Threaten Exit to Avoid Discipline.** We offer evidence in favor of the assumption that party leaders cannot observe brokers' efforts or effectiveness directly, but try to evaluate these efforts through various monitoring devices. At the same time, our fieldwork and broker survey demonstrate that brokers sometimes threaten to abandon their party leader and join forces with an opposing one, from another faction of their party or even sometimes from another party. The threat is that they will take "their" voters with them.

6. **One's Position in the Party Hierarchy Influences One's Distributive Preferences.** Our broker-mediated theory implies that brokers who operate at the neighborhood level will be inclined to channel resources to loyal supporters, whereas their higher-ups in the party would prefer that resources go to responsive, swing voters. Chapter 5 explores this implication further. However, our broker survey offers additional evidence that distributive preferences vary with a person's location in the party hierarchy. City councilors, people who had risen somewhat in the party to the point where they had run for municipal office, overwhelmingly endorsed the idea that scarce resources should go to districts with many

swing voters. Although many low-level brokers also endorsed this idea, they did so in substantially smaller numbers than did the city councilors.

In sum, we show that brokers play a vital role in intermediating distributive relationships with voters, while also imposing costs on parties. The evidence we offer suports our analytical move of disaggregating clientelist parties. Understanding the divergent incentives of brokers and party leaders sheds substantial new light on the logic of clientelist distribution.

4.1 WHO ARE THE BROKERS?

We begin with descriptive information about the brokers we surveyed and, by extension, those in the Argentine provinces from which our samples were drawn. The central source of information around which this chapter revolves is a sample survey that we conducted, beginning in 2009, of about 800 brokers in four Argentine regions – the provinces of Córdoba, Misiones, and San Luis, and the "urban cone" (*Conurbano*) of Greater Buenos Aires.[3] All were face-to-face interviews. These surveys were designed to illuminate brokers' preferences, motivations, and constraints and their interactions with voters and with party higher-ups. We believe that ours is the largest and most detailed survey of political brokers ever undertaken.

Generating a probability sample of brokers is challenging, because a ready-made sampling frame – that is, a list of brokers from which one could draw a random sample – does not exist. As described further in Appendix A, our approach to this problem is two-fold. First, we developed a probability sample of city councilors. We did this by randomly sampling municipalities from four Argentine provinces and then randomly sampling city councilors from each of those municipalities. Once municipalities were identified, it was straightforward to obtain a list of councilors and thus a sampling frame for councilors in the municipality.

As a second step, we then asked city councilors in our interviews: (1) the number of non-elected activists who work for them; and, later in the survey, (2) a list of the names and contact numbers for those activists. We then sampled at random from the latter list. We therefore generated a probability sample of city councilors; challenges of sample selection (e.g., in the provision of the lists) may imply some deviation from a pure probability sample for non-elected activists (see Appendix A). We consider both city councilors – who in general did territorial work in neighborhoods before being elected as councilors – and the non-elected activists who work for them to be brokers, though they are at different levels of organizational responsibility. Our complex, multi-stage cluster sampling design implies that the most reliable way to attach standard errors to our estimates is by using the bootstrap, described in Appendix A.

---

[3] As mentioned, this survey is described in detail in Appendix A.

About 56 percent of our sample were men, 44 percent women.[4] They were not as a group either uneducated or very poor by Argentine standards; most could be described as lower middle class. Nearly half reported monthly earnings of 3,000 pesos or less, and 60 percent below 4,000. The average Argentine monthly income is about 2,300 pesos.[5] The modal respondent was a secondary school graduate (22 percent), though 20 percent of respondents said they were college graduates.[6] Half of the sample had some some postsecondary education.

The mean age of our sample was 48; the youngest broker was 21, and the oldest 87. The average number of years they had "militated" in their party was 18; the average number of years working for the same local boss (*referente*) was 11. Significantly, a full 71 percent had worked for the same party throughout their career.

A broad range of experiences initiated our respondents into political life. Some said that a family member, friend, or work associate got them involved. Some were initially drawn into their activities through a party youth organization. Some began working in a particular campaign, doing simple tasks such as passing out flyers, putting up posters, or "distributing votes" (meaning ballots). Others casually attended a rally or candidate's speech.

These initial experiences led eventually to professional or at least paid involvement with their party. Whether the brokers are full-time party professionals is a complex question. When asked, 83 percent said that they had other paid work, separate from their political activities. Yet the figure may be misleading. The largest single occupation mentioned was "public employment." Even excluding city councilors, it was mentioned by 30 percent of brokers. But in not a few instances, their public-sector jobs were secured, and retained, by virtue of their work for the party. (Others described themselves as merchants, self-employed, independent professionals, private sector white-collar employees, or retirees.)

As mentioned, our strategy was to sample local city council members and then their non-elected activists. Of the 800 respondents, 284 described themselves as holding an elected office – in almost all cases, a seat on the city council. A few mentioned their position in the municipal cabinet or administration – secretary of governance, secretary of sport, fiscal oversight board (*tribunal de cuentas*). Several mentioned their position in the local party (e.g., leader of their party delegation on the city council). Thus the sample can be described as comprising local party actors, about one-quarter of whom had ascended to the level of holding local office. Thirty-eight percent had run for office at least once; 62 percent never had.[7]

Turning to party affiliation, not surprisingly the largest number (52 percent) were affiliated with the Peronist party; 22 percent were Radicals; 6 percent

---

[4] The bootstrapped standard error on the 56 percent is 5 percent.
[5] As measured by the INDEC, the official statistical agency, in the final quarter of 2011.
[6] The bootstrapped standard error is 8 percent.
[7] The bootstrapped standard error is 6 percent.

were from *Renovador*, a regional party from the province of Misiones that is a coalition of the Peronists and Radicals; and 4 percent Union PRO, a rightist party. The remainder were brokers from smaller parties, whereas 16 percent reported no affiliation.

Our richest data come from Argentina. However, we introduce, when appropriate, evidence from other countries. Our research and many excellent secondary studies suggest that the roles brokers play in Argentina are in many ways parallel to those played by brokers in other democracies, as we discuss later.

4.2 TESTING ASSUMPTIONS AND HYPOTHESES OF THE BROKER-MEDIATED THEORY

4.2.1 Brokers Know Their Clients

In the broker-mediated theory, it is the social embeddedness of brokers with constituents, and the information that this embeddedness provides, that makes brokers valuable to parties. Indeed, clientelism *requires* brokers: only locally embedded agents of the machine command the knowledge of voter preferences and partisan inclinations needed to turn the politically motivated distribution of benefits into electoral support. In contrast to other kinds of parties, political machines' penetration into constituents' social networks and daily lives allows them to infer the partisan orientation and actions of voters, if not perfectly, at least reasonably well.

Evidence that brokers do have this knowledge draws on our extensive fieldwork and prior research. That they have this knowledge is consistent with a large literature on clientelism in Argentina and in other countries.[8] In our fieldwork, we were struck by the familiarity of brokers with "their" constituents. We interviewed brokers who could rattle off the names, telephone numbers, family characteristics, work situations, and health status of their voters, from memory. Yet because it is fundamental to our theory that brokers command much detailed (and politically relevant information) about voters, a first-order empirical task is to examine more systematic evidence on this question.

Among the information that brokers claim to know about their voters is for whom they vote. As part of our survey of brokers, we asked:

When a neighbor with whom you have a lot of dealings votes for a candidate you do not support, do you think you will realize that the neighbor voted in this manner?[9]

Nearly 80 percent of brokers said yes (Figure 4.1).

---

[8] Brusco, Nazareno, and Stokes 2004, Stokes 2005; see also Auyero 2001.
[9] All translations from the Spanish are ours. The Spanish-language survey instrument is posted at www.thaddunning.com.

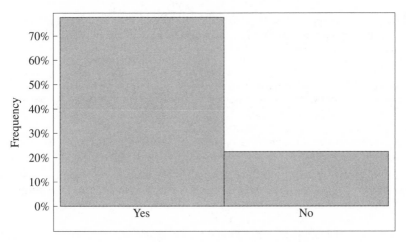

FIGURE 4.1. Can Brokers Infer Voters' Choices? N = 773.

Many voters share the belief that their electoral choices can't be kept secret from brokers. In our 2003 survey of voters, we asked "Even though the vote is secret, do you believe that party operatives can find out how a person in your neighborhood has voted?"[10] Keep in mind that, in a narrow sense, the Argentine ballot is secret and has been since 1912. Nevertheless, 37 percent of the sample responded that party operatives can find out how a person voted, 51 percent that they cannot, and the remaining 12 percent didn't know.

As a follow-up, we asked those voters who said the party could ascertain their vote choice how the party managed this. The most frequent answer was "I don't know" (206). Others said they didn't know but offered some speculative explanations (48), whereas others said that the party somehow marked the ballots (99) or found out by "asking around, investigating, speaking with neighbors" (89), or that party operatives spied on people in the voting booth (46) or that technology and computers were somehow involved (47). Some answered simply that brokers would ask voters (33).

In our fieldwork – in line with the large number of "don't know" responses – some voters perceived brokers' ability to discern their vote choice as mysterious. We interviewed one couple who were stupified by local brokers' ability to discern particular voters' choices:

Question: When people come and give things out during the campaign, are they people whom you know?

Husband: Yes, they're people from here, they're neighbors. Here everyone knows each other. "Small town, big hell." (*Pueblo chico, infierno grande.*)

Question: Do they know how you voted?

[10] See Appendix B.

Husband: For many years we've seen, people will say, "So-and-so voted for so-and-so." And [the candidate] wins, and they come and say, "You voted for so-and-so." I don't know how they do it, but they know.

Wife: We were at the *unidad básica* [a neighborhood Peronist locale] and they say to me, "[Your cousin] voted for Eloy" [the given name of a Radical-party candidate]. And I asked my cousin, "did you vote for Eloy?" And she said "yes"! They knew that my cousin had voted for Eloy![11]

What is mysterious for voters is basic craft knowledge for brokers. In a 2002 interview, we asked a local Peronist operative in the province of Córdoba whether it was possible for him to discover, after an election, how people in his neighborhood had voted. His answer – which we quoted in part in the epigram to this chapter – was as follows:

"In the sector that one works in, yes, you know how to find out, yes. Because you've already been working there with those people, you go around observing the affinities of each person, by way of the campaign events in the neighborhood, or when they come to you and request some medicine or a box of milk, and sometimes they give you a hard time and complain, and you go along identifying people . . . besides I've been working there for 20 years and I know who is a Peronist and who isn't or who might have an affinity and vote for the Peronists."

Notice what this broker is claiming. He can distinguish not just party affiliation – who is a Peronist – but more subtle categories, such as people who have an "affinity" and might be induced to vote for the party, even if they are not part of the party's core constituency. In other words, he can distinguish loyalists from swing voters who might nevertheless be responsive to the broker's help in obtaining gifts.

Close familiarity allows brokers to make inferences from subtle cues. Another grassroots party organizer in Argentina explained, "you know if a neighbor voted against your party if he can't look you in the eye on Election Day."[12]

These accounts of how brokers learn their constituents' voting preferences and actions resonate with the views of brokers in our survey. According to the vast majority of respondents, the relevant information arises out of the day-to-day interactions between brokers and neighbors, often people who have known each other for a long time. What's more, the implicit job description of a broker involves retaining close contacts with people in his or her neighborhood, keeping track of who needs what assistance and who might be available to participate in rallies, meetings, and other party events. In our survey, we asked an open-ended follow-up question to the one just cited, asking brokers *how* they would know if a voter had voted for some other candidate. Respondents

[11] Interview conducted by Valeria Brusco, Lucas Lázaro, and Susan Stokes, July 2003.
[12] Stokes 2005, p. 317.

indicated that their daily conversations with voters allowed them to draw inferences from attitudes or affect. The following comments are typical:

"In the neighborhood, everyone knows each other."

"It's a community. We all know each other."

"Through open daily, direct dealings with people."

"Through mannerisms, discussion, dialogue, attitude, a look or gesture."

"You see it in their faces."

"They are transparent."

"It's difficult to hide things when we interact."

"Because he is my neighbor, I know him."

"Because here we all know each other; the one who didn't vote with you tries to avoid you."

"Because the next day he regrets not having done what he said he would do."

One broker told a story about a neighbor who asked for corrugated iron to make a garage; the broker did not give the iron and saw the neighbor "eating at the site/headquarters of another party . . . he didn't look at me for two days."

Other brokers gave other explanations, yet these also emphasized the importance of the repeated interactions between brokers and various neighbors. Brokers emphasized the distributive exchange between themselves and voters, the technology of voting, or the presence of networks of local informants in the following terms:

"Because they stop asking for things."

"When someone is going to vote with you, he asks you for the ballot; when he doesn't ask, he's not going to vote with you."[13]

"I have many intimate allies who bring this information to me."

Beyond voting behavior, respondents also emphasized their knowledge of the partisan and ideological orientations of their clients and potential clients:

"Generally, through daily chats, one notes the ideology that the neighbor has."

"The neighbors are very identified with respect to political orientations."

"The communities know who is with the party."

"We politicians have a good sense of smell."

Thus our systematic data from a probability sample of brokers confirm what our fieldwork (and that of others) suggested. Brokers believe that they can infer

---

[13] This quote illustrates the role of the party-created ballot or "ticket" as opposed to Australian ballot in facilitating vote buying.

the preferences and behaviors of their voters – even when voters try to hide them. In total, more than 90 percent of responses to the open-ended follow-up question emphasized in some way the importance of daily interactions or conversations with voters. Only a few brokers mentioned that "the quantity of votes" received at the local polling station (*mesa*) helped them infer the voting behavior of their clients. This overwhelming result shows that – especially in the presence of the secret ballot – the social embeddedness of brokers in their neighborhoods is crucial for inferring individual voting behavior.

Another indication of brokers' confidence that they know their constituents came from a question about voters feigning positions or preferences that they do not really hold. We asked brokers in our survey the following question:

Some people play hard-to-get and suggest they will only go vote, or will only vote for the party or candidate that you support, if you give them benefits. In your neighborhood, would you say that there are:

1. Many people like this
2. Some people like this
3. Few people like this
4. No people like this

About 67 percent of brokers said there are "many" or "some" voters in their neighborhood who play "hard to get" (left panel of Figure 4.2). We then asked a follow-up question: "How difficult is it to distinguish between those who will turn out to vote only if they receive a benefit from those who will turn out to vote in any case – very easy, easy, neither easy nor difficult, difficult, or very difficult?" About 67 percent of brokers said it was very easy or easy to identify these people (right panel of Figure 4.2).

A second follow-up question asked respondents how they could tell the true swing voters (or potential abstainers) from those who would mimic them. Respondents again emphasized their long trajectories living side-by-side with their neighbors.[14] Answers such as the following were typical:

"I know the people of the neighborhood."

"Knowing the trajectory of the person."

"Because here we all know each other."

"Because we've lived together all our lives."

The back-and-forth between brokers and "their" voters are sometimes initiated by the voters, sometimes by the brokers. When voters request favors from

---

[14] Although many brokers answered this question by emphasizing that they know their neighbors intimately, many answers were a variant of "they [voters] tell you directly" that they want a benefit or will only vote for the party if given a benefit. Such answers are also illuminating of the close ties between brokers and voters, yet for these respondents, the contrast intended in our question between what voters say they will do and what the broker knows they *really* will do – even if playing hard to get – may have been lost.

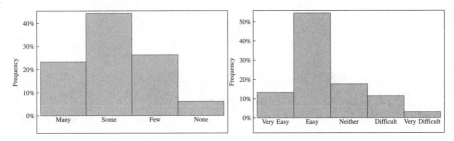

FIGURE 4.2. How Many Voters Play "Hard to Get"? (Left Panel), and Can Brokers Easily Tell? (Right Panel), N = 774, 773.

brokers – assistance in finding a job or rations of food or medicine – brokers later cash in their chits by requesting network participation from voters, asking them to participate in a rally or post flyers or vote in a primary election.[15] That they also expect these voters to support the party in general elections goes without saying. We asked brokers what proportion of voters who received goods had requested them, and to what proportion of voters they had extended help without voters asking for it. The question wordings were:

Out of every 10 voters that you have ever helped, to how many have you extended help without them asking for it?"

and

Out of every 10 voters that you have ever helped, how many asked for help directly?

More brokers identify requests as originating with voters than the other way around (Figure 4.3). However, the modal answer to both questions is 5 out of 10, or half: sometimes voters ask for help and sometimes brokers offer it.

Our surveys of Argentine *voters* also underline the long-lived relationships and (informal) networks in which brokers and voters are enmeshed, through which voters sometimes approach brokers for help. Relatively small numbers of respondents said they had received direct gifts or assistance – only 7 percent of respondents in our 2003 survey of poorer voters, for instance (though see our discussion in Chapter 2 of social desirability bias and of credible estimates of the prevalence of clientelist gifts.)[16] Yet whenever we asked voters, "If you

---

[15] Voting in general elections is compulsory in Argentina, but voting in primaries is a "favor" that a voter can choose to perform.

[16] The question read, "During electoral campaigns, party operatives and neighborhood political leaders often give people things or assistance. In the last presidential campaign, did you receive any of the following?" The respondent was then given a card that listed items that might have been handed out and forms of assistance (*ayudas*) that they might have received. The items included food, mattresses, subsidies, clothing, money, medications, housing, and roofing materials; the assistance included help with legal paperwork, medical attention, obtaining student scholarships, payment or cancellation of bills for public services or taxes, and jobs.

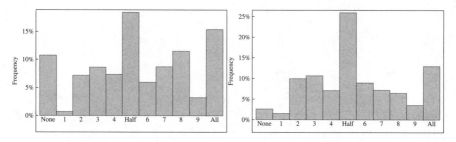

FIGURE 4.3. Percent of Voters to Whom Brokers Have Offered Benefits (Left Panel), and Percent Who Have Asked for Help (Right Panel) (Vertical Bar Indicates Average Response). N = 742, 742.

were facing a grave family problem, for example, related to a job or health, would you turn to a party representative [puntero, referente]?" – and we did so in voter surveys in 2001/2002, 2003, and 2009 – about one-third of the sample answered that they would. For many residents of low-income neighborhoods, a local party operative could offer solutions to very personal, family crises.

The findings are a testimony to the contrasting functions of party machines, which directly mediate voters' access to state benefits and even labor-market opportunities, and bureaucratic parties in advanced democracies, which rarely today play these roles. It is difficult to imagine large numbers of Swedes, Americans, or Spaniards saying that they would turn to a political party representative if faced with a family health or employment emergency.

That voters frequently initiate requests for aid does not mean that brokers respond to these requests without regard for the political inclinations of the voter or political impact of the assistance. Brokers can say no to voters' requests. Some brokers undoubtedly engage in "constituency service," as we defined that term in Chapter 1, interceding on the behalf of constituents, with no criteria for attending to constituents' needs beyond that they live in the broker's neighborhood or sector. However, frequently brokers are guided by the likely political impact of their problem-solving strategies and mete out their time and assistance preferentially, depending on voters' electoral responsiveness or willingness to invest in a broker's local power base.

We shall see evidence that politics comes into play in a later section, where we report brokers' perception that certain kinds of voters – those who are loyal supporters, and to some extent those who are swing and hence electorally responsive – are likely beneficiaries of party largess. As Auyero contends, clientelism involves poor people getting help through "personal problem-solving networks" – which does not preclude the extraction of a political price from the voter, such as a vote, participation in a rally, or some other benefit to the broker.[17]

---

[17] Auyero 2001.

In Venezuela as well, brokers acquire detailed, electorally relevant information about "their" voters. We discussed in Chapter 2 the efforts to which pro-Chávez party leaders went to extract, systematize, and diffuse this information. The opposition also used clientelistic strategies, and also went to lengths to extract information about constituents.

In the lead-up to the Venezuelan legislative elections of 2010, the political opposition invested in clientelism and in pork-barrel strategies as well. In the Caracas slum of Petare – formerly a stronghold for Chavismo, after Chávez's rise to power in 1999 – opposition candidates began to gain a toehold, in part by recruiting disaffected activists and operatives who had previously worked with Acción Democrática (AD) and COPEI.[18] The opposition gradually gained support in the Caracas municipality of Sucre and even in Petare (which is located in Sucre), and opposition candidate Carlos Ocariz won the mayoralty in 2008. One of the disaffected brokers recruited by the opposition Justice First (*Primero Justicia* party) who gave her first name as Betti, had spent nearly 35 years with AD and had also briefly worked with COPEI (she left because AD "didn't value one the way one deserved" but the leaders of COPEI were "just the same"). But she had "never stopped communicating with neighbors" who were not all with Chávez. After Ocariz approached her about working with him, she worked "house by house . . . sharing coffees" with her neighbors.

Betti and other brokers like her provide important information about their clients to party leaders. During the 2010 legislative election campaign, the opposition incumbent in the municipality divided Petare into 38 informal "zones" and recruited "zone chiefs" (*jefes zonales*) – that is, brokers – to manage each of these zones on behalf of the opposition party Primera Justicia. Betti, as a zone chief, was responsible for 13 sectors (blocks) that comprised one of these zones. The brokers were recruited from the panoply of parties that comprised the opposition Unity Table, including Primero Justicia, the Movement to Socialism (MAS), COPEI, and AD, as well as disaffected brokers from the *chavista* United Socialist Party of Venezuela (PSUV). Political workers in the mayor's office refer to these brokers as "mini-mayors" (*mini-alcaldes*) and as "the eyes of the mayor in the street" (*los ojos del alcalde en la calle*). Each of these zone chiefs in turn had six "promoters" (*promotores*) who worked with him or her in the zone, and the promoters in turn helped many residents. The zone chiefs and their promoters are given responsibility for turning people out not just for elections but also for rallies and other events in non-election season and are given explicit quotas (e.g., one broker might be required to turn out 100 voters). According to workers in the mayor's office, this system becomes a channel for distributing jobs as well as access for favors. For example, street sweeping is done by the municipality, and the jobs are given to the zone chiefs

---

[18] These two parties, which were predominant in the pre-Chávez era, have almost entirely lost popular support during the period preceding and following Chávez's first election.

or are under their control for allocation to followers. As one might imagine, this control over economic resources gives brokers substantial local power. It also allows brokers to gain substantial information about the neighborhoods under their purviews.[19]

In sum, brokers do have privileged knowledge of the voters they organize. This knowledge arises from brokers' long-term involvement in local social networks and from their ongoing if sometimes intermittent interactions with their clients. Relationships between voters and brokers are repeated and sustained and involve substantial opportunities for brokers to infer the political preferences and actions of individual voters. These relationships also give brokers a privileged ability to discriminate between individual voters when allocating benefits.

4.2.2 Targeting Loyalists (and Some Swing Voters)

How do brokers use their knowledge of individual voters to distribute access to scarce resources? What types of voters do they prioritize? And how do the objectives of brokers, such as building political careers or broadening local power bases, shape their distributive strategies? We take up the question of targeting first and then investigate the broader question of the types of activities in which brokers are engaged.

Chapter 2 explained in some detail the tendency of machines to channel resources to party loyalists – not exclusively, but often predominantly and to a degree certainly unanticipated in theories of distributive politics. Our surveys of Argentine brokers reveal again the marked tendency of brokers to target loyal co-partisans, while not excluding swing voters. Our broker survey included the following set of questions, asked as a survey experiment. Approximately one-half of brokers were assigned at random to be asked the following question:

Suppose that the mayor of a hypothetical municipality called a broker and gave him access to 10 social-assistance programs with which to mobilize voters. The broker has 40 neighbors who need assistance. Suppose that all of them always turn out to vote. Among them, there are **neighbors who prefer the party of the broker and others who are indifferent between the parties.** To which type of neighbors would the broker give more programs?

The bolded text indicates that the hypothetical choice was between Certain/Loyal and Certain/Swing voters. The other half of the sample was asked the same question, but here we asked whom a broker would choose between (1) voters who are certain to turn out but are indifferent between the parties (Certain/Swing Voters) and (2) voters at risk of abstaining who prefer the party of the broker (Potential/Loyal voters).

---

[19] One political worker we interviewed had read Auyero's description of clientelism in the Conurbano of Buenos Aires, Argentina, and commented that it had sounded just like Petare.

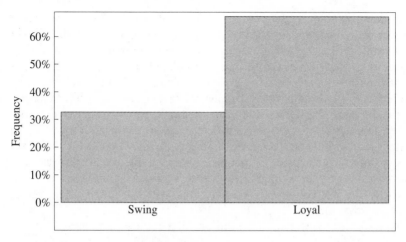

FIGURE 4.4. Brokers' Preference for Loyal Voters (Survey Experiment). N = 682.

The results are reported in Figure 4.4, which gives the percentage of respondents who indicated that the broker would give to loyal voters and the percentage who indicated they would give to swing voters, pooling across the two versions of the question. In responding to the first version of the question, two-thirds of the surveyed brokers said that the broker would distribute more programs to voters who are certain to vote and prefer the party of the broker – that is, to Certain/Loyal voters. Just over 30 percent said the broker would favor voters who are certain to vote but are indifferent between the parties – that is, Certain/Swing voters. If received theories reviewed in Chapter 2 are right, we would expect these percentages to be reversed.

In response to the second version of the question, about 69 percent said the broker would give to party supporters who are at risk of abstaining (i.e., potential/loyal voters). Just 31 percent said they would give to certain/swing voters. The disinclination brokers expressed to target swing voters who are certain to vote especially sharply contradicts many of the theories of distributive politics.

We also posed a non-experimental, hypothetical question to brokers in our survey, this time asking them to consider voters who were at some risk of abstaining (i.e., they were Potential Voters). Every broker was asked to compare Potential Voters who preferred the party of the broker with Potential Voters who were indifferent between the parties.[20] In response to this question, brokers again overwhelmingly chose Loyal/Potential over Swing/Potential voters.

[20] For the "Potential Voters" version of the question, we asked "Returning to the hypothetical municipality we mentioned before, now let's suppose that the broker cannot count on his neighbors to turn out to vote of their own initiative. Among them, there are neighbors who prefer the party of the broker and others who are indifferent between the parties. To which type of neighbors would the broker give more programs – to those who do no always vote and

ice in Figure 4.4 would be fairly easily explained if the logic were
he vote" – increase turnout among supporters. But the broker
ls starkly that, given a choice between different kinds of voters,
... s strongly predicted to choose the loyal supporter, regardless of
whether the party supporter is at risk of abstaining. Indeed, the preference for
loyal voters is if anything slightly stronger when the voter is certain to vote,
though the difference between the 70 percent and 69 percent is not statistically
significant. Thus respondents expect a hypothetical broker to favor loyal people
who always turn out to vote even more than they do loyal people who may not
turn out to vote (in both cases in comparison with indifferent voters who are
certain to turn out to vote). Again, this result is hard to square with received
theories in which machines give rewards to loyal voters as long as these voters
are at risk of abstaining.[21]

In Chapter 2 we reviewed evidence indicating that the preponderance of loyalists among the beneficiaries of machines was not an artifact of endogenous
party affinities, turnout buying, or subcontracting. Still another possible explanation is that brokers worry that distributing largess to swing voters would
lead to resentment among "loyalists," who would then be in danger of defecting. Another way of saying this is that the construct of "loyalists" may be
logically plausible but actually an empty category: maybe there are no voters
whose support can be taken for granted. To explore this possibility, we posed
the following question:

Suppose that, in a very competitive election, a broker distributes access to social programs to voters who are not affiliated with his party. What would be the reaction of
voters who are sympathetic to the party and who have supported it in the past? Would
they:

(1) Not change their behavior
(2) Fail to turn out to vote
(3) Turn out to vote but vote for a different candidate or party?

About 63 percent of respondents said the loyal voter would not change her
behavior. Thirty-two percent thought she would vote for another candidate or
party and about 8 percent thought she would not turn out. Although a third
of respondents did worry about the defection of loyalists, most did not. A
majority of brokers believe that the loyal supporter as we have conceived her –
an ideological or partisan supporter who would continue to support her party
even absent a benefit – is not an empty category.

who prefer the candidate of the broker, or those who do not always vote and are indifferent
between the parties?"

[21] This does not imply that turnout buying cannot be effective. When we asked brokers "Would
you expect a neighbor who does not always vote to decide to turn out if s/he receives a social
program?" about 68 percent said yes. Our point is simply that the evidence does not suggest
that turnout buying provides the main reason for targeting loyal voters.

As a follow-up to the experimental question about the hypothetical broker who is called on to distribute social-assistance programs before an election, we asked brokers to explain their response, in an open-ended format. Their comments point toward another important fact: it is often ambiguous whether the respondent is referring to past loyalty to the *party* or to the *broker*. Indeed, the latter interpretation is suggested by phrases that brokers used to explain their choice. Giving to loyalists would allow the broker to "continue assuring himself of *his* votes"[22] or "to assure himself of the votes of *his* voters."[23] This interpretation is also consistent with our field work, as well as with the field-work of researchers such as Camp and Szwarcberg.[24] Brokers may be giving benefits to loyal voters to assure their loyalty not to the party but to *the broker*. This interpretation takes us to alternative possibilities that are more consistent with the broker-mediated model.

Still, some responses were suggestive of brokers' fearing that loyalists who were ignored might defect. Some respondents used the verb "to assure" (*asegurar*) – giving the impression that respondents saw these voters as possibly voting for the party of their own accord but only being certain to do so if they received some direct benefit. For instance, the broker would give the benefit to the loyal supporter:

"Because it would assure [the votes of] those followers."

"Because he has them assured. They always vote [for the party] but that's because they were always given [programs]."

If brokers viewed most loyalists as in danger of defecting if taken off the gravy train, this fear did not come through in great numbers in response to the questions reported in Chapter 2. As we showed there, many brokers think that the majority of voters in their neighborhoods are loyalists who are prone to vote for the party, even absent targeted benefits provided by the party (see Figure 2.9). It may be that this was simply a face-saving response or a self-serving belief among brokers who would prefer not to see themselves as purchasing people's loyalty with benefits. Yet both in field work and in the broker survey, we found brokers to be quite candid and pragmatic in their explanations of how they and their colleagues operated. Their frank admission – described later – that many brokers pocket party resources is just one example. We tend, then, to take at face value brokers' assertion that they count quite a number of loyal supporters among their constituents, as we do the view of many that these voters' electoral support is not at risk should party largess be expended elsewhere.

In addition to asking brokers how many people living in their neighbor-hoods were certain to turn out to vote and were avid adherents to their

[22] Emphasis added; translation of *Sigue asegurando sus votos.*
[23] Emphasis added; translation of *para asegurarse los votos de los suyos.*
[24] Camp 2012; Szwarcberg 2009.

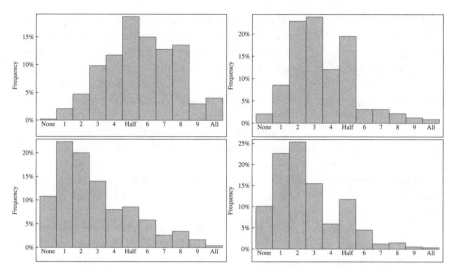

FIGURE 4.5. Distribution of Brokers' Voters (Certain/Loyal, Top-Left Panel; Certain/Swing, Top-Right Panel; Potential/Swing, Bottom-Left Panel; Potential/Loyal, Bottom-Right Panel). N = 773, 753, 739, 741.

party – Certain/Loyal voters – we asked about the presence of Certain/Swing voters, Potential/Loyal voters, and Potential/Swing voters. The results can be seen in Figure 4.5. What jumps out from this figure are the large (asserted) percentage of Certain/Loyal voters (top-left panel), especially compared with the smaller percentage of Certain/Swing voters (top-right panel); the small percentage of Potential voters (unsurprisingly in Argentina, with its formally compulsory voting – panels 3 and 4). Note also the much higher concentration of non-abstainers rather than potential abstainers among Loyal voters (top-left versus bottom-panel).[25] All of this evidence about the perceived distribution of voters in brokers' own neighborhoods – and their tendency not to abandon the party if denied clientelistic benefits – tends to go against an explanation whereby brokers shower benefits on loyalists out of fear that they will lose the loyalists' votes should they not do so.

The phenomenon of brokers favoring loyalists is by no means unique to Argentine clientelism. Earlier we reviewed relevant evidence from India, Venezuela, and Mexico. In India, to recap, our survey data from the southern state of Karnataka showed that party members disproportionately received jobs and benefits from village councils when the council president was a co-partisan.[26] In addition, we found that citizens who share the party of the council president are 13 percentage points more likely than other citizens to say they

---

[25] This may suggest that ideology/partisanship and propensity to abstain are not independent.

[26] Appendix D describes this survey in more detail.

had received a gift from a political party or candidate before an election, in return for turning out to vote – a highly statistically significant difference that is also substantively large.

To summarize, our systematic research in Argentina, India, and Venezuela shows that brokers view their networks as heavily populated by loyal voters who always turn out to vote and whose electoral support is not contingent on the voters' receiving minor gifts. Alongside of these loyalists, brokers also describe their networks as composed of less committed voters. From the standpoint of the partisan inclinations of voters, networks are heterogeneous. And in their dealings with swing voters, brokers are well aware of the electoral payoffs that their parties can reap when they give out minor gifts and favors. By implication they are aware of the loss of votes for their party when they direct favors toward party loyalists.

That brokers are prone to targeting loyalists does not mean that their efforts are exclusively aimed at dogged partisans. Instead, the evidence – consistent with the broker-mediated theory – points toward brokers' favoring loyalists but building heterogeneous networks of followers.

To probe the types of voters whom brokers tended to target, we asked the following question:

Of every 10 people whom you have helped, how many were already sympathizers of the party?

As Figure 4.6 shows, over one-quarter of the sample responded "5 out of 10," about 10 percent responded "All," and about 6 percent responded "None." Although the figure hints at some intriguing heterogeneity across brokers, we do not find substantial heterogeneity by province, or across brokers who are elected councilors and those who are not.[27] For present purposes, the major point is that the modal answer is "Half" – suggesting that many brokers do indeed have heterogeneous networks, consisting of both previous supporters as well as nonsupporters of the party.

The thinking of swing-voter theorists is at odds with that of many brokers, but not all of them. In response to our question about how a broker would allocate 10 social programs, only around 31–32 percent of surveyed brokers said they would target voters who are certain to turn out and who were relatively indifferent in their party affinities – the response that prevailing theories would predict (see Figure 4.4). In a follow-up, open-ended question, among the minority who chose this Certain/Swing response, around 15 to 20 percent gave the precise rationale of these theorists: a peso spent on a loyal voter is a

---

[27] For example, the mean response is 5.76 in Buenos Aires, 5.35 in Misiones 5.53 in San Luis, and 5.21 in Córdoba. Among elected councilors, it is 4.69, whereas among non-elected brokers, it is 5.42.

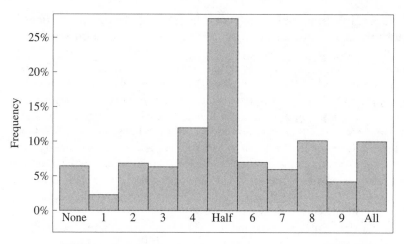

FIGURE 4.6. Brokers' Heterogeneous Networks: Number of Clients Out of 10 Who Were Already Party Sympathizers (Vertical Bar Indicates Average Response). N = 654.

peso wasted. One broker explained the logic of targeting swing voters in the following terms:

"To capture new votes; he's already got the others captive."[28]

This broker and many others would therefore reach out to swing voters to increase his electoral market share.[29]

Fieldwork – ours and that of other investigators – indicates that voters who receive benefits are often expected to reciprocate by participating in the broker's network-building activities: putting up posters, attending rallies, or voting in primaries. Although in the next section we review evidence that brokers require network participation with an eye toward building their own local power, many also view organization building as an effective route to winning elections.[30] We asked brokers:

Out of every 10 voters that accompany a broker to a political rally, how many do you think will vote for the candidate of the broker in a primary election?

and then we repeated the question, replacing "primary election" with "general election." In all cases, brokers thought that the great preponderance of voters

---

[28] *"Para captar votos nuevos, a los otros ya los tiene cautivos."*

[29] We did not find substantial heterogeneity in responses to this question as a function either of region or of position (i.e., being an elected councilman or working for an elected councilman). About 27 percent of respondents in Buenos Aires and 25 percent of respondents in each of Córdoba, Misiones, and San Luis reported that half of the people they have helped were already party supporters. Other features of the distribution of responses appear similar across provinces. Hence, about 28 percent of councilors and 24 percent of non-elected brokers said that half of their beneficiaries consisted of supporters.

[30] Auyero 2001.

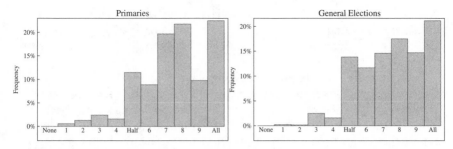

FIGURE 4.7. Network Participation and Voting Behavior: Number of Rally Attendees Out of 10 Who Will Vote For Broker's Candidate (Vertical Bar Indicates Average Response). N = 759, 761.

would indeed vote for the candidate preferred by the broker (Figure 4.7). Apparently, heterogeneous networks have some electoral impact.

On balance, the evidence about clientelist networks and strategies is consistent with the broker-mediated theory. Brokers expend party resources on loyalists. To some extent they do so because some "loyalists" will abandon the party if they are ignored. To some extent they do so because they want to bring reluctant voters among the loyalists to the polls. However, frequently they do so for neither reason. They simply want to build up their local network of supporters and can do so most cheaply by recruiting voters who prefer their party. We offer more evidence on this last point in the next section. Brokers also care about their party winning elections, which induces them to deliver some benefits to swing voters in search of votes.

4.2.3 Networks and Rent Seeking

Argentina

The broker-mediated theory pivots around the idea that brokers are rewarded for building large networks and that they build networks for reasons other than winning elections. Is the evidence consistent with these assumptions?

If turnout buying is clearly *not* the main reason for targeting loyal voters in this context – and if rewards really do go to long-time supporters who would probably support the party even absent clientelist inducements – why *do* brokers target loyal individual voters? The broker-mediated theory posits two reasons.

One reason, consistent with Szwarcberg's findings, is that by building large networks of followers, brokers can send a signal of their strength and competence to party leaders, thereby securing "employment" or, more generally, advancing their careers.[31] Because networks are cheaper to build with partisan or ideological sympathizers of the party, much of brokers' network-building

---

[31] Sczwarzberg 2008.

effort is focused on loyal voters. A corollary to this idea is that various modes of formal or informal intraparty competition – primaries, for instance – may also give local operatives incentives to build large networks of sympathetic followers.

A second reason why brokers "waste" resources on loyalists is that building large local power bases may itself provide a more diffuse kind of "rent" to brokers, even beyond the point at which these power bases are electorally useful for the party. Brokers may extract various kinds of rents from parties and use these rents for a variety of purposes – including the building of a local power base of followers. Thus the targeting of loyal voters can also be seen as a part of the rent-seeking behavior explored in the model of the previous chapter.

Results from our broker survey show that when brokers offer access to social programs to people who already prefer the party, the brokers are reinforcing their local organizational structure and territorial control. To those in our samples who predicted that brokers would favor loyal voters, we asked, *why?* They gave the following kinds of answers:

"Because it is important to the broker to maintain the structure of his internal perquisites."

"It gives him more possibilities to manage convocations [e.g. of rallies or strikes]."

"To take care of people who are always faithful, loyal to the party."

"Because he is rewarding loyalty and affection for the party."

The first statements suggest that enhancing the power of the *broker* – not boosting the electoral fortunes of the party – is a key reason why brokers target partisan sympathizers of the party. The second two quotes emphasize that voters may also be rewarded for loyalty to the party, not just to the broker. Still, a sizeable number of responses underscored the personal obligation that the broker was under to return the favor extended by the voter's participation in political activities. For example, one broker said that a supporter would be given a social program "to reward the accompaniment [*Para premiar el acompanamiento*]."[32] Such phrases suggest the ways in which brokers are seeking to obtain accompaniment – for example, network participation – from voters.

The broker-mediated theory assumes that brokers care both about their party's winning elections and about extracting rents – skimming resources from the party, building their local power by allocating too many resources

---

[32] Of course, this type of response is sometimes ambiguous. Did the respondent mean that a *referente* needs to reciprocate to keep the person on his/her side and voting for the party? Or was this a more normative and/or psychological comment, that it's difficult not to reciprocate when someone has helped you in the past? We address these questions in more detail elsewhere.

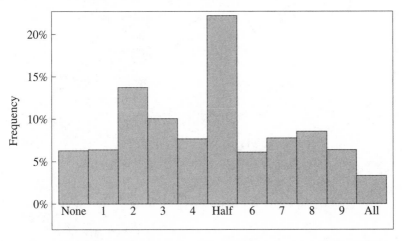

FIGURE 4.8. Rent-Seeking by Brokers: Number of Brokers Out of 10 Who Keep Party Benefits for Themselves. N = 640.

to loyalists, perhaps saving on effort. To investigate rent seeking, we asked respondents to our broker survey:

Out of every 10 brokers, how many do you think keep for themselves benefits that the party gives them to distribute to voters?

The answers suggest substantial rent seeking. In total, among the 86 percent of brokers who answered this question, more than 90 percent suggested that at least some brokers extract benefits not intended for them by the party (Figure 4.8). Nearly 25 percent of the sample said that "half" of brokers keep resources intended for voters. A mere 6 percent claimed that no brokers extract rents. Note that social desirability might induce brokers to minimize any rent seeking, so their willingness to acknowledge widespread rent seeking of the crudest form is striking.

The broker survey turned up a good deal of evidence of brokers building local organizations by providing resources to clients in exchange for their participation in rallies. We asked brokers:

Out of every 10 brokers who have the possibility to distribute benefits in exchange for attendance at rallies, how many would you say choose to do so?[33]

Figure 4.9 indicates that most brokers do engage in this form of organization/ participation buying, at least according to their peers. Thirteen percent say that all brokers would do this, whereas about three quarters say that three or more

---

[33] The wording in the survey instrument asked brokers how many would "*not* choose to do so"; for clarity, we recoded the data as an increasing measure of payments for rally participation, so that 0 became 10, 1 became 9, and so forth.

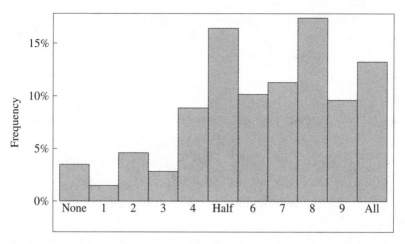

FIGURE 4.9. Organization Building by Brokers: Number of Brokers Out of 10 Who Distribute Benefits in Exchange for Rally Attendance. N = 731.

brokers of every 10 would engage in this kind of participation buying; only 4 percent say none would.

Brokers simultaneously extract rents while engaging in organization building. As a follow-up to the preceding question, about how brokers get people to take part in network activities, we asked:

Thinking of the brokers who, having the possibility to distribute benefits in exchange for participation in rallies and elections, choose not to do so, what do you think explains this decisions?
(1) Because they think it does not get results.
(2) Because they prefer to keep the benefits themselves.
(3) Because they think participation should be voluntary.
(4) Other.

Of those who answered this question (about 91 percent of respondents), fully 30 percent suggested that brokers keep resources for themselves. (About half gave the perhaps socially desirable response that participation should be voluntary, whereas 11 percent said participation buying does not work.)[34]

Here again, when asked about the actions and motivations of their fellow brokers, large numbers quite frankly describe them as extracting rents – saving on effort, recruiting loyalists because of the ease and benefits (to the brokers) of doing so, and skimming party resources for their own use.

India

In India, as in Argentina, brokers have opportunities and incentives to extract rents, and they exert substantial effort in network building. Local council members and presidents are rewarded by their parties for turning out the vote

---

[34] Nine percent said "other."

at election time. These rewards create strong incentives for brokers to allocate benefits to co-partisans. After all, leaders, unlike brokers, cannot easily discern electorally responsive (swing) voters from hard-core loyalists, so heavy turnout or other visible signs of widespread participation will naturally be interpreted by leaders as indicating that the local brokers are energetic and capable. Brokers are intimately involved with building local party organizations, and they often target partisan supporters with benefits.

In interviews, council members talked about their intimate relationships with "their" voters in terms that were strikingly similar to some of the comments of the Argentine brokers. In the villages we visited, voters readily identified council members with particular parties, but they also readily identified themselves with their preferred representatives. Future research in India should probe the relationship between brokers and voters in the kind of detail allowed by our surveys in Argentina, but preliminary evidence suggests a tendency of brokers cultivate networks of loyal followers, whom they seek to mobilize with gifts and favors.[35]

What, then, about rent seeking in India, another central objective of brokers in our model? As Bussell noted, extracting rents is particularly important for elected officials, because of the high cost of campaigns and the expectation that parties will extend tickets to candidates who can finance part of the cost.[36] Oldenburg, as well as Wade, have analyzed the role of mediation by brokers and in particular the cycle of rents that flows through brokers, from officials to citizens in the form of electoral bribes or from citizens to officials in the form of bribes for services (often via the bureaucracy).[37] In the case of land consolidation in the state of Uttar Pradesh, for instance, Oldenburg shows that middlemen play an important role in facilitating bribe payments from citizens and also keep a large portion of the bribe.[38] As for our own research in India, we have already noted the discrepancy between the official monetary return to elected posts in village councils and what individuals are willing to spend on campaigns to win these posts. This gap may in itself indicate an important role for rent extraction.

4.2.4 Winning Elections

We have seen that many brokers do not invest all their effort in helping their party win. They shirk, skim resources, or invest in their own local power base at the party's expense. The very local scale on which brokers operate – a scale that has to be small if the broker is to be able to provide the information and monitoring of voters that clientelism requires – means that their actions are

---

[35] Dunning and Nilekani 2012.
[36] Bussell 2012.
[37] Oldenburg 1987; Wade 1985.
[38] Oldenburg 1987: 521–522. Ironically, according to Oldenburg, it was the relatively *low* level of bureaucratic corruption in the process of land consolidation that allowed middlemen to exploit the *perception* of high corruption to induce citizens to pay them to pass on bribes.

unlikely to make the difference between their party's winning or losing, even in elections in moderate-sized municipalities, certainly in provincial or national elections. The temptation is to leave the hard work and sacrifice for the party's cause to other brokers.[39]

Still, brokers are rarely indifferent about their party's electoral prospects. In the opening discussion of this chapter, we mentioned several reasons why they want their party to win. In general they feel strong attachments to their party. Framed, yellowing photographs of Juan Domingo and Eva Perón graced the walls of many Peronist operatives whom we interviewed, whether the interviews were conducted in public spaces or in the brokers' homes. Radical party centers often feature murals with images from that party's pantheon, especially of Hipólito Yrigoyen. This is far from a peculiarity of Argentine politics. More than mere cults of personality, the prevalence of these images speaks of partisan and to some degree ideological convictions of brokers. Partisan attachments are fed by the same sorts of self-identification and emotions that also feed attachments to sports teams among many people. Of course, working to boost a party's vote share is not so simple as working for the Peronists or the Radicals or other parties. A broker might well feel himself or herself to be working for one faction or candidacy of (say) the Peronists and not another, or for one local boss (*referente*) and not another.

Our interviews and broker survey in Argentina trace the career paths of brokers. Many first worked for the party because they were swept up in youthful enthusiasm for a particular candidate. Others became proselytizers for their party's program or vision. We would not expect such people to be indifferent to their party's electoral fortunes, even if they had some self-interested reasons not to exert themselves fully on its behalf and even if their efforts would make only a small difference in whether their party won or lost. What's more, even despite some significant shuffling of brokers among distinct party factions or, on occasion, from one political party to another, for the most part these individuals have committed years, often decades, to promoting the party's cause. Recall that more than 70 percent of brokers in our survey had never changed parties and that the average broker had toiled for 14 years on behalf of his or her party and 11 years on behalf of his or her local boss. The figure of the broker is hence deeply ambiguous: he is at once an extreme version of a loyal voter but also someone who plays his own game and in so doing may work against the party's interests.

Brokers' commitment to their party is not just a matter of ideological conviction or deep partisan identification. Brokers draw resources from their parties and build their careers around the party. When their party or faction loses, they lose access to the kinds of resources around which they construct their local followings. What's more, if their livelihood comes from state employment

---

[39] Camp 2012 analyzed a formal model in which this collective-action problem plays a central role.

or patronage, the consequences of their patron's losing control over the public sector can be personally catastrophic. Even factional disputes can get in the way of brokers' drawing benefits from the party.

An event in the recent history of the province of Córdoba starkly illustrates the costs that lost access to patronage impose on brokers. In this case, the loss of state resources was the fallout not of a lost election but of the breakup of the marriage of a Peronist governor and his wife, the latter having served as the Secretary of Government in her husband's provincial cabinet. Juan Manuel de la Sota was elected governor of Córdoba in 1999 and was reelected in 2003; in 2005, he and his wife, Olga Riutort, divorced. Their split reverberated throughout the provincial Peronist party and state government. A party worker who had been a city council candidate on Riutort's dissident Peronist list recalled:

We [Peronists] had about 15,000 public sector workers [*contratados*]. After the political divorce happened, on December 31 one thousand letters went out informing people that they were now out of the government. This is something the government can do, legally it can do it, even if it represents a failure of ethics and of sentiment, to throw out some guy who lives on his salary, it's crazy ... This is the way the state, and any party, handles things.[40]

Brokers come in different flavors. Some are "pragmatists," in Szwarcberg's categorization, who readily trade minor benefits for electoral support.[41] Others are "idealists," who believe in their party's ideals and program and would prefer to work to boost its fortunes and spread the word. Probably these instincts are mixed in the minds of many brokers. A broker whom Szwarcberg interviewed expressed the frustration of someone who is an idealist by nature but who understood the advantages that material handouts offered: "Unfortunately, voters listen to you, they are interested in you, but they need things. Then, if you do not have money, if you can't give them things, they can't support you. They support whomever has things to give away, no matter who she or he is."[42]

4.2.5 Leaders' Efforts to Monitor Brokers and Brokers' Efforts to Avoid Discipline

Argentina

From a party leader's perspective, the challenge is to make use of brokers' efforts on behalf of the party while minimizing the rents that brokers extract. Just as brokers come up with many ways to monitor voters, leaders are inventive when it comes to monitoring brokers. In the Argentine municipality of Florencio Varela, located within greater Buenos Aires, Camp found that the mayor

[40] Interview conducted by Valeria Brusco 2003.
[41] Szwarcberg 2013 (forthcoming).
[42] Szwarcberg 2013, p. 27.

maintained a detailed database with information about his party's brokers.[43] The database included telephone numbers of some voters in each broker's neighborhood. The mayor's office periodically phoned a smattering of voters to inquire whether certain benefits that the party had disbursed through its brokers had ended up in the hands of voters. The implication was that incompetent or self-promoting brokers might not pass the benefits along; this was an elaborate effort to catch them.

In our Argentina brokers' survey, many brokers concurred that their work was evaluated in electoral terms. Many brokers identified electoral performance as a key factor that their parties used to evaluate the brokers' efforts. A preponderance of brokers asserted that providing a large number of votes in the general election was among the most important ways for a broker to boost his or her political career.

This finding is intuitive – after all, winning elections should be most valued by party leaders. Yet it is not always easy to judge brokers by returns in their neighborhoods. Even party insiders do not necessarily have access to turnout figures or party vote share on a neighborhood-by-neighborhood basis. And even if they did, electoral performance is a noisy signal of brokers' efforts. Unobserved factors can thwart energetic efforts of a "good" broker and mask a mediocre performance by a "bad" one. We should therefore not be surprised that many brokers in our survey saw other activities as crucial to their reputations with party leaders. We asked:

If you had to state what is most important for a *referente* who is interested in a political career, would you say that it is best to mobilize voters for a political rally, for a primary election, or for a general election?

The left panel of Figure 4.10 shows that about 64 percent of respondents answered "a general election." Yet a full 36 percent mentioned primary elections or rallies as most important for the broker's career – quite a striking result, given that the purpose of broker-mediated distribution, for party leaders, is presumably to win general elections.

Some close observers of Argentine elections have suggested that clientelism mainly operates during intra-party competition.[44] Our results indicate that primaries are not the whole (or even the major) story behind vote buying in Argentina. These findings are all the more noteworthy given that we conducted the surveys during a period of particularly intense factionalism and intra-party competition in Argentina, competition that presumably heightened the importance of vote-buying during primaries. However, consistent with our theoretical model, our evidence does suggest that party leaders are expected to use both primaries and rallies to judge brokers' effectiveness. A sizeable

---

[43] Camp 2012.
[44] See De Luca et al. 2006.

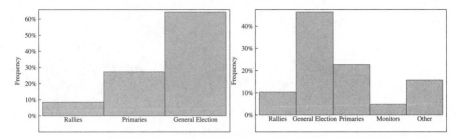

FIGURE 4.10. Most Important Perceived Criterion Party Leaders Use to Evaluate Brokers (as Perceived by Brokers). N = 735, 749.

minority of brokers view mobilizing voters for rallies or for primary elections as even more important than mobilizing them for general elections.

Our survey elicited brokers' views about how party leaders evaluated them with a wider of response categories. We asked:

When party leaders evaluate the political work of *referentes*, what aspect weighs most heavily in their evaluation?

(1) The number of people whom the *referente* takes to rallies.
(2) The number of votes the party receives from the *referente's* neighborhood in a general election.
(3) The number of votes that a candidate receives in a primary election.
(4) The number of election judges/monitors (*fiscales*) whom the referente provides for the party.
(5) Other information?

Although the most frequent answer is again "a general election" (see right panel of Figure 4.11), here this option no longer enjoys a simple majority. Instead, about 54 percent of brokers cited one of the other options – rallies, primaries, election judges, and other – as the most single important aspect for evaluating the success of monitors, with the distribution of responses being about evenly split across these options (though the frequency is somewhat lower in the case of election judges).[45]

Notice that when brokers turn people out to rallies, provide election judges or monitors (*fiscales*), and elicit voter participation in primaries, they are signaling the size of their networks. Election judges/monitors – who give out envelopes at polling places, register voters' participation, and tally votes – are often clients who have received benefits from the broker and reciprocate by playing these roles. Brokers also organize the clients in their networks to

---

[45] We also asked what is the second-most important activity used to evaluate a broker. Among those who answered this question, 111/590 = 18.8 percent said "rallies;" 158/590 = 26.8 percent said "general elections;" 208/590 = 35.3 percent said "primary elections;" 80/590 = 13.6 percent said "election judges;" and 33/590 = 5.6 percent said "other."

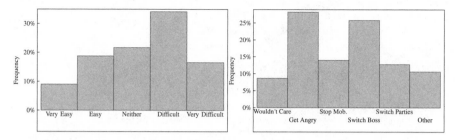

FIGURE 4.11. Broker Exit Options and Party Resources: Perceived Ease with Which Party Leaders Can Remove Resources (Left Panel) and Brokers' Probable Response (Right Panel).

attend rallies, providing buses for transportation and sometimes food, alcohol, or even marijuana for those who attend.[46] The respondents in our broker survey who chose the "other information" response to the question about evaluating the work of brokers also frequently emphasized the importance of repeated interaction with voters and of network-building, often in terms of organizing their "territory." In response to a follow-up open-ended question, they explained their view about what is most important for evaluating brokers in the following typical terms:

"Closeness to the people"

"Daily contact, militance, and how much they cover the capital"

"Form of organization"

"The image of the broker in the neighborhood"

"Territorial work"[47]

"The degree of insertion of the broker, reaching distinct sectors, and the general acceptance [of the broker by voters]"

"Presence with the people, listening to the people"

That brokers expect party leaders to value these efforts, as well as valuing brokers' contributions to the party's votes in a general election, is consistent with our approach in the "hiring model" of the previous chapter. If leaders glean something important about a broker's capacities from the size of the network that the broker constructs, and if primary elections also play an important

---

[46] Auyero 2001, Sczwarzberg 2008. Election judges may sometimes play a key role in electoral fraud as well, or at least in careful monitoring of the electoral process. One Peronist broker in the Conurbano of Buenos Aires described a judge who had been hired by an opposition candidate seeking to "buy" a local machine. This monitor did not notice that the opposition leader's ballots were actually printed for a nearby municipality – so ballots from that area were disqualified. Interview, July 2009.

[47] "*Trabajo territorial.*"

role in evaluating brokers, then we should expect to see – and do see – brokers prioritizing network-related activities.

Leaders attempt to use whatever information they can glean about their brokers' efforts and capacities to condition benefits they send to brokers. Leaders can threaten to discipline brokers by taking away resources from those who extract rents. The key question is how credible, from the vantage point of brokers, is the threat? We asked brokers:

Imagine that a political leader thinks he can augment the number of votes by taking resources away from one broker and transferring them to another. The broker who would lose the resources has few voters and they are all loyal to him. How difficult would it be for the political leader to do this?

As the left panel of Figure 4.11 shows, although responses were quite scattered, the modal answer was "difficult," whereas almost half the sample said "difficult" or "very difficult."[48]

Why are party leaders unable to freely shift resources away from brokers, even from ones who are extracting rents or using those resources in electorally inefficient ways? One explanation is that brokers have substantial exit options, either in the form of defection to leaders from the same party or leaders of a different party. We asked the follow-up question:

What would the broker who lost resources do? Would he:

(1) Not care
(2) Get angry but do nothing
(3) Cease to mobilize voters
(4) Go work for another leader of his same party
(5) Go to work for a leader of another party
(6) Something else?

Nearly 40 percent of the sample said the broker would shift his/her efforts to another leader (with a greater proportion, indicating a shift within rather than outside the party). Taken together, respondents who mentioned an exit option of some kind – ceasing to mobilize voters, switching to another faction or to another party – constituted half the sample (right panel of Figure 4.11).

In turn, about 28 percent said that the broker would get angry but nothing more – a response suggestive of the view that there is no exit option. Indeed, the modal answer was "get angry but not do anything." Moreover, of those who said it would "difficult" or "very difficult" for party leaders to switch resources from one broker to another (left panel of Figure 4.11), about 35 percent said that a broker stripped of resources "wouldn't care" or "would get angry but wouldn't do anything," whereas another 15 percent said that the broker would stop mobilizing. Just 11 percent said the resource-deprived broker would switch parties. These opinions are consistent with what we learned

---

[48] Elsewhere, we explore the heterogeneity of responses across distinct strata of brokers.

about brokers' career paths, in particular that 71 percent worked for the same party throughout their careers. Thus, although there is some evidence that exit options matter, they may not provide the only opportunity that brokers have to extract rents from the party. The imperfect ability of leaders to detect brokers' impact on the party's electoral fortunes, as in the model of the previous chapter, also plays a role.

Leaders' Efforts to Discipline Brokers: India and Venezuela

The opportunities that brokers enjoy to extract rents, and the incentive leaders have to come up with strong monitoring devices, is not idiosyncratic to Argentine politics. In India, party leaders in the states and even in the national government use their ability to promote the careers of underlings as a disciplining device. Party leaders in India play an important role in structuring career advancement for local politicians – for instance, for council members and presidents who aspire to candidacies for subdistrict or district councils. Party leaders at higher levels are frequently in contact with their affiliates on village councils, and leaders, including members of state legislative assemblies, are sometimes present at village council meetings.[49] Thus the idea developed in Chapter 3 that brokers who build large organizations are "hired" by parties seems quite relevant in the Indian context.

In Venezuela as well, party higher-ups try to monitor the party's brokers. Given the scope for agency loss among Venezuelan brokers – whether *chavistas* or opposition operatives – leaders there invest substantial effort in monitoring the actions of their brokers. In the opposition stronghold of Petare, the mayor's office went to great lengths to subvert rent seeking or wasteful targeting on the part of brokers. The structure of zone chiefs and promoters working under them, described earlier, is overseen by several coordinators working out of the mayor's office.[50] These coordinators and the mayor's support staff designed a survey of neighbors and gave the task of conducting the survey to the brokers. Reminiscent of the Florencio Varela mayor's efforts in Argentina, the mayor's staff planned to conduct random call-backs to voters to solicit any complaints about brokers.

Zone chiefs and their promoters were also assigned specific vote quotas for the legislative elections: they were supposed to increase the vote total in each polling station under their command by a specified number over the total gained by the opposition in the previous mayoral election of 2008. To achieve this goal, each promotor was obliged to recruit "mobilizers" (*movilizadores*)

[49] Wilkinson 2007. Our field research suggests that parties also contribute to the cost of horse trading and vote buying at the council level. For example, in councils that are split along partisan lines, parties are said to help to supply the funds necessary to buy members' votes and thus obtain majorities for important council decisions.

[50] One was seen as particularly relevant because he grew up in the most impoverished part of Petare and thus has substantial credibility with voters there.

who were in turn responsible for recruiting 10 voters who would promise to turn out to vote for the mayor. The number of mobilizers that each broker had to recruit was assigned by the mayor's office, on the basis of surveys of electoral results by zone. By the time of the September 2010 legislative elections, the mayor had 360 brokers working with him, and the mayor's office thought it might have organized as many as 60,000 to 80,000 voters in this fashion. Operatives clearly believed in the electoral efficacy of this structure. As one municipal coordinator put it when we asked him why they had constructed this elaborate hierarchy of brokers, "Machines win elections."[51] To be sure, vote quotas are noisy indicators of brokers' effort, because the mapping from effort to electoral outcomes is far from tight. Nonetheless, this does indicate attempts by party leaders to use votes and vote shares to monitor brokers.

These machines and the local knowledge they generated very likely played a role in the targeted distribution of benefits to voters. At rallies for opposition candidates in the Sucre neighborhoods of Winché (in the *parroquia* of Caucaguita) and Dolorita, two days before the legislative elections, the mayor presented checks ranging in amounts from 1,200 to 2,000 Bolívares (about US$300–$500 at official exchange rates) to neighbors. Beneficiaries had been selected in advance, their names and identity numbers (*cédulas*) appearing on a spreadsheet compiled by mayor's staff; the neighbors came up one by one to pick up the checks, as the mayor called their names. In Winché, the mayor made a point that his party had never asked anyone about their political affiliation before giving assistance (many people applauded in apparent agreement); in Dolorita, he noted that this "help" (*ayuda*) was just a little something to tide neighbors over during times of economic crisis and was not being given simply because there was an election in two days.[52]

At the same time, the opposition incumbent in Sucre appears to have followed a mixed strategy, involving the provision of valued public goods as well as targeted inducements. Perhaps because they understood that the clientelist strategy would leak resources through broker rent extraction, officials in the Petare mayoral administration did not rely on clientelism alone but also invested in the improvement of public goods and services. The mayor's office has invested substantial resources in tracking violent crime and in deploying neighborhood police to try to combat it; crime ranks consistently in public-opinion surveys as the most important public policy issue to Venezuelans, and the opposition in Petare has been given credit for reducing it (even if crime rates are, in truth, stubbornly high). Thus both machine politics and public-good provision have their political role.

---

[51] Interviews, Caracas, September 2010.

[52] In fact, we could not pinpoint the selection criteria for these people, other than that selection was based on "economic need." The recipients were mostly but not exclusively women.

Whatever the source of their bargaining power, brokers appear to possess substantial autonomy and considerable ability to extract rents from party leaders. Although our model does not explore many aspects of the intra-party bargaining between brokers and leaders – a topic powerfully analyzed by Camp – our analysis in the previous chapter does suggest that brokers can use their agency advantages to pull rents from party leaders, and the evidence in this section is consistent with that assertion.[53]

4.2.6 Positions in the Party Hierarchy and Preferences Over Which Voters to Target

If the broker-mediated theory is accurate, we might expect distribution to swing voters to be more enthusiastically embraced the higher one ascends in the party hierarchy. In Chapter 5, we compare distributive practices when they are under the control of actors at the extremes of party ladder: high-level officials in central offices versus lowly activists and brokers. In this section, we explore these preferences among party actors who are more proximate to one another: city councilors and grassroots brokers.

The brokers whom we surveyed in Argentina, as noted, fell into two categories. Most (516 out of 800) were neighborhood-level party operatives. The remaining 284 held the elected office of city council member, and a few of these served in other capacities in the municipal administration. We take advantage of this stratification to study the impact of party position on distributive preferences. We asked:

Imagine that your party is in the midst of a very competitive electoral campaign. You work in a neighborhood that has voted historically for the party's candidates. There is another broker who works in a neighborhood where half of the voters are undecided. How would you prefer that the political boss (*jefe político*) distribute resources? Should he give more resources to you, recognizing the loyalty of your neighborhood, or should he prioritize the other broker, whose neighborhood has many undecided voters?

The framing of the question emphasized the electoral advantages of targeting swing districts, and even low-level brokers endorsed this strategy at a rate of two to one. However, the endorsement was closer to universal among city councilors. Support for targeting loyalist strongholds was just 15 percent among the somewhat more highly placed party operatives; it rose to 28 percent among low-level brokers (see Table 4.1).

One explanation for this difference is that it reflects a selection mechanism. Some brokers are more attuned to the needs of the party or more susceptible to the incentives party leaders deploy to encourage brokers to adhere to the party's electoral interests. These well-behaved brokers (from the leadership's vantage point) rise in the party hierarchy. Another explanation is that the difference

---

[53] See Camp 2012 for further discussion.

TABLE 4.1. *Preference for Distribution Among Different Types of Party Actors*

	Swing District	Loyal District
City councilor	85.3%	14.7%
Broker	72.3%	27.8%

The table presents weighted estimates of percentages in the population of brokers, where the weights are the inverse of the sampling probabilities, N = 714.

reflects an adaptation mechanism. Party operatives begin to see things more from the leadership's point of view once they rise in the hierarchy. Our surveys do not allow us to easily adjudicate between these mechanisms, but either explanation is consistent with the broker-mediated theory.

4.3 CONCLUSION

What are the broader implications of the evidence presented in this chapter? One is that brokers think they have substantial knowledge of the preferences and behaviors of their clients – the kind of information that is valuable to parties but that party actors at a further remove from the neighborhoods lack. We have also seen that brokers pursue a variety of goals, including organization building and electoral mobilization. Their statements about how fellow brokers use resources implicitly acknowledge both electoral and rent-seeking activities. They candidly acknowledge that brokers use their positions to pocket resources and to build their own power bases – retaining at least some benefits that party leaders would like to pass on to voters. Party leaders use career incentives to attempt to minimize rents, and brokers can threaten to exit, taking their voters with them, but neither side entirely solves its problems, and a certain level of agency loss remains inevitable. In these regards, the evidence presented in this chapter largely substantiates the main claims of the broker-mediated model.

Looking ahead, the four next chapters further explore assumptions and implications of the broker-mediated model. The next chapter investigates further the observable implication that distributive preferences should be a function of an actor's position in the party hierarchy (Chapter 5). We then explore a distinct dimension of the model, its implications for the impact of poverty on clientelism (Chapter 6). Next we turn to the macro-historical implications: if party machines pivot around an imperfect agency relationship between brokers and leaders, under what historical conditions does this relationship remain a solid grounding for machines, and when does this grounding soften and decay? (Chapters 7 and 8).

5

A Disjunction Between the Strategies of Leaders and Brokers?

At the end of the last chapter, we noted that if our broker-mediated theory is accurate, people at distinct rungs in the party ladder will hold predictably different preferences over which types of voters should receive material rewards. Party leaders should favor distributing resources to responsive voters; other things (than voter partisanship) being equal, they prefer that party resources end up in the pockets of uncommitted voters. Brokers have greater incentives to target loyal partisans, though – as we have seen, both theoretically and empirically – they also expend some resources on swing voters. In this chapter we test this same hypothesis, but now at extremes of the party hierarchy. We use evidence of distribution of benefits among states, provinces, municipalities, and electoral districts. Such intergovernmental transfers should reflect the distributive preferences of elite partisan actors.

Evaluating the implications of the theory with real-world evidence is not a simple task. Many forces are at work in the distributive strategies of party leaders. Even in our theory, party leaders under some circumstances share with brokers an incentive to distribute to loyal supporters – for instance, when they are incumbents trying to buy back support after bad outcomes (large negative δ, in our model). Even if our model accurately captures the incentives brokers have to work against the interests of party leaders, the leaders are also likely to be subject to countervailing pressures. They may find themselves tacking back and forth between pleasing core supporters – to encourage high turnout or discourage potential competitors who might poach their constituents – and courting independents. We discuss later the array of institutional factors that influence party leaders' distributive preferences.

Yet another difficulty is that most studies of distributive politics tell us about what kinds of regions, provinces, or localities ruling parties favor when they divvy up the pie. However, few tell us which kinds of individuals end up benefiting. When governments allocate public goods – when we are in the domain of pork-barrel politics – the problem is mitigated; it is safe to assume that leaders who send local public goods to marginal districts are hoping to win over swing voters.[1] But the problem is greater when the goods involved are targeted – when, in the terms of our conceptual scheme, we are in the realm of non-conditional individual benefits or of clientelism. Even in these settings, the probability that a randomly selected individual is a swing voter is greater in marginal districts than in ones that are "safe" for one party or another.[2] Nevertheless, the possibility exists that – in an example that Johansson offers – "half of the population" in a district "is extreme conservative and the rest communists" and "none would even consider to switch" their vote, however generous the payoffs they receive.[3] A few studies circumvent this difficulty by studying the impact of district-level public opinion on distributive strategies. Others, like our own, study distribution directly at the level of individuals. If individual-level data show that loyal voters, and non-abstainers, are the primary beneficiaries of brokers' largess, yet in the same settings leaders direct resources to swing districts, the presumption is strong that leaders and brokers are working at cross-purposes. This is the research strategy we pursue later in this chapter.

5.1 THEORIES OF DISTRIBUTION BY PARTY LEADERS

Although some scholars present evidence regarding the distributive strategies of governments[4] in a given setting as though it were dispositive about the general logic of such distributions, Rodden and Wilkinson argue persuasively that one should not expect a uniform logic across varying institutional settings.[5] A crucial institutional variable is whether the body that decides which districts get what is a single unitary actor or a collection of actors with diverse interests. Presidential systems in which the executive controls distribution unilaterally are an instance of the first kind of setting, as are parliamentary systems at moments of single-party government. The single-unitary-actor assumption must be suspended in the following settings: presidential systems in which legislatures play a large role in determining distribution or in which parties are weak and the president needs to hold together legislative coalitions in favor of his policies, single-party parliamentary governments with highly factionalized ruling parties (e.g., the Liberal Democratic Party (LDP) in Japan), and minority and coalition governments.

---

[1] Although, as discussed later, they may also be attempting to increase turnout among loyalists in marginal districts.

[2] Deacon and Shapiro 1975, and Schady 2000.

[3] Johansson 2003, p. 888.

[4] We use phrases such as "government transfers" or "ruling-party transfers" as a short-hand; opposition party leaders also make decisions about how to expend their party's scarce resources.

[5] Rodden and Wilkinson 2004.

With multiple decision makers, the theoretical literature underscores parties' extracting benefits for their constituents in proportion to their number of cabinet positions or seats in the legislature (Gamson), or to their status as formateur party among coalition members (Baron and Ferejohn), or to their bargaining weights.[6] Even small parties that are pivotal for a coalition, making the difference between a government standing or falling, can extract out-of-proportion resources for their constituents. Israeli politics often provides the intuition behind this proposition, though policy concessions in addition to material benefits are presumably what small parties extract.

When a single unitary actor – a president with control over budgets and strong parties, a prime minister whose party rules alone – is responsible for deciding intergovernmental transfers, the theory of such transfers overlaps with the theories of distributive politics we reviewed in Chapter 2. These governments are expected to deploy discretionary resources with electoral objectives in mind. The electoral logic is – in many theoretical treatments – that benefits go to "swing" districts, which are uniquely responsive to largess. They are uniquely responsive in that (in the now-familiar Dixit-and-Londregan refrain), opposition strongholds are written off, whereas "safe" districts are taken for granted.

Another key dimension of institutional variation is whether elections are in single or multiple districts. Examples of single-district elections are national legislative elections in which voters choose among alternative party lists in a single national district or direct presidential elections. In single-district elections, every individual vote is potentially pivotal and the theory generally predicts that resources go to regions or types of voters who are most responsive.

Multidistrict elections include legislative elections with more than one district and indirect presidential elections (e.g., through an electoral college). In multidistrict elections, the most obvious strategy is to expend resources preferentially on districts where a victory will produce the last assembly seat required to bring the party into government or the last electoral-college vote required to create a plurality in favor of the party's presidential candidate. In this connection, Cox alerts us to some ambiguity in the notion of a "swing" district.[7] Are they places heavily populated by swing – ideologically indifferent – voters? Or are they districts that make the difference between a party's winning or losing an election? To avoid confusion, we use the term "swing district" to refer to a subnational jurisdiction in which many indifferent voters reside and "pivotal district" for one that can make or break a party's effort to win control of government, whatever the distribution of voter preferences within it. A "marginal district" is one in which the gap between winners and first losers is small.

Party leaders in multidistrict contests are expected to direct resources toward pivotal districts. Among pivotal districts, resources are predicted to go to

[6] Gamson 1961, Baron and Ferejohn 1989, Ansolabehere et al. 2005.
[7] Cox 2009.

marginal ones, where the party's vote share is expected to be very close to the margin between winning and losing.

The degree of centralization of government is also a crucial institutional variable influencing distributive strategies. In highly centralized systems, regional and local administrators are appointed by central authorities and policy is determined by the national government. In such settings, questions of opposition-party control over resources transferred from the center, and problems of credit claiming, are absent. By contrast, the single-unitary actor assumption is inappropriate in federal systems. Here the partisan identity of subnational governments is crucial. Consider the following situation. Party A controls the national government. Region R will be pivotal in the next parliamentary elections: if A wins in R, it continues to control the national government; if it loses, Party B will replace it in power. The leaders of Party A know that the outcome in R is likely to be close, and there are many swing voters in R. R is swing, marginal, and pivotal; Party A should spend lavishly there.

Now assume that Party B controls the regional government of R. Party A may be dissuaded from expending resources there, for two reasons. The first has to do with credit claiming. If voters in R give credit to Party B (the regional government) for projects undertaken there, then distributive largess by Party A will yield additional votes for Party B. The second disincentive for spending has to do with control. If Party B anticipates that a central government–sponsored program will help Party A defeat it in the next election, it may use its regional control to slow down the implementation of the program or waste resources in such a way that the yield in votes for Party A is reduced. Given a choice between spending resources in two regions, both of which are simultaneously marginal and pivotal, Party A will prefer the region in which it controls the regional government over one in which regional government is under Party B's control.[8]

For clarity, we introduce some additional terminology, displayed in Table 5.1. Districts heavily populated by swing voters are (as noted) swing districts, those heavily populated by loyal supporters are "loyal districts," and those heavily populated by opposition voters are "opposition districts." We call districts governed by the ruling party at the center "aligned districts," those controlled by ideologically rival parties "rival districts," and those controlled by coalition partners or supporters of a president's legislative agenda "neutral districts."

Just as theorists developed models to explain loyal individual supporters' sometimes receiving discretionary rewards, so they have developed models to explain intergovernmental transfers sometimes going to loyal districts. One

---

[8] For theoretical development of some of these ideas, see Arulampala et al. 2009 and Dixit and Londregan 1998. The nature of programs is also a crucial consideration, because central governments even in highly federalized settings may be able to design programs so that distributive decisions circumvent subnational authorities.

TABLE 5.1. *Terminology for Types of Subnational Districts by Partisanship of Voters and of District Governments*

	Oppose	Indifferent	Loyal
Voters	Opposition	Swing	Loyal
Subnational Governments	Rival	Neutral	Aligned

reason why a district that already produces many votes for a party may still receive its largess is that it is pivotal. The risk that the district could go the wrong way, though small, is more catastrophic if losing the district means losing control over the government. Another reason why risk-averse politicians might extend largess to loyal districts is that powerful incumbents may wish to avoid even the remote possibility of losing their own seats and be willing to trade off maximizing their party's vote share, or its share of seats in the legislature, in favor of their own job security. Yet a third reason for party leaders to spend on loyal districts, underscored by Cox, is to discourage ideologically proximate competitor parties from entering the race.[9] Hence the need for coordination, as well as for risk reduction, can induce party leaders to prefer spending on loyal districts.

Another factor that we expect to impinge on distributive allocations is the degree to which – in decentralized systems with multi-district elections – the jurisdictions of subnational governments and electoral districts overlap. At one extreme, consider a country in which the overlap is perfect – where (say) provinces are both electoral districts and sub-national governmental jurisdictions. An example is presidential elections in the United States, where electoral-college districts perfectly overlap with state government jurisdictions. In such settings, the partisanship of the regional or local leadership will make a difference in the strategies of central authorities. These considerations help explain the Federal Emergency Management Agency (FEMA) violation of programmatic distribution, mentioned in Chapter 2.[10] The state of Florida overlapped perfectly with the electoral-college district of Florida; the "district" was expected in the 2004 presidential elections to be both marginal (it had been excruciatingly so in 2000) and pivotal (as it had certainly been, again, in 2000). That it was also an aligned state – the party of the governor matched that of the national executive – was perhaps less important in its attracting funds, though this is difficult to know without information about whether federal FEMA authorities needed to collaborate with state party authorities to carry out the discriminatory distribution. Certainly, distributive benefits to an aligned state would have avoided problems of credit claiming by a rival subnational authority.

[9] Cox 2009.
[10] Chen 2009.

At the other extreme, in settings in which election districts and regional or local governmental jurisdictions do not overlap at all, we expect party leaders at the center to take the partisanship of subnational governments much less into account. Policy makers who want to keep programs from being "politicized" have been known to purposely draw program boundaries that cross-cut jurisdictional and electoral boundaries; this was the case of some New Deal programs, though the effectiveness of these depoliticizing efforts was not complete.[11]

In addition to loyal districts' potentially being pivotal, what other explanations do theorists offer for discretionary benefits going to them? Cox discusses three.[12] One involves coordination, as mentioned earlier: the national party may shower benefits on loyal districts to drive up vote shares and discourage ideologically proximate competitors. Another involves polarization. Highly polarized distributions of voters may encourage the channeling of benefits to loyal districts: given a choice between loyal and opposition districts, a party may anticipate winning more votes by turning out loyalists who might otherwise abstain than by persuading opposition voters. Low and variable turnout, furthermore, encourages a strategy of mobilization of loyalists, and parties may channel benefits preferentially to loyal districts to encourage co-partisans to go to the polls. There are even instances of payments aimed at keeping opposition voters away from the polls. Abstention buying, or what Cox and Kousser call "deflationary fraud," implies heightened spending in rival districts. Cox and Kousser found newspaper references to 44 cases of abstention buying in rural New York State in the 1880s and 1890s.[13] In addition, Chen, who studied the impact of FEMA spending in Florida in 2004, demonstrated that receipt of FEMA funds increased turnout among loyalists but also suppressed turnout among opposition voters.[14]

Polarization and mobilization do not imply the kinds of agency problems between brokers and party leaders underscored by our theory; the need to increase turnout in a polarized electorate will create incentives for party leaders *and* disciplined brokers alike to target loyalists. Similarly, if leaders and brokers are single-mindedly focused on winning elections by dissuading ideologically proximate parties from entering the race, coordination will require spending on loyalists, with no agency problems implied. However, if the coordination is geared toward keeping powerful brokers from switching parties or

[11] We discuss this instance more fully in Chapter 8.
[12] Cox 2005, 2007.
[13] See Cox and Kousser 1981. In a more recent, though less well-documented case, Ed Rollins, Christie Todd Whitman's 1993 New Jersey gubernatorial campaign manager, told reporters that his campaign had paid black ministers not to preach get-out-the-vote messages to their congregations and had offered to match Democratic Party "walking around money." Rollins later retracted the claims, and no evidence of payments were uncovered. See the discussion in Karlan 1994.
[14] Chen 2010.

switching among factions in parties, then coordination-inspired spending on loyalist districts does arise from brokers' being imperfect agents of their party leaders.[15] This situation is closer to the one that we find to be widespread among machines in contemporary developing democracies. Yet another factor that makes voters responsive in our model is valence shocks. If a negative shock leaves loyal supporters disinclined to cast a vote for the party, even if their underlying partisanship has not been affected, then leaders will, along with brokers, favor loyal supporters.

The broader point is that evidence about the distributive actions of leaders and brokers must be interpreted carefully if one is to use this information to adjudicate between unitary and broker-mediated models of distributive politics.

5.2 DO SWING DISTRICTS RECEIVE PARTY LARGESS?

Is there any evidence that political parties engage in swing-district strategies? If the answer were no, or if this were an infrequent strategy, this would constitute a priori evidence against the broker-mediated model. But the evidence points in the opposite direction. Research around the world uncovers frequent political discrimination in favor of marginal, and in many cases plausibly swing, districts, and, in some cases, against loyal districts. In fact, if the preponderance of evidence is that brokers favor loyal individuals, the preponderance of evidence is that party leaders favor marginal districts.

Not all of the cases discussed here are ones of machine politics. Many are cases of pork-barrel or nonconditional individual benefits – that is, nonprogrammatic policies but in the absence of parties that rely heavily on brokers. Such instances, however, are still germane to our theory; we expect to find political parties free of intermediaries pursuing a swing-district logic. This is the expectation when other the strategies mentioned earlier are not at play, such as turnout buying, coordination, or risk-aversion among incumbents.

Consider the following examples:

- In Spain, expenditures on roads, railways, and other infrastructure in the late 1980s and early 1990s were greater in regions with smaller margins of victory in the previous election. "The safer the incumbents feel, the less they try to buy votes with infrastructure."[16]
- In Australia in the early 1990s, the allocation of pork in the form of sports stadiums was deployed "to influence electoral outcomes in those electoral

---

[15] See Camp 2012 and Szwarcberg 2009.
[16] Castells and Solé-Ollé 2005, p. 1200. They study infrastructure investment from 1987 and 1996, a period in which the leftist Socialist Workers Party of Spain, Partido Socialista Obrero Español (PSOE) was in power nationally. They also find that leftist regional governments received larger disbursements.

districts of primary strategic concern: marginal seats and seats held by cabinet ministers especially those with small electoral margins."[17]

- In Canada between 1988 and 2001, regional development grants for small businesses, nongovernmental organizations, and local authorities went disproportionately to marginal ridings, as well as to ones in which the member of parliament was a cabinet minister – especially the cabinet minister in charge of regional development![18]

- In Sweden, swing municipalities – ones with large numbers of voters who were indifferent between the parties – received more, and more generous, environmental grants in the run-up to national elections in 1998.[19] They also received larger fiscal transfers from the central government in the 15-year period after 1981, controlling for the efficiency and equality criteria that formally influenced these transfers.[20]

- In Portugal, over a 30-year period beginning in 1972, central authorities delivered grants to municipalities with a bias toward swing districts. The researchers concluded that there was "strong evidence in favor" of the hypothesis that "politicians target swing voters," those residing in places where the margin of victory in previous elections was small. The authors find "no support" for the idea that "politicians favor their supporters," meaning loyal districts.[21]

- In Albania in the 1990s, soon after the transition to democracy, the central government initiated a program of block grants for rural communes, which in turn was spent on families for income support. "[T]he extent to which a commune is pivotal has a positive effect on the size of the block grant received, while distance from being a swing commune has a negative effect on the size of grant received."[22]

- In Peru, the Fujimori government in the early 1990s spent disproportionate "social fund" (FONCODES) monies, for nutrition and family planning, credit, school renovation, water, and sanitation programs, in localities that had supported the president in his first election bid and in ones in which the margin of victory was close. It also spent disproportionately on districts

---

[17] Denmark 2000, p. 909. The study – as mentioned in Chapter 2 – focuses on the early 1990s, a period in which the Labour Party was in power nationally, and also finds that constituencies represented by Labour members of parliament received larger allocations. Nonprogrammatic distributive politics is also studied by Worthington and Dollery 1998.

[18] Milligan and Smart 2005. The period they study was 1988 to 2001. Crampton 2004 also finds evidence of nonprogrammatic distributive politics in Canada favoring swing ridings in the West, though not throughout the country.

[19] Dahlberg and Johansson 2002.

[20] Johansson 2003.

[21] Veiga and Pinho 2007, pp. 469–470.

[22] Case 2001, p. 415.

where support for the government eroded sharply between the president's first election in 1990 and in a vote in 1993.[23]

- In South Korea between 1988 and 1997, "regional distributive patterns of national subsidies were affected by electoral margins between the two leading candidates in a province...the governments tended to distribute national subsidies to electorally competitive 'swing' regions."[24]
- In Ghana, political manipulation endured despite the use of formulas in the allocation of intergovernmental grants. Districts "with lower difference between the vote shares of the two parties in the previous presidential election receive higher DACF [District Assembly Common Fund] allocations and disbursements." There is no evidence "that DACF transfers are targeted to the incumbent's core supporters."[25] The political neutrality of formulas was circumvented by over-disbursing funds to marginal districts and by multiplying districts in marginal areas.

Certainly not all party leaders everywhere pursue marginal-district or swing-voter strategies. In several of the countries mentioned, governments spent disproportionate resources both on swing and on loyal districts. Nor were all instances of swing strategies ones that involved machine-style parties; many, instead, involve bureaucratic parties. Still, the pervasiveness of party leaders favoring marginal and swing districts, whether or not they sit atop an organization of brokers, speaks to the power of the swing-as-responsive-voter logic and reinforces the sense that brokers who favor loyal constituents are working against their leaders' interests.

Table 5.2 summarizes the results of a number of studies. It shows that, although the marginal district result was common, it was not universal.

Among the countries with the least consistent empirical findings is the United States. Its prominence in the academic literature, the persistence of nonprogrammatic politics (usually described, in a kind of short-hand, as "pork-barrel politics") despite its wealth, and the inconsistency of the findings, warrant an expanded discussion of this case.

The United States: Loyal District Results A series of careful studies by Ansolabehere, Levitt, and Snyder finds that partisan control of government makes a difference in the distribution of spending among states and among

[23] Schady 2000. The 1993 vote was in a referendum to approve a new constitution, but the "yes" position on the constitution was closely associated with the president. Fujimori had suspended the previous constitution during a 1992 coup d'etat, and his party had basically drafted the new one single-handedly.

[24] Kwon 2005, p. 324. However, note that Horiuchi and Lee 2008 have divergent findings for Korea. Over a later time period, but a broader range of expenditures, they find incumbent presidents favoring districts that offered them strong support and weak support, while spending less in districts where their level of support was intermediate.

[25] Banful 2010, p. 2. She noted Miguel and Zaidi's 2003 finding that educational expenditures in Ghana in 1998 were higher in districts that voted overwhelmingly for the president's party, but did not explain the divergence in the findings.

TABLE 5.2. *Ecological Studies of Non-Programmatic Distributive Politics, Coded by Leaders' Distributive Strategy*

Country	Author, Pub. Year	Time Period	Program	Strategy Discerned
United States	Wright 1974	1933–1940	New Deal federal spending in states	Swing
United States	Levitt and Snyder 1995	1984–1990	Federal spending in Congressional districts	Loyal
United States	Herron and Theodus 2004	1999–2000	State assembly to districts (Illinois)	Swing
United States	Bikers and Stein 2000	1993–1994	Federal spending in Congressional districts	Programmatic
United States	Ansolabehere and Snyder 2006	1957–1997	State governments to counties	Loyal
United States	Chen 2008	2004	Federal emergency aid in Florida	Loyal more, swing less
United States	Berry et al. 2010	1984–2007	Federal spending in Congressional districts	Swing
Canada	Crampton 2004	Mid-1990s	Job-creation fund	Swing
Canada	Miligan and Smart 2005	1988–2001	Regional development grants	Swing, rival
Australia	Worthington and Dollery 1998	1981–1982, 1991–1992	Commonwealth grants to states	Mixed
Australia	Denemark 2000	Early 1990s	Sports stadiums	Swing aligned
Spain	Castells and Sol-Oll 2005	Late 1980s– early 1990s	National infrastructure spending in regions	Swing
Portugal	Veiga and Pinho 2007	1979–2002	Municipal grants	Swing, rival
Sweden	Dahlberg and Johansson 2002	1998 to municipalities	Environmental grants	Swing
Sweden	Johansson 2003	1981–1995	Central government spending in municipalities	Swing
South Korea	Horiuchi and Lee 2008	1993–2002	National spending in muncipalities	Loyal and opposition

(continued)

TABLE 5.2 *(continued)*

Country	Author, Pub. Year	Time Period	Program	Strategy Discerned
South Korea	Kwon 2005	1988–1997	National/ministerial spending in regions	Swing
India	Rodden and Wilkinson 2004	1957–2003	National spending in states	Swing; rival
India	Cole 2007	1992–1999	Agricultural credits to states	Swing
India	Khemani 2007	1972–1995	Fiscal transfers to states	Swing, aligned
India	Vaishnav and Sircar 2010	1977–2007	School buildings in Tamil Nadu	Swing
Albania	Case 2000	1990s	Block grants for income support to rural communes	Swing, pivotal
Mexico	Molinar and Weldon 1994	Early 1990s	PRONASOL funds center to states	Swing (win back defecting supporters)
Mexico	Bruhn 1996	Early 1990s	PRONASOL funds to municipalities districts	Loyal
Mexico	Hiskey 1999	Early 1990s	PRONASOL funds to municipalities	Loyal
Mexico	Magaloni 2006 Smart 2005	1990s	PRONASOL funds to municipalities	Swing (wing back defecting supporters)
Mexico	Magaloni, Diaz-Cayeros, and Estevez 2007	1990s,	PRONASOL funds to municipalities	Mixed
Brazil	Ames 2001	Early posttransition	Central government to municipalities	Loyal
Brazil	Rodden and Arretche 2003	1991–2000	Center's transfers to states	Loyal
Peru	Schady 2000	1991–1995	Antipoverty, development funds from center to counties	Swing (win back defecting supporters)
Venezuela	Hawkins 2010	2005	Targeted "Mission" benefits to municipalities	Swing

Country	Author, Pub. Year	Time Period	Program	Strategy Discerned
Argentina	Calvo and Murillo 2004	1987–2000	Fiscal transfers from center to provinces	Loyal
Argentina	Lodola, 2005	1995–1999	Workfare transfers from center to municipalities	Loyal, and protesting
Argentina	Gordin, 2006	1983–2003	Fiscal and housing transfers to provinces	Rival
Argentina	Nazareno Stokes, and Brusco 2006	1995–1999	Workfare transfers to municipalities	Swing
Ghana	Banful 2010	1994–2005	Formula-based intergovernmental transfers	Swing

counties and that partisan distribution favors places that provide larger numbers of votes for the governing party. Hence these authors consistently uncover a loyal-district result. They also offer some evidence that the logic behind this strategy is mobilization or turnout buying.

Levitt and Snyder studied federal spending in Congressional districts during a period of uninterrupted Democratic control of Congress, from 1984 to 1990. They found that spending was a positive function of the number of Democratic votes in a district, though they found no electoral effect on targeted transfers to individuals.[26] Ansolabehere and Snyder, in turn, studied the flow of resources from state governments to counties. They summarize their findings thus: "(i) Counties that traditionally give the highest vote share to the governing party receive larger shares of state transfers to local governments. (ii) When control of state government changes, the distribution of funds shifts in the direction of the new governing party... Finally, we find that increased spending in a county increases voter turnout in subsequent elections."[27]

The United States: Marginal District Results However, several studies of the United States uncover marginal- or swing-district distributive strategies. To explain why New Deal spending was heavier in Western states than in the

---

[26] Levitt and Snyder 1995. Yet, as mentioned in Chapter 2, the "bias" they uncovered appears fairly programmatic: partisan influence reflects distinctive programs and ideologies. Bicker and Stein's research supports this interpretation: they found that changes in partisan control of Congress cause changes in the type of federal spending, with Democrats spending more on transfers and entitlements and Republicans on conditional liability programs. See Bickers and Stein 2000.

[27] Ansolabehere and Snyder 2006, p. 547.

more unemployment-ravaged South, Wright studied the impact of the "political productivity" of spending on the amounts disbursed. Political productivity included the past variability in outcomes of presidential votes in the state, the predicted closeness of the vote in the 1936 presidential election, and each state's weight in the electoral college. Predicted closeness – marginality – indeed played an important role, driving up spending on Works Progress Administration (WPA) and other depression-era programs.[28]

Whereas the FDR administration appears to have been concerned with future presidential contests, presidents who care about their legislative agenda can be expected to deploy resources to try to increase their party's share of seats in Congress. Hence, Berry et al. reasoned, "presidents ought to direct a disproportionate share of federal outlays to electorally vulnerable members of their own party, and a disproportionate share of cuts to electorally vulnerable members of the opposition party."[29] They indeed found that representatives of the president's party attracted more federal spending across the period 1984–2007, especially those from his party who were in marginal districts and hence vulnerable. "[R]epresentatives who were elected in close races receive about 7–9% more federal spending," which was nearly double the advantage of coming from the president's party alone.[30] Yet they also found that marginal representatives from rival parties receive more benefits, suggesting that not just nonconditional benefits to individuals but effort by representatives who are in trouble inflates spending in congressional districts.

An especially brazen instance of nonprogrammatic distributive politics favoring swing districts is the one mentioned earlier from the state of Illinois.[31] In the run-up to state assembly elections in 2000, the legislature distributed 1.5 billion dollars from a "Member Initiative Spending" program. The spending went to an array of projects, including road improvement, emergency vehicles, and playgrounds. Decisions about the allocation of funds was in the hands of four individuals: the Democratic and Republican leaders of the lower and upper chambers. Herron and Theodus described the application procedure thus: if a legislator decided that his district had a particular need, he would go to his respective party leader and request funds. There were no formal rules for what constituted need, no limits on how much a given district could receive, and no requirement that the four caucus leaders act collectively or deliberate.

Herron and Theodus were unable to detect any need-related criteria for distributing funds: low district income, low housing values, and high population growth rates played no role. Political factors drove the program. Districts that had been won by large margins, or in which the legislator ran unopposed,

[28] Wright 1974.
[29] Berry et al. 2010, p. 789.
[30] Berry et al., p. 792.
[31] This is the case mentioned in Chapter 2, studied by Herron and Theodus 2004.

received significantly fewer dollars. So did districts with ideologically extreme representatives, suggesting that the bias toward marginal districts was also a bias toward swing districts. The exceptions were the districts of the four caucus leaders, which, though safe, benefited handsomely from the program. Against the interpretation that vulnerable members were simply more energetic in seeking out funds, the authors cited an interview with an official from the House Speakers Research Staff, who explained the funding priorities thus: "the highest amount of member initiative funding, from $1.5 to $2.5 million annually, went to politically vulnerable members of the House Democratic caucus. The next largest amount, $1.2 million, went to majority leaders and appropriation chairs, followed by appropriation committee members with $650,000, and simple members with $375,000."[32]

The picture in the United States is thus mixed, with some careful studies showing that swing or marginal districts are favored, others revealing loyal-voter or safe-district bias. To the extent that party leaders in the United States target loyal districts, this strategy is at least in part aimed at driving up turnout. Levitt and Snyder showed a substantial positive boost of federal spending on incumbents' vote shares – an additional $100 per capita translates into a 2 percent increase in the popular vote for incumbent members of congress – but the authors do not parse this increase between turnout buying and vote buying.[33] FEMA spending drove up support for George W. Bush in Florida in 2004. Chen found poor Florida voters, and Republicans, especially responsive. "[S]ome of the new Bush voters induced by FEMA aid were Democratic converts who would otherwise have voted for John Kerry. In poor precincts, an increase in FEMA aid actually causes a statistically significant decrease in the absolute number of votes for John Kerry."[34]

In sum, a swing-voter strategy comes through most clearly in the United States in multidistrict elections, when members of Congress or state assemblies have an interest in driving up the vote share of marginal members and hence controlling more seats, or when presidents are concerned about their own prospects in the electoral college or their party's control over congress. A loyal-voter or aligned-district strategy comes through most clearly in single-district elections, such as those of governors. The explanation for why the U.S. Congress seems often to favor loyal districts may have to do with turnout, but also perhaps with programmatic priorities; recall Bickers and Stein's conclusion that distinct spending priorities by the parties reflected their ideological commitments to transfers (the Democrats) and contingent liability (the Republicans).[35]

---

[32] Herron and Theodus 2004, p. 305.
[33] Levitt and Snyder 1997, p. 33.
[34] Chen 2008, p. 14.
[35] Bickers and Stein 2000.

5.3 LEADERS AND BROKERS IN FOUR DEVELOPING DEMOCRACIES

The previous discussion indicates that when party leaders control nonprogrammatic distribution, the beneficiaries are often – though not always – marginal districts. Yet the inferential step from a marginal-district strategy to a swing-voter strategy can be problematic. Unless we know from public opinion polls that many swing voters inhabit the districts that benefit from largess (as in Dahlberg and Johansson's studies of Sweden), or that the favored districts are represented by ideologically centrist legislators (as in Herron and Theodus's study of Illinois), or that monies going to marginal districts shift vote choices in favor of the benefactor party (as in Chen's study of Florida), ecological evidence is less than decisive. In this section we take a different tack: we study aggregate distributive patterns in places where we also have individual evidence that brokers favor loyal (and non-abstaining) voters. We therefore take a closer look at four developing democracies, all of which are home to political machines engaged in clientelism: Mexico, India, Venezuela, and Argentina. In Venezuela, not only do we have evidence regarding individual and aggregate distributions, we also have evidence at both levels regarding the same programs. In Mexico, India, and Argentina, the program fit is less tight. Still, from rich primary information and secondary sources, a clear picture emerges of strategic disjunctions between leaders and brokers in these four important clientelistic democracies.

5.3.1 Distribution to Swing States and Municipalities in Mexico

We saw in Chapter 2 that largess distributed by operatives of Mexico's then-ruling party, the PRI, went preferentially to voters who had previously declared themselves to be supporters of the party and who expected to turn out to vote in the upcoming 2000 elections. Consistent with the patterns we uncovered in Argentina, Venezuela, and India, brokers from Mexico's PRI favored loyal supporters when doling out campaign gifts.

Not so when rewards were in the hands of party leaders. In this case, rather than favoring bastions of loyal supporters, Mexican national authorities and PRI leaders deployed public resources in constituencies where voters were switching their allegiance away from the party.

In the final decades of PRI rule, when its hegemony was challenged and it began to lose provincial and local elections, distributive politics intensified. President Carlos Salinas (1988–1994), who defeated a leftist contender only with the help of an eleventh-hour manipulation of the vote count, created a huge program, the National Solidarity Program, or PRONASOL, "an innovative social spending program designed to win back popular support for the government in a context of neoliberal policies."[36] PRONASOL was an umbrella

---

[36] Bruhn 1996, p. 152.

program that accounted for nearly 8 percent of all social spending in Mexico in the early 1990s. It provided support for everything from community development schemes to credit for small manufacturing firms to scholarships for poor children. PRONASOL funds were also used for major infrastructure projects, such as road-, hospital-, and school-building programs. President Salinas was ideologically and politically at odds with much of the PRI party organization, and PRONASOL was designed to bypass party control. Decisions about where to allocate funds were centralized in the office of the president, and an independent bureaucracy channeled funds to local organizations.

PRONASOL was the Mexican public spending program most heavily and systematically studied by social scientists. Their studies are basically unanimous in the view that the government used PRONASOL to pursue electoral, as well as developmental, goals. Most of these studies also agree that the driving electoral strategy behind PRONASOL was not to reward loyal supporters but to win back constituencies that had, or were in danger of, defecting to the left.[37] Regarding the allocation of funds among Mexico's 31 states, Molinar and Weldon concluded that they went preferentially to states in which the opposition PRD had made significant gains, rather than in secure PRI strongholds.[38] Likewise, Bruhn found that states that voted heavily in 1988 for Salinas's leftist challenger, Cuauhtémoc Cárdenas, received disproportionate PRONASOL funding and benefited from a reorientation of funding, even when poverty levels, economic growth rates, and other socioeconomic factors are taken into account.[39] Focusing on distribution at a lower level of aggregation, across municipalities, Magaloni reported some findings consistent with those of Molinar and Weldon: "PRONASOL was, to a large extent, designed to convince voters in vulnerable municipalities not to invest their partisan loyalties in the PRD."[40] Magaloni, Diaz-Cayeros, and Estévez found similar trends.[41] Public and club goods tended to go to swing districts, though inflated levels of individualized benefits went to loyal districts.

5.3.2 Distributive Disjunction in India

In Chapter 2 we offered evidence that loyal voters and non-abstainers received targeted benefits in India. Citizens in the state of Karnataka who shared the party identity of a candidate were 10 to 13 percentage points more likely to receive a gift from that candidate's party than were non–co-partisans. In addition, Indian citizens who identified with the party of their village council president were 13 percentage points more likely than non–co-partisans to report having turned out to vote in exchange for a campaign gift. Indian brokers, like

---

[37] A partially discordant view is that of Hiskey 1999.
[38] Molinar and Weldon 1994.
[39] Bruhn 1996.
[40] Magaloni 2006, p. 136.
[41] Magaloni, Diaz-Cayeros, and Estévez 2007.

their counterparts in Argentina and Mexico, favor their loyal supporters, and among them supporters who are at little risk of abstaining.

But when party leaders in New Delhi or state capitals control the allocation of expenditures, they are less prone to shower largess on loyalists. Arulampala et al. showed that discretionary spending by the central Indian government between 1974 and 1997 went to marginal electoral districts in aligned states.[42] Both the partisanship of state governments and marginality mattered. Among aligned states, the national ruling party favored ones with many marginal constituencies, and among states with many marginal constituencies, the national party favored aligned ones. Arulampala and co-authors' explanation for the favoring of marginal constituencies is that party officials hoped to sway swing voters; their explanation for the favoring of aligned states is that officials at the center wanted their party to claim credit for the benefits delivered.

Cole, who studied the Indian government's distribution of agricultural credits, found that credit to banks jumps in election years and – in those years – "more loans are made in districts in which the ruling state party had a narrow margin of victory (or a narrow loss), than in less competitive districts."[43] Khemani, who studied fiscal transfers, and Vaishnav and Sircar, who studied the distribution of school building funds across constituencies in Tamil Nadu, both uncovered marginal/aligned-state strategies.[44] Khemani wrote that politically motivated "transfers ... are greater to those co-partisan [aligned] states where the party controls a smaller proportion of districts or seats allotted to the state in the national legislature." Hence "affiliated states that are 'swing' receive more transfers."[45] In Tamil Nadu over a three-decade period, party leaders might prefer to reward loyal constituencies but "when more than half of the ruling coalition's victories come in closely-fought ('swing') constituencies the ruling party alters its post-election targeting strategy to reward pivotal areas ... In swing constituencies where the margin of victory is slim, politicians must make desperate promises to sweeten the pot."[46]

Rodden and Wilkinson, in turn, found that during a period of Congress Party hegemony (1972–1989), discretionary resources went to both safe Congress states and to marginal states; they found that swing (marginal) states always attract disproportionate resources, regardless of the state's partisan alignment.[47]

Our theoretically predicted pattern of a disjunction between the distributive strategies of party leaders and brokers finds support, then, in India.

---

[42] Arulampala et al. 2009.
[43] Cole 2009, p. 220.
[44] Khemani 2007, Vaishnav and Sircar 2010.
[45] Khemani 2007, p. 466.
[46] Vaishnav and Sircar 2010, p. 20.
[47] Rodden and Wilkinson 2004.

5.3.3 Distribution to Swing Municipalities in Venezuela

The literature on geographic distribution of targeted spending in Venezuela is sparse. However, Hawkins offered evidence quite in line with that of the Mexican and Indian patterns.[48] He considered distributions of targeted educational slots in two Missions (the social programs called *Ribas* and *Sucre*) in 2005, as a function of local development levels, poverty rates, and levels of support for Chávez in the 2000 election. He concluded that "Mission benefits are generally targeted to marginal districts."[49] In light of his analysis, he expects "the distribution of scholarships and students to be at a maximum in marginal municipalities."[50] By contrast, as we reported earlier, Hawkins found that individual recipients of these program were more pro-Chávez than were others living in the same neighborhoods and communities at the same point in time. Hence the central government sent targeted programs to swing municipalities, which local operatives then sent to loyal supporters. One might suppose that these loyal beneficiaries were in danger of abstaining and that the pattern observed is simply a case of turnout buying. However, recall our finding in Chapter 2, that people whom the Chávez government defined as "non-abstainers" were favored in this distribution.

5.3.4 Distribution to Swing Municipalities and Provinces in Argentina

We have seen that distributive politics at the micro level in Argentina, from party brokers to individuals, is dominated by a strategy of targeting loyal voters – loyalists who are also non-abstainers – though indifferent or swing voters were not completely left out of the distributive game. We turn now to evidence regarding aggregate distributions. A substantial literature examines distributive politics in Argentina, illuminating the nature of intergovernmental transfers from the center to the provinces and from the center or provincial governments to municipalities.[51] A common finding is that politics does indeed intervene in decisions about where to spend public resources. And all of the studies reviewed evaluate the impact of electoral politics in single-district elections, in which parties try to maximize their votes overall, without concern for the district in which they are cast. What's more, compulsory voting laws mean that turnout is high and stable. Hence, to the extent that higher levels of spending go to places in which elections had been close, the party controlling the distribution is likely to be aiming at swing or undecided voters. These are swing-district, rather than pivotal- or marginal-district, results.

Concerning the exact nature of the political manipulation, Calvo and Murillo found a bias in the allocation of federal resources (and higher levels of

---

[48] Hawkins 2010.
[49] Hawkins 2010, p. 217.
[50] Hawkins 2010, p. 200.
[51] Remmer 2007 studied levels of patronage spending on personnel by provincial governments.

spending in general) in provinces with higher Peronist vote shares, though this finding holds across Peronist and non-Peronist presidential administrations. The authors saw this bias as an artifact of electoral institutions and heavy representation of Peronist supporters in over-represented provinces.[52] In turn, Gibson and Calvo, and Gordin, studied the distribution of National Treasury Contributions (*Aportes del Tesoro Nacional*, or ATN) funds from the central government to the provinces.[53] Provincial governments transfer ATN funds to municipalities, where they can be invested in local public goods such as roads and bridges, or simply to cover gaps in municipal budgets. Studying a single year (1994) during the Peronist Menem administration, Gibson and Calvo showed bivariate correlations between ATN transfers and "peripheral" provinces, ones that also tend to be more heavily Peronist.

Gordin studied a longer time span and included a broader set of econometric controls. He found relatively little impact of economic and developmental factors in the central authorities' decisions about how to allocate funds across the provinces. However, he did uncover electoral factors that shape distributive choices. Rival provinces – those ruled by opposition governors – attracted significantly more ATN funding than did aligned ones – those controlled by the party that ruled at the center. The same is true of distributions of FON-AVI funds, a federal housing program. In explaining these results, Gordin underlined Argentina's substantial de facto centralism, constitutional arrangements notwithstanding; this centralism means that central governments have to worry little about provincial administrations' exerting control, or claiming credit, for nationally sponsored programs. Hence they may be more willing than are Indian governments, for example, to use federal largess to try to win over swing or mildly opposed voters.

Our own fine-grained analysis of intra-provincial distributions of ATN funds yields results in line with Gordin's. Rather than rewarding local governments in places that had offered strong electoral support, a provincial administration appears to have used ATN funds to win over swing districts and even poach in rival constituencies. That the period we study, the early 2000s, was one during which the Peronists' major opponents found themselves in disarray may have emboldened the provincial Peronist administration to attempt to win over swing and even opposition constituencies. The strategy stands in contrast to Argentine brokers' heavy targeting of loyalists among individual supporters.

We scrutinize the intra-provincial politics of distribution in one province, Córdoba, in the early 2000s. Data availability weighed in our choice of this province to study, but so did the very large number of municipalities in the province – more than 400. We focus on the impact of election returns in the prior (1998) gubernatorial election, specifically the impact of local levels of support for the governing party on the amount of ATN funds channeled to

[52] Calvo and Murillo 2004.
[53] Gibson and Calvo 2001; Gordin 2006.

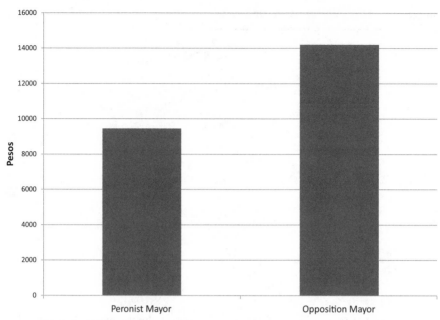

FIGURE 5.1. Average ATN Funding, Córdoba Municipalities, 2000–2002. *Source:* Authors' Compilation, N = 417.

a given municipality. Figure 5.1 compares the average ATN funding paid out to municipal administrations controlled by the Peronists (the governor's party, 200 mayors) and by opposition mayors (226), in most cases from the Radical Party. It shows that average ATN spending in opposition municipalities was fifty percent larger than in Peronist ones.

To further study the impact of opposition control and of vote shares in the prior election on the distribution of ATN funds, we regressed ATN funding on prior electoral outcomes in each municipality in the 1998 gubernatorial election (see Table 5.3). We examined political effects on two dependent variables: the average funding across three years (2000, 2001, and 2002, *Average ATN*) and the level of ATN funding among municipalities that received any funds (*Some ATN*). Our key independent variables were the absolute difference in vote shares between the winning party and the first loser (*Margin*); in almost all cases, this was the margin of Peronist over Radical votes shares, or vice versa. We also study the impact of partisan identities of mayors. (The Peronists were in control of both the national and provincial governments at this time.) The indicator *Rival* takes the value of 1 when a non-Peronist party was in control of the municipality, zero when the mayor was a Peronist. We include controls for population size and for the proportion of households falling below an official poverty line. The effect of poverty rates was never statistically different from zero; therefore, we omit it in the reported estimations.

TABLE 5.3. *ATN Funds to Municipalities*

	(1) Average ATN	(2) Some ATN
Margin	−208.5	−331.0*
	(−1.94)	(−2.36)
Rival	7760.1***	2652.0
	(2.89)	(0.71)
Population	1.541***	1.603***
	(11.66)	(10.31)
Constant	5141.3	13094.0**
	(1.94)	(3.41)
N	408	298
R^2	0.278	0.295

Municipalities in Córdoba, Argentina, 2000–2002.
OLS regressions, t statistics in parentheses.
* $p < 0.05$, ** $p < 0.01$, *** $p < 0.001$.

The Peronist leadership in Buenos Aires and in the capital of Córdoba did not appear mainly interested in rewarding high levels of support for the Peronist party in earlier elections. Rival municipalities had higher average levels of ATN spending than did Peronist ones, though they were not more likely to receive some, rather than no, ATN funds. In both models, the trend is toward smaller differences in vote shares between the 1998 Peronist gubernatorial candidate and his rivals being associated with larger average levels of spending over the following years.

The tendency of the central Peronist authorities to pour resources into rival and marginal municipalities suggests a swing-voter strategy, not a loyal-voter one. This stands in sharp contrast to the patterns we observe in Argentina when distribution is under the control of brokers and the recipients are individuals.

Partisan bias toward swing municipalities is also in evidence in a workfare program, *Plan Trabajar* (Program Work), though here the scholarship is not uniform in its findings. *Trabajar* was initiated by the second Menem administration in the mid-1990s and was carried over into the Radical-Alianza administration of Fernando de la Rúa in 1999–2001. It was ostensibly a program to benefit unemployed workers, paying them a small wage in return for their labor in infrastructure projects. The projects were proposed by local governments and by nongovernmental organizations. At its height, *Trabajar* targeted 300,000 individuals. Focusing on the second national Peronist administration of Carlos Menem, Lodola found that the provincial vote share of the Peronist party had a positive impact on the provinces' shares of *Trabajar* funds.[54]

[54] Lodola 2005.

By contrast, Weitz-Shapiro demonstrated a swing-district logic to *Trabajar* distributions under the de la Rúa administration. The smaller the difference in vote shares between the winner and first loser at the provincial level, the greater the positive deviation of *Trabajar* spending over its ideal level.[55] She also found that *Trabajar* funds went disproportionately to provinces that had many protests, in the form of road blockages.

More in line with Weitz-Shapiro than with Lodola's results, Nazareno and co-authors uncovered political bias in *Plan Trabajar* in favor of municipalities in which the prior elections had been close. Although they uncovered no clear political manipulation in a non-election year, in the election year of 1999 they found *Trabajar* funds going disproportionately to Peronist municipalities that had been won by a small margin. Hence, in this instance, both partisan alignment and swing status drove up the allocation of targeted workfare benefits. Summarizing their findings regarding mayoral budgets, in turn, Nazareno and his co-authors wrote that "neither of the two traditional parties [Peronists or Radicals] rewarded loyal voters; they did not intensify patronage spending in places in which they had received broad support of the population." Peronist mayors in particular pursued a strategy of "channeling patronage toward marginal [swing] voters."[56]

5.4 CONCLUSION

Leaders of political parties who deploy public resources for electoral ends will consider a number of questions. Will spending programs help our party, or will control over them, and credit for them, be hijacked by the opposition? Do we need to drive up vote shares across the board, or is what matters most winning over voters in certain marginal or pivotal constituencies? Should we spend extra funds in districts that are traditionally friendly toward the party, in the hope of high participation, or should we deploy scarce resources in places where there are more fence-sitters? Evidence of non-programmatic use of public resources reviewed in this chapter suggests a range of answers to these questions. But we are struck with the frequency with which high-level party strategists seemed to lean toward using public monies to try to influence swing voters. This was not always the choice they made; nor can we always infer from their spending in marginal *districts* that their ultimate target was swing *voters*. Given the prevalence of a loyal-voter strategy among the brokers who worked for these leaders, however, the degree of disjunction between leaders' and brokers' strategies is striking. This key prediction of the broker-mediated model is, then, largely sustained.

---

[55] She detected no partisan manipulation under Menem administration. Weitz-Shapiro 2006.
[56] Nazareno et al. 2006, p. 69.

6

Clientelism and Poverty

6.1 INTRODUCTION: POVERTY OF NATIONS AND OF VOTERS

Part II of this book constructs a model of clientelism that pivots around the behavior of types of individuals – party leaders, brokers, and voters. Part III examines macro-dynamics of clientelism: why it persists and what forces may undermine it, with an emphasis on historical developments at the national level.

The current chapter marks a transition between micro and macro concerns. Here we study the link between clientelism and poverty. The broker-mediated model in Chapter 3 included assumptions about how wealthy and poor voters differ in the utility they derive from expressions of political loyalties and from money. These assumptions, and what may lie behind them, are our focus here. The national experiences of shifts from clientelism to nonconditional distribution, to pork-barrel politics, and even to programmatic distribution, explored in Part III, have much to do with changes in income levels and in income distribution. Hence, before shifting to these accounts, it is helpful to pause and examine more closely the evidence about poverty and clientelism.

Imagine drawing a country at random from a list of all those in which competitive national elections are regularly held. If one had to guess whether clientelism was widely practiced in the country selected, one's guess would probably be improved by knowing how wealthy the country is – its per capita gross domestic product (GDP) and income distribution. The poorer the country, the more likely that its politics would be clientelistic.

Imagine drawing a voter at random from the electoral list of a country where clientelism is widely practiced. If one had to guess whether the person selected had ever obtained access to social assistance in exchange for his or her vote, one's guess would certainly be improved by knowing the voter's income and where it placed him or her on the economic ladder. The poorer the voter, the more likely the voter would be to have "sold" his or her vote.

That clientelism is isomorphic with poverty seems self-evident. Indeed, in the theoretical treatments discussed in Chapter 2, the idea that benefits flow disproportionately to poor voters is more an assumption than a result. Many historical examples can be cited of political machines homing in on the poor. Blue-collar and immigrant neighborhoods were the places where the ward-healers of political machines in U.S. cities sought votes; it was the working-class "river wards," not the middle-class "newspaper wards," in the words of Wilson and Banfield, where machines operated.[1] The poor cities of Naples and Palermo in the Mezzogiorno, not the more prosperous cities of Milan or Bologna, were the ones where the Italian Christian Democratic party exchanged patronage for votes in the 1950s through the 1970s and where clientelism was still rife in the 1980s.[2] Other examples could be cited of political machines targeting the poor.

In this chapter we review evidence suggestive of a link at the level of countries – *suggestive*, only, because of the difficulties of devising national-level measures that are comparable across countries. (In Chapter 8, we offer over-time evidence from two countries that economic development encourages a shift from clientelist to programmatic strategies.) And we review evidence – much more readily gathered – of a link between poverty and clientelism among individuals within any given polity. A now-substantial body of research, like that reviewed in Chapter 2, consistently indicates an association between poverty and vote selling among individual citizens.

After reviewing the evidence, we delve more deeply into explanations for why party machines target poor voters.[3] This is a matter of debate among scholars. For some, the votes of poor people are simply cheaper than those of the wealthy: the poor value a given material reward more highly and hence are more responsive to machine largess. Others stress the uncertainty of programmatic promises that candidates make in campaigns and poor voters' acute sensitivity to risk. The latter view has found proponents among some World Bank researchers, among others. The differences between these two explanations are real and carry distinct practical implications. If the risk-reduction explanation is right, then imperative mandates and other institutions that force politicians' pronouncements into line with their actions would undermine clientelism.[4] But if machines simply target the poor because they are willing to sell their votes for a lower price, then such measures would be ineffective. There may also be normative implications, which we probe more deeply in Chapter 9. After all,

---

[1] Banfield and Wilson 1963.

[2] On clientelism in southern Italy, see Chubb 1981, 1982, Putnam 1993; on pork-barrel spending and patronage in the Italian Chamber of Deputies, see Golden and Picci 2011.

[3] We defer to the next part of the book an explanation of why poor *countries* are more likely than wealthy ones to feature vote buying.

[4] Assuming, of course, that such measures and institutions would be effective in increasing politicians' credibility.

if vote selling reflects a personal distaste for risk, then perhaps it should not be seen as compromising voter autonomy.

We turn to survey evidence from African and Latin American countries, as well as to a richer survey designed specifically to test these mechanisms, which we deployed in Argentina.

6.2 NATIONAL POVERTY AND NONPROGRAMMATIC DISTRIBUTION

Cross-national surveys are suggestive of substantially higher levels of vote buying in poor than in wealthy democracies. They point toward more vote buying in poorer than in wealthier world regions and to some extent to more vote buying in poorer than in wealthier countries within regions.

To study poverty and vote buying, we make use of surveys. Of course, self-reported vote selling raises concerns about social-desirability bias, with under-estimation of the frequency of vote buying – as the list experiments reported by Gonzalez-Ocantos et al. suggest. Still, as long as the degree of social-desirability bias is fairly constant, or at least unrelated to covariates such as poverty whose descriptive relationship to vote buying we seek to uncover, survey evidence offers insights into cross-national variation in vote-buying. What's more, some survey questions attempt to reduce this bias by asking people about their observations of parties buying the votes of other people, or of parties' efforts to buy their votes, without having to relay whether this effort succeeded.

One source for cross-national comparisons are the regional Barometer surveys, especially in Africa and Latin America. In 2005, Afrobarometer asked survey respondents in 18 sub-Saharan African countries, "during the [most recent] election, how often (if ever) did a candidate or someone from a political party offer you something, like food or a gift, in return for your vote?" Possible answers were "never," "once or twice," "a few times," "often," or "don't know."[5] In 2002, Latinobarometer surveys posed the following question i 17 Latin American countries: "Have you known of someone in the last elections who was pressured or received something to change his vote in a certain way?" The subsequent question was, "And can you tell me if this has happened to you?"[6] Given the differences between the form of the question (if not, so much, the substance), one would not want to read too much into cross-regional differences in the responses. Still, it is noteworthy that on average 20 percent of African respondents said they had been offered an electoral bribe, whereas on average only about 7 percent of Latin American respondents said this.[7] There are, of course, many differences between Africa and Latin America, but prominent among them is the large gap in average incomes. The mean GDP

[5] From Harding 2008.
[6] Latinobarometer. Various years. Latinobarometer Corporation, www.latinobarometro.org.
[7] Surveys using unobtrusive measures of campaign gifts – see our discussion later in this chapter – suggest that actual levels are considerably higher.

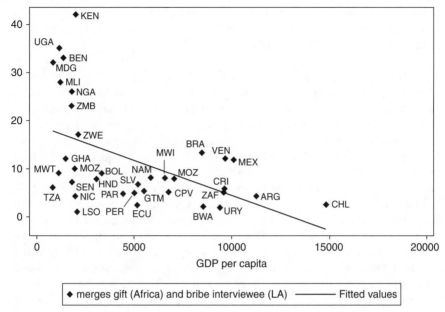

FIGURE 6.1. Africa and Latin America: Percent Received Gift by GDP per Capita.

per capita for African countries coded as democracies in 2005, at the time the surveys were conducted, was around $2,800; for Latin American countries in 2002, it was just over $7,000.

Figure 6.1 is a coordinate plane that locates each Latin American and African country by the percentages of people who said they had been the targets of vote buying (vertical axis) and by the country's per capita GDP (horizontal axis).[8] The fitted line shows that, on average among these countries, higher GDP per capita was associated with lower levels of clientelism. Yet if indeed higher average incomes discourage clientelism, the effect is far from inevitable. The figure reveals a number of countries with surprisingly widespread clientelism, given their level of development (e.g., Brazil, Mexico, and Venezuela), and ones that are surprisingly free of it, despite low incomes (e.g., Lesotho and Tanzania).

The Eurobarometer surveys do not ask any equivalent question. Presumably, the numbers of people who would answer yes would be tiny, at least in the region's older democracies. One can perform the thought experiment of inserting these countries into Figure 6.1. Their annual GDP per capita is generally more than $30,000, and they would have near-zero positive "responses" to the vote-buying question. The conclusion would be a stronger negative correlation between national income and national rates of vote buying among the pooled democracies of Latin America, Africa, and Western Europe.

---

[8] Data on electoral bribes are from Afrobarometer country surveys in 2005 and Latinobarometer country surveys in 2002. GDP per capita from Penn World Tables 6.3.

That wealthy countries are on the whole less clientelistic than poor ones is borne out by the work of Kitschelt and his collaborators.[9] These researchers conducted expert surveys with more than 1,400 respondents in 88 countries. The experts were asked to score the political parties in their countries according to how clientelistic they perceived them to be.[10] Although precise scores are unavailable – and the authors recognize that there is undoubtedly a lot of measurement error – early results are highly suggestive of national-level associations between wealth and programmatic politics, and between poverty and clientelism. Experts in only 4 of 20 advanced democracies judged their parties to be more clientelistic than did experts from any other regions.[11] The four wealthy outliers, in declining order of clientelism, were Italy, Greece, Portugal, and Spain. Spain was more clientelistic than Slovenia, the Czech Republic, and Latvia; Italy more so than those countries and than Poland, Estonia, and Botswana. A few other outliers stand out: Japan is highly clientelistic though wealthy, and Israel and South Korea are not far behind. Still, basically, the wealthy, advanced democracies have little clientelism. African and Latin American countries, by contrast, are clustered at low-to-middle income levels and are viewed by their own political experts as practicing widespread clientelism. Post-communist countries are the least tightly clustered and include some of the most clientelistic party systems (Montenegro) but also moderately clientelistic ones (Latvia, the Czech Republic, Slovenia), at least in the views of their national experts.

The link between average income and clientelism, though still present, appears weaker when we focus within regions of the world. Regarding Latin American countries, Figure 6.2 draws on a different set of surveys, those conducted by the Latin American Public Opinion Program (LAPOP). In 2010, interviewers asked samples in 16 Latin American countries, "In recent years and thinking about election campaigns, has a candidate or someone from a political party offered you something like a favor, food, or any other benefit or thing in return for your vote?"[12] Figure 6.2 locates these Latin American countries by the level of clientelism revealed in the LAPOP survey and by annual GDP per capita. Although (as we shall see) the LAPOP surveys reveal strong associations of poverty and clientelism at the level of individuals, the association between national-level underdevelopment and clientelism in this case is weak. Some poor countries had high levels of clientelism (Bolivia, Paraguay), and some wealthier ones had low levels (Chile, Uruguay). Others fall far from the regression line, with either "too little" (Ecuador, Nicaragua) or "too much" (Argentina, Mexico) effort at vote buying.

---

[9] See a series of papers including Kitschelt 2011.

[10] The precise measure is referred to by the authors as "clientelistic effort."

[11] See their Figure 3, pp. 20–21.

[12] Faughnan and Zechmeister 2011, p. 1. Data on GDP per capita come from Penn World Tables 7.1.

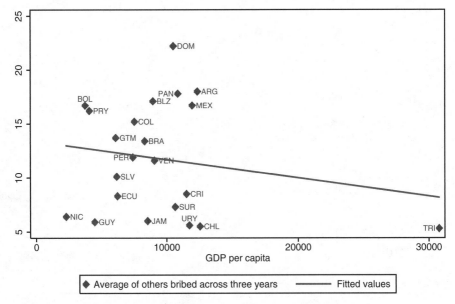

FIGURE 6.2. Latin America: 2010 Campaign Gifts by GDP per Capita.

Responses to a somewhat different question, posed four to eight years earlier, tell a similar story.[13] In 2002 (as mentioned), and in 2005 and 2006, the Latinobarometer asked, "Did you know of someone in the last elections who was pressured or received something to change his vote in a certain way?," with possible answers "yes," "no," or "don't know."[14] Figure 6.3 reports the average percentage answering yes across the three surveys, plotted against the average GDP per capita in each country during these three years.[15] Again the figure is suggestive of a quieting impact of national wealth on vote buying, though obviously other things are also going on. Again Mexico displays too much clientelism for its level of development. Chile, and to a slightly lesser degree Uruguay and Costa Rica, again appear as wealthier countries with correspondingly little vote buying.

We have offered some evidence of an association between regional and national wealth, on one side, and the prevalence of electoral clientelism on the other. Chapter 8 examines more deeply a transition away from clientelism during periods of national economic development in Britain and the United States – though this trajectory is far from inevitable. These historical experiences are suggestive of changes that economic development traces in electorates, changes that encourage programmatic strategies. At the most basic level,

[13] Latinobarometer again, as opposed to LAPOP.
[14] Latinobarometer. Various years. Latinobarometer Corporation, www.latinobarometro.org.
[15] GDP figures are from the Penn World Tables 6.3.

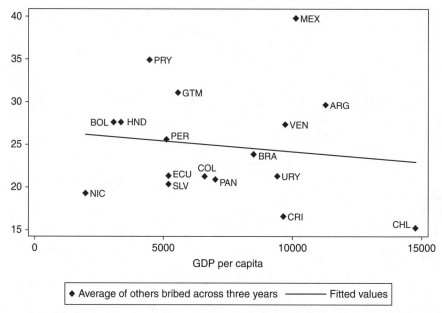

FIGURE 6.3. Latin America: Average Percentage of Respondents Observing Campaign Gifts by GDP per Capita.

industrialization and economic growth can shift the social structure of populations and, eventually, of electorates such that middle-income voters come to prevail numerically over the poor. If low-income voters are particularly responsive to material largess – as our analysis later in this chapter suggests – one can think of them as decreasingly motivated, as their income rises, by material offers, and increasingly motivated by the expressive value of supporting their preferred party or policy orientation in elections. At the same time, growth in the size of the electorate can make machines, densely networked as they are, less efficient than are parties that rely on broadcast appeals. Public debates about programs produce rules and criteria of distribution and pave the way for programmatic distribution. In addition, campaign appeals, which allow party leaders to side-step their brokers, can reach larger numbers of voters as literacy rates grow and as technological change lessens reliance on face-to-face communications between parties and brokers.

6.3 INDIVIDUAL POVERTY AND NONPROGRAMMATIC DISTRIBUTION

We have up until now simply assumed an association between clientelism and individual-level poverty that we have not yet demonstrated. A variety of evidence points toward poor people being preferentially targeted by party machines. Some of the same surveys that we have just been discussing provide evidence of this link. Drawing on the LAPOP surveys, Faughnan and

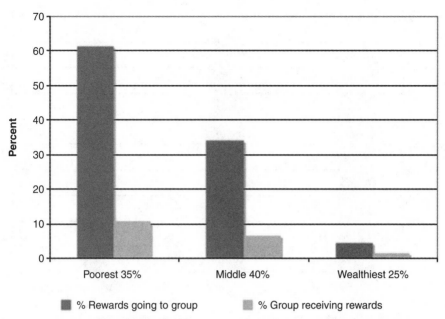

FIGURE 6.4. Argentina: Income and Targeted Rewards. *Source*: Authors' Survey Data, N = 1,750.

Zechmeister pooled 36,601 responses across 22 countries in Latin America and the Caribbean and estimated a multivariate logistic regression model to predict "yes" answers to the question cited earlier: "...has a candidate or someone from a political party offered you something like a favor, food, or any other benefit or thing in return for your vote?" Income, grouped by quintiles, had a statistically significant negative effect on someone's answering yes, and one that was larger than other attributes – being a younger voter, being a man, or living in a rural area.[16] (Education, by contrast, has no independent association with vote selling in the LAPOP surveys.[17])

Our original surveys in Argentina and Venezuela suggest that income and receipt of campaign gifts are negatively related (see Figures 6.4 and 6.5, respectively). In Argentina, just under 60 percent of all rewards went to the poorest 35 percent of the sample, and around 11 percent of the respondents in this poorest group reported receiving gifts; around 35 percent of all rewards went to the middle 40 percent of the income distribution (and around 7 percent of this group received gifts), whereas under 5 percent of the rewards went to the richest 25 percent (and only a tiny fraction of this group received gifts). The

[16] They compare standardized coefficients; see their Figure 2 and the associated discussion, pp. 2–3. Note that the model includes country fixed effects, which have a large independent effect on vote buying.
[17] That is, education controlling for income.

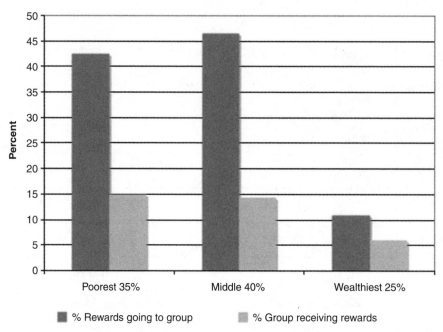

FIGURE 6.5. Venezuela: Income and Targeted Rewards. *Source*: Authors' Survey Data, N = 574.

Venezuelan results are not monotonic: a slightly larger percentage of middle-than lower-income respondents reported having been offered campaign gifts. But the data do reveal a sharp drop-off of offers of campaign gifts at upper-income levels.

Individual-level evidence from other countries suggests similar patterns. Breeding's survey in rural and urban wards near Bangalore in the Indian state of Karnataka found that nearly 90 percent of voters in the poorest group (incomes under 1,000 rupees per month) received campaign gifts, with the reported percentages decreasing to 53 percent, 40 percent, 23 percent, 31 percent, and 21 percent, in the subsequent income categories.[18] In this context – as in Argentina and Venezuela – discrete individual benefits of low monetary value prevailed, such as "private household consumer items (e.g., cycles, sewing machines, sarees, stainless steel *dabbas*), ration cards . . . and other private benefits such as money for school fees." Overall, 49 percent of 1,446 respondents reported receiving some kind of a private vote bank benefit – a material gift from a political party to the citizen – in Breeding's survey.

As in Latin America and India, poor voters in Africa also appear to be the most likely ones to be approached by parties to sell their votes. Drawing on

[18] Breeding 2011, Table 1. Monthly incomes corresponding with these income groups are 1,001–5,000 rupees, 5,001–10,000 rupees, 10,001–15,000 rupees, 15,001–20,000 rupees, and above 20,000 rupees, respectively; Breeding 2011, p. 73.

the same Afrobarometer survey question mentioned earlier – "during the [most recent] election, how often (if ever) did a candidate or someone from a political party offer you something, like food or a gift, in return for your vote?" – Harding estimated a multilevel model of vote buying, allowing him to take into account both individual- and country-level effects. He found that poverty has the largest impact on vote buying: "An individual with the highest possible level of poverty is 23% more likely to be offered something for his vote than an otherwise identical voter at the lowest level of poverty."[19] At the same time, "individuals in countries with a greater per capita GDP have a lower likelihood of being offered money or gifts in exchange for their votes."[20]

In sum, there is strong evidence across a range of countries and historical time periods that clientelist politics are "poor people's politics," to quote the title of Auyero's study of Argentina.[21] The evidence is consistent with the conventional wisdom among scholars and others: poor people are more likely than the wealthy to sell their votes. The next question is: why?

6.4 WHY DO MACHINES TARGET THE POOR?

6.4.1 Diminishing Marginal Utility of Incomes

One common sense way to connect individuals' poverty with clientelism is through the diminishing marginal utility of income, and indeed this assumption is incorporated into many theories, including our own in Chapter 3. The connection can be traced through the following syllogism: people's propensity to vote for a party is a function of how much the party's largess has increased their utility of income; poor people's utility of income is increased more than rich people's by a gift of any given monetary value; therefore, parties focus their largess on the poor. The minor premise – that a gift boosts the utility income of poor people more than of rich people – follows directly from the assumption of diminishing marginal utility of income. The assumption is widespread among theorists. For instance, a basic assumption that Dixit and Londregan made is that "poor voters switch more readily in response to economic benefits because the incremental dollar matters more to them."[22]

The diminishing marginal utility explanation gains power when we consider two alternative decision rules that any voter might follow: (1) vote for the party with the most appealing program; or (2) vote for the party that offers the greatest material reward in return for one's vote. In the narrowest material

---

[19] Harding 2008, p. 15. To measure poverty he used factor analysis to construct an index, based on questions about a respondent's having gone without things such as food, water, and medical treatment in the past year.

[20] Harding 2008, p. 15.

[21] This is the title of Auyero's 2001 book.

[22] Dixit and Londregan 1996, pp. 1137, 1143. Dixit and Londregan adopted this assumption as a technical convenience. Empirical evidence of diminishing marginal utility from income can be found in Diener and Biswas-Diener 2002 and Inglehart 2000.

sense, only a party that offers a material benefit conditional on a vote is offering the second sort of reward. As appealing as a candidate's policies might be, nothing is at stake – in a narrowly material sense – for a voter unless that voter is trading his or her vote for a benefit. This is true for two reasons: his or her vote is unlikely to make the difference between a preferred platform's winning or losing, and he or she will receive a benefit that is programmatically offered and delivered, independent of his or her vote.

To make the point more clearly, we return to the mathematical representation of a voter's utility function presented in Chapter 2:

$$U_i(b_i, \sigma_i, \sigma_P) = -(\sigma_i - \sigma_P)^2 + b_i,$$

where σ_i is the location of individual i or party P on the ideological dimension and b_i the discrete material benefit that a party may give to a voter. The first expression on the right-hand side, the quadratic-loss function, can be interpreted as the disutility a person experiences when he or she votes for a party or candidate that is relatively distant from his or her policy bliss point. This is an expressive benefit. In turn, b_i is the utility the voter derives from a targeted benefit. This is a material benefit. We might think of voters as varying in how heavily they weigh expressive versus material benefits. If $\kappa \in (0, 1)$ is the weight they place on expressive benefits and $(1 - \kappa)$ the weight they place on material ones, then we can rewrite the utility function as

$$U_i(b_i, \sigma_i, \sigma_P, \theta_i) = -\kappa_i(\sigma_i - \sigma_P)^2 + (1 - \kappa_i)b_i.$$

One interpretation of the common finding that poor people are particularly inclined to sell their votes is that κ increases with income, so that poorer voters are less likely to pursue the expressive benefits than to accept material payoffs, even if these payoffs are paltry.

It will be relevant to the discussion in the next section that the preceding holds true even if (as we have assumed) there is *no uncertainty* attached to the delivery of programmatic benefits.

That poor people's votes are cheaper to buy is reflected in the low unit cost of the benefits that machines distribute – tin roofing materials and bags of food are more often the currency of clientelism than luxury cars or high-end televisions.[23] As a Peronist organizer in Córdoba, Argentina, told the authors:

> We work constantly, trying to get [the voters] minimal things, medications, medical devices, boxes of food, a subsidy, a bus fare, to get them things, get them what they really need. That's the way to keep their votes.[24]

---

[23] This does not imply that quite high-value items are never offered directly to voters. Two days before the Venezuelan legislative elections of 2010, one of the authors (Dunning) observed local activists from Chávez's coalition unloading refrigerators from a truck in the poor Caracas neighborhood of Petare. Opposition candidates, meanwhile, were literally distributing checks to voters at rallies throughout the area.

[24] Authors' interview, January 2003.

In India as well, as noted previously, discrete individual benefits such as "... vate household consumer item," of low monetary value are the most common rewards.[25] A straightforward interpretation is that these are gifts that match poor people's needs and that machines get a bigger "bang for their buck" giving gifts to the poor than they would to middle class or wealthy voters.[26]

6.4.2 Uncertainty and Risk

A different explanation for why it is the poor who sell their votes focuses on the uncertainty of campaign promises. Here the syllogism is: clientelist distribution appeals to people who are risk-averse; poor people are risk-averse; therefore, clientelist distribution goes to the poor. This explanation *also* builds on diminishing marginal utility of incomes, which implies that the poor are especially averse to risk. The asymmetry between a big reduction of utility that comes from a loss versus a smaller boost to utility that comes from a gain is implied by the concavity of the function relating income to utility.[27] What is distinctive about the risk explanation is the additional claim that benefits delivered programmatically are more riskier than those delivered by machines.

Kitschelt suggested the attractiveness of clientelist distribution to poor, risk-averse voters. For "poor and uneducated citizens," he wrote, the appeal of "clientelist exchanges always trumps that of indirect programmatic linkages promising uncertain and distant rewards to voters."[28] Similarly, Wantchekon contended that individualized rewards, wielded by incumbents, undercut the opposition by underscoring the lack of credibility of their offers: "Discretion over when and how to spend government resources allows the incumbent to undermine the credibility of opposition candidates by, for instance, making up-front payments to voters."[29] In turn, Keefer, and Keefer and Vlaicu, explained clientelism as a strategy that politicians turn to when their programmatic promises are not credible.[30] Keefer wrote that the "inability of political competitors to make credible promises to citizens leads [the competitors] to prefer clientelist policies."[31]

---

[25] Breeding 2011, p. 73.

[26] We borrow the phrase from Calvo and Murillo 2004, who used it in a similar context.

[27] It is worth noting, however, that some economists question whether diminishing marginal utility of income is a plausible explanation for aversion to risk; see Rabin 2000.

[28] Kitschelt 2000, p. 857. See also Kitschelt 2007.

[29] Wantchekon 2003, p. 401.

[30] Keefer 2007, and Keefer and Vlaicu 2008.

[31] Keefer 2007, p. 804. As we saw in Chapter 2, an important body of work links clientelist mobilization to another kind of risk reduction, that of politicians or political parties. Cox and McCubbins 1986 contended that risk-averse politicians will distribute individualized goods to loyal supporters (rather than to swing voters); the responsiveness of loyalists is less variable and such investments less risky. Magaloni, Diaz-Cayeros, and Estévez 2007 also treated clientelist distributions as a low-risk investment and posited that just as investors diversify their investment portfolios, parties diversify their mobilization strategies.

Desposato noted the apparent paradox of a person's supporting a party that gives him or her small amounts of medicine rather than one that offers to build a hospital that would serve him or her.[32] He resolved the paradox by underscoring the uncertainty of programmatic offers. "Poor, risk-averse voters may well prefer private goods rather than policy promises..."[33]

Note that the concavity of the function relating income to utilities makes the poor both more risk-averse than the wealthy – more sensitive to small losses of income – but also responsive to machine largess than the wealthy – more sensitive to small increases in income. The concave functional form explains the empirical regularity of poor people being targeted by machines, with no theoretical need to assume that programmatic benefits are especially uncertain. Parsimony is on the side of the diminishing marginal income approach; it requires fewer assumptions. But parsimony is only one consideration; a more important one is realism.

The key empirical question thus becomes: are poor people, and in particular poor people who sell their votes, especially incredulous of politicians' pronouncements? Before turning to some empirical tests, we note that it is not inevitable that programmatic distribution is highly uncertain. Claims that it is call to mind unreliable politicians on the hustings, promising the moon. However, programmatic benefits also take the form, say, of cash deposited onto an ATM-style card, managed by a bureaucracy of civil servants – even in countries, like Mexico, where clientelism persists. Does the Mexican voter necessarily view cash benefits delivered through the *Progreso* or *Oportunidades* program as less certain than those offered by *La Efectiva*, to harken back to the examples that opened our book? Even when candidates or party manifestos offer programs that do not already exist, their words should not be automatically written off as cheap talk. If politicians are involved in repeated interactions with voters or if they will be punished electorally for making promises that they then break, they have incentives to make credible promises.[34] Keefer and Vlaicu are certainly right that institutional fragilities in new democracies can subvert the predictability of campaign statements and undermine their credibility. Yet if politicians have incentives to build reputations for reliability (in Downs's terms), they also have incentives to build credible institutions.

6.4.3 Risky Programs or Cheaper Votes? Empirical Evidence

Our empirical strategy is to treat the diminishing marginal utility of income (an assumption common to both explanations) as axiomatic and to bring data

---

[32] Desposato 2006, p. 59.
[33] Desposato 2006, p. 59.
[34] See, e.g., Downs 1957, p. 105; Harrington 1993, Alvarez 1997, and Stokes 2001. For the view that some voters embrace ambiguity in electoral appeals, see Tomz and Van Houweling 2009.

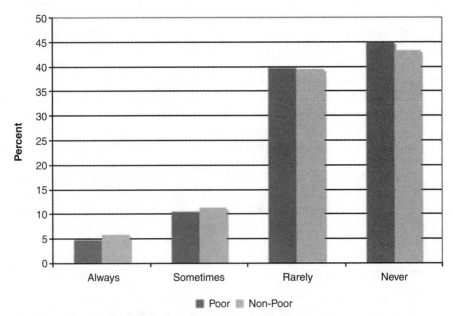

FIGURE 6.6. African Respondents Believing Politicians' Promises, by Poor and Non-Poor. *Source*: AfroBarometer Survey Data, N = 24,687.

to bear on the question of whether poor people who sell their votes perceive campaign promises as lacking credibility. We make use of survey data from Africa and Latin America. As noted, in 2005, the Afrobarometer surveys asked people in 18 African countries whether they had exchanged their votes for a gift and whether they viewed politicians' promises as credible. If the risk explanation is supported, we would expect poor people in general, and those who sold their votes in particular, to be especially incredulous of politicians' promises.

The relevant question is the following: "In your opinion, how often do politicians keep their campaign promises after elections?" Possible answers were "often," "always," "rarely," or "never." African politicians did not do very well on this question: a mere 15 percent of respondents answered "often" or "always," and the modal answer was "never" (43 percent). To measure poverty, the survey asked a number of questions that probed the material deprivations that respondents might endure, such as, "Over the past year, how often, if ever, have you or anyone in your family gone without enough food to eat?" Figure 6.6 shows levels of credulity among poor and non-poor respondents. It reveals no strong or monotonic association.

Turning now to beliefs in politicians' credibility among those who do and who do not report selling their votes, again the differences are slight and the relationship between levels of incredulity and clientelism is non-monotonic.[35] And among the poor, the correlation between receiving a gift and doubting politicians' promises was actually negative, though not significantly different from zero. If anything, poor clients in Africa were slightly *more* credulous of campaign promises than were poor nonclients.

The African finding anticipates an even stronger one in a Latin American setting, again going against the risk explanation. Our 2003 survey of Argentine voters probed individuals' attitudes toward risk, their involvement in machine networks and receipt of benefits, and their views of the credibility of politicians' programmatic promises. These data allow us to investigate several questions: (1) Are poor people more risk-averse? (2) Are poor people more prone to perceive programmatic appeals as risky? (3) Does risk aversion make voters more likely to be clients (i.e., to have received clientelist transfers)? And (4) are people who are especially incredulous of politicians' programmatic offers and campaign platforms also especially prone to clientelism?

Following Buendía, we asked questions that probed people's attitudes toward three kinds of risk:[36]

1. **Generalized risk:** Which phrase do you agree with more: "Better a bird in hand than one hundred in flight," or "He who doesn't risk, doesn't gain"?
2. **Public-policy risk:** Which phrase do you agree with more: Implementing new and attractive but untested policies is necessary for progress," or "Implementing new and attractive but untested policies is dangerous"?
3. **Employment-related risk:** Which phrase do you agree with more: "A good job is one in which you don't earn much but it's certain and stable," or "A good job is one in which you earn a lot but it is unstable"?[37]

We also asked a series of questions (described in Chapter 2) about receipt of benefits and participation in clientelist networks:

(1) **Receipt of benefits:** During electoral campaigns, party operatives and neighborhood political leaders often give people things or assistance. In the last presidential campaign, did you receive any of the following? (The respondent was then given a list of items that might have been handed out and forms of assistance that might have been received).

[35] The correlation coefficient relating "yes" responses to the question "Did you receive a gift in exchange for your vote?" and "How often do politicians keep their campaign promises after election" (coded from always to never) was 0.01; with an N of 24,455, the significance level was 0.05. Among poor people, the correlation coefficient is −0.004; with an N of 8,983, the significance level was 0.73.

[36] Buendía 2000.

[37] Majorities of respondents chose the more risk-accepting response to the general question (60 percent) and to the policy question (61 percent); the employment question elicited overwhelming distaste for risk (91 percent). We found high correlations between responses to generalized and work-related risk questions and between generalized and policy-related risk questions; responses to work- and policy-related risk were negatively correlated.

(2) **Networks:** If you were facing a grave family problem, for example related to a job or health, would you turn to a party broker or operative [*puntero, referente*]?

Finally, we also asked about the credibility of campaign pronouncements:

How likely is it that a politician will fulfill his campaign promises if he wins the election?

We asked this question about politicians in general and then asked about politicians from specific parties. Our surveys also gathered data on individual covariates, such as age, gender, education, and party affiliation.

Majorities of our samples chose the more risk-accepting response to the general question (60 percent) and to the policy question (61 percent); the employment question elicited overwhelming distaste for risk (91 percent). We found significant correlations between responses to generalized and work-related risk questions and between generalized and policy-related risk questions; responses to work- and policy-related risk were negatively correlated.[38]

Poor People *Are* More Risk Averse. With our Argentine data, we first tested the proposition that poor voters are more risk-averse than are wealthier ones. We inspected correlations between income levels and answers to our risk questions and found positive correlations between income and generalized risk acceptance, income and risk acceptance, related to policies, and income and employment-related risk acceptance.[39] We also estimated probit models (not shown) of the probability of a person's choosing a risk-accepting or risk-averse response as a function of income, education, and a series of control variables. Again, income levels significantly influenced people's attitude toward risk, and in the expected direction: poor people were more risk-averse. In simulations, shifting from the minimum to the maximum income category (holding all other variables at their sample means) increased the probability of a risk-accepting response to the generalized risk question from 56 percent to 75 percent.[40]

Income was less clearly related to tastes for risky public policies or jobs. We found no effect of income on our sample's willingness to experiment with untried policies or distaste for risky employment, although those with more years of schooling were more accepting of experimentation.

In sum, the assumption that poor people are more risk-averse finds some support among our samples, particularly when we consider generalized risk.

The Poor Are *Not* More Prone to Perceive Programs as Risky. The next proposition to be tested is whether the poor are especially prone to see programmatic offers as high risk.

---

[38] Bivariate correlations are 0.12 (significant at the 99 percent level) between generalized and policy risk, 0.07 (significant at 99 percent) between generalized and work-related, and −0.05 (significant at 95 percent) between policy and work-related risk.

[39] Correlation coefficients were 0.12 ($p = 99$ percent), 0.08 ($p = 98$ percent), and 0.05 ($p = 97$ percent).

[40] Younger respondents, those with more schooling, and women were also more risk-accepting by this measure.

If (following Kitschelt, Wantchekon, Keefer and Vlaicu, and Desposato) people enter into clientelist relations because programmatic promises lack credibility, then we might expect poor people to be especially incredulous of politicians' campaign promises.[41] To gauge the credulity of the poor in our Argentine samples, we studied people's perceptions of the risk attached to campaign promises.

Politicians rarely fulfill all of their campaign pledges. This statement holds for all democracies, but Argentine voters at the time that we conducted the surveys had especially good reasons to doubt the credibility of politicians. Carlos Menem in his first administration (1989–1995) carried off a particularly spectacular bait-and-switch maneuver, running for office as a pro–big government Peronist and then quickly transforming into a devout neoliberal. Argentines had plenty of opportunities to witness policy switches at lower levels of government, as well as incompetence and corruption.

To assess the credibility of parties and the degree of risk that our samples attached to their promises, we asked, "*How likely is it that a politician will fulfill his campaign promises if he wins the election? Very likely, likely, not very likely, or unlikely.*" We asked about politicians in general and then followed with questions about Peronist and Radical politicians. By asking about "politicians" and their promises, we steered respondents away from interpreting this question as referring to clientelist distributions, which as we have shown are carried out not by political leaders and office seekers but by local operatives (*punteros, referentes*). The responses revealed a good deal of incredulity regarding politicians: about three-quarters of our sample thought it "not very likely" or "unlikely" that politicians would fulfill their promises.

Yet, as in Africa, income was unrelated to people's views of the credibility of either party. Ordered probit estimations (not shown) revealed no association of income with the perception that politicians lacked credibility. Income was also unassociated with people's perceptions of the credibility of the Radical Party or the Peronist Party. What we did find were strong partisan effects: Peronist partisanship increased the credibility of the Peronists, and Radical partisanship of the Radicals. We also found that people who evinced risk acceptance with regard to public policy, saying that untested policies had to be implemented for progress to take place, were especially skeptical of the credibility of either party, a belief structure that must be fraught with frustration.

Clients Are *Not* More Risk Averse. By contrast, people who received campaign gifts or campaign-period access to social programs were no more risk-averse than others in our samples. Recall that we asked, "During electoral campaigns, party operatives and neighborhood political leaders often give people goods or assistance. In the last presidential campaign, did you receive any of the following?" The respondent was then given a card that listed items that might have been handed out and forms of assistance (*ayudas*) that they might

---

[41] Alteratively, the rich and poor might attribute the same level of risk to programmatic promises, but the poor are more allergic to that risk; see later.

have received. The items included food, mattresses, subsidies, clothing, money, medications, housing, and roofing materials; the assistance included help with legal paperwork, medical attention, obtaining student scholarships, payment or cancelation of bills for public services or taxes, and jobs.

There were no significant correlations between a person's reporting having received a gift and any of our measures or risk. In fact, the sign on the coefficient relating risk to clientelism was "wrong" from the perspective of the risk-aversion approach.

Because respondents might be wary of acknowledging to an interviewer that they had received a campaign handout, we used other questions to probe for clientelism. As noted earlier, we asked, "If you were facing a grave family problem, for example related to a job or health, would you turn to a party representative for help?" By this measure, the profile of the client emerges clearly. Multivariate models produce an image of the client as a low-income woman with little formal education. However, the client is *more* risk accepting, regardless of whether the measure is generalized risk or an index that sums risk-accepting postures across the three questions.[42]

It's worth dwelling on the risk result. Imagine that we drew two of the poorest people in our samples, two people who were also similar in terms of many other traits and attitudes that we measured. If one of them were risk-averse, her probability of turning to a local political actor for personal assistance would be 32 percent. If the other were risk accepting, this probability would be 39 percent.[43] The effect is not enormous, but it runs directly against the predictions of the risk-aversion approach.

Clients Are *Not* Prone to Perceive Programmatic Appeals as Risky. If clientelism were a refuge for voters with a distaste for risky programmatic promises, we would expect clients to be people who attribute a particularly high level of risk to programmatic offers. But the evidence weighed against this proposition. In our Argentine samples, people who attached more risk to politicians' campaign promises were *less* likely to be clients. People who found politicians' promises credible were more likely to report having received campaign handouts. And those who were relatively credulous of programmatic campaign promises were *more* likely to consider turning to a party operative to help in a crisis. The results do not change substantially whether we ask about the credibility of promises by Peronists or Radical candidates. Hence we find little support for the proposition that clientelist voters are ones who see programmatic offers as especially risky.

Should risk aversion be a better explanation than merely diminishing marginal utility of income for clientelist parties' targeting the poor, we would

---

[42] The estimated probit and ordered probit models (not shown) included other demographic controls and clustered standard errors by province.

[43] Simulated expected probabilities, calculated using *Clarify*, were 64 percent to 71 percent for the risk-averse case and 37 percent and 42 percent for the risk-accepting one.

expect any apparent income effect to disappear in the presence of controls for risk and uncertainty of campaign offers. But this is not the case. The income effect is not only robust but also strong. Assuming two risk-accepting people, one among the poorest in our sample and the other among the wealthiest, the poor one is more than twice as likely to receive a campaign gift than is the wealthy one. Between these two risk-accepting people, the poor one is more than three times as likely to turn to a party operative for help if her income is at the minimum for our sample than if it is at the maximum.[44]

In short, poor Argentines were much more likely to be clients, whatever their taste for risk.

We have contrasted two answers to the question, Why do clientelist parties target the poor? One answer emphasizes diminishing marginal utilities from income: a targeted benefit of a given nominal value increases the utility income of poor voters more than of wealthy ones. If a voter in systems in which clientelism is widespread face a choice between casting a ballot in exchange for a reward, even if a small one, or casting a vote that expresses partisanship or preference for certain policies, the lower his or her income, the more likely he or she is to choose the reward. We contrasted this approach with one that emphasizes the risk aversion of the poor. In this view, voters see themselves as choosing between a small reward delivered with certainty and a campaign promise that may or may not materialize. Risk-averse persons, the poor prominent among them, will be drawn toward clientelism.

Our empirical tests confirmed one assumption of the risk-aversion approach: poor people tended to be risk-averse. But in other ways, this approach failed to find support in African or Latin American settings. Although poor people did evince a greater aversion toward risk, more risk-averse individuals did *not* receive clientelist benefits, nor did they participate in clientelistic networks, at higher rates than risk seekers. Most damaging to the risk-aversion interpretation, people who attached more risk to politicians' campaign promises in our sample are actually *less* likely to be clients. If anything, risk *acceptance* is more associated with being targeted for clientelist benefits than risk aversion.

We suggested earlier that the diminishing marginal returns and risk-aversion explanations of the link between poverty and clientelism have distinct practical implications. If it had turned out that clientelism among the poor was driven by risk aversion, the most appropriate measures would have been ones that lowered the risk of politicians' failing to follow through on campaign promises. An array of institutional fixes to improve mandate responsiveness

---

[44] The first simulations drew from ordered probits of the gift variable. Holding all other variables at their sample means, the probability of the poorest person receiving a gift was 9 percent (95 percent confidence intervals: 6%–12%), the wealthiest person, 4 percent (3%–6%). The second simulations drew from probit models of the *puntero* variable. At the minimum income, the simulated estimated probability of turning to the operative was 50 percent (95 percent confidence interval, 42%–58%); at the maximum income it was 15 percent (11%–19%).

have been used or at least considered, such as written instruction
tors, referendums on initiatives that were not vetted during cam
provisions for the recall of office holders who violate mandates.[45]
the merits of these proposals, our analysis suggests that they will ı ͺ ͺͺͺ
clientelism.

---

[45] This last provision exists for mayors in Colombia. For a skeptical view of imperative mandates, see Manin 1997.

PART III

THE MACRO-LOGIC OF VOTE BUYING: WHAT EXPLAINS THE RISE AND DECLINE OF POLITICAL MACHINES?

7

Party Leaders Against the Machine

In Part II of this book, we studied the micro-logic of broker-mediated distribution. Our focus was on understanding the incentives that guide the behavior of brokers, as well as those facing voters and party leaders. The goal of Part II was to understand what drives brokers to build ideologically heterogeneous networks of voters, ones that are notably heavy in loyal supporters. We sought to explain how brokers may extract rents from party leaders. Our formal model in Chapter 3 generated insights into the political inefficiencies that broker-mediated distribution of benefits can produce, from the point of view of vote-maximizing political leaders. Our evidence presented in Chapters 4 and 5 showed that the incentives of party leaders and brokers can indeed diverge in ways that have important consequences for the political logic of transfers both to individual voters and to aggregates of voters, such as those residing in provinces, municipalities, or districts. We have seen that brokers can help to make vote buying effective; yet the reliance on brokers can also diminish the political efficacy of clientelist parties as vote-seeking organizations.[1] Thus our argument suggests that clientelism carries electoral costs as well as benefits for political leaders.

What, then, explains the incentives of party leaders to perpetuate a system of broker-mediated distribution in the first place? This question takes us toward a broader terrain, one focused on the rise and decline of clientelism in various countries over time. Understanding what gives rise to clientelism, and what kills it, is more uncertain territory: the questions are bigger and messier, the evidence necessarily more tentative. Yet insights about the micrologic of broker-mediated distribution contribute substantially to illuminating

---

[1] Although the structure of our model is quite different, our focus on the inefficiencies that clientelism can generate due to the diverging interests of brokers and party leaders echoes the pioneering work of Camp 2010.

the macro-history of clientelism. Explaining the rise and fall (and sometimes the reappearance) of clientelism in both historical and contemporary perspective is an important goal. In this third part of the book, we take several theoretical and empirical steps in that direction by showing how a focus on tensions between party leaders and brokers contributes to understanding this macro-history. Although we are not able to test conclusively all of the theoretical arguments we develop in this part of the book, we demonstrate the ways in which our broker-mediated theory can help explain transitions to and from clientelist systems and use comparative case-study evidence to probe the plausibility of our arguments.

In this chapter, we provide the theoretical foundations for our subsequent exploration of comparative case-study evidence. We extend the model of Chapter 3 to study the incentives of party leaders to invest in broker-mediated clientelistic spending, as opposed to nonclientelistic welfare benefits. These nonclientelistic benefits can be either programmatic or nonprogrammatic, in the terms of our conceptual typology in the first chapter; they may take the form of pork-barrel politics or the noncontingent delivery to individuals. Whether programmatic or not, here individuals' receipt of benefits are not contingent on vote choice or other political behaviors, and, in particular, benefits are not distributed through brokers. A central difference between machine politics and noncontingent modes of distribution is that in the latter, local armies of brokers are not required to mediate between party leaders and voters. Rather, benefits may be distributed through a relatively impersonal bureaucracy, in which the bureaucrats are not direct party employees, or they may even take the form of direct cash transfers into citizens' bank accounts – a form of benefit delivery that has become increasingly common in the twenty-first century.[2] Our analysis, then, is an effort to understand the political costs and benefits to party leaders of two broadly differing strategies: buying individuals' votes via brokers, or setting up systems of programmatic or nonprogrammatic spending that do not involve mediation by brokers.

Our analysis suggests several conclusions. Although nonclientelistic spending cuts out the brokers – thus potentially making the delivery of benefits to voters less costly to party leaders – unmediated transfers also entail political costs. With means-tested programs, for instance, all eligible individuals in a particular income category receive benefits, which may imply that "too many" voters receive benefits from the point of view of political optimality. In this case, from the standpoint of party leaders, some benefits are "wasted" on unresponsive voters who are eligible for transfers. The same was true under clientelism: brokers "wasted" significant resources on loyal supporters. Therefore, a crucial analytical question is, What conditions make unmediated distribution more or

---

[2] Although nonclientelistic distribution may involve the construction of relatively depoliticized bureaucracies, it need not take this form. On conditional cash transfers, see De La O, 2012.

less inefficient for party leaders? We explore and compare these sources of inefficiencies in this chapter.

Given these sources of inefficiencies, we show that the total value of welfare benefits received by voters can be higher for nonclientelistic forms of spending, and the ability of party leaders to target benefits to swing voters can be even weaker under nonclientelistic than clientelistic systems. Thus despite the tendency of brokers to over-target loyalists, clientelism can still sometimes allow better targeting of voters than nonclientelistic spending. This observation also has normative consequences, to which we return in the final part of this book.

In light of the fact that clientelism also brings costs to leaders – in particular, agency problems imply that brokers can extract rents from party leaders – nonclientelistic spending can under some conditions be more attractive to leaders than clientelism, despite the electoral waste it can entail. Here, the comparative statics results we discussed in Chapter 3 are especially important for understanding the conditions under which nonclientelistic spending does become more attractive to party leaders, relative to clientelism. In this chapter, we develop predictions about several factors that help explain transitions from clientelism to nonclientelistic forms of spending, or vice versa.

In brief, our claims build centrally on the following observations about factors that shape the relative efficacy of clientelism:

- **Returns to Scale.** Adding an additional broker to a party machine expands the size of a party's voter network by a fixed amount, due to the intensity and frequency of interactions between brokers and voters that are required to sustain clientelism. By contrast, certain other forms of nonclientelistic mobilization, including expenditures on public goods, may involve increasing returns to scale. Investments in bureaucratic delivery systems can bring increasing returns, as can publicizing distributive platforms through the mass media. In our analysis that follows, we focus especially on the size of the electorate as a factor that conditions the influence of returns-to-scale considerations.
- **Capacity to Monitor.** The effectiveness of clientelism depends on the quality of the interactions between brokers and clients and especially on the discernibility of vote choice and other political behaviors. Institutional and social factors make brokers more able to monitor voters in some settings than in others.
- **Poverty.** Because diminishing marginal utility of income makes the votes of poorer citizens cheaper for brokers to buy (Chapter 6), political machines tend to target the poor. Although nonclientelistic spending can target the poor as well, rising incomes may intensify rent seeking by brokers, which makes clientelism less attractive to party leaders. Middle-class and high-income voters may also place greater value on the expressive utility of supporting preferred parties, whereas low-income voters may place more value on the material utility of accepting a payment.

- **Costs of Programmatic Communication.** The lower the costs party leaders face in circumventing brokers and communicating directly with voters, the greater the payoff from nonclientelistic strategies.

We expand on each of these claims in the next section before developing their formal underpinnings in the context of our model.

Two initial points about these observations should be made. First, our theoretical analysis here is focused on the *incentives* of party leaders to "subvert the machine" – that is, to shift to nonclientelistic modes of benefit provision that do not rely on party-affiliated local brokers. As our subsequent analyses make clear, however, the *capacities* of party leaders to do so vary widely across cases, sometimes as a function of institutional differences across settings. Our comparison of the U.S. and British cases in the nineteenth and early twentieth centuries highlights this point, as we find that the structure of U.S. federalism made a wholesale eradication of the machine much more difficult for national party leaders (Chapter 8).

Second, our macro account seeks to discern the factors that shape returns to scale, monitoring capacity, poverty, and the costs of communication. Thus we explain the rise, decline, and sometimes re-emergence of clientelism by focusing on factors such as the size of electorates, the degree of urbanization, average incomes in the electorate, and the possibilities for mass communication. These factors may themselves be powerfully shaped by economic development. For instance, the possible link between industrialization and these factors is discussed later (in connection with Figure 7.1) and explored more fully in Chapter 8, in which we emphasize that industrialization in Britain and the United States crucially shaped each of these factors. Thus our argument appears to share some features of classic modernization theories of political development.[3] Indeed, some arguments familiar from modernization theory are important in our argument.

However, it is important to be clear that in our account, each of these factors matters because of our central focus in this book: the reliance of political machines on armies of brokers (or electoral "agents" as they were called in nineteenth-century Britain). For each of the preceding bulleted observations, understanding the micro-logic of broker-mediated distribution – our focus in Part II of the book – is key. This micro-logic suggests *why* factors such as population growth, poverty, or industrialization should relate to the rise, fall, and sometimes re-emergence of clientelism. Our process-tracing historical accounts thus pinpoint specific ways in which economic development and other factors shaped the costs and benefits of clientelism to political leaders – and, in particular, influenced the agency costs involved in broker-mediated

---

[3] Lipset 1959.

distribution – and thus illuminate how such macro factors serve to perpetuate or undermine clientelism.

7.1 BROKER-MEDIATED THEORY AND THE RETURNS TO CLIENTELISM

Party leaders must decide whether to expend a marginal scarce resource (money, time, effort) on clientelist or nonclientelistic (programmatic or non-programmatic) distributive strategies. To maximize the party's vote share, the leaders seek to spend on the strategy with the highest marginal return in votes. Expenditures on clientelism go toward buying votes, paying brokers, and sustaining the networks on which clientelism relies. Expenditures on programmatic strategies are for governing-related costs (e.g., expanding public services or creating new universal policies)[4] and for campaign-related costs – e.g., communicating and announcing programs (perhaps through the print and broadcast media).

In comparing the electoral returns to programmatic versus clientelistic distribution, it is worth keeping in mind that the time frame of decisions to allocate to the two strategies may be different. Public spending priorities and programmatic commitments evolve over relatively long periods of time and hence are sunk costs by the time of election campaigns. Still, a party that finds itself in a transitional situation between clientelism and programmatic strategies will need to decide whether to deploy scarce resources on benefits to individuals channeled through the machine or on campaign pronouncements extolling past policies and proposing future ones.

What, then, explains the marginal value of deploying resources on clientelist strategies? Our model of Chapter 3 already provides several predictions about what makes clientelism more or less politically efficient for leaders. Principally, these are factors that increase or decrease the incentives of brokers to extract rents, either for their pecuniary benefit or to build their own local power bases. For example, when voters value benefits over ideology, the return to brokers of targeting responsive voters is greater, relative to extracting rents – because targeting more sharply elevates the probability that their party wins. By contrast, a more ideological electorate makes clientelism more wasteful, in that brokers have stronger incentives to extract rents.[5] Similarly, the ability of brokers to turn resources into votes – which depends on their own capacity to monitor voters and their local knowledge of voter preferences and behaviors – also shapes the returns to clientelism: when brokers are more effective as monitors of voters, the political efficacy of clientelism increases.[6] Average income in the electorate also matters: poverty may increase the returns to clientelism by making voters (who on average will have larger marginal utilities of income in

[4] Programmatic strategies can also entail costly efforts to impose programmatic unity on a party.
[5] This is captured by the κ term in the model of Chapter 3.
[6] This is captured by the comparative statics of η in the model of Chapter 3.

poorer societies) more responsive to transfers, whereas the growth of average income weakens these returns and thus increases the incentives of brokers to extract rents. Finally, the impact of individual brokers on electoral outcomes, and the extent to which they care about these outcomes (e.g., the extent to which they care about winning office) also influences brokers' incentives: when the variability of electoral outcomes increases, so that valence shocks become more important, or when elections are less competitive, clientelism is less efficient from the point of view of party leaders, in that brokers have stronger incentives to extract rents. (For a full discussion of these comparative statics results, see Section 3.1.)

What are the returns to unmediated forms of spending, whether programmatic or nonprogrammatic? To investigate fully the choice of leaders between clientelist and nonclientelist strategies, we also need to understand the costs and benefits of these latter strategies. A central issue here revolves around returns to scale. Clientelism, as we argue here, involves relatively constant returns to scale: the small-scale linkages between voters and brokers that are so central to the monitoring and information gathering role of brokers must be replicated for each broker, always for relatively small groups of voters. Each broker can only feasibly engage in the necessary long-term relationships with a certain number of voters, and so the returns to adding an additional broker to the network may therefore be relatively constant.

By contrast, unmediated spending may involve increasing returns to scale, with heavy initial or sunk costs but constant or declining fixed costs. This may be especially true, for instance, of efforts to cultivate a partisan "brand" and programmatic identity that a party may use to persuade or mobilize voters. It may also be true of the creation of bureaucratic agencies that use income, employment, or demographic characteristics to award eligibility for benefits – rather than using partisan orientation or actions on election day, which may require intense and frequent contact between brokers and voters as opposed to the more distant and occasional contact between bureaucrats and citizens. (We expand on these themes later.) Scale matters in another way as well: establishing group-based eligibility criteria may expand the number of people who receive benefits – because loyal, swing, and opposition voters must all be included if they fit the impersonal criteria – but it may also contract the size of the eligible groups, because now benefits can be delivered directly on the basis of eligibility criteria rather than through brokers who may end up targeting too many of the "wrong" kinds of voters. Thus understanding how returns to scale shape the attractiveness of nonclientelistic strategies is critical.

In the next section, we further assess the relative costs and benefits of clientelist versus nonclientelist strategies on theoretical grounds by extending the model of Chapter 3. One important lesson of this analysis is that a number of factors can influence the returns to distributive strategies, and so seeking to identify a master causal variable may not always be productive. Industrialization and economic development, however, often play a crucial role, as our case studies suggest: they can shape the returns to both kinds of strategies through a number of channels. Most crucially, our analysis suggests specific reasons why economic growth and development matter for transitions to programmatic politics – an explanation rooted in the micro-logic of broker-mediated distribution. In particular, our theory suggests four factors that influence the marginal electoral return to clientelist and nonclientelist strategies, each of which is in turn shaped by industrialization and economic development. We expand on these four factors now before turning to our model.

7.1.1 Returns to Scale

Given the smaller returns to scale in mediated strategies, the larger the electorate, the more attractive we expect programmatic strategies to be. Clientelist parties are elaborate information-gathering devices, with implications for party organization. To monitor voters effectively and deliver benefits in a fine-tuned manner, brokers must be in constant and close contact with small numbers of voters. In Chapter 4, we saw many examples of the ways in which brokers in Argentina, Venezuela, and elsewhere gather fine-grained information about "their" voters: brokers know the partisan proclivities of voters in their network, observe their participation in rallies and other events, and believe they can infer the vote choices of these voters, even in the presence of a secret ballot. Yet the intimate quotidian interactions required to obtain this knowledge cannot be sustained with each voter if a broker's network grows too large. Hence the foundations of the machine must be replicated over and over again as the electorate grows. Moreover, because of the complexity of organizing armies of brokers, adding additional brokers may increase vote shares less when the number of brokers is already large. For this reason, clientelism may involve diminishing rather than constant returns to scale.

By contrast, campaign expenditures on policy signals yield increasing returns. The broadcasting of messages through radio and newspapers involves large start-up costs, but the marginal cost of reaching an additional community or voter is negligible. Parties that bypass brokers and rely on bureaucracies to distribute benefits also reduce the agency problems inherent in clientelism.[7] Where once the criteria for distribution were an individual's partisan orientation, the depth of his partisan affinities, and his actions on election day, now the criteria are his income, employment status, or demographic characteristics. Securing reliable information needed to make clientelism work requires that brokers maintain close contact with their constituent neighbors. Securing reliable information needed to make programmatic distribution work can be achieved through more distant and occasional contact. In the absence of the pronounced information asymmetries that brokers have vis-à-vis party leaders,

---

[7] Of course, agency problems can persist under programmatic politics, especially when bureaucratic capacity is low. See, especially, Huber and McCarty 2004.

bureaucrats are more reliable agents of the leaders who employ them, at least relative to political brokers.

The growing efficiency of programmatic politics as the national and district electorates grow is one link between industrialization and the decline of clientelism. Industrialization can expand the size of the electorate in two ways. In its early stages, industrialization often fosters population growth.[8] Not just the national electorate, but electoral districts, may become more populous under the stimulus of industrialization. When constituencies are attached to towns or boroughs, as they were in Britain, a growing population will mechanically increase the number of voters in the constituency. Of course, legislatures may also be increased in size, for instance, by creating new districts; yet it is plausible that an upper bound on the size of legislatures exists in representative democracy, so that population growth implies that each legislator represents an increasingly large electorate.[9] What's more, the same kinds of political pressures that lead to expansions of the franchise with industrialization also make small constituencies appear increasingly anachronistic. Larger constituencies, as much as a larger electorate writ large, tend to reduce the efficiency of clientelism.

In Chapter 8, we discuss further the ways in which industrialization may shape characteristics of the electorate. Our focus here on returns to scale, then, provides one plausible reason why industrialization encourages a shift away from clientelism and to programmatic strategies: it engenders a larger electorate (see Figure 7.1).

7.1.2 Discernibility of Vote Choice

The less discernible voters' choices, the smaller the marginal electoral returns from clientelism.[10] Voters whose choices are completely opaque can defect from the implicit agreement that lies behind the bribe. They can accept payoffs and vote as they please. Such voters cannot credibly commit to complying. When this is true, vote buying should unravel.[11] Again, the micro-logic of

---

[8] Industrialization eventually leads to a "demographic transition" to lower birth rates. However, the early stages of industrialization produce large income differentials between agricultural and industrial sectors, causing movements of people into industrial economies. Hence polities and regions that industrialize initially experience sharp population increases. This was the British and American experience in the nineteenth century.

[9] For instance, as we note in Chapter 8, the average size of a constituency in the U.S. House of Representatives at the time of the Civil War (1861–1865) was around 16,000 voters; today, the figure is more than 640,000 citizens (Frederick 2008).

[10] *Discernible* is better than *observable*: the activity of monitoring voters' actions goes beyond observing their vote in a poll book or on a ballot.

[11] Of course, voters may believe their vote is not private, even without brokers and with a well-enforced secret ballot: see Gerber et al. 2011 for evidence that substantial proportions of the electorate in the United States today believes the vote is not secret.

broker-mediated distribution is central, because brokers provide the monitoring capacity necessary to make vote choice discernible to political machines. Both voting technologies and social contexts can shape the discernibility of vote choice.

In tying the increasing opacity of the vote to the reduced effectiveness of vote buying, we do not wish to suggest that distributive politics has no impact on voters' choices even when these choices are completely secret and undiscernible. Programmatic and highly bureaucratized parties engage in programmatic distribution, pork-barrel politics, and nonconditional benefits to individuals, all aimed at winning votes; none relies on parties' discerning individuals' votes. When voters' choices are opaque to parties and parties lack the ability to hold individual voters to account for their votes, voters may still be responsive to distributive strategies. They may be responsive to the extent that they view current largess as predictive of future largess, should the party in power be reelected; or to the extent that largess engenders good will, which then translates into electoral support; or to the extent that voters who receive largess are pressed by norms of reciprocity to return the favor with a vote.[12]

These alternative mechanisms – expectation of future benefits even without accountability, good will, or a normative need to reciprocate – are likely, however, to be less robust than is "perverse accountability," meaning credible threats by the party to withdraw rewards to individuals.[13] The voter who gives his vote to a party that built schools in his district because he expects future benefits to flow to his district does not cause future community investments to happen with his vote, in the sense that he can cause an on-going flow of future benefits to himself and his family (or avoid their withdrawal) when he trades his vote for benefits. Recalling the broker quoted earlier, "if you do not have money, if you can't give [voters] things, they can't support you. They support whomever has things to give away."[14]

Given the particular forcefulness of distributive strategies when parties can discern voters' choices, what are the factors shaping this discernibility? The most obvious factor is voting technologies. Under public or *viva voce* voting, individuals' votes are fully observable, though keeping track of whether voters turn out and which party they vote for, and conditioning delivery of rewards on these actions, still requires some organizational depth. Written ballots provide greater secrecy, especially when they are filled out in closed booths and when they have a standardized format. The Australian ballot most diminishes the observability of voters' choices. The Australian ballot is produced by public entities (not parties), distributed on or shortly before election day, and bear the names of all parties' candidates for a given office.

---

[12] On the last, see Lawson and Greene 2011. These alternative mechanisms can also be at work under clientelism. That is, voters who are in danger of having benefits withdrawn will be all the less likely to defect to the extent that good will or norms of reciprocity are at work.

[13] See Stokes 2005.

[14] Szwarcberg 2013, p. 27.

Parties and reformers keen to encourage programmatic politics and to undermine party machines pursue ballot reform, often – as we shall see – against
the objections of brokers who anticipated their role being undercut.[15] In this
sense ballot reform is an indicator of shifts away from clientelism, rather than
a cause. Yet as Aidt and Jensen demonstrated with data from Britain, the
U.S. states, and Latin America, economic development increased the probability of parties' shifting to the secret ballot. Indeed, although causal inferences
about the effects of economic development are surely tricky, these authors
conclude that "modernization can predict the timing of the secret ballot very
well."[16]

In addition to voting technologies, the social context of voting also influences the discernibility of the vote. Voting behavior can be monitored at a
lower cost in rural communities and small towns than in big cities; the multifaceted nature of social relations in smaller communities makes it easier for
brokers to infer electoral choices.[17] Bensel made this point with respect to mid-
nineteenth-century America: "Because rural voters were thickly embedded in
their communities, they invariably carried their social and political histories
to the polls with them. Their neighbors, serving as party observers or election
judges, knew their names and political leanings..."[18] The interconnectedness
of rural life can to some degree be replicated by party machines that operate in urban settings and make use of brokers who are tightly integrated into
neighborhood social networks.

By moving people from small towns to more anonymous cities, and by
encouraging political leaders to adopt the secret ballot, industrialization and
economic growth undermine vote buying.

7.1.3 Numerical Weight of Low-Income Voters in the Electorate

Because the responsiveness of voters to electoral bribes diminishes with income,
brokers may have greater incentives to extract rents or engage in other politically wasteful activities when voters are on average richer. By contrast, the
responsiveness of voters to programmatic appeals does not diminish with
income. Indeed, because literacy rates and print media exposure tend to be
higher among wealthier voters, responsiveness to programmatic strategies tends
to be a positive function of income. The relative numbers of poor versus middle-
class voters, in turn, decline with declining poverty in the larger society. When
the electorate is on average poorer, mediated distribution is more attractive

---

[15] In the United States, the push for the Australian ballot was in part an effort to eliminate
bribery and circumvent machines, but another motivation was to reintroduce de facto literacy
requirements, through the back door. See the discussion in McCormick 1981a and Keyssar
2001.
[16] Aidt and Jensen 2011, p. 6.
[17] For evidence, see Stokes 2005, Faughnan and Zechmeister 2011.
[18] Bensel 2004, p. xii.

to party leaders, whereas rising incomes increase the appeal of unmediated strategies.

If poor voters are more responsive to a bribe or a treat than are higher-income voters, are they not also more responsive to material programmatic appeals?[19] Indeed, they will be. However, with programmatic distribution, the spigot is not turned off when a person fails to vote the "right" way. Consider a low-income voter who faces the choice between inducing an ongoing flow of benefits by voting for the machine or contributing what is basically a symbolic or expressive vote for the party offering programs that will help him or her materially. (His or her vote is "symbolic" in that it is not pivotal, and the party, should it win, will extend benefits to the voter independent of his or her actions on election day.) The urgency of need might well lead the poor voter to vote for the machine. If the voter's income rises and the treat or bribe appears to be more and more trivial, we would expect the voter to be more willing to register support for the party whose program is most attractive.

Moreover, diminishing numbers of poor voters in the electorate makes the vote-buying activities of brokers less effective. In our model, this increases the incentives of brokers to divert their efforts to rent seeking. Maintaining large armies of local brokers therefore becomes a less optimal vote-getting strategy for party leaders as poverty declines, providing another way that economic development can serve to undermine clientelism.

The impact of industrial growth on the mean income of the electorate is not unidirectional, however. On the one hand, industrialization increases the income of the population. To the extent that income levels of the subset of the population that has the right to vote reflect those of the broader population, industrialization exerts upward pressure on the median income of voters. This effect occurs because poverty, by absolute measures, becomes less widespread as societies industrialize, purely as a function of economic growth. What's more, industrialization in the advanced democracies eventually produced greater income equality than in the pre-industrial period.[20]

But on the other hand, economic growth creates political pressures to extend the franchise. Each extension brings into the electorate people who before were excluded by income or literacy requirements: the lower economic strata.[21] Therefore, a short-run effect of industrial growth is to make the electorate poorer. In general, the decline of poverty in the electorate due to economic growth is gradual, its increase due to expansions of the franchise is discontinuous and abrupt.

In sum, by (eventually) engendering a wealthier electorate, industrialization undermines vote buying.

---

[19] This point has been made by Lippert-Rasmussen 2011.
[20] See Lindert 2000.
[21] Extension of the suffrage to women was an exception.

7.1.4 Costs of Mass Communication

Programmatic politics involves expenditures on public goods and targeting of individuals. Both kinds of expenditures are publicly pronounced. As a consequence, other things being equal, the lower the costs party leaders face in circumventing brokers and communicating directly with voters, the greater the pay-off from programmatic strategies. Higher literacy rates, allowing for wider circulation of newspapers, encourage programmatic strategies, as do greater penetration of print and broadcast media.[22]

The costs of communicating with voters may be mediated through electoral systems. Executive elections, legislative elections under plurality rules, and open-list proportional systems give individual candidates incentives to broadcast their personal policy intentions and traits to voters, incentives that are much muted in proportional and closed-list systems. It is often assumed that voting systems that encourage a "personal vote" also encourage clientelism.[23] In fact, choosing candidates based on their personal appeals and clientelism are better conceived as substitutes than as complements. The reason is that candidates who can make personal appeals can also circumvent the party machinery.

Anyone who has lived through the communications revolution of the late twentieth century knows that technological innovation can be an autonomous driver of reduced costs and heightened speed of communication. Yet it is also the case that the industrial revolution of the nineteenth century played a role in expanding the scope, and reducing the costs, of communications that politicians deployed to reach voters directly. The industrial revolution also enlarged the market for newspapers and fed breakthroughs such as the telegraph. We shall see that in Britain, innovations in communications were probably not immediate drivers of the rise of programmatic politics. However, they did mean that inexpensive techniques were available to politicians who wanted to sidestep party machines and campaign by communicating directly with voters.

Another reason, then, why industrialization undermined vote buying in today's advanced democracies is that it encouraged the rise of modes of direct communication with voters, allowing political leaders to sidestep brokers.

In sum, industrialization and economic development may be neither necessary nor sufficient to cause nonclientelistic politics. Yet because development may often influence the effectiveness of brokers, the responsiveness of voters, and the relative costs and benefits of clientelistic politics, it can tip the balance toward the erosion of clientelism – as our historical and contemporary case studies in the next chapter suggest. The countervailing effects of industrialization on income levels of the electorate and on the ultimate prevalence of vote buying are illustrated in Figure 7.1.

---

[22] Our assumption here is that voters can't directly observe government activities and that parties incur costs when they signal their programmatic achievements and intentions.

[23] On electoral systems and the personal vote, see Carey and Shugart 1995.

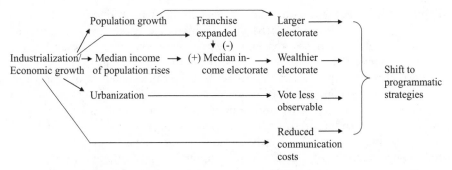

FIGURE 7.1. Factors Encouraging Shift to Programmatic Politics.

We return to these themes in the next chapter. However, to further ground our analysis in the interplay between party leaders, brokers, and voters, and to generate further comparative statics predictions that we investigate next, we first return to the formal model developed in Chapter 3.

7.2 CLIENTELISM AND PROGRAMMATIC POLITICS: A MODEL

To analyze the incentives of party leaders to invest in clientelism or instead in other forms of non–broker-mediated spending, we modify the model of Chapter 3, now allowing for a prior choice of leaders over types of spending.[24] The timing of the game is similar as in Chapter 3, with the main difference being that leaders now must allocate their budget between clientelistic (broker-mediated) and nonclientelistic (nonmediated) spending. Thus:

1. Each broker organizes a network of followers, promising each follower a benefit of b^i if the voter participates in her network.
2. Leaders of the machine party M observe the size of brokers' networks and decide which broker to hire. The party also allocates non–broker-mediated, group-specific transfers f^J for all J (described later) and distribute remaining resources of size $\Omega = \Delta - \sum_J \alpha^J f^J$ to their chosen broker (the budget constraint is also described later).
3. Elections take place. If party M wins office, the broker distributes resources to voters in his network, extracts any unspent resources as rents, and reaps the continuation value of his or her party staying in power.

As in Chapter 3, this reduced-form game assumes commitment to brokers' distributive strategies; again, the rationale is that brokers and voters are in fact

---

[24] We reiterate key features of the model here, but to follow the discussion, readers may find it helpful to have read Chapter 3.

immersed in a repeated game that allows commitment to distributive strate-gies.[25] Modeling this full repeated game would come at the cost of additional complexity but would not substantially illuminate the core issues we high-light. Despite its simplicity, analysis of this game sheds light on several key issues that may shape leaders' incentives to invest in clientelism or instead in nonclientelistic group-specific transfers.

Note in particular that we now suppose that the party's budget consists of two types of spending: resources transferred to brokers for vote buying and group-specific transfers that bypass brokers. Thus the party leader now has a total budget $\Delta \equiv \Omega + \sum_J \alpha^J f^J$. As in Chapter 3, Ω is the amount of resources transferred to brokers. By contrast, here f^J is a per-capita transfer to group $J \in R, M, P$, with R for "rich," M for "middle-class," and P for "poor."[26] These per-capita transfers $\{f^R, f^M, f^P\}$ are unmediated, and, although they can be targeted to specific groups, everybody in the targeted group is eligible for and receives the transfer. That is, although a program might be means-tested (so that only, say, poor citizens receive the benefit), eligible beneficiaries can't be discriminated against or favored on the basis of their partisan preferences or political behaviors. Because α^J is the population share of group J, $\sum_J \alpha^J f^J$ is the total amount of the group-specific transfers.[27]

The key point is that the group-specific transfers cut out the intermedi-aries: brokers are not required for their distribution.[28] These transfers may be programmatic, in the sense of Chapter 1, or they could also involve nonpro-grammatic group-based transfers; our main objective here is to investigate the incentives to spend on broker-mediated clientelist benefits or on nonmediated transfers. Thus we assume that total spending can be allocated toward either clientelistic or nonclientelistic spending, or both; the goal of the analysis is to determine the optimal mix of types of spending, as a function of the model parameters.

Individual income is then the sum of the group-specific endowment y^J, the group-specific per-capita transfer f^J provided by the incumbent party, and the individual benefit provided by the broker, b^{iJ}. Quasilinear utility over endowment income and transfers is thus

$$H(y^J + \eta b^{iJ}) + f^J. \tag{7.1}$$

As in Chapter 3, b^{iJ} is the benefit paid by the broker to voter i in group J, and η measures the "effectiveness" of the broker hired by party M in targeting

---

[25] See Stokes 2005.

[26] The notation here uses upper-case $J \in R, M, P$, in contrast to Chapter 3.

[27] It is also the average amount of transfers: recall that the total population size is normalized to 1.

[28] Here, we constrain the f^J and Ω to be nonnegative: this implies, for instance, that resources can be dedicated to clientelism via brokers, but party leaders cannot leave brokers with negative income. These assumptions are not essential for what follows, however.

resources to voters.[29] Unlike in Chapter 3, voters now add to their endowment incomes an additional type of income that they receive from parties: the group transfer f^J. Notice that η does not multiply utility over the group transfer f^J, because the broker's effectiveness does not influence the enjoyment of this transfer (because the transfer is not mediated by the broker). Also, although the benefits b^{iJ} are indexed by i because each voter can receive a differently sized benefit, the group transfers f^J cannot be targeted this precisely. More fine-grained targeting would require brokers. To capture possible returns-to-scale effects, we assume that utility is linear in f^J; this contrasts with $H(\cdot)$, a concave utility function.

As in Chapter 3, non-network participants, and those who prefer party M on ideological grounds, vote sincerely. An opposition voter i in group J may be induced to participate in the network of party M's broker, and to vote for party M, if and only if

$$\kappa[H(y^J + \eta b^{iJ}) + f^J] - c \geq \kappa H(y^J) + \sigma^{iJ} + \delta. \tag{7.2}$$

As in Chapter 3, κ is a parameter measuring the value that voters place on material benefits, relative to ideology, whereas c is the (material) cost in terms of time and effort of network participation. Also, as before, σ^{iJ} is the "ideological" preference of voter i in group J. This variable is distributed uniformly on $[\frac{-1}{2\phi^J}, \frac{1}{2\phi^J}]$; thus it has mean zero in each group, with positive values indicating a preference for party B and negative values indicating a preference for party M. Finally, δ is again the aggregate popularity shock and is distributed uniformly on $[\frac{-1}{2\psi}, \frac{1}{2\psi}]$. Thus a large positive realization of δ helps party O, whereas a large negative realization helps party M.

Brokers behave in the current model just as in the one in Chapter 3. A broker who is hired by party M to distribute resources to voters receives a postelection payoff R if her party wins. In addition, the broker may extract pecuniary "rents" r by failing to pass on some measure of resources to voters. If a broker k is hired by party M, her expected utility is therefore

$$EU^k = p_M(r + R). \tag{7.3}$$

Here, p_M is the probability that the broker's party wins office, which gives the broker access to the continuation value of holding office, R. However, r gives the (endogenous) rents chosen by the broker. If a broker is not hired by party M, his or her reservation utility is normalized to zero.

7.2.1 Analysis

With these preliminaries, we can begin the analysis of the model. First, we derive the expected vote share and the probability of victory of party M as a

---

[29] For convenience we drop the subscript k on η.

function of its policy choices. Note that an arbitrary voter in group J who is indifferent between parties M and O has ideology parameter σ^{ij} given by

$$\sigma^{ij} = \kappa[H(y^J + \eta b^{ij}) + f^J) - H(y^J)] - c - \delta. \tag{7.4}$$

In general, given some equilibrium choice f^{J*} and some realization of δ, there could be multiple pairs (σ^{ij}, b^{ij}) for which equation (7.4) would hold. In fact, just as in Chapter 3, if brokers target voters who prefer party O on ideological grounds (i.e., voters who prefer party O when there are no group transfers or individual benefits, and δ is set at its expected value of zero), they will set b^{ij} such that (7.2) holds with equality. Thus it is again useful to define the *largest* value of σ^{ij} such that the equality in (7.4) holds, conditional on some equilibrium choice f^{J*} and on the benefit distribution schedule of brokers. We use the notation $\tilde{\sigma}^{J*}$ for this value:

$$\tilde{\sigma}^{J*} = \kappa[H(y^J + \eta b^{J*}) + f^{J*} - H(y^J)] - c - \delta. \tag{7.5}$$

Again, this is simply definitional: given some benefit distribution schedule and some choice of f^J, $\tilde{\sigma}^{J*}$ is the "most opposed" voter in group J who is made just indifferent between the parties by the combination of transfers. As in Chapter 3, it is straightforward to show that any voter i in group J with $\sigma^{ij} \leq \tilde{\sigma}^{J*}$ votes for party M: voters with $\sigma^{ij} < \kappa H(y^J) - \delta$ – that is, those who prefer party M on ideological grounds, even absent any per-capita transfers or clientelistic benefits – will by definition have ideological preferences at least as small as $\tilde{\sigma}^{J*}$. In addition, any voters whose votes are bought will be paid their reservation value by brokers, so voters in group J with $\sigma^{ij} < \tilde{\sigma}^{J*}$ will be paid $b^{ij} < b^{J*}$.

We can now generically define party M's vote share in each group J, which is just the proportion of voters with $\sigma^{ij} \leq \tilde{\sigma}^{J*}$, given the choice of f^J for each group J. That is, defining $\tilde{\pi}^J$ as the vote share in each group J, we have

$$\tilde{\pi}^J = \int_{\frac{-1}{2\phi^J}}^{\tilde{\sigma}^{J*}} \phi^J \, dz$$

$$= \int_{\frac{-1}{2\phi^J}}^{\kappa[H(y^J + \eta b^{J*}) + f^{J*} - H(y^J)] - c - \delta} \phi^J \, dz$$

$$= \frac{1}{2} + \phi^J [\kappa[H(y^J + \eta b^{J*}) + f^{J*} - H(y^J)] - c - \delta. \tag{7.6}$$

Next, the party's overall vote share is the weighted sum of the vote share in each group, where the weights are given by the proportionate size of each group:

that is, $\sum_J \alpha^J \tilde{\pi}^J$. The probability that party M wins office is thus

$$\tilde{p}_M = Pr\left(\sum_J \alpha^J \tilde{\pi}^J \geq \frac{1}{2}\right)$$

$$= Pr\left(\sum_J \alpha^J \left[\frac{1}{2} + \phi^J \left[\kappa[H(y^J + \eta b^{J*}) + f^{J*} - H(y^J)] - c - \delta\right] \geq \frac{1}{2}\right)$$

$$= Pr\left(\frac{\kappa}{\phi}\sum_J \alpha^J \phi^J \left[\kappa[H(y^J + \eta b^{J*}) + f^{J*} - H(y^J)] - c \geq \delta\right), \qquad (7.7)$$

where as in Chapter 3, $\phi = \sum_J \alpha^J \phi^J$ is the average of ϕ^J across the three groups $J = P, M, R$. We denote this probability by $\tilde{p}_M$ to distinguish it from the probability defined in Chapter 3. To define this ex-ante probability of victory, we simply integrate the density of the random variable δ over its domain, up to the critical value defined in (7.7). Thus

$$\tilde{p}_M = \frac{1}{2} + \psi\left[\frac{\kappa}{\phi}\sum_J \alpha^J \phi^J [H(y^J + \eta b^{J*}) + f^{J*} - H(y^J)] - c\right]. \qquad (7.8)$$

We assume that party leaders will maximize this probability of victory. The question then becomes whether they will do so by prioritizing clientelist transfers through brokers or instead by prioritizing unmediated, group-based transfers. We turn next to this question.

7.3 WHEN DO LEADERS CHOOSE MACHINE POLITICS?

To understand leaders' incentives, it is useful to analyze an extreme case. Suppose that leaders have a dichotomous choice between dedicating all funding to nonclientelistic transfers or to devoting all resources to mediated distribution through brokers. If they opt for an entirely nonclientelistic strategy, $\Omega = 0$ and $b^{ji} = 0$ for all i and all J. If they opt entirely for a clientelistic strategy, $f^J = 0$ for all J, and we simply have the setting of Chapter 3, in which unmediated group-based transfers were not available.

Clearly, it can only be optimal for office-seeking party leaders to set $\Omega = 0$ if the probability of winning without clientelism is greater than the probability of winning with clientelism, so the analysis comes down to comparison of these two probabilities. Let $\tilde{p}_{M,NC}$ be the probability of winning conditional on $\Omega = 0$, that is,

$$\tilde{p}_{M,NC} = \frac{1}{2} + \psi\left[\frac{\kappa}{\phi}\sum_J \alpha^J \phi^J f^{J*}\right], \qquad (7.9)$$

where " NC" represents "no clientelism." Note that here the terms for clientelist benefits b^{iJ} and the cost of network participation c both drop out: there is no broker-mediated distribution. Next, let $\tilde{p}_{M,C}$ be the probability that party M wins conditional on $f^J = 0$ for all J, and thus $\Omega = \Delta$. That is,

$$\tilde{p}_{M,C} = \frac{1}{2} + \psi \left[\frac{\kappa}{\phi} \left[\sum_J \alpha^J \phi^J H(y^J + \eta b^{J*}) - H(y^J) \right] - c \right], \qquad (7.10)$$

where "C" stands for "clientelism."

A sufficient condition for $\tilde{p}_{M,NC} \geq \tilde{p}_{M,C}$ to hold is then that $H(y^J) + f^{J*} \geq H(y^J + \eta b^{J*})$ for all J.[30] When will this condition be met? Examination of the relevant budget constraints suggests a first answer. In the "no clientelism" case, the budget constraint is simply $\Delta = \alpha^R f^R + \alpha^M f^M + \alpha^P f^P$, because here all spending goes to nonmediated group-specific transfers. In the "clientelism" case, however, the budget constraint is $\Delta = \Omega$. As in Chapter 3, $\Omega = \sum_J \bar{b}^J + r^*$, where $\bar{b}^J$ is the total resources the party's broker distributes to each income group, and r^* gives equilibrium rents extracted by the broker. Note then that in the clientelistic case, the amount of resources spent on direct transfers in each group J – and thus the value of b^{J*} – depends on equilibrium rent extraction r^*.

The first observation to make here is that some portion of the resources dedicated to clientelism by party leaders are extracted as rents by brokers – and thus have no impact on the party's probability of victory. Indeed, without nonclientelistic transfers, the structure of the model is just as in Chapter 3. There, we showed that equilibrium rents extracted by the party's broker are given by

$$r* = \frac{\tilde{p}_{M,C}\phi}{\eta\psi\kappa \sum_J \alpha^J \phi^J H'(y^J + \eta b^{J*})} - R, \qquad (7.11)$$

where here we have simply substituted $\tilde{p}_{M,C}$ for p_M in Chapter 3. Recall that here, ϕ is again the average group-specific density of the ideology parameter σ^{iJ}, and R is the exogenous value to brokers of their party holding future office; other parameters are as defined in the previous subsection. The intuition behind equation (7.11) is that brokers trade off the utility from rents they can extract from party leaders against rent-seeking's negative impact on the probability of victory.

This equation, already analyzed in Chapter 3, provides several initial comparative statics results. As before, brokers will be less prone to extract rents, and hence party leaders will be more prone to retain their machines, when:

1. The density of the random variable δ – that is, ψ – is larger. When ψ increases, electoral outcomes become less noisy; thus brokers have less

---

[30] This follows because $\tilde{p}_{M,NC} \geq \tilde{p}_{M,C}$ if $c \geq \frac{\kappa}{\phi}[\sum_J \alpha^J \phi^J [H(y^J + \eta b^{J*}) - H(y^J) - f^{J*}]$. Because c is non-negative, this is satisfied whenever $H(y^J + \eta b^{J*}) - H(y^J) - f^{J*} \leq 0$. Rearranging terms gives the sufficient condition noted in the text.

scope for extracting rents without sharply driving down the probability of victory.

2. Voters value benefits more highly relative to ideology, that is, κ increases. A preference for material over ideological or expressive benefits makes voters more responsive to brokers' transfers, which heightens the returns to targeting swing voters relative to extracting rents.

3. The broker is more effective, that is, η is higher, again because in this case voters are more responsive to transfers.

4. The exogenous returns to winning office, R, increase; as brokers care more about winning elections, they increasingly target voters with benefits instead of extracting rents.

5. Voters are on average poorer, that is, the average group-specific marginal utility of income is higher, so that brokers have stronger incentives to target voters. Thus poverty increases the marginal benefit of a clientelistic transfer, making voters more responsive to transfers and reducing the incentives of brokers to extract rents.

6. Elections are more competitive (formally, when the probability of victory declines; here, with one incumbent party transferring resources, the ex-ante probability of victory is more than one-half, so a decline in the probability of victory means elections are becoming more competitive). Again, here targeting voters becomes more attractive to brokers, relative to extracting rents.

All of these factors make clientelism more attractive for party leaders, relative to unmediated strategies – group-specific programmatic or nonprogrammatic transfers that are not targeted to individuals and made conditional on their vote choice.

Because our focus is on the role and importance of brokers, we emphasize the parameter η. This parameter measures the effectiveness of brokers in transferring resources into benefits for voters and thus into votes for the party. These benefits are conditional on network participation (and at least implicitly on vote choice).[31] Where vote choice is less discernible, the electorate is larger, and clients are more urbanized (or less concentrated in particular ethnic neighborhoods), η may reasonably be expected to be lower, driving up the returns to rent-seeking by brokers.

Because party leaders are trading off the returns to clientelism against the returns to non–broker mediated spending, any factors that increase rent seeking by brokers will make the latter strategies more attractive. Indeed, group-based spending is more attractive when $H(y^J) + f^{J*} \geq H(y^J + \eta b^{J*})$. Because overall resources transferred to brokers are $\Omega \sum_J \bar{b}^J + r^*$, as $r*$ goes up, fewer (swing) voters will be bought in equilibrium, and the returns to clientelism to party leaders will decrease.

---

[31] See Stokes 2005.

7.3.1 Returns to Scale and Group-Based Transfers

The analysis thus far only considers one side of the issue: how the extent of rent seeking by brokers shapes the returns to clientelism. What shapes the returns to unmediated group transfers in this model?

Here, issues of scale are key. Group-based transfers cut out the middleman and eliminate rent seeking by brokers. Yet, by getting rid of brokers, party leaders also restrict their ability to target individual voters – for instance, swing or weakly opposed voters. Indeed, all voters in a given group (here, defined by income category) receive the per-capita transfer targeted at their group. As a result, many voters who would vote for the party regardless of transfers (loyal voters), as well as those who are very opposed to the party and are probably not going to vote for it even given transfers, receive benefits. The amount of political "waste" could thus be even greater under nonmediated group-based transfers than under clientelism. Yet, because utility in group-based transfers is linear, the scale effects are different than for clientelist transfers, which are subject to diminishing returns. Finally, the payment of benefits to all voters in a given category implies that unmediated distribution can be an expensive strategy.

To see these points formally, let us derive an expression for $\sum_J \alpha^J \bar{b}^J$, the total amount of clientelistic benefits. Note that due to the competition between brokers, the broker who is hired by the party must offer network members at least as much as the next most productive broker, that is, the broker with η_{k-1}. The benefit b^{ij} must also be large enough that voters in the network are just indifferent between participating and not, that is, $\kappa H(y^J + \eta_{k-1} b^{ij}) - c = \sigma^{ij}$. Thus, for all voters who participate in the broker's network,

$$b^{iJ} = \frac{1}{\eta_{k-1}} \left[H^{-1} \left(\frac{\sigma^{ij} + c}{\kappa} \right) - y^J \right], \tag{7.12}$$

where H^{-1} is the inverse function of H.[32] In each group J, then, the total amount of resources $\bar{b}^J$ is given by

$$\bar{b}^J = \int \left[\frac{1}{\eta_{k-1}} \left[H^{-1}(\frac{\sigma^{iJ} + c}{\kappa}) - y^J \right] \right] d\sigma^{iJ}, \tag{7.13}$$

where the integral is taken over members of the broker's network. The total amount of the benefits is then just the weighted sum of this quantity over each group, that is, $\sum_J \alpha^J \bar{b}^J$.

How does this compare to the quantity spent on benefits with nonmediated group-specific transfers? Recall that if $\hat{p}_{M,NC}$ is going to be as big as $\hat{p}_{M,C}$, so that leaders do not choose clientelism, it must be the case that as many voters would vote for the party with nonclientelistic transfers as under clientelism. Thus the most expensive swing voter in the broker's network under clientelism

---

[32] $H(\cdot)$ is monotonically increasing and thus one-to-one, so the inverse function $H^{-1}(\cdot)$ exists.

must also vote for the party under universalism. Again, a sufficient condition for this to be true is that $H(y^J) + f^J = H(y^J + \eta b^{J*})$. Recalling that b^{J*} is defined as the value of the benefit paid to the swing voter with $\sigma^{iJ} = \sigma^{J*}$ and substituting σ^{J*} into (7.12), we have

$$f^J = \frac{1}{\eta_{k-1}} H^{-1} \left(\frac{\sigma^{J*} + c}{\kappa} \right) - y^J \tag{7.14}$$

for all J.[33] Then, the total amount spent under universalism in each group J is

$$\bar{f}^J = \int_{\frac{-1}{2\phi^J}}^{\frac{1}{2\phi^J}} \left[\frac{1}{\eta_{k-1}} H^{-1} \left(\frac{\sigma^{J*} + c}{\kappa} \right) - y^J \right] d\sigma^{iJ}, \tag{7.15}$$

with the total amount of universalistic benefits across all groups being the weighted sum $\sum_J \alpha^J \bar{f}^J$.

Comparison of equations (7.13) and (7.15) suggests that the benefits paid under unmediated strategies can be more expensive than clientelism for two reasons. First, under clientelism, the amount paid to each voter can be tailored to that voter's participation constraint. This can be seen formally by the fact that σ^{iJ} appears in the numerator of the inverse function in (7.13), whereas σ^{J*} appears in the numerator in (7.15). This is the virtue of brokers for party leaders: brokers provide privileged information about the ideological or partisan proclivities of individual voters, and they can tailor payments in a way that is not possible when group-specific distributions are paid to every eligible voter in a group. With unmediated transfers, by contrast, party leaders have no way to discriminate between voters on the basis of their partisan or ideological affiliations, and so they must pay each citizen in a given group the same amount.[34] Here, b^{J*} is the largest value of b^{iJ}, that is, it is the value paid to the "most expensive" voter in group J. So the inequality $f^J \geq b^{J*}$ implies that for each group J, the transfer that the party pays to all members of the group must be at least as large as the clientelist benefit paid to the most expensive voter in the broker's network. Unmediated spending thus also involves substantial electoral "waste," though the source is different than the waste under broker-mediated distribution: here, every voter in a particular group receives the subsidy for which he or she is eligible – regardless of political ideology or affiliation.

---

[33] Notice that although we are analyzing here the cost of universalism, parameters relevant to clientelism – such as the productivity of the next most competent broker, η_{k-1} – appear in Equation 7.14 because the benefit of universalism must be as big as the benefit paid to the most expensive swing voter under clientelism, and these parameters are relevant to the latter.

[34] Obviously, in reality groups could be divided according to a variety of observable criteria, besides income. In principle, recorded measures of political tendency such as party membership could be used by leaders, even absent brokers. However, the point here is that without dense insertion into local social networks by brokers, conditioning benefit receipt on finer-grained information about political loyalties is typically infeasible.

What's more, not only is the per-capita transfer larger without brokers, but also the benefit is paid to every member of a given group. Formally, this can be seen from the fact that the integral in (7.15) is taken over all members in a group, whereas in (7.13) it is only taken over members of a broker's network. Again, this is due to the fact that all voters eligible for the benefit are paid the benefit. Thus nonmediated transfers forego the political advantages of clientelism – the fact that brokers can tailor the size of bribes to individual voters' circumstances.

In sum, both kinds of distribution involve electorally "wasteful" spending: clientelism involves distributing benefits through brokers, who extract rents and can also target inefficiently; nonmediated transfers eliminate rent seeking but may involve even more waste by targeting unresponsive voters. Which source of waste will be larger depends in part on the comparative statics results discussed previously.

7.4 TESTING THE THEORY

The analysis in this chapter captures some of the tradeoffs that party leaders face in deciding whether to build networks of brokers engaged in clientelistic transfers or engage instead in unmediated kinds of distributive politics – such as conditional cash transfers or various forms of bureaucratic, means-tested programs we consider in subsequent chapters.

We have found that several factors may influence the attractiveness of clientelism to party leaders. First, the equilibrium value of rent seeking by brokers is critical. If brokers extract lots of rents, then much of leaders' total resource pie will be dissipated, implying that fewer resources are spent on targeted benefits for swing voters. Rent seeking should in turn increase when brokers are less effective at turning resources into votes and thus, on the margin, find it more attractive to capture rents instead. Such declining efficiency of clientelistic transfers may be due to changes in the size or composition of the electorate, institutional innovations that make inferring vote choice more difficult, or broader social changes that complicate the sustained interactions between brokers and their clients required to make clientelism effective. Poverty makes voters more responsive to clientelistic benefits, given diminishing marginal utility of income; when poverty declines, vote buying becomes more expensive, increasing the incentives of brokers to divert income to other purposes. Finally, the informational asymmetries that characterize relations between party leaders and their intermediaries imply that in evaluating brokers, party leaders may substitute observable metrics, such as the size of brokers' local networks, for unobservables, such as the extent to which brokers target and persuade swing voters. However, the use of such metrics may increase incentives for brokers to build large networks by mobilizing lots of "cheap" loyal voters, which makes clientelism as a whole a not-fully-effective form of distributive politics, and it undercuts a basic rationale for the existence of brokers – because their superior local information should, in principle, allow them to target individual swing voters. Party leaders should well understand these difficulties. At high enough levels of rent seeking and inefficient targeting, leaders might be willing to do away with the machine and switch to more universalistic forms of social-service provision.

The analysis in this chapter highlights the fact that unmediated spending involves another kind of electoral "waste." Because every voter in a particular group receives the subsidy for which he or she is eligible – regardless of political ideology or affiliation – the ability to target swing voters with such spending may be even weaker than under clientelism. To make unmediated transfers "pay" politically as well as clientelism does, every voter in each group (here, poor, middle income, or rich) must be paid enough so as to make the most expensive "swing voter" bought under clientelism also willing to vote for the party if given unmediated transfers. This result implies that group-based unmediated spending can be an expensive form of distributive politics.[35] Still, if clientelism involves enough waste by brokers or enough inefficiencies in targeting, transitions to group-based targeting can be attractive. Moreover, if parties can target relatively narrow or well-defined groups of voters, leaders may happily slough off their machines and adopt unmediated distributive strategies. For instance, this would be the case if swing voters can be readily identified on the basis of some geographic or other attribute and then given group-based transfers. Another possibility – not explored in this theoretical chapter but implied by the analysis – is that, in light of the brokers' extraction of substantial funds in the form of rents under clientelism, transfers made through a universal welfare state win greater support from nonbeneficiaries than they do when made through clientelism.

In sum, transitioning from clientelism to unmediated distribution cuts out the middle man – the broker or electoral "agent." This shift eliminates the rents captured by the broker. It also eliminates payments to loyal voters by brokers, payments that are electorally suboptimal for party leaders. Yet unmediated distribution also carries political costs. Gaining greater theoretical understanding about when the costs of clientelism may outweigh its benefits, thus heightening incentives to transition to other forms of distributive politics, has been the goal of this chapter.

Perhaps the key theoretical move here is simply to highlight the importance of principal-agent problems in the relations between party leaders and brokers. Indeed, our analysis suggests that leaders tolerate their electoral agents with

---

[35] There are a number of further normative as well as positive implications of this analysis. For example, notice that according our analysis, unmediated transfers lead to benefits for more people in a group. This has important implications. Suppose that the poor are to be targeted under both clientelism and under universalism. The analysis suggests that as a group, they will receive more under universalism. We investigate the positive implications of this observation in subsequent empirical chapters, and we reflect on the normative implications in Chapter 9.

some distaste; when underlying conditions become less favorable to clientelism, we might expect party leaders to hasten transitions to other forms of distributive politics. We investigate exactly this interpretation of the demise of clientelism – as an attack by leaders against the power of their inefficient brokers – in the next chapter and also evaluate the comparative statics predictions developed in this chapter.

Testing the ideas presented in this chapter is very far from straightforward. As we move from the micro to the macro realms, the questions become even bigger; the concepts fuzzier and more difficult to operationalize and measure, and the counterfactuals more challenging to evaluate. To mention but a few of the difficulties: (1) the size of rents extracted by brokers is typically unobservable in a systematic way, as is the value brokers place on winning office relative to rent extraction; (2) measures of the efficacy of clientelism (i.e., η in our model) or the weight voters place on benefits relative to ideology (i.e., κ) are similarly difficult to discern; and (3) for well-known reasons, the causal impact of factors that may shape the efficacy of clientelism is especially challenging to infer.[36] Moreover, the processes through which clientelist or programmatic forms of political competition and benefit provision are "chosen" can unfold over relatively long periods of time. Thus the impact of variables such as industrialization or economic growth may have a cumulative influence on leaders' incentives and (for example) undermine the attractiveness of clientelism relative to programmatic strategies, yet those impacts may be felt over a relatively long time period, and it is not clear as an a priori matter when a given degree of industrialization should cumulate enough to tip the balance from one strategy to another. This does not gainsay the theoretical usefulness of models of strategic choice that analyze sharp tradeoffs between menus of options, such as the model we have analyzed. It does suggest that moving from theory to testing is not going to be clear-cut in this more macro area. The challenges involved in operationalizing and measuring key variables, such as rent extraction by brokers or even vote buying itself, also imply that large-N cross-national empirical work (for instance, cross-national regression analysis) may not be the most suitable strategy for our research problem.[37]

In the next chapter, we opt instead for structured comparisons of two historical cases – Britain and the United States during the nineteenth and early twentieth centuries. These are cases in which clientelism, vote buying, and broker-mediated distribution were once rife but had largely dissipated by the end of the nineteenth century (Britain) or the mid-twentieth century (the United States). The causes of the decline in vote buying in these countries have been previously analyzed, and we draw extensively on this secondary literature. Our

---

[36] For instance, although industrialization may shape the costs of communication or the size of the population, these latter factors may in turn spur industrialization and economic growth.

[37] Measurement of the key variables is only one of the major difficulties that may arise in cross-national regression analysis, of course; confounding by unobserved heterogeneity is another.

theoretical focus in this chapter on the potential inefficiencies of vote buying and on the advantages of programmatic strategies – and in particular on
how industrialization and associated changes such as population growth and
declining communication costs can increase the costs of clientelism as well as
the benefits of alternative modes of persuasion and mobilization – brings new
understanding of these historical cases. In particular, our focus on the tension
between party leaders and brokers focuses our attention on how the intra-
party dynamics of reform shaped inter-party agreements to reform the political
system. Thus although much previous scholarship has focused on campaigns
by outsiders and reformers in hastening the decline of electoral corruption
and machine politics (and justifiably so, given their clearly important role), we
argue that the transition from clientelism cannot be understood without understanding how social and economic changes altered the incentives of political
leaders, as well as their capacities to shift away from a clientelist equilibrium.
Although the British and U.S. cases demonstrate many similarities, important
differences in their historical trajectories and in the timing of the transition
from clientelism help us to test as well as to further refine the theory.

The strength of our within-case analyses is that they allow us to assess
key elements of our theory – especially the ways in which tensions between
party leaders and brokers over distributive strategies are apparent, and also
how economic and social changes affect those tensions. Still, our comparative
case-study strategy coupled with extensive within-case analysis is not without
substantial inferential perils. Perhaps most importantly, assessing the causal
impact of changes such as industrialization is challenging, for the reasons signaled earlier, and within cases, many factors change over time that may also
affect the outcomes of interest. The evidence presented and conclusions reached
in Chapters 8 and 9 are therefore necessarily tentative. Nonetheless, even if this
evidence does not permit complete testing of our theory, it does suggest the usefulness of our focus on leaders and brokers. Clientelism does not always emerge
or persist because of the wishes of political leaders alone, and when it dies, it
often does so in part as a result of leaders moving against the machine.

8

What Killed Vote Buying in Britain and the United States?

8.1 INTRODUCTION

In nineteenth-century Britain and the United States, vote buying was commonplace. Parties gave voters cash, food, alcohol, health care, poverty relief, and myriad other benefits in exchange for their votes. To gain leverage over them, parties gathered information about voters' debts, their crimes, even their infidelities.

Today, these forms of distributive politics have basically disappeared from both countries, as they have from most other advanced democracies where they once were practiced. Although money shapes politics in twenty-first-century Britain and even more so in the United States, the practices of clientelism have virtually disappeared. The details of electoral corruption in nineteenth-century Britain and America therefore have a startling feel today. Consider some examples:

- A commission on electoral bribery reported to the House of Commons in 1835 that, in Stafford, £14 were paid per vote cast in a hotly contested election. Polling proceeded over several days, and electors were called to cast their vote in alphabetical order. Those with surnames beginning with A's and B's didn't get much for their votes, "but if the polling lasted two days, the names which began with an S or a W were of the greatest value."[1] "At Leicester," also in 1835, "as soon as the canvass began public houses were opened by each party in the various villages near the borough. The voters were collected as soon as possible, generally locked up until the polling, and according to an election agent, [they were] 'pretty well corned.'"[2]

---

[1] Seymour 1970[1915], p. 172.
[2] Seymour 1970[1915], p. 173.

- Across the Atlantic Ocean, a party official in Newark, New Jersey, offered the following description of Election Day, 1888:

  "[A] room is secured, generally in the rear of a saloon ... At this precinct there are a half-dozen men located outside with a pocketful of brass checks ... When a floater comes along, the outside agents simply make a bargain with him. If the price is $2, they simply give him 2 checks ... The purchaser sees that the man votes right and tells him to see John Jones in the room at the back of the saloon ... The voter has simply to get his check cashed."[3]

- In addition to giving out cash on or around Election Day and to treating voters with food and alcohol, British and American parties also secured votes by providing a range of services and assistance, and not just in the brief time before elections but continuously. Like the Tammany Democratic machine, with its emergency relief services, British election agents worked in parallel with religious and charitable organizations to offer voters social insurance. Hence:

  In corporation towns the distribution of charities was an efficacious means of winning votes. In Bristol the control of such distribution was vested entirely in the hands of the Conservatives and formed a ready means of influencing the votes of the poorer classes, as were the Christmas gifts distributed by church wardens and vestries. At Coventry the use of Bablake Hospital was granted only to those electors who had voted in the interest of the Liberal Corporation which controlled it. If an impecunious voter applied for assistance from a poor-law board, instead of retailing the size of his family and the misfortunes which had fallen upon his work, he found it more worth while to begin his plea by stating the colour of his politics.[4]

What, then, killed vote buying in Britain and the United States? The explanation we offer in this chapter focuses on changes in the electorate, changes that were the effects of industrialization and economic growth. We show that industrialization in both countries increased the size and average income of the electorate, made it harder for parties to discern people's votes and monitor their electoral behavior, and reduced the costs of direct communication between candidates and voters, allowing candidates to circumvent brokers. Given the conflicts between leaders and brokers – an unavoidable result of the imperfect agency that brokers rendered to leaders – under changed circumstances, leaders were only too happy to slough off their machines.

Industrialization and economic growth eventually spelled the demise of clientelism in both countries. However, it lingered longer and persisted at higher levels of economic development in the United States. One gets a sense both of the overall decline in both countries and of the longer persistence in the U.S. by comparing the numbers of legal claims of fraudulent elections to the House of Commons and the House of Representatives. In both countries, losing candidates who believed the election had been flawed had formal

---

[3] Reynolds 1988, p. 54.
[4] Seymour 1970[1915], p. 179; this comes from a report from 1835.

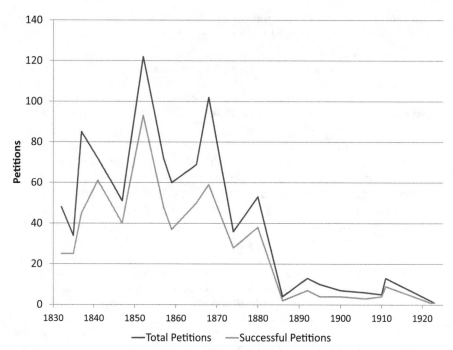

FIGURE 8.1. Petitions Challenging Elections to British House of Commons, 1832–1923. *Source:* Data are from Seymour 1915 and O'Leary 1962.

redress.[5] Figure 8.1 displays the number of petitions claiming fraudulent elections in the U.K. Figure 8.2 displays petitions as a percentage of the total number of seats in the House of Commons (which varied between 658 and 670 throughout this period). Petitions were at their height in the mid-nineteenth century. They declined to a degree after the introduction of the secret ballot in 1872. But they declined more definitively after key electoral reforms passed in the early 1880s. During the remaining years of the nineteenth century, and with the dawn of the twentieth century, accusations of vote buying virtually disappeared.

In some ways the history of electoral challenges in U.S. House elections, displayed in Figures 8.3 and 8.4, tells a similar story – from relatively high levels in the mid-to-late nineteenth century followed by steep decline.[6] The difference lies in the early decades of the twentieth century: whereas petitions

[5] The legal procedures were instituted in the House of Commons as part of the Great Reform Act of 1832. In the U.S. they had existed on an ad hoc basis since the first Congress and were formalized and regularized in 1851. See Seymour 1915 for the history of the procedures in Britain and Jenkins 2004 and Kuo et al. 2011 in the United States.

[6] Figures 8.3 and 8.4 include information from Jenkins 2004. His counts of contested elections, though not historical trends, are slightly different from those found in Kuo et al. 2011.

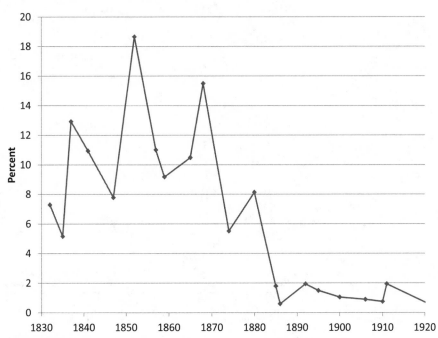

FIGURE 8.2. Petitions Challenging British Elections, as Percentage of Total Members of Parliament, 1832–1923. *Source:* Data are from Seymour 1915 and from O'Leary 1962.

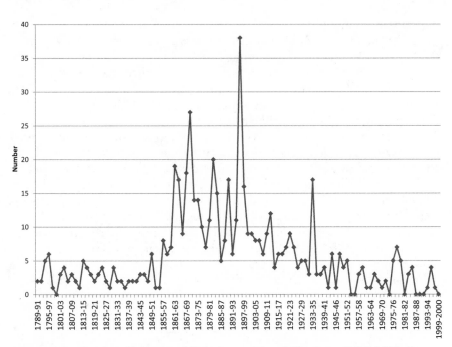

FIGURE 8.3. Number of Contested U.S. Congressional Elections, 1789–2000. *Source:* Data are from Jenkins 2004.

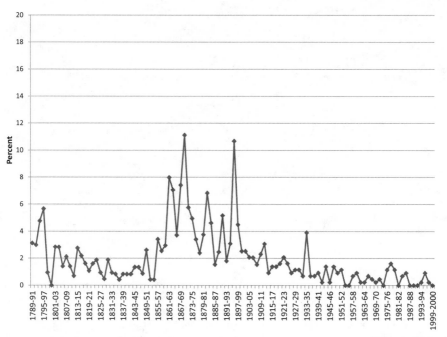

FIGURE 8.4. Contested U.S. Congressional Elections as a Percentage of Total Seats, 1789–2000. *Source:* Data are from Jenkins 2004.

basically ended in the U.K. before the First World War, challenges persisted in the United States right through the Progressive Era and into the early years of the New Deal.

A few vote-buying machines persisted in the United States well into the twentieth century. One was Louisiana's Plaquemines Parish machine, headed by Leander Perez, whereby voters were still in the 1950s and 1960s routinely paid a few dollars for their votes.[7] Even if out-and-out vote buying was anachronistic in the post–World War II period, if the secondary literature is any guide nonprogrammatic distribution persists to this day in the United States. Studies of the United States cited in earlier chapters uncovered biased distribution of federal dollars to states and of state dollars to counties and to state-assembly districts, both for public spending projects (pork) and for targeted benefits (nonconditional benefits to individuals). By contrast, we are aware of only one study that reveals nonprogrammatic distribution in the U.K., in the allocation of government grants to local authorities.[8] Even this study does not point toward consistent or glaring use of such strategies.

[7] Jeansonne 1977.
[8] See John and Ward 2001.

With only two national cases to compare, we cannot definitively adjudicate among several plausible explanations for the quicker and more definitive demise of British clientelism. It may be linked to differences in the nature of electorates of the two countries. Nineteenth-century America featured immigrants who lived in ethnically distinctive urban communities, had considerable unmet economic and social needs, and were rapidly incorporated into the electorate. Urban machines flourished in immigrant communities. However, we – like some contemporary observers in the United States – are also struck by sharp differences in the two countries' institutional settings. The demise of electoral corruption was hastened in Britain, as we shall see, by effective anticorruption legislation. The career of this sort of legislation in the United States was uneven. The federal structure of the American government and the rise of powerful statewide party organizations were barriers to antimachine reforms. State parties channeled substantial financial resources into campaigns, whereas campaigns were largely self-financed by candidates in the U.K., giving politicians an incentive to pursue reforms that would limit expenditures on electoral agents. American statewide parties also coordinated many campaigns at several levels of government, both primary and general elections, many of them beyond the jurisdiction of Congress. With resistance from machine bosses and, in some cases, from the courts, the U.S. Congress could not at a blow kill vote buying by placing tight regulations on campaign spending. In 1883, the British House of Commons did exactly that.

That said, the same intra-party dynamics drove electoral reform in the two industrializing countries. Party leaders – Tories and Liberals, Democrats and Republicans – saw a common interest in attacking their own election agents and machines. About the U.S. states' late nineteenth-century adoption of the government-produced or "official" ballot, Reynolds wrote, "Assisted by the reformers, the Democratic and Republican leadership used the official ballot to wrest control over the election from the hands of machine operatives."[9] Ballot reform, like other anticorruption measures, was not simply a byproduct of Mugwump and progressive reformers, as is commonly supposed. Reformers could not have succeeded had they not entered into an implicit alliance with party leaders. Leaders were centrally driven by a desire to eliminate the "treachery" regularly committed against them by local machines.

To the reformers the machine meant venality, corruption, and bribery; its unprincipled minions controlled the machinery of elections, demanded and misspent great sums of cash, and stood in the way of honest balloting. *To the partisan leaders the local machine*

---

[9] Reynolds 1988, p. 49. Pressure for civil-service reform in late nineteenth-century America also emanated in part from party leaders, including presidents, who viewed reform as promising "to rebuild the autonomy and prestige of their offices" (Skowronek 1982, p. 55). Skowronek also noted, however, that presidents and other party leaders who claimed to oppose patronage sometimes were simply in an internal power struggle to control it.

was a source of insubordination and untrustworthiness – an increasingly expensive and unwieldy instrument for carrying out the will of the true party organization.[10]

Intra-party conflict between leaders and brokers also drove reform in Britain. Conservative and Liberal leaders were aligned in their hostility toward their electoral intermediaries. As O'Leary explained, the "desire to wipe out the tribe of electioneering parasites . . . proved to be a common goal transcending party differences," which explains the "surprising degree of accord between the leaders of the [Liberal and Conservative] parties during the debates between 1880 and 1883."[11]

Although party leaders in both countries came to view themselves as better off without brokers, any individual's use of bribery to win elections could stymie legislative action.[12] The historian Charles Seymour captured well the collective desire to eliminate vote buying and how it could be quashed by individual Members of Parliament's incentives to defect. In the early decades after the Great Reform Act of 1832, MPs viewed themselves as in peril of losing office should they support the reforms needed to end electoral bribery.

The average member [of the House of Commons] might really prefer a free election; bribery meant expense, and it meant that the skill of the election agent was trusted as more efficacious than the candidate's native powers, an admission that few members liked to make. But there was always a modicum of candidates who preferred to insure their seats by a liberal scattering of gold; in self-protection the others must place themselves in the hands of their agents, thus tacitly accepting, if not approving, corrupt work.[13]

In Britain, after changes wrought by industrialization had eroded the electoral benefits from a "liberal scattering of gold," these obstacles were more easily overcome.

In the United States, legislators had to clear these obstacles to collective action many times over, in the 48 states. States adopted reforms, rejected them, and saw them tested by state and federal judges. Congress tried to regulate elections of their members and sometimes found themselves thwarted by internal dissent or by the courts. Although these complex processes ran their course, in the meantime, state and national political committees became coordinators of myriad campaigns and funnels for money that ran from the trust – banks, insurance companies, manufacturers, corporations – to statewide parties and to city machines.

Many American political leaders took inspiration from the British Anti-Corrupt Practices Act of 1883. However, as Sikes explained, the simple solution of limiting candidates' own expenditures was impotent in the American setting:

[10] Reynolds and McCormick 1986, p. 851, emphasis added.

[11] O'Leary 1962, p. 229.

[12] Camp 2010 explains how obstacles to collective action can interfere with brokers' incentives to work for their parties.

[13] Seymour 1970[1915], p. 199.

To control by law a candidate for parliament who personally or by his agent manages his own campaign, and whose canvass is distinct by itself is a comparatively simple matter. To deal with a dozen or more candidates, all running for office at the same time on a party ticket and voted for within the same election district, none of whom may have anything to do with the actual conduct of the campaign, is a task of much greater complexity . . . [14]

That American party committees, not candidates, were responsible for the "actual conduct of campaigns" extended to the financing of campaigns as well. Corporate finance of campaigns was a post–Civil War phenomenon but became regularized and systematic in the late 1890s.[15] British candidates' mistrust of their election agents was especially bitter, given that the funds used for bribing and treating frequently came out of the candidates' own pockets. Given the generous corporate monies available to parties, the incentive for reform was weaker in the United States.

Our explanation for the contrasting pace of the emergence of programmatic politics in these two countries contrasts with Shefter's influential account.[16] Late nineteenth-century Britain, in Shefter's view, represented a case in which an entrenched politics of patronage was avoided. Constituencies for universalism arose within both Liberal and Conservative parties before each took on the task of mobilizing popular electoral support. The United States presents a more complicated panorama. The Western states were like Britain and staved off patronage politics; the Eastern states combined early mass democracy and late constituencies for universalism and hence became persistently patronagebound.[17] The crux of the difference between Britain and the Eastern United States, in Shefter's account, is the early onset of American mass democracy, and hence American parties' habituation to patronage politics before an effective constituency against it took shape.[18] "One strongly suspects that had universal suffrage been adopted in England prior to the formation of a constituency for

---

[14] Sikes 1928, p. 125.

[15] See Mayhew 1986 and Mutch 1988.

[16] Shefter 1977, 1994. The explanandum of Shefter's study and ours are not identical. Although his "universalism" is like our programmatic politics, he is focused on the use of public employment as an electoral tool, whereas our focus is on clientelism and vote buying, of which patronage may be a sub-category. It is tempting to try to rectify the two accounts by pointing out that civil service positions in Britain were coveted by aristocratic and bourgeoise families, so that it is natural to consider a "constituency for universalism" centrally involving Oxbridge-educated men of the landed and mercantile classes. In contrast, our more central focus on flows of smaller benefits and assistance would naturally entail struggles among party actors trying to entice middling and low-income voters.

[17] Mayhew 1986 offered a more nuanced geography of patronage-prone states, or ones in which the parties maintain "traditional party organizations." These include northeastern and mid-Atlantic states, but also several midwestern ones.

[18] Or, more precisely, American parties in the East.

bureaucratic autonomy the outcome of the struggle between the practition-
ers and opponents of patronage politics would have been quite different. In
that event Britain would have recapitulated the experience of the United States
during the Jacksonian Era."[19]

The vigor with which British parties used treats, bribes, and other nonuni-
versalist inducements to boost their vote tallies, going back – as we shall see –
at least to the Great Reform Act of 1832, leads us to doubt Shefter's account.
Well before universal suffrage, Liberal and Conservative candidates and their
agents were accustomed to competing by using particularistic blandishments.
The coalition that developed against patronage and electoral bribery in Britain
and the United States was comprised not of bureaucrats and the educated
middle classes who favored meritocracy so much as between reformists and
party leaders, the latter chafing under their own machines. Their motivation
was not to preserve the civil service for their elite-educated sons but to circumvent unreliable brokers. If there was a critical moment at which the two
countries' experiences diverged, it was with the American party leaders' failure to institutionalize universalism before the parties became too complex, the
campaigns they ran too multicandidate and multilevel, and before campaign
funding became too plentiful to be easily controlled by reformers. Yet these
"failures" were in a sense constitutional, reflecting a highly federalized system
of government, independent state parties, and a central government hemmed
in both by state governments and by the courts.

8.2 BRITAIN

Reviewing the historiography about Victorian politics in Britain, it is hard not
to be struck by the very deep tensions that frequently afflicted the relationship between leaders and brokers. These conflicts are rendered vividly in the
period's political fiction. The rapacious and unreliable electoral agent was a
frequent figure in the Victorian novel. Some of the darkest accounts come from
writers with personal experiences as candidates. Anthony Trollope drew on his
experience as a Liberal candidate for the corrupt district of Beverly in 1868
for his 1871 political novel *Ralph the Heir*. And Trollope's character George
Vavasor, in his 1865 novel *Can You Forgive Her*, was bled to the point of
bankruptcy by his electoral agent.

Why did clientelism as practiced by these fictional agents and their flesh-and-
blood counterparts not survive to the end of the Victorian era? In what follows,
we first discuss the rise and decline of electoral corruption in nineteenth-century
Britain, with its notable drop-off in the last two decades of the century. On
average, 67 formal charges of electoral corruption followed each election that
took place between 1832 through 1880. Between 1885 and 1900, the average
fell to nine. We then explore the conditions that encouraged this decline. These

[19] Shefter 1977, p. 441.

include the growth and (eventually) growing affluence of the electorate, as well as the increasing opacity of electoral choices and politicians' easier access to mass communications at the end of the century. These shifts changed the calculations of politicians, who for many decades had chafed under the burden of their brokers and electoral agents. Political leaders later passed legislation – some of it measures that had been proposed earlier but failed – that further increased the opacity of the vote, regulated levels of campaign spending, and drove up the risks and costs for candidates who were caught, or whose agents were caught, buying votes.

Our focus on industrialization as the unmoved mover of political change echoes earlier accounts of nineteenth-century democratization and of the crystallization of party voting in the British electorate.[20] Our topic is not entirely unrelated to these, though here democratization lies not in the expansion of the franchise but in its increasingly free exercise. Also, our concern is less with the rise of parties than with a profound shift in their manner of eliciting voters' support. Yet rather than gesturing toward social pressure from below as the link between industrialization and democratization, or noting the inefficiency of private members' bills in a dynamic, industrializing economy, our account shifts the focus to intraparty conflict. Industrial-era changes eventually resolved this conflict against electoral agents and in favor of programmatic politics.

8.2.1 The Timing of the Decline of Clientelism in Britain

It is inevitable that the voters should be influenced in some manner or other. The flexibility of political influence is well known; at one time it is embodied in patent, flagrant, and unashamed corruption; under different conditions it becomes insidious and impalpable. In earlier days a constituency was purchased like a church living or an army commission. It was the property of the buyer . . . Such customs fell into disuse with the passage of time, and individual voters were bought with money or presents. Then instead of purchasing individuals the candidate bought whole communities, by entertainments and picnics. The step between this stage and that in which classes and trades are won by promises of legislation is not very broad.

– Charles Seymour, Electoral Reform in England and Wales[21]

To work out the timing of Seymour's sequence from individual vote buying and treating to electoral promises made to "classes and trades," it is helpful look to the frequency of reports of bribery and petitions and to the prominence of party manifestos and campaign statements.

In the late eighteenth century, the out-and-out purchasing of votes, commonly referred to in Britain as electoral bribery, was relatively less important

---

[20] Acemoglu and Robinson 2006 also connected the expansion of the franchise in nineteenth-century Britain to industrialization, but their explanation underscores the creation of popular pressure and social movements. Cox 1987 explained the emergence of the cabinet and parties as the end result of industrial growth.

[21] Seymour 1970[1915], p. 453.

than was the "insidious and impalpable" influence on electoral choices exercised by landowners, notables, and employers over people who depended on
them.[22] In the views of contemporaries, the Great Reform Act of 1832 encouraged a shift from influence to bribery. Viscount Palmerston lamented in 1839
that "the extent to which bribery and corruption was carried at the last election,
has exceeded anything that has ever been stated within these walls." Seymour
concurs:

> Before 1832 the great lords had, with few exceptions, complete control of the small
> boroughs . . . But after the Reform Act the patrons lost their control to a large extent
> and must strain every nerve to influence the election; where they had before com-
> manded, now they must buy. The close boroughs had been opened and instead of a
> corrupt corporation there was a numerous electorate, composed often of persons whose
> circumstances laid them open to temptation.[23]

The reform made it "necessary for the ambitious rich who desired to buy seats
in parliament to purchase, not the borough itself, but the voters."[24]

Note the allusion here to the short-run effect of the expanded franchise: it
drove down the median income of the electorate. Newly expanded to include
leaseholders in the counties, this more "numerous electorate" was now – in contrast to before the reform – composed of a greater number of "persons whose
circumstances laid them open to temptation." Franchise-expanding reforms,
then, made vote buying a more attractive strategy; only long-run economic
development would improve the material conditions of the electorate and drive
down the numbers of voters for whom the treat or access to poor relief was
worth the sale of his vote.

The heyday of "patent, flagrant, and unashamed" electoral corruption was
the half century after the Great Reform Act of 1832. The Great Reform Act's
extension of the franchise and retention of the rights of freemen gave candidates
and their agents the incentive and additional means to manipulate the vote. The
1832 reform also established electoral registries for the first time. In its wake,
registration societies appeared throughout the land. Lawyers attached to these
societies helped register voters and also specialized in the competitive effort
to strike voters from the lists. These lawyers were the precursors to electoral
agents, the registration societies the precursors to the Liberal and Conservative
party associations.[25]

There is broad agreement that vote buying became widespread after 1832
and declined sharply in the late 1880s. During the remaining years of the
nineteenth century, and with the dawn of the twentieth century, accusations
of vote buying fell to a trickle. Figures 8.1 and 8.2 suggest a structural shift

---

[22] O'Gorman 1989.

[23] Seymour 1970[1915], p. 170. For more recent accounts of the Great Reform Act see Smith
2004, and Salmon 2003. Scott 1969 outlines a similar sequence, though in more abstract terms,
from votes that were commanded to votes that had to be purchased.

[24] Seymour 1970[1915], p. 196. Orr's (2006) assessment is similar.

[25] See the discussion in O'Leary 1962, p. 16 and passim.

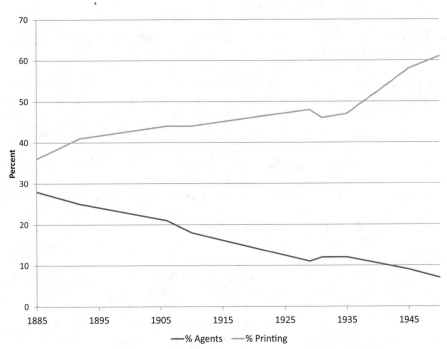

FIGURE 8.5. Trends in British Campaign Spending on Agents and Printing, 1885–1960. *Source:* Data are from Craig 1989.

in the late 1880s, from relatively high (though varying) to fairly insignificant numbers of accusations thereafter. A 1906 petition accusing a candidate of bribery and the subsequent appointment of a royal investigatory commission provoked much discussion; two generations earlier, such accusations had been routine.[26] In 1911, the election court heard petitions of alleged corruption in an Irish constituency. Other such cases followed, very intermittently, in subsequent decades. When a case came before election judges in 2010, many educated Britons were unaware of the court's existence.[27]

If the decline in accusations of bribery reflected a real shift away from broker-mediated distribution and toward programmatic politics, we would expect to find changes in the composition of campaign expenditures in the late nineteenth century, away from agents and toward direct communications by leaders. Indeed, campaigners' official reports, compiled by Craig, show a secular shift, beginning in the 1880s (see Figure 8.5).[28] The electoral agent received

[26] Seymour 1970[1915], pp. 448–450.

[27] During the 2010 general election campaign, the Labour Party candidate from Oldham East and Saddleworth accused his Liberal Democratic rival of taking illegal foreign donations and being sponsored by "extremists." The Labour candidate won the election. The Liberal Democrat brought a petition to the election court, claiming that his opponent had made false statements about him; the court ordered a new election. In this case, the allegation was not of bribery but of libel.

[28] Craig 1989.

ever-smaller shares. Expenditures on agents fell from nearly 30 percent in 1885 to less than 10 percent a half-century later. Expenditures on printing rose steadily, by World War II amounting to £6 of every £10 spent.

Well before World War II, in the final decades of the Victorian era, electioneering increasingly involved public pronouncements of campaign pledges, reported through a much-enlarged printed press. William Gladstone's later career embodies both trends. His "chief electoral device" became in the late 1870s "the active mobilization of public opinion behind a clearly articulated set of proposals"[29] – articulated, what's more, in the setting of the mass rally and in the context of a burgeoning newspaper culture. Gladstone's soaring speeches in the 1879 Midlothian campaign had as an intended audience not just the many people who were physically present but also reporters from news agencies such as the *Exchange Telegraph*. With little interest in party bureaucracies, indeed aloof even from his parliamentary party, Gladstone "depended upon words – and increasingly upon words reported in the press – to achieve high political visibility."[30]

By the 1880s, party leaders understood the increasing power of direct communications with voters and the shrinking space for the treat or the bribe. In the debates leading to the passage of the crucial 1883 Corrupt and Illegal Practices Act, some Conservative back-benchers objected to the bill's proposed campaign spending limits. The Tory leader John Gorst countered that expenditures need not be high: "All that was really required was that the constituencies should have the means of amply being informed, or informing themselves, of the character, qualifications and political views of the candidates."[31]

8.2.2 Industrialization and the Decline of Clientelism in Britain

"By the second quarter of the nineteenth century Britain had become the home of the first urban industrialized economy in the modern world" writes Hoppen. Although he and other historians of this period have found economic growth rates less impressive, on revision, than the term "industrial revolution" might suggest, still the change was revolutionary in that its "effects were sustained."[32] Industrialization in Britain set off a series of crucial transformations in the electorate. The electorate became more numerous. Industrialization made British society and, in a less linear way, the British electorate, wealthier. The electorate became more urban and hence more anonymous. Industrialization made Britain a society in which ambitious politicians could communicate directly with mass constituencies. All of these changes eroded the effectiveness of the electoral agent, with his treat and his bribe. Ultimately, a larger and

---

[29] Hoppen 2000, p. 592.
[30] Hoppen 2000, p. 633, see also Jenkins 2002.
[31] Hansard April 27, 1882, cclxviii, cited in O'Leary 1962, p. 165.
[32] Hoppen 2000, p. 276.

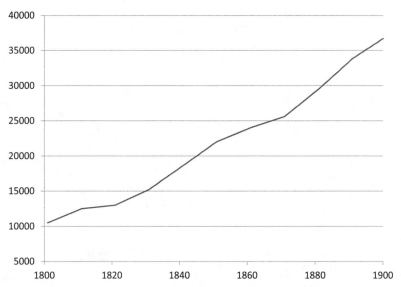

FIGURE 8.6. Population of Britain, 1800–1900 (1,000s). *Source:* Data are from Jeffries 2005.

more urban electorate and one populated by relatively fewer poor people made bribery less attractive to office seekers than were programmatic appeals.

A Larger Electorate

Contrary to Malthusian predictions, Britain in the nineteenth century experienced, simultaneously, considerable economic growth and considerable population growth. The population rose from about 8 million in 1801 to more than 30 million a century later (see Figure 8.6).[33] In part simply as a reflection of population growth, the size of the electorate in Victorian Britain exploded (see Figure 8.7). However, this mechanical effect was overshadowed by political change: successive new categories of men were given the right to vote. Extensions of the franchise meant that growth of the electorate outpaced that of the broader population. Although the population grew by a factor of three, the electorate grew by a factor of nine: from 435,000 in 1830 to 4.4 million in 1888. Much of this growth came in spurts around the electoral reforms. The electorate was 49 percent larger in 1833 than in 1831, an increase due almost entirely to the Great Reform Act of 1832. It grew by 88 percent in the years surrounding the Reform Act of 1867, by 67 percent in the years surrounding the 1883 reform.[34] Both population growth and pressure to expand the franchise were traceable, in part, to industrialization.

---

[33] Population statistics are from Jeffries 2005.
[34] Seymour 1970[1915], Appendix 1, p. 533.

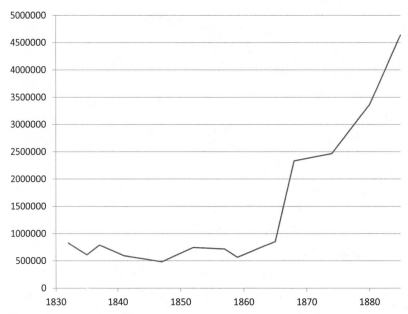

FIGURE 8.7. Votes Cast in British Parliamentary Elections, 1832–1923. *Source:* Data are from Craig 1989.

Just as important as a more numerous total electorate was the larger size of constituencies. The reform of 1832 took representation in Westminster away from many small, rotten, and pocket boroughs and redistributed their seats to larger boroughs such as in the Midlands, Lancashire, and Yorkshire, which, with the growth of industry, had gained in importance, though not to that point in political representation. The redistribution (what Americans would call "redistricting") of 1867–1868 under Disraeli entirely disenfranchised seven towns with populations of less than 5,000 and shifted 35 seats away from towns with populations of less than 10,000. The redistribution of 1885 under Gladstone increased the number of seats in the industrial centers of Manchester, Sheffield, Birmingham, and Liverpool. Figure 8.8 displays the average number of votes cast per member of parliament. The figure reveals a strong upward trend, beginning in the 1870s.

Several authors have drawn connections between the size of the electorate as a whole, the size of borough constituencies (especially in the industrializing north), and the decline of bribery and patronage. Indeed, a central justification for reforming the constituencies was that larger districts would undercut corrupt practices. Recent studies as well attribute cleaner elections in late compared with early Victorian Britain to the larger constituencies. In the era of mass constituencies, O'Leary contended, "the cost of electioneering on the old lines would be quite prohibitive" – the old lines being through electoral agents

FIGURE 8.8. Votes Cast per Member of the House of Commons, 1832–1918. *Source:* Data are from Craig 1989.

who engaged in treating, bribing, and intimidation.[35] Regarding patronage, O'Gorman wrote:

[E]ven before 1832 the number of electors was already so great as to render patronage in many constituencies of little consequence. Perhaps in the closed boroughs ... patronage might have been an effective instrument of political control, but even in these places it was far from being an adequate and reliable method of controlling a parliamentary constituency.[36]

Cox also noted the reduced attractiveness of electoral bribery in larger constituencies:

Certainly a fixed amount of money would buy a smaller proportion of total votes in larger towns if the average price of votes was not less. Even if the price of votes was less (in proportion to the greater number of voters) ... the costs of arranging to bribe many more electors, not to mention the increased risk of being caught, made bribery a less attractive electoral option ... In contrast, a given policy promise – to disestablish the Irish church, for example – would almost certainly appeal to a larger number of voters in larger towns and may have appealed to a larger proportion. One suspects therefore that candidates in the larger and more independent boroughs engaged in the politics

[35] O'Leary 1962, p. 231.
[36] O'Gorman 2001, p. 67.

FIGURE 8.9. Campaign Expenditures per Voter in Britain, 1857–1959. *Source:* Data are from Craig 1989.

of opinion more thoroughly than their colleagues in the smaller towns because it made more electoral sense to do so.[37]

These are astute interpretations and they arrive at the right basic conclusion: larger constituencies made patronage and vote buying less attractive. What Cox in particular hinted at, without quite enunciating, is that as constituencies grew, the unit cost of votes declined, when elicited through programmatic appeals. In contrast – as we have suggested – the monitoring and delivery roles that must be carried out by brokers, and hence the party's dense organizational structure, meant that economies of scale are basically absent in clientelist politics. Not just "arranging to bribe" but holding the bribe's recipient to account was a costly matter, one that was labor-intensive, requiring close and continuous contact between large numbers of electoral agents and individual voters. When the national electorate and local constituencies grew, party programs and print appeals became well worth the investment they required.

If these arguments are correct, as parties shifted from clientelism to programmatic strategies, we should observe a fall in the per-vote cost of campaigning. And indeed a sharp decline did occur in Britain. Figure 8.9 displays the total amounts spent by candidates, divided by the number of votes cast, across all

[37] Cox 1987, p. 57.

elections in which candidates reported expenditures and in which most constituencies were contested.[38] Beginning in 1857, candidates were required to
make detailed reports of campaign spending to election auditors. Because of
unreported expenditures on bribery, the figures for 1857–1885 understate the
levels of spending; the downward trend in reality would have been even steeper
than it appears in the figure. The Corrupt and Illegal Practices Act of 1883
imposed spending limits and tightened reporting procedures. Therefore, the
figures beginning with the 1885 election are more reliable.

Figure 8.9 reveals a marked decline in campaign expenditures per vote cast.
Expenditures in 1900 were about one-quarter, on a per-vote basis, of what
they had been at their peak in the mid-nineteenth century.

Certainly machine politics survives in very large electorates. Rather than
automatically ending clientelist strategies, increasingly populous electorates
are one factor that tends to drive up the relative implicit price of votes acquired
through bribery and hence to make programmatic politics more attractive.

A Wealthier Electorate

Chapter 6 showed evidence that poor countries are prone to clientelism and
that poor people are prone to be clients. We noted that poor people are likely
to be driven to "vote for" immediate benefits, like a bag of food or some cash,
whereas wealthier people are more willing to cast expressive votes in favor
of their preferred candidates, parties, or programs. We now turn to evidence
that the British electorate eventually became wealthier and hence less "open to
temptation."

The poverty, unemployment, and squalor of the "slums" (a term first used in
this sense in the 1840s) conveyed by Charles Dickens, and the penury suffered
by dislocated agricultural workers depicted by Mary Gaskell, were essential
features of the Victorian period. Certainly poverty was widespread. Estimates
of the percentage of inhabitants whose family earnings at the end of the century
were insufficient to meet their basic needs ranged from 27 percent in York to
31 percent in London.[39] Yet notwithstanding rural displacement and urban
squalor, Britain became a significantly wealthier society in the nineteenth century. Output increased steadily over the century, though faster in some periods
than others. Income distribution was highly unequal: estimates put the Gini
index at 49 in 1867. Inequality did not in all respects follow a Kuznets trajectory. It did not increase in the early stages of industrialization, but it did
subside in the first decades of the twentieth century.[40] In addition, real wages in

---

[38] These elections are 1857, 1859, 1865, 1868, 1874, 1880, 1885, 1892, 1906, 1910, 1929,
1931, 1935, 1945, and 1950. Few candidates ran unopposed after 1918, but we include them
to follow the spending trend well into the period of programmatic strategies. Candidates who
ran unopposed spent almost nothing. Calculations are based on information in Craig 1989.

[39] Hoppen 2000, p. 62.

[40] See Lindert 2000, pp. 173–175. The change should not be overstated: Lindert reports Gini
estimates for England and Wales of 59.3 in 1801 and 49.0 in 1867. He shows that income

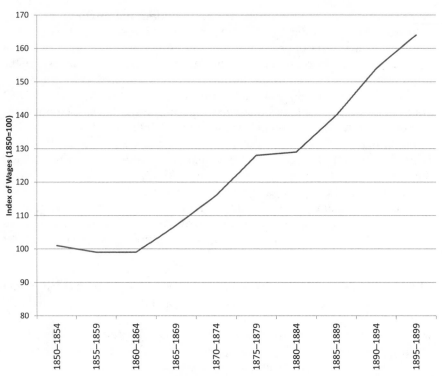

FIGURE 8.10. Real Wages in British Manufacturing, 1850–1899. *Source:* Hoppen 2000.

manufactures grew (see Figure 8.10). A mechanical effect of growing wealth of the general *population* would have been to reduce poverty rates and dependency in the *electorate*.

Economic growth also increased pressure to open the suffrage. Latter nineteenth-century electoral reforms nearly doubled the percentage of the adult male population entitled to vote, from 17 percent in 1861 to 30 percent in 1871, and doubled it again, to 61 percent in 1871, before finally reaching nearly 100 percent in 1918.[41] The short-term effect of suffrage-broadening reforms – in 1867 and 1885, more than in 1832 – was, however, to bring new strata of lower-income voters into the electorate. That the extension of the suffrage to poorer voters might encourage bribery was something that contemporaries warned of. In debates leading to the 1867 reform, which eventually established the household suffrage, nearly all predicted "an increase of electoral

---

inequality increased again between 1868 and 1911, but declined fairly steadily thereafter, until the 1960s.

[41] Hoppen 2000, p. 653.

corruption as a result of the extension of the franchise to the classes most open to temptation."[42]

The complexities of the evolving Victorian suffrage, and the shortcomings of statistics on poverty and incomes in the period, make precise estimates of the income structure of the electorate over time treacherous. It's difficult to know with precision at what point rising incomes in the population would have outpaced the reductions in average income of the electorate that resulted from successive expansions of the suffrage to the lower strata. We might stipulate that the short-term effect of expansions of the franchise in 1867 and in 1883 was to depress median incomes in the electorate faster than the offsetting rise in incomes in the general population boosted them. Still, the upward trend in the median income of the electorate would have become more pronounced than the downward one as the unenfranchised segment of the population became a smaller fraction of the whole. With universal suffrage – established in 1918[43] – income levels of the electorate came basically to reflect the income structure of the population. Even by the closing decades of the nineteenth century, the dominant trend was probably one of voting populations who were increasingly economically secure.

Changes in the structure of incomes in the twentieth century may help explain why the shift away from vote buying became permanent. From the end of the Great War until 1970, Britain experienced a sustained (and well-documented) shift toward greater equality of income distribution.[44] It also became an affluent country. Hence, as a long-run effect of changes that began in the latter Victorian era, a more prosperous electorate made vote buying a less tempting strategy for office seekers.

A Less Discernible Vote

In the first decades after the 1832 reform, small borough and county constituencies were places where electoral agents could closely monitor the actions of voters. The party association sent the agent out:

through the boroughs to discover the private circumstances of the voter and make use of any embarrassment as a club to influence votes. [Agents carried ledgers with] a space for special circumstances which might give an opportunity for political blackmail, such as debts, mortgages, need of money in trade, commercial relations, and even the most private domestic matters.[45]

As population flowed away from villages and small towns and into the larger manufacturing areas, fine-grained surveillance of voters became harder to carry out.

---

[42] Seymour 1970[1915], p. 277.
[43] Women were also enfranchised in 1918, but were subjected to property qualifications until 1928.
[44] Lindert 2000.
[45] Seymour 1970[1915], p. 184.

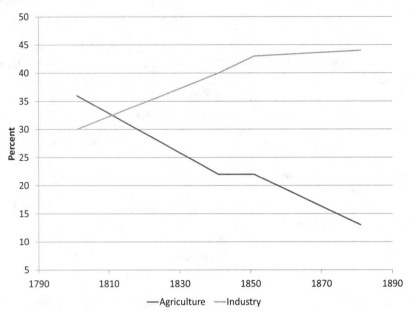

FIGURE 8.11. Proportions of British Labor Force in Agriculture and Industry, 1800–1880. *Source:* Data from Hoppen 2000.

Over the century, an ever-larger segment of the British population came to live in large towns and cities. Lying behind this population movement was a sharp change in the composition of the labor force, from agriculture to industry (see Figure 8.11). In 1801, towns with fewer than 2,500 inhabitants accounted for more than two-thirds of the population; in 1891 they accounted for only one-quarter. Some of this population movement was away from county constituencies and toward middle-size or large urban boroughs, such as Manchester or London.

In the larger town and city boroughs where newly enfranchised artisans and working- and middle-class men arrived, embarrassment and blackmail were less feasible. The very act of moving also gave voters greater anonymity, making their electoral actions and preferences less easily discovered.

These demographic changes undoubtedly caused difficulties for party agents who needed to identify vulnerable voters and deliver benefits and treats to them. However, the most important change in this regard was not an exogenous social transformation but a reform very much fashioned by politicians: the 1872 introduction of the written ballot. In the United States, ballot reform was a multistaged process, and written ballots were in use long before secrecy was achieved. Britain, by contrast, leapt all at once from recording votes openly in poll books to the Australian ballot, which dissociated parties from the production and distribution of ballots at the same time that it promoted electoral secrecy. Later in this chapter we discuss the circumstances leading to this dramatic change, which quite intentionally, and with one blow, made the votes of individuals much harder to discern.

The ballot complicated but did not eliminate electoral bribery. There is some evidence of a post-ballot disarticulation of the market for votes. The price of votes fell after the introduction of the ballot, in one documented case from £5 to 5 shillings.[46] The ballot meant that the candidate's agent was buying not a vote but some probability of a vote, a commodity of lesser value. Voters began accepting bribes from multiple competing candidates. The fall in the price of a vote and voters' inability to commit to a single buyer signaled a partial unraveling of the market for votes. But the unraveling was only partial. Voters were still seen as susceptible to pressure: "by demanding pledges, the agent was often able to exert as strong influence as in the days of open voting."[47] And claims of electoral corruption persisted.

Declining Costs of Mass Communication

Political aspirants' use of print media to publicly announce their policy proposals had a long history in England and in Britain. In the seventeenth century, the preferred medium was the author-produced pamphlet or broadside. The use of the term "manifesto" to describe these pamphlets has been traced to the 1640s,[48] and electioneering via printed platforms occurred as early as 1679. With the emergence of a party system in the early eighteenth century, the Whigs and Tories regularly set out their positions in printed manifestos.[49] The public sphere was, then, vigorous well before the nineteenth century.[50]

What evolved in the nineteenth century were newspapers: printed texts appearing on a regular basis and for a mass audience, containing information about current events as well as political opinions and party propaganda. The newspaper replaced the broadside and pamphlet as the key medium defining the public sphere. Newspaper circulation doubled between 1801 and 1839, from 16 million stamps a year to 29 million.[51] The supply of newspapers also exploded, from 266 in 1824 to more than 2 million in 1886, the sharpest rise taking place between the 1860s and the turn of the century.[52]

The explosion of relatively inexpensive printed newspapers, and their penetration into ever-broader strata of ever-more-literate British society, meant

---

[46] Seymour 1970[1915], p. 435.
[47] Seymour 1970[1915], p. 433.
[48] Peacey 2004.
[49] Knights 1994.
[50] Pincus 2006.
[51] Christie 1970, cited in O'Gorman 2001, p. 75.
[52] Vincent 1966, cited in Cox 1987, p. 13. The greater ease of direct communication with voters afforded by the growing saturation of newspapers was not entirely unrelated to the actions of government (hence we call this a "mainly exogenous" factor), because the reduction in the regulated price of stamps and of paper contributed to this change.

that aspirants for office could communicate programmatic appeals to their constituents with little difficulty.

Inexpensive newspapers and growing literacy also changed the electorate in ways that made vote buying less effective. Party leaders were aware of these changes, perceiving in the 1880s that "the epoch of aristocratic, and even of middle class, influence was passing rapidly and that the new mass electorate, through increased education and a cheap press, would become politically free and independent in a sense that their predecessors would not have thought possible."[53]

These developments were not disconnected from growing dominance of the political party over individual members, a trend traced by several authors. In explaining this change, Cox focused on the growing importance of the cabinet in control of policy. When the outcome that mattered most to voters was which party controlled the cabinet, rather than the personal identity of a constituent's local member, voting strategies shifted toward parties.[54] Yet Cox's explanation shares with our own the sense that industrialization was a prime mover of these processes: it made private bills inefficient, rendered vote buying too costly, and shifted the demographic traits of the electorate in ways that left it less easily bribed.

8.2.3 Parliamentary Reforms in Context

A common answer to the question, What killed vote buying in Britain? is that legislative reformism did.[55] Proponents of this view rarely ask, however, *why* party leaders in Parliament were willing to undertake reforms when their parties had relied on vote buying for decades. They also do not explain why reforms that had been debated earlier in the century were only successfully passed in its closing decades.

Legislative-reform explanations for the decline of electoral bribery focus on a series of legislative acts to which we have alluded: the Corrupt Practices Act of 1854, which clarified legal definitions of bribery and established a system of auditors to monitor spending; the reform act of 1867, which judicialized the petition process; the 1872 introduction of the ballot; and the Corrupt and Illegal Practices Act of 1883. Without doubt, the cumulative impact of these acts was to help end vote buying in Britain. Our claim, however, is that the acts would not have passed had structural, or if you will exogenous, changes not made them palatable to party leaders and to members of parliament. Members had always despised their electoral agents and been embarrassed by bribery.

---

[53] O'Leary 1962, p. 231.

[54] Cox 1987.

[55] However, *which* reform mattered most varies from author to author. Eggers and Spirling 2011 pointed to the 1868 judicialization of petitions claiming election fraud, Seymour 1915 and O'Leary 1962 to the 1883 anticorruption act, and Kam 2009 to the 1885 shift to single-member districts.

But they found the courage of their convictions only when they saw clear ways to undermine the agent without losing their own posts or placing their party at a disadvantage.

If not industrialization and changes in the electorate, what else might account for the timing of reforms and their role in reducing clientelism? One might imagine that parliament was fully committed to reform from early in the century but had to go through a trial-and-error process before it finally lit onto effective measures. Another alternative might be that members became persuaded, through deliberative processes, to support reforms that they had earlier rejected. Not political self-interest but principled beliefs stood in the way of effective reforms. A late-century shift in beliefs about how voters should vote and how candidates should campaign might have been a necessary condition for effective reforms, reforms that, once undertaken, eliminated bribery.

That effective antibribery legislation had to await institutional innovation does not square with the record. Instead, either the same measures had been circulating for decades before they were adopted (as in the ballot), or weak versions of measures were adopted where it was fairly clear that stronger medicine was required.

The crude buying of votes had long been a crime in English common law, and the first antitreating law was enacted in 1696.[56] In the eighteenth and early nineteenth century, electoral bribery was perennially the stuff of scandal. The Corrupt Practices Act of 1854 for the first time defined in detail which practices constituted electoral corruption. Later reforms would build on this more explicit set of definitions. Yet in assessing reforms adopted before 1867, Seymour found that "all of the changes suggested were slight and none succeeded in winning the acceptance of both Houses."[57] One description of the pre-1865 cause of franchise reform could well be applied to the overlapping cause of anticorruption reform: "though it generated sporadic bouts of ill-coordinated activity," it "came to resemble nothing so much as a corpse on a dissecting table."[58] Not until industrialization had transformed the electorate in the ways detailed earlier were party leaders able to collude against their own electoral agents and put a stop to it.

A more significant act was the reform of 1867. It shifted jurisdiction over trials for electoral bribery from Parliament to High Court judges. Since the seventeenth century, claimants – mostly losing candidates – could petition parliament to overturn the results of elections that they alleged were corrupt.[59]

---

[56] O'Leary 1962, p. 11.

[57] Seymour 1970[1915], p. 202.

[58] Hoppen 2000, p. 237.

[59] In addition to shifting jurisdiction over these cases to judges, the 1867 reform moved the trials from London to the district in which corruption was claimed. Boroughs that investigatory commissions found to be incurably corrupt lost their privilege of representation altogether. Totnes, Reigate, Lancaster, and Yarmouth lost their seats in 1867, Beverly and Bridgewater in 1870; Seymour 1970[1915], pp. 423–424. Not antibribery provisions but the expansion of the

However, the House of Commons was often unwilling to punish one of their own, and cross-party collusion ended many investigations. The agreement to forgo charges for treating was regarded by electoral agents as "an honorable treaty."[60] Partisanship played a part in the petition process: Conservative candidates accused of bribery were somewhat more likely to have their defenses heard by Conservative-chaired committees, Liberals by Liberal-chaired committees, and the partisan identity of the chair influenced the outcome of the case.[61]

The written ballot, seen by supporters as the key to freeing voters from bribery and intimidation, had ardent and eloquent supporters in the House of Commons in the 1830s and 1840s. Beginning in 1838, they proposed the ballot year after year, with growing weariness; not until 1872 did it pass. A not dissimilar story can be told of parliamentary committees that investigated vote buying. The House of Commons first formed such a committee in 1835. The witnesses it summoned were "of the same type as were to appear before similar committees during the next forty years."[62] Yet not until the 1880s did Parliamentary action effectively kill vote buying.

Investigations, commissions, and reforms through mid-century did not eliminate vote buying in Britain. From 1868 to 1884, between one-third and one-half of constituencies experienced bribery.[63] Intimidation was also still widespread. A parliamentary investigation in 1868 uncovered many cases of employers punishing underlings who ignored their instructions to vote for the employer's preferred candidate. In one instance, a mill owner from Ashton-under-Lyne dismissed 40 employees who disobeyed his instructions to vote for the Liberal candidate.[64]

Corruption receded definitively in the wake of the Corrupt and Illegal Practices Act of 1883. Indeed, O'Leary holds that the 1883 act "eliminated" corruption.[65] This late-Victorian reform, as we have seen, imposed strict regulations on the composition and overall levels of campaign spending, barred the use of paid canvassers, and put in place procedures for the investigation and punishment of violations. Thus it became risky for election agents to spend funds illegally on bribes.

---

franchise was the most important element of the 1867 reform. The Conservative government of Disraeli passed what amounted to a "household franchise": the right to vote for all male heads of household, without qualifications based on length of residency or rates paid.

[60] Seymour 1970[1915], p. 189.

[61] Eggers and Spirling 2011. These authors identified an asymmetry in partisan bias, however: Conservatives were punished by Liberal committee heads but Liberals MPs were not punished by Conservative heads.

[62] O'Leary 1962, p. 19.

[63] Hoppen 2000, p. 285, Hanham 1959, p. 263.

[64] Hartington Select Committee report, cited in Woodall 1974, p. 469.

[65] Rix 2008 is skeptical of the term "elimination." However, she concluded that the 1883 act reduced bribery and continued a trend that would culminate in the early twentieth century.

Hence, if the Reform Act of 1832 ushered in a period of heightened corruption and intimidation, effective anticorruption legislation was delayed for two generations. Parliamentary leaders were well aware that imposing strict controls on spending would be required. However, they were only capable of passing effective legislation when their members believed that alternative electoral strategies had become more effective than clientelism.

The history of the introduction of the written ballot illustrates well that neither novel institutions nor persuasive justification were what delayed effective antibribery reforms. This history also inveighs against the idea that popular pressure was the key to forging more democratic and transparent electoral practices. The ballot was debated for decades but did not come close to passage until late in the Victorian era. The idea of a secret ballot was broadly popular, resonating in particular with workers and "middling sorts" for decades. It had been the second demand of the People's Charter, tightly linked to the Chartists' first demand of "a vote for every man twenty-one years of age, of sound mind, and not undergoing punishment for crime." Yet nineteenth-century parliaments remained remarkably unresponsive to popular movements. The Chartists' petitions were met with parliamentary indifference, if not hostility, and their championing of the written ballot probably hurt its prospects. When, in 1839, Chartists wheeled their first petition – three miles long and containing 1,280,000 signatures – into the House of Commons, the reception was chilly. A motion merely to discuss the petition failed, 235 votes to 46. Many members were disengaged from the debate, including Disraeli, who during the debate "spent his time leisurely eating oranges."[66]

Radical candidates like George Grote of and Mark Philips of Manchester campaigned in 1831 promising to press parliament to introduce the ballot. They were easily elected, Grote with more votes than had ever been cast for a member from London. For a decade Grote advocated eloquently in the House of Commons for the ballot, but gave up and retired from Parliament in 1841. The movement for the ballot languished, only to pass more than a generation later.

When the House of Commons finally passed the ballot in 1872, it did *not* do so because parliamentary leaders were finally won over, in the abstract, to the merits of secret voting. Even forward-thinking Liberals such as John Stuart Mill remained opposed to it on principle. Mill, then a Liberal MP, wrote of the proposed shift to secret voting, "Remove publicity and its checks, then all the mean motive of mankind . . . skulk to the polling-booth under a disguising cloak."[67] Gladstone himself was never more than lukewarm toward secret voting. He preferred instead "the idea of voters as independent gentlemen who strode to the poll with their head high and the courage to declare their

---

[66] Vallance 2009, p. 379.
[67] Cited in Woodall 1974, p. 468.

choice without fear or favour."[68] After an 1871 Parliamentary speech and vote in favor of the ballot, Gladstone recorded in his diary "Spoke on ballot, and voted in 324-230 with mind satisfied & as to feeling a lingering reluctance."[69] What changed were not Gladstone's convictions but his need for allies. He committed himself to its passage to gain Radical support for his government. In particular, Gladstone garnered the Radicals' support by offering John Bright a place in his cabinet and promising to press for passage of the ballot.

By the time the ballot was introduced, few in the House of Commons seemed willing to fight hard against it. Indeed, it eventually passed with the support of Conservative and Liberal leaders. The sense from the Parliamentary debate is that, despite enduring scruples, party leaders perceived much less at stake in allowing voters to escape being held to account. By 1872, as we have seen, even a former Conservative Principal Agent John Gorst could confidently tell nervous Tory backbenchers that they could win elections simply by informing constituents about their "character, qualifications, and political views."[70] The electorate was well along in a process of transformation that made them less vulnerable to bribery.

Stepping back, industrialization made Britain a wealthier country and a more democratic one. By the turn of the nineteenth to twentieth centuries, it was well on its way to being a prosperous country. Certainly large segments of the society remained poor and vulnerable. However, the numbers of voters willing to give up their vote for a day at the public house was shrinking, just as the number who would render their vote in return for cash or access to hospital attention was also in sharp decline. The ease of modern mass communications provided alternative avenues for reaching voters, now with words rather than with treats. In addition, the size of constituencies rendered electoral strategies that required close monitoring of voters' actions inefficient.

Industrializing produced vigorous, even violent, social movements, ones that demanded democratic reform and autonomy for the electors. It was on its way to being a society in which the organized working class found fairly direct representation through its own political party. But on the whole the attack on clientelism was carried out by a more traditional political elite. Radicals militated for universal suffrage, the ballot, and proportionality in representation; Whigs and Tories for redistribution of constituencies and rationalization of the suffrage; Liberal governments drove up the cost of vote buying by making detection easier and penalties harsher; and all agreed – for self-interested reasons, as much as for the public good – to reduce and closely monitor campaign expenditures. Perennial tensions between party leaders and their agents in the constituencies made electoral reform attractive to the former, as long as it did not impose obvious electoral costs.

---

[68] Jenkins 2002, p. 355.
[69] Cited in Jenkins 2002, p. 356.
[70] See note 30.

8.3 THE UNITED STATES

8.3.1 Timing of the Decline of American Clientelism

The heyday of American clientelism was the second half of the nineteenth century. Its decline began during the Progressive Era, but it persisted, in the form of political machines, entrenched in the cities and amongst immigrant voters, into later decades. Its full demise came only in the second half of the twentieth century.

An exchange of favors for votes was an essential part of nineteenth-century American elections. Bensel offered many examples to support his general contention that, in the mid-nineteenth century United States, "For many men... the act of voting was a social transaction in which they handed in a party ticket in return for a shot of whiskey, a pair of boots, or a small amount of money." This remained true during the Gilded Age, the golden era of party politics. Party appeals to voters were economic, sectional, ethnic, and religious. But electoral politics in the Gilded Age also featured vote buying: the exchange of cash, food, alcohol, and other small items for votes. The 1888 election in Newark, New Jersey, cited earlier, in which party operatives gave voters chits redeemable for cash, was not unusual. An 1887 study of New York City politics estimated that one-fifth of voters were bribed. Twenty-five years later, an investigation into bribery in Adams County, Ohio, identified 1,679 voters who acknowledged receiving payments for their votes, 26 percent of the county's voters.[71]

American clientelism was dealt a blow by ballot reform. Between 1889 and 1896, state assemblies introduced the "official" (Australian) ballot. The ballot reduced the effectiveness of the kind of exchange that Bensel described, especially in rural areas and small towns. Because payments to individuals give them a selective incentive to go to the polls, it is not surprising that the Australian ballot was followed by a decline in turnout. In the years between the Civil War and the critical election of 1896, turnout achieved its highest levels in American history. After 1896, it dropped sharply.[72] The decline in turnout was especially pronounced among low-income and rural voters. Single-ticket voting and the stability of electoral choices also fell off sharply in the first decades of the twentieth century. Ballot reform hence is part of the explanation for the turn-of-the-century demise of partisanship. In addition to high turnout rates, the late nineteenth century partisan period was characterized by widespread single-party voting and stability of party vote shares over time in localities. All declined after the turn of the century. The greater difficulty parties faced

---

[71] The New York Figure is from Ivins 1887, the Ohio figure in Blair 1912; both are cited in Sikes 1928, p. 8.
[72] See Kleppner 1982, Rosenstone and Hansen 1993.

in exchanging money or treats for votes was certainly a crucial cause of the demise of partisanship.[73]

Historians also note the rising importance of party platforms in the late nineteenth century, another sign that vote buying was yielding to electoral strategies that, in Hoppen's phrase, "depended upon words." In New Jersey, for instance, whereas the major parties' manifestos in the 1880s were "brief and opaque," increasingly after 1900 they "articulated a more definite set of policies."[74]

The turn-of-the-century decline of vote buying meant that exchanges of votes for small bribes – cash, a hod of coal, a Thanksgiving turkey – was more a nineteenth than a twentieth century phenomenon. Yet clientelism persisted through the Progressive Era and even into the fledgling period of the welfare state. The currency of twentieth-century clientelism was patronage and biased access to public programs. Its organizational expression was the urban party machine.[75] Voters who received benefits or public-sector jobs were accountable to machines that were deeply networked organizations, their tentacles reaching through ward and precinct captains into working-class neighborhoods, churches, and meeting halls. The machines were named for cities in which they operated, and for the mayors or party leaders who presided over them. On the Democratic side were Tweed of Tammany Hall in Manhattan, Kelly and Nash, and later, Daley in Chicago and Hague in Jersey City. On the Republican side, they were named for McMane, later Durham and Vare, in Philadelphia, Magee in Pittsburgh, Cox in Cincinnati and Sheehan in Buffalo. Beyond these big-city machines were ones in smaller cities, including Perez in Plaquemines Parish, Louisiana (a Democrat). Although machines belonged to cities, patronage was equally a phenomenon of national politics and featured interactions of presidents, congressmen, and city bosses.

Franklin Roosevelt's Works Progress Administration (WPA) embodied a mix of programmatic public spending and clientelism. Roosevelt was both the architect of the New Deal and a product of New York state politics, having served as a state senator and governor. In New York he first opposed and then made accommodations with the Tammany Hall machine. President Roosevelt's minister of relief, Harry Hopkins, tried to keep the WPA from being politicized. To avoid congressional and machine manipulations, Hopkins delineated program boundaries that cross-cut congressional districts and county and city limits.[76] After the Democrats won the 1936 election in a landslide, and after Hopkins moved to become Roosevelt's chief political advisor, the WPA became more politicized. A mix of transparent formulas and electoral

[73] See Converse 1972; see also Burnham 1965, 1974.

[74] Reynolds 1988, p. 94.

[75] Patronage had a long history in American politics, going back to the Jacksonian Era and the "spoils" system and transforming during Reconstruction into a tool of partisan politics. See James 2005.

[76] Erie 1988, p. 132. See also Dorsett 1977.

responsiveness guided the federal government's distribution of WPA funds across states. Wright showed that electoral responsiveness guided state-level distributions, although Wallis showed that need also played a large part.[77] However, once the funds arrived in machine cities, electoral considerations became paramount.[78]

WPA projects doubled the number of public-sector jobs available in Depression-ravaged cities like New York, Jersey City, and Chicago. In Pittsburg, one-third of Democratic ward and precinct captains became WPA project supervisors, helping to consolidate that city's Lawrence machine. The Kelly-Nash machine in Chicago used WPA funds to hire extra canvassers before elections, and "Boss Hague," to whom the entire New Jersey Democratic congressional delegation owed favors, appropriated a percentage of WPA workers' salaries to pay for campaign expenses.[79] New York's Tammany Hall machine required party affiliation for applicants for the Civil Works Administration (CWA), a 1933–1934 employment relief program. One Tammany employee boasted, "This is how we make Democrats."[80]

Patronage helped secure electoral victories. In a recent paper, Folke, Hirano, and Snyder showed that the adoption of civil service reforms reduced the reelection prospects of incumbent statewide office holders.[81] Their findings confirm the sense that machines, such as Jersey City's patronage "army" of 20,000, were indeed effective. The voting population of Jersey City was 120,000. The Hague machine instructed public-sector workers "to secure the votes of family and friends. If each worker brought in two more votes, the machine was guaranteed victory..."[82]

Machines also politicized access to new federal pension and welfare programs. Erie explained that Chicago's Kelly-Nash machine operatives "served as welfare brokers. To expedite Social Security and [Aid to Families with Dependent Children] eligibility... precinct captains initiated client contacts with social service agencies. By 1936 two-thirds of the machine's lieutenants reported serving as employment and welfare brokers, up from one-third in 1928."[83]

In southern states, where populations remained more rural and poverty rates high, vote buying remained endemic well into the twentieth century. This was the case even though the hegemony of the Democratic Party and the disenfranchisement of blacks reduced the need and hence willingness of candidates to pay for votes. However, in places where elections were competitive, vote buying persisted well into the twentieth century. Poll taxes afforded opportunities for

[77] Wright 1974, Wallis 1987.
[78] See Erie 1988, p. 136.
[79] Erie 1988, p. 129–130.
[80] Caro, 1974, quoted in Erie 1988, p. 131.
[81] Folke, Hirano, and Snyder 2011.
[82] Erie 1988, p. 124.
[83] Erie 1988, p. 134.

buying votes. As an example, Key cited a late-1940s Arkansas campaign that "put a thousand dollars or so into a county a day or two before the October 1 deadline to cover poll taxes. The holder of the poll-tax receipt is, of course, given to understand that he will support the administration candidate the following year."[84] Anti-bribery legislation in the post–15th amendment South was sometimes aimed at keeping Republican candidates from paying the poll taxes of black voters.[85]

Today, party machines are a thing of the past. The welfare state in twenty-first-century America is, generally speaking, thoroughly rule-bound, bureaucratized, and insulated from to partisan manipulation. Research into distributive politics in contemporary United States discerns programmatic politics, as when a change of partisan control of congress changes spending patterns in ways predictable from the parties' ideologies; pork-barrel politics, as when spending on sports and recreation facilities rises with the electoral vulnerability of the assemblyman or woman; and nonconditional benefits to individuals, as when spending on food stamps rises with the incumbent party's vote share in a congressional district.[86] But no clientelism.

That said, machine politics left deep imprints in American politics, some observable still. Both major parties rely on nonpartisan organizations that work hard to turn voters out and to shape their electoral choices. Their efforts include "walking-around money," presumably paid to campaign workers. In Baltimore, even as late as the 1970s, "on election day, DiPietro's precinct workers will arrive at the polls early and hand out $15 to each worker, as payment for such chores as distributing sample ballots … "[87] Churches also influence voters and work to boost turnout: evangelicals on the Republican side, black churches alongside of labor unions on the Democratic side. Nominally nonpartisan civic organizations link these churches even more closely to the parties, a leading example being the Moral Majority or Family Research Council's role as nexuses between the Republican Party and evangelical churches. What's more, parties command highly detailed information, down to the individual voter (and individual small donor). State and national parties – Democrats and Republicans – retain highly detailed databases that record information about individual voters, their party registration, turnout history, past party contributions, consumer patterns, and more.[88]

If detailed information about voters was what leaders "bought" when they employed brokers, have parties in the United States in the digital era returned to a kind of modernized clientelism? Whatever the answer to that question, three features distinguish contemporary party strategies from machine politics as it

[84] Key 1950, p. 594.

[85] Sikes 1928, p.24.

[86] See, respectively, Bickers and Stein 2000, Herron and Theodus 2004, and Ansolabehere and Snyder 2006.

[87] Weisskopf 1978, p. 8. We are grateful to David Mayhew for the reference.

[88] For a description of these databases, see Hersh and Schaffner 2011.

existed until a half century ago. First, the voting public is no longer composed of large segments of people who are very poor. When accusations of vote buying do appear in the contemporary United States, they tend to be in poor rural redoubts. The Appalachian region of eastern Kentucky is one of the few places where prosecutions for violations of federal vote-buying statutes persist even into the twenty-first century.[89] Compared with the usual ways in which parties mobilize electoral support across the country, these cases are isolated and anachronistic.

A second difference is that parties now lack the capacity to target (or exclude) individual voters from receiving (or being denied) state benefits or services. Even the FEMA case of partisan bias in the delivery of disaster relief, discussed in Chapter 5, was one in which good will, not credible threats of denial of future benefits, drove voters' responsiveness to largesse.[90] Today's consultants with their databases do not play the same role as the armies of live human beings, brokers, who – in the eras of Tweed or Plunkitt – could hold voters accountable for their actions at the polls.

The American electorate of the later twentieth and twenty-first centuries, finally, is unlike that of the nineteenth and early twentieth centuries, which had nowhere to turn but to party agents or the charitable organizations, in search of transfers or protection from risk. Now government fulfills these functions. Isolated manipulations of programs as in the FEMA case notwithstanding, the vast majority of social spending by governments at all levels in the United States, especially that going to individual beneficiaries, is constrained by rules, means tests, and other abstract formulae.[91]

---

[89] Hence in 2010 federal prosecutors accused four men of vote buying in Perry County. According to the AP, they were accused of paying people $20 each to cast ballots for a given candidate in a 2010 primary election for a U.S. Senate seat. A similar prosection in took place in Pike County in 2004; see "Where Prosecutors Say Votes are Sold," *New York Times*, August 29, 2004. See also Sabato and Simpson 1996.

[90] See Chen 2004, 2009.

[91] Another practice, still widely used today, that is reminiscent of the heyday of the American machine is the use of party resources to convey voters to the polls, known as hauling. This spending is legal, though sometimes it is suspected of ending up in the pockets of voters and hence of bleeding into illegal vote buying (as in the Eastern Kentucky case alluded to earlier). As an example of legal hauling, in the 2010 midterm elections, the Philadelphia Democratic Party reverted to the use of "street money" to turn out the vote. As one state legislator commented, "You got this huge debate of the 21st century politics versus the 19th century, ... I think you need a combination of both. What happens is the people on the street operation say 'OK, you need the commercials and the direct mail and all this stuff. But you also need to ensure that you are out there working.' This is a form of making sure you have full coverage." (The quote is from State Assembly Representative Dwight Evans, in "Philly Dems Lean on Tactics Shunned by Obama to get Sestak Elected," October 27, 2010, Sam Stein, *The Huffington Post*.) And social-science research confirms that get-out-the-vote campaigns are at their most effective in the United States when they involve personalized contact, over the telephone or, even more so, face-to-face canvassing. See, e.g., Gerber and Green 2000.

Party interests certainly influence the distribution of public material resources in the United States today. Changes in the level of funding and rules of distribution follow changes in party control of congress and the presidency.[92] But the resulting patterns of distribution are usually predictable from public debates and from the formalized rules of distribution; that is, they are programmatic.[93] Even in instances of nonprogrammatic distributive politics, such as the FEMA and (perhaps) Faith Based Initiative examples discussed earlier, the parties in power lack the capacity of the machines of old to hold voters to account. Writing in the 1980s, Erie noted that the party machines are "now in eclipse. Government bureaucracies and labor unions have assumed the welfare and employment functions once fulfilled by the machines. Civil service reform has limited their supply of patronage jobs. Their ethnic constituents have moved to the suburbs."[94] Banfield and Wilson, sketching in the early 1960s the machine "in its classical form," were writing about a vanishing phenomenon: "no big city today has a city-wide machine that is like the model... "[95]

Yet in contrast to Britain, the death of electoral clientelism in the United States was delayed and gradual. Its final demise came with reform mayors in the 1950s in Philadelphia, Jersey City, and Boston; the early 1960s in New York; the mid-1970s in Chicago; and later still in Albany and Baltimore.

The American experience, then, raises two questions. Why did American industrialization, outpacing as it did British industrialization after the Civil War, not eliminate clientelism as quickly and definitively as it had in Britain? The answer has partly to do with differences in the impact of industrialization on the electorate, but also with the relative ineffectiveness of anticorruption reform in the United States. What explains this ineffectiveness?

8.3.2 Industrialization and the Gradual Decline of Clientelism in the United States

The trends that explain the demise of clientelism in nineteenth-century Britain – the growth and growing affluence of the electorate, the greater opacity of the vote with the secret ballot and an increasingly urban and mobile electorate, the rising prominence of mass circulation newspapers linking political aspirants to increasingly literate electorates – were common to nineteenth-century America and help explain the decline of vote buying in that country as well. Yet America's development differed in several crucial ways from Britain's. These differences, as well as a more complex environment for antimachine reforms, together explain the persistence of patronage and machine politics in the United States later and at higher levels of industrialization than in Britain.

The franchise was always a more popular right in the United States, with relatively modest property qualifications in the late-eighteenth century, and

---

[92] See the citations in Chapter 2.
[93] See especially Bickers and Stein 2000, Levitt and Snyder 1995.
[94] Erie 1988, p. 4.
[95] Banfield and Wilson 1963, p. 116.

even those were basically eliminated by the mid-nineteenth century. (Racial and gender qualifications, obviously, persisted much longer.) The more popular franchise meant that the electorate was more tilted than the British toward poor voters, ones more willing to trade their vote for a material reward. Industrialization created a hunger for workers that was fed in large measure by immigration, and immigrant men were rapidly incorporated into the electorate. Income distribution remained more unequal in the nineteenth century United States than in Britain; in the United States, but not in Britain, health, physical stature, and other basic measures of welfare declined in the latter nineteenth century.

Hence, despite industrial growth – indeed, in some senses because of it – broad swaths of the American electorate remained economically vulnerable well into the twentieth century. Immigrant communities also reproduced some of the informational qualities of small towns, allowing political brokers to closely monitor constituents' electoral behavior, even though they resided in large cities.Only with the Depression, the New Deal, and World War II did income inequality subside somewhat. Hence by the second half of the twentieth century, the United States had developed into an industrial power in which prosperity was more equally shared.[96] The offspring of immigrants, like working-class native-born citizens, moved from the cities to the suburbs and became indifferent to the rewards that the machine might offer. In the middle-class "newspaper wards," unlike the working-class "river wards," the hod of coal and Thanksgiving turkey – as Banfield and Wilson remind us – had become a joke.[97]

A Larger U.S. Electorate

Clientelism persisted in the United States despite a large and growing electorate. In the first decades of the nineteenth century, the United States was an expansive and labor-hungry country. The population grew from less than 4 million in 1790 to 10 million in 1820, 35 million in 1865, and 75 million in 1900. The United States thus began the nineteenth century with about half of the population of Britain but surged ahead of Britain in the 1840s. (See Figure 8.12.)

Even at the founding, the U.S. states conceded the right to vote to a relatively broad array of men. In 1790, 60–70 percent of adult white men had the right to vote. Property requirements began to be dismantled after 1790 and had basically been eliminated by 1850, and by 1855 taxpaying was not a qualification for voting. Hence, at mid-century, there were almost no economic qualifications for voting.[98]

---

[96] As in Britain, however, beginning in the last quarter of the twentieth century, income equality declined.

[97] Banfield and Wilson 1963.

[98] See the discussion in Keyssar 2001.

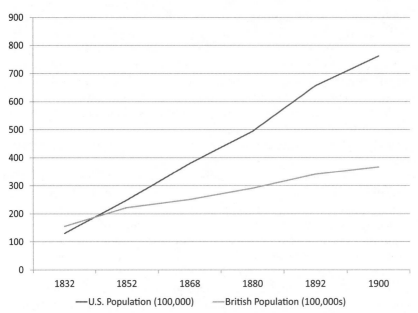

FIGURE 8.12. Populations of Britain (England, Scotland, and Wales) and the United States, 1832–1900. *Source:* Jeffries 2005 and U.S. Census Bureau 1949.

Nineteenth-century immigration helped swell both the population and the electorate. Immigrants arrived from Germany and Ireland early in the nineteenth century. They arrived from Italy and Eastern Europe after 1880. Cities were the destination of most Irish, Italian, and Eastern European immigrants. In 1854 alone, 428,000 European immigrants arrived in the United States. Keyssar noted that the 3 million foreigners who arrived between 1845 and 1854 were equivalent to 15 percent of the 1845 population.[99] In 1870, New York and Philadelphia were the only cities with populations over half a million; by 1910, eight cities contained half a million people, and three of them – New York, Chicago, and Philadelphia – each had more than 1.5 million.

Immigrants were quickly absorbed into the electorate. To attract settlers, between 1850 and 1889, 18 states enacted alien voting provisions, allowing noncitizen "declarants" the right to vote.[100] (These provisions were later repealed.) Between the 1840s and the Civil War, immigrants were easily granted citizenship. Irish immigrants were particularly ready participants in elections. The number of Irish-American voters in New York and Boston tripled between 1850 and 1855; by the latter year, more than one in five voters in those cities was an Irish immigrant. Nativist reactions began to crystallize at mid-century.

---

[99] Keyssar 2001, p.

[100] See Keyssar 2001, p. 36, and appendix 12. "Declarants" were people who had declared their intention to be naturalized.

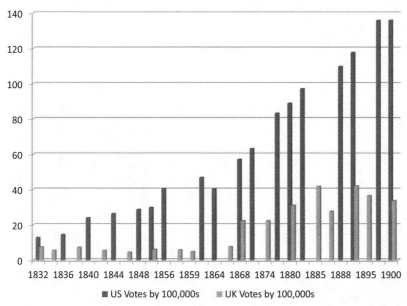

FIGURE 8.13. Votes Cast for U.S. Presidents and British MPs, 1832–1900. *Source:* Data from Leip 2005 and Craig 1989.

In the 1850s, the Know-Nothings pressed, with only limited success, for literacy requirements for voting in many states, and the federal government ratcheted up the regulation of elections and of naturalization.

The greater longevity of clientelism in the United States than in the Britain was despite a sharper growth in the overall U.S. electorate. The surging U.S. population and modest qualifications for voting (for white men) led to a large national electorate. The number of votes cast for president was around 100,000 in 1820, around 1 million in 1832, 8 million at the centennial of the founding, and 13.5 million in 1900. Despite sagging turnout – a phenomenon, as we saw, that began after 1896 – still the number of voters continued to climb, reaching 50 million in 1940.

In 1865, at the end of the Civil War, the population of the United States was 35 million, and 5.7 million votes were cast in the presidential election in 1868, or about one in six. The 13.5 million people who cast votes in the presidential elections of 1900 represented about 16 percent of the 85 million people living in the country; in the British general election of 1900, about 1.2 million votes were cast in a country whose population was around 30 million.

Figures 8.13 and 8.14 allow a comparison of the size of the active electorate relative to the general populations in the United States and in Great Britain. Figure 8.13 shows a persistently larger electorate in the United States. Before the 1840s, when the U.S. population surpassed Britain's, the larger U.S.

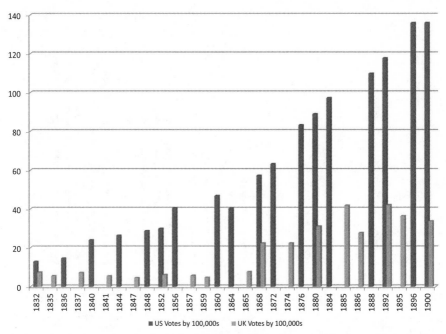

FIGURE 8.14. Votes Cast in the United States and Britain as a Percentage of Population, 1832–1900. *Source:* Data from Leip 2005 and Craig 1989.

electorate was entirely due to that country's more expansive franchise. The British electorate increased sharply after the second great reform of 1867, but still the U.S. electorate remained much larger, now fed by rapid population growth and rapid conversion of immigrants into voters. Figure 8.14 shows that, even after Britain's 1885 reform, the proportion of the U.S. population that voted was twice that of Britain's. With – by then – a much larger population, nearly four times as many votes were cast for U.S. president in 1900 than in the British general election of that same year.

The delayed demise of clientelism, as measured against its demise in Britain, was, then, despite a persistently larger electorate in America. The machine cities were populated by hundreds of thousands, in some cases millions, of voters. We posit, instead, that other factors, in particular high poverty rates, large numbers of voters populating immigrants communities, and – perhaps above all – the contrasting institutional setting, should be central to these comparisons.

8.3.3 Wealth and Poverty in the U.S. Electorate

The main reason for the decline and near disappearance of the city-wide machine was – and is – the growing unwillingness of voters to accept the inducements that it offered. The petty favors and "friendship" of the precinct captains declined in value as immigrants were assimilated, public welfare programs were vastly extended, and per capita incomes rose steadily and sharply in war and postwar prosperity. To the voter who in case of need could turn to a professional social workers and receive as a matter of course unemployment compensation, aid to dependent children, old-age assistance, and all the rest, the precinct captain's hod of coal was a joke.[101]

Nineteenth-century industrialization of the United States, which accelerated after the Civil War, produced a larger economy and a wealthier society. In the period from 1820 to 1850, per capita income grew about 20 percent; it roughly doubled between the end of the Civil War and turn of the century. Yet nineteenth-century economic expansion did less to reduce poverty in the United States than in Britain. The United States was and is a highly unequal country, in particular in comparison with other early industrializers. In the nineteenth century, it experienced a near-steady increase in income inequality. The U.S. Gini index peaked at close to 70 in 1890 and declined to 49 in 1930. Hence although the economy grew rapidly in the nineteenth century, so did poverty. The period between 1790 and 1870 was one of a lowering of stature and life expectancy, and health got worse. "[A]cross the 19th century, population grew faster, skills per worker grew slower, and the skilled/unskilled pay ratio widened" in comparison with the period 1929–1948.[102]

Some poor voters were country folk whose families had been long resident in the United States, or who had arrived with the German migrations of the early nineteenth century. Others were city dwellers, whether working-class Protestant Yankees or – more numerous, certainly in many of the largest cities – Irish, German, Italian, or Eastern European immigrants. The immigrants who fed the labor-hungry industrial centers were, as we have seen, quickly naturalized and enfranchised. They became voters whose needs were great and whose exposure to economic and social risk was significant. Describing elections in immigrant communities in Philadelphia in 1905, Abernethy commented that "Ballot boxes were stuffed by ambitious ward leaders, voters were purchased for as little as twenty-five cents or a drink of whiskey, and voting lists were padded with phantom voters."[103]

Only with some equalization of the distribution of income, between the 1930s and the 1970s, as well as rapid post–World War II economic expansion, did the center of gravity of the electorate shift from working- to middle-class voters. This was a key factor lying behind the belated demise of American clientelism.

Despite industrialization, economic growth, and a large electorate, the party machines saw poor native-born citizens and immigrants as people whose votes could be secured with offers of whiskey, boots, or even a low-paying city

---

[101] Banfield and Wilson 1963, p. 121.
[102] Lindert 2000, p. 205, citing Williamson and Lindert 1980.
[103] Abernethy 1963 p. 5.

job. And members of Congress and even presidents had an incentive to channel federal resources to the machines. Presidents who shunned machines and patronage, like Rutherford Hayes, risked isolation and defections from within their party; those like FDR, who shrewdly combined programmatic mobilization and cooperation with machines, won. Postwar prosperity and the move of immigrant populations to the suburbs (as Banfield and Wilson suggested) eventually made machine politics obsolete.

8.3.4 Costs of Mass Communication in the United States

As in Britain, rising literacy and technical improvements meant that ambitious politicians who wanted to broadcast policy proposals and programs could turn to newspapers. An explosion of newspapers occurred at the beginning of the nineteenth century, fostered by their distribution, at very low costs, through the U.S. Postal Service.[104] Although the press had always played a central role in party politics, Reynolds placed the rise of campaigning in the newspapers in the first decades of the twentieth century. "Full-page partisan advertising, virtually unknown in the nineteenth century, became a central component of twentieth century campaigns." He noted that the New Jersey Democratic Party created a publicity bureau for the 1907 gubernatorial campaign, institutionalizing "a new relationship between politicians and the press."[105]

8.3.5 Opacity of the Vote in the United States

Also as in Britain, and as in developing democracies today, multifaceted social relationships in nineteenth century towns were a support to vote buying. As Bensel explained, in small towns, voters were frequently "embedded in long-term personal relationships" with the agents who engaged them in these exchanges, relationships that helped the agents hold voters accountable for their choices.[106] In rural areas of New York State in the late nineteenth century, party managers "had sufficient information to follow a policy of not only paying 'floaters' to cast ballots for their parties, but also of rewarding opponents for not voting."[107]

A case of vote buying in rural Ohio at the close of the Civil War, reported by Bensel, illustrates what an important asset rich local knowledge was to party agents, even in the period when agents could still observe individual ballots. A Republican Party agent in Knox County, Ohio, in 1866 offered to pay a Mrs. Beach $10. If both Mrs. Beach and her 21-year-old son, a first-time voter,

---

[104] See John 1995.

[105] Reynolds 1988, p. 95.

[106] Bensel 2004, p. ix. For an excellent description of the voting process in mid-nineteenth-century America, see Bensel 2004, pp. 9–14.

[107] Cox and Kousser 1981, p. 655.

would cast ballots for the Republican candidate, each would receive $5. Under interrogation, party agent Coe explained that:

two or three of [William's] associates that frolicked and caroused around ... were democrats, and he was inclined to run with them ... a young blacksmith – I don't know is name; he works with Higgins; Ira Barr, who made his boasts that he was going to make a democrat of [William] ... We did not know how [William] stood, nor what his politics were; but we saw him often in bad company, and feared he would be led astray, and this was done in order to bring him in the way he should go at an early day [i.e., in his first election]. Coe gave William a Republican ballot, marked so that he could inspect it after the election. But the ballot that William eventually cast, retrieved for Coe by a Republican election judge, showed that William had erased the printed names of Republican candidates for governor and sheriff and written in Democratic ones. Only Mrs. Beach received $5.[108]

Hence even before the official ballot was introduced – a change we discuss later – when party agents could more easily monitor voters' actions, the inter-connectedness of rural and small-town social relations meant that party agents – themselves community members – commanded detailed information about individuals, families, and work relationships. As in Britain, the shift of population from the countryside to the cities (described earlier) brought with it a greater anonymity of voters, their actions less easily observed by party agents.

That said, immigration and ethnic residential concentration had the effect of reproducing these intimate and multifaceted social relations, to some degree, in the cities. Immigrant neighborhoods were places where precinct captains and ward heelers knew a great deal about their constituents. The personal connection between brokers and other operatives, on one side, and voters, on the other, took on special importance to immigrants in new and unfamiliar surroundings. They were especially responsive to people like the Philadelphia ward boss described by Varbero, who cultivated recent Italian immigrants with a mix of personal and material appeals: "Baldi's hold on the community was secured in the fashion of the traditional ward boss. Personable and apparently benevolent, bank president Baldi often dispensed dollars in exchange for allegiance, a simple and time-honored formula for success in the American city."[109]

The cities were full of people who – whether they had arrived from the countryside or from a foreign land – felt great need; unlike in Britain, they were likely to have the right to vote. They were the stuff on which party machines were built, and their presence goes some way to explaining the persistence of

---

[108] Cited in Bensel 2004, pp. 47–48. Bensel reported that Coe also gave a ballot to William Beach's father. Suspecting that the father planned to vote Republican in any case, and might himself vote with William's ballot – allowing William to take the bribe and despite voting Democratic – Coe marked the father's ticket with the words "our country" and marked the son's ballot with the same words but spelled backwards.

[109] Varbero 1975, p. 285. We are grateful to David Mayhew for the reference.

clienetlism in America for decades after it had basically been extinguished in Britain.

8.3.6 Clientelism and Legislative Reforms

Clientelism flourished in nineteenth and twentieth-century America despite being illegal. Electoral bribery was recognized as a crime in common law before the passage of antibribery statutes. State constitutions also contained antibribery sections in their organic laws. The following identical language appeared in 12 state constitutions:

Laws shall be made to exclude from office, from suffrage, and from serving as jurors, those who shall hereafter be convicted of bribery... The privilege of free suffrage shall be supported by laws regulating elections, and prohibiting under adequate penalties, all undue influence thereon from power, bribery, tumult, or other improper conduct.[110]

Seventeen states also included language in their constitutions disqualifying people found guilty of buying votes from holding office.[111]

Still bribery persisted, as we have seen. When authors such as Earl R. Sikes or Helen M. Rocca of the League of Women Voters wrote about vote buying in 1928, they used the present tense.[112] As did V.O. Key, observing Southern society in 1950.

The first wave of anticlientelist legislation meant to give teeth to constitutional and common law began with an 1890 New York State act, which attempted to limit campaign spending, bar certain kinds of expenditures, and publicize the sources of campaign contributions. The New York act was "feeble" in that it applied only to candidates and not to political committees.[113] By 1900, 17 states had passed laws regulating the use of money in elections, in part to discourage bribery, in part to limit the influence of corporations in politics.[114] In 1925, Congress passed the Federal Corrupt Practices Act. In addition to restrictions on campaign contributions, the 1925 act made it unlawful to promise employment to gain political support, to offer or give a bribe to influence votes, and to accept such a bribe and for public officials to solicit campaign contributions from public employees.

Legislative assaults on patronage, as on vote buying, also began in the late nineteenth century. Attempting to follow European and British examples, American reformers passed the Pendleton Civil Service Act in 1883. But

---

[110] Quoted in Sikes 1928, pp. 10–11. The states including this language were Alabama (1819), California (1849), Connecticut (1818), Florida (1839), Kansas (1885), Kentucky (1799), Louisiana (1812), Mississippi (1817), Oregon (1857), South Carolina (1868), and Texas (1866).

[111] Alabama, Illinois, Indiana, Kansas, Kentucky, Louisiana, Maryland, Massachusetts, Mississippi, Missouri, New Hampshire, Ohio, Oregon, Pennsylvania, Rhode Island, and Texas; Sikes 1928, pp. 10–11.

[112] Rocca 1928.

[113] Sikes 1928, p. 125. For a recent account, see Abu El-Haj 2011.

[114] See McCormick 1981b.

the act had limited effectiveness. Of roughly 200,000 positions in the federal government, more than half remained outside the Pendleton Act's civil-service rules.[115] Subsequent measures, under the administrations of Rutherford Hayes, Grover Cleveland, and – most vigorously – Theodore Roosevelt, reduced but did not root out patronage. As a result, well into the twentieth century party bosses employed "patronage, services, contracts, and franchises . . . to maintain power. Bosses purchased voter support with offers of public jobs and services rather than by appeals to traditional loyalties or to class interests."[116]

Federal corrupt practices legislation had to navigate around a number of legal obstacles. One was the ambiguous legal definition of political parties: were they private associations, and hence beyond the reach of legislation, or were they organizations involved in the election of Congress and hence subject to Congressional control? A second, not unrelated, obstacle was the courts' views of primary elections. Were they internal party matters, or were they the first stage of elections? The Supreme Court's majority decision in the 1921 *U.S. v. Newberry* case held primary elections to be methods by which party members chose candidates and hence not subject to Congressional regulation. In 1923, Texas passed a law making it illegal for blacks to vote in primaries. The "white primary" law was upheld by a district court in Texas. The Supreme Court reversed this decision, but on the grounds that it violated the 14th and 15th amendments of the constitution. The Court's decision left intact the construct of parties as private associations and primaries as their internal affairs, at least regarding the raising and deployment of funds.

As in Britain, in the United States as well the introduction of the Australian ballot was a blow against clientelism. And as in Britain, ballot reform in America was as much an assault by party leaders on agents and bosses as by nonpartisan reformers on parties. Revising a conventional wisdom that Progressive-era reformers forced ballot reform on reluctant parties, two leading American political historians described ballot reform as an effort to "outlaw 'treachery'" – the treachery here being the failure of party bosses and local ballot handlers to act in the interests of the candidates.[117] Local party captains could affix an "unofficial" candidate's name at the top of the ticket; they could substitute one faction's ticket for another's; they could produce "pasters" with names of friends at the head of tickets and distribute these to voters; they could "bolt" and they could "trade." "Even a candidate who had faithfully paid his assessment to the party to ensure that his name was printed on the correct ballots might discover that failure to pay a local district captain resulted in the exclusion of his ballot from the bunches. Even individual ticket pedlars at the polls might require a candidate to pay a fee to ensure that voters had

---

[115] Skowronek 1982, p. 69.

[116] Erie 1988, p. 2.

[117] The title of Reynolds and McCormick's 1986 essay is "Outlawing 'Treachery': Split Tickets and Ballot Laws in New York and New Jersey, 1880–1910."

an opportunity to cast the candidate's ballot."[118] In short, party leaders had myriad reasons to mistrust their own machines and to tighten their control over ballots.

The ballot and other anticlientelism reforms bore the clear imprint of Mugwumps and Progressive reformers. Yet – as Reynolds and McCormick emphasized – these reformers often saw themselves as members of parties, rather than antiparty activists. They included people such as William Mills Ivins, a Democrat New York lawyer, who were appalled at the vast sums of money in campaigns and widespread buying of votes. However, it was party leaders, in the state legislatures and in Congress, who distrusted the machines that they had relied on, who were the driving forces behind reforms.

Reynolds and McCormick made clear, as we have tried to in our account of British ballot and other reforms, that these political alliances need to be understood against the backdrop of industrialization and a changing electorate. They wrote that "candidates and leaders were paying the pedlars to put the right tickets into the right hands, and they expected better treatment for their money." They continued:

Perhaps in an earlier day when the electorate was smaller and more deferential, the party organization had been able to deliver the vote with fewer hitches, but if that had ever been the case, it was no longer true by the 1880s. Considered in this light, it is hardly surprising that candidates and major party officials looked favorably on the proposals to restrict local leaders and to eliminate ticket pedlars entirely."[119]

8.4 CONCLUSION

The decline of electoral bribery in Britain in the United States tells us a good deal about how it worked, at the time when it remained vital in both countries. Vote buying focused on the poor; when the poor and vulnerable among the electorate shrank and the middle class grew, relatively fewer votes could be purchased with cash or minor consumption goods. The equivalent resources could attract more voters through persuasive discourse and publicity. Vote buying required close contact between brokers and voters, given its fine-grained functions of monitoring voters and delivering goods and services to them; when the electorate as a whole, and electoral districts, became more populous, the political machine became a more costly organization through which to obtain votes. The premium that machine politics places on local knowledge of constituents creates rent-seeking opportunities for brokers; when party leaders could shift to direct appeals to voters without risking their own seats and their party's prospects, they happily sloughed off their machines.

---

[118] Reynolds and McCormick 1986, p. 847.
[119] Reynolds and McCormick 1986, p. 848. In a similar vein, Winkler 2000, p. 877, wrote, "Party reforms sought to deprive local bosses of control over elections."

PART IV

CLIENTELISM AND DEMOCRATIC THEORY

9

What's Wrong with Buying Votes?

9.1 DISTRIBUTIVE POLITICS AND DEMOCRATIC THEORY

Distributive strategies can be divided into two categories: those with public and binding rules about who gets what, and those in which these rules are absent or hidden. We began this study by emphasizing the contrast as a conceptual one, but one that was driven by real-world empirics. Here we shift lenses and consider this distinction from the point of view of political philosophy. What would contemporary theorists of justice say about programmatic and nonprogrammatic strategies? Given that reason and deliberation are at the center of normative democratic theory as it has evolved over the past half century, nonprogrammatic strategies appear to be antithetical to notions of just distribution.

Consider the theory of justice proposed by Rawls.[1] Just distributions are ones that would be acceptable to free, equal, and rational citizens in the original position, people who do not know what their endowments in the society that they are constructing will be. Hidden criteria cannot be evaluated by these citizens. Hence how the particular distributive outcomes that these criteria might produce measure up to standards of justice is unknowable. Or consider the theory of justice put forth by Barry.[2] Here distributive rules are just when they would be accepted as fair by reasonable people who would be harmed by them. It follows that rules of distribution that remain hidden from public view can never be shown to be just.

More than that, we strongly suspect that injustice and secrecy are causally linked. Our conjecture is that distributive rules remain hidden precisely in cases in which they would be most likely to fail tests of fairness and justice. They are kept out of public view precisely because their patent unfairness would hurt

[1] Rawls 1971.
[2] Barry 1995, see also Scanlon 1998.

the prospects of the office seekers who deploy them. A rule that says "invest in recreational facilities in places where the ruling party is in danger of losing," as in the Australian case, or "allocate environmental grants in places with many swing voters," as in the Swedish case, or "lavish public funds in the districts of powerful incumbents," as in the Illinois or Canadian cases, or "offer access to antipoverty programs preferentially to responsive voters," as in several Latin American cases would, if made public, fail the test of fairness and likely hurt the party that voiced it. Our conjecture is that public political discourse filters out unfair distributive rules; this filtering produces an association between unjust and hidden principles of distribution.

It might appear that not much more need be said about the normative status of clientelism, vote buying, or other varieties of nonprogrammatic distribution. But more needs to be said, for two reasons. One is that the departure from democratic norms of justice, not to mention equality and autonomy, is more acute under some nonprogrammatic practices than under others. One task of this chapter is to highlight these differences, in light of our empirical study. Second, partisan bias and clientelism are sometimes justified on consequentialist grounds. Beneficial consequences might mitigate, or even neutralize, violations of democratic norms. Markets for votes are sometimes seen as having the beneficial effects of increasing participation, or of encouraging redistribution, or of enhancing efficiency. We take up each claim in this chapter.

We consider the consequences of distributive strategies for individuals. However, elections and other democratic acts are public phenomena, in which the public has interests. Democratic theorists have long identified a public interest in using elections as vehicles for representation, which requires that elections communicate the preferences and sentiments of the citizenry. They have also identified an interest in elections as mechanisms of accountability, in which an incumbent is either renewed or turned out of office in light of his or her performance during the term that is ending.[3] Most fundamentally, elections are moments for choosing political leaders, as a function of the electorates' actions at the polls. When scholars consider the impact of vote trafficking, they have appropriately weighed these public considerations, as shall we.[4] Whatever their effects on individuals, one must consider whether and to what extent nonprogrammatic practices promote or interfere with representation, accountability, and the choice of leaders.

Between the individual and polity-wide consequences, nonprogrammatic strategies also hold consequences for classes of citizens – for clients, for instance, or for the poor. These consequences have been ignored in prior studies, a shortcoming we hope to avoid.

As a prelude to this discussion, it is worth commenting on the concepts of freedom, autonomy, and equality. The image of the citizen emerging from

---

[3] For the history of these ideas and contemporary views, see, e.g., Pitkin 1967 and Manin 1997.
[4] See, in particular, Karlan 1994.

normative democratic theory is a person who is free and equal. We adopt from political philosophy a notion of freedom that is linked to autonomy. Autonomy of citizens as voters does not mean that they are insulated from public reason, which Rawls defined as "the reasoning of legislators, executives (presidents, for example), and judges ... candidates in political elections, and of party leaders and others who work in their campaigns," as well as of voters themselves.[5] Autonomous citizens are influenced by public reason but are not coerced; this is one important sense in which they are free. Democratic deliberation requires that public discussions of policies precede votes and participants do not attempt to change each other's behavior with threats of sanctions and coercive force.[6]

Yet where to draw the line between influence and coercion is not always clear. For the sake of making the strongest possible case against the easy view that vote buying harms vote sellers, we stipulate that voters facing nonprogrammatic parties find themselves in situations that fall short of full coercion. This is more obviously true under what we have termed "partisan bias." A voter whose district has been lavished with pork, for instance, retains sufficient autonomy that he or she can ignore the pork and vote on other grounds, without personal material consequence. More controversially, one might hold that a voter whose actions are monitored by a machine can choose to allow the grim trigger to be pulled: he or she can forfeit benefits and vote against the party. The voter might be interpreted as willingly paying a price (in forgone benefits) to "purchase" the freedom to choose to vote against his or her erstwhile benefactor's wishes. Although in comparison with the beneficiary of pork, his or her autonomy is more curtailed, we have little doubt that many voters have made just this choice.

Why not simply interpret vote sellers as people who make a free choice to reap a targeted benefit, however modest, over voting for a candidate or party on some other grounds? The difficulty with this formulation is that it ignores a fundamental asymmetry between decisions under clientelism and other kinds of electoral decisions. Recalling our discussion from Chapter 6, a voter whose decision rule is "support the candidate offering policies most to one's liking" will not enjoy any material benefit or suffer any material harm as a direct consequence of that choice. In mass elections, individuals' choices basically never change the outcome, even more so in programmatic settings, where the rule boundedness of distribution further severs any connection between one's vote and one's receipt of benefits.

Not so under clientelism. As we have noted several times, the effect of linking a person's material welfare to his or her vote creates a basic asymmetry between expressive voting and vote selling. No matter how appealing a promised program or how gratifying an incumbent's programmatic accomplishments, support flows away from those who "do not have money to give"

---

[5] Rawls 1996, p. 382.
[6] See Mansbridge 2010.

and toward those who "have things to give away."[7] The asymmetry also gives rise to a collective action problem for clients. Even if they strongly prefer the policies on offer from one party, they may be induced to vote against it if what they care about is their own material well-being. Overcoming the collective action problem would require a degree of coordination that is difficult for mass electorates to achieve.

This basic difference between voters' decision making under vote buying versus under programmatic politics helps answer another question: if poor voters weigh material considerations especially heavily in their voting decisions, is it not the case that programmatic appeals to material self-interest also create political inequalities between poor and wealthier voters? That is, if a central difficulty that vote trafficking poses for democracy is that it involves distinct responses from poor and wealthy voters, then public appeals to material self-interest also pose difficulties for democracy and should perhaps be banned.[8] Such a ban would be tantamount to insisting "that the franchise be exercised without taint of individual benefit," to return to the U.S. Supreme Court's formulation – and few would so insist.[9]

What makes vote trafficking toxic for the poor is not that they may be especially strongly influenced by appeals to self-interest, but that they are bribed into not pressing their material interests on their representatives who shape public policy, whereas wealthy voters avoid being so bribed. A bag of rice given in exchange for a vote trumps the expression of support for, say, a more generous welfare state. Under vote buying, public policy will tilt away from the interests of the class of vote sellers; their votes do not communicate policy preferences prospectively, nor do they communicate judgments of policy or performance retrospectively. This prejudicial effect of vote trafficking on poor voters is a consequence of parties having limited budgets and finding the poor to be most responsive. Were a machine to begin buying votes at the top of the income distribution, the rich would suffer these same prejudicial effects.

These considerations bring us to the question of equality. A fundamental tenet of democratic theory is that citizens have equal political rights. When parts of the citizenry are induced to make expressive choices in elections and the others discouraged from doing so, this basic equality has been breached. The citizenry is now composed of people whose rights may formally be equal but who will exercise them in disquietingly different ways.

Another conceivable argument in favor of allowing people to sell their votes is that doing is merely allows them to mitigate risk. If the delivery of policy promises is inherently risky and some people have a distaste for risk, we might view the ability to sell one's vote for a sure (even if small) benefit as an expression of individual distaste for risk. Earlier we reviewed evidence that weighed

---

[7] To cite, again, the nonclientelist party organizer interviewed by Szwarcberg 2013.
[8] See Lippert-Rasmussen 2010.
[9] *Brown v. Hartlage* p. 456 of U.S. 57.

against the interpretation of clientelism as risk aversion. Even if some people were motivated to sell their votes as a way of reducing electoral risk, the fact that people with low incomes are likely to be more averse to risk (see Chapter 6) would raise disturbing questions about class-based inequality. Poor and risk-averse voters would be communicating less about their policy preferences and involved less in holding office holders to account.

9.2 NONPROGRAMMATIC DISTRIBUTION AND THE DIVERSITY OF HARMS

In this section we consider the particular deleterious consequences – to individual voters, classes of voters, and to the public – attached to particular types of nonprogrammatic strategies. These considerations produce a rough ranking by severity of harm, and we discuss them from least to most harmful. The discussion is summarized in Table 9.1.

9.2.1 Partisan Bias: Nonconditional Benefits to Individuals and Pork

For reasons already discussed, the voter who faces no conditionality has greater autonomy than the voter who faces possible sanctions if he defects. The voter whose district has been supplied with local public goods can vote against the incumbents without personal harm. He or she can vote against the incumbent even despite its having paved the roads in his or her district rather than another one that needed them more, or even though it gave him or her access to an antipoverty program while more needy people went without. The voter will not suffer any direct consequences should he or she defect. And he or she votes free of coercion or threats of sanctions. Because they are relatively autonomy preserving, we find pork-barrel politics and nonconditional benefits to individuals to be less deleterious to democracy than is clientelism.

Yet they are not harmless. At the most basic level, because the real criteria guiding distribution are hidden, they are likely to be unjust. Indeed, in neo-Kantian terms, they are basically unjust by definition.[10] They are also inefficient, if efficiency means allocating resources appropriately to achieve socially defined ends.

We posit that pork-barrel politics is somewhat less harmful than is nonconditional benefits to individuals. The individual targeting entailed in the electoral diversion of public programs is likely to be less visible than is pork-barrel politics and hence more insidious. Politicized allocations of antipoverty funds

---

[10] The formulation that we used earlier, that hidden criteria cannot be shown to be just by the methods proposed by neo-Kantian philosophers, is more accurate. Just distributions might in theory be realized through programs whose criteria remain obscure, but the nonpublic, non-deliberative quality of such hypothetical programs would mean that their justice could never be evaluated by citizens.

TABLE 9.1. *Nonprogrammatic Distribution: Summary of Harms*

Type of Non-programmatic Strategy	Harm to Individual Voters	Harm to Class of Voters or Citizens	Harm to Polity
Pork-barrel politics	Individuals in nonprivileged constituencies lose public goods		Inefficient allocation of resources
Nonconditional benefits to individuals	Nonprivileged individuals lose access to public programs		Inefficient allocation of resources
Organization buying	Opportunity costs of time	Loss of benefits to rightful beneficiaries	Inefficient allocation of resources
Pure turnout buying	Potential loss of autonomy	*Benefit* of higher turnout of low-income citizens	Biasing of election results, potential blunting of accountability
Fused vote/ turnout buying	Loss of autonomy		Blunting of mandates, accountability
Vote buying	Loss of autonomy	Reduced influence over public policy	Blunting of mandates, accountability
Abstention buying	Loss of autonomy, reduced participation	Reduced influence over public policy	Biasing of election results, blunting of mandates, accountability depressed participation

among families or emergency funds among the victims of natural disasters may be slower to come to light than the politicized allocation of bridges or schools.

9.2.2 Clientelism

Organization Buying

A central finding of our study is that voters who receive payments are frequently loyal partisans who sell not their vote or their electoral participation but their involvement in their brokers' networks. Because party loyalists are cheaper to organize, the people becoming active in networks are mainly supporters of the party. Also, they suffer no expressive disutility from voting for a party whose program or identity they disdain. The main cost to these people is the opportunity cost of the time spent on organizational activities – attending rallies and the like – and the inconveniences involved.[11] The primary losers in this case are not the voters or the polity at large, but party leaders, from whom brokers extract rents.

We underscore, then, as an important contribution of our study that it uncovers the prevalence of a form of nonprogrammatic, even clientelistic politics, which, ironically, is relatively harmless.

Yet organization buying is not entirely benign. Its main deleterious public effect is to redirect resources away from their rightful beneficiaries to loyal supporters. In other words, it is socially inefficient, in the sense offered earlier, of interfering with the achievement of democratically established distributive goals.

Pure Turnout Buying

A machine that only pays people to turn out, but not to change their vote, will target its own loyal supporters who are in danger of abstaining. We find this a relatively harmless version of clientelism. It switches no one's vote, meaning that it is relatively autonomy preserving.

Turnout buying also boosts participation.[12] A strong piece of evidence that clientelism increases turnout is that, historically, antibribery, antimachine reforms had the effect of driving turnout down. Converse has shown that the introduction of the Australian ballot in the United States increased abstention.

To the extent that turnout buying favors the poor – following the logic of Chapter 6, we expect them to be most responsive, given diminishing marginal utility of income – it may counter abstentionism among low-income groups. The introduction of the Australian ballot in the United States increased abstention in particular among populations who would otherwise have sold their votes: the urban poor, rural voters. For this reason, historians have sometimes looked askance at the introduction of the ballot or other antitrafficking reforms, seeing in them lightly cloaked efforts by social elites to exclude poor and illiterate voters.[13]

Yet there are three negative features of pure turnout buying. One is that it may leach easily into vote buying.[14] Even a party that legitimately wants only to "get out the vote" without influencing vote choice might be interpreted as pressuring voters to return the favor of a campaign gift or a ride to the polls

---

[11] These inconveniences are not always minor. Szwarcberg 2009 reported a case in which a young mother was asked by her broker to attend a rally and had to leave her baby in the inadequate care of a teenage neighbor. The baby suffered a serious accident, with lasting consequences. Ironically, the broker – having, in an indirect sense, caused the accident – also transported the baby to a clinic and hence probably helped save its life.

[12] The case for vote buying as – at least in part – turnout buying has been made by Lindbeck and Weibull 1987, Cox 2009, and Nichter 2008.

[13] Keyssar 2001; Reynolds 1988.

[14] This problem is analyzed in Karlan 1994.

with their votes. Even if the turnout seller is a supporter of the party (as we generally expect to be the case, otherwise it would not try to mobilize him or her), but a supporter who doesn't want to vote for it this time around, any incentive to get him or her to the polls may also to be interpreted as an effort to win his or her vote.

Furthermore, the autonomy-preserving quality of pure turnout buying depends on the reasons why a voter would otherwise abstain. If a loyalist chooses to abstain to avoid bearing the costs of voting, then offsetting these costs without seeking to influence the vote seems unobjectionable.[15] However, consider the case of the loyalist who chooses to abstain because he or she is unhappy with his or her party but can't bear the thought of voting for its opponent. The loyalist is in effect choosing to cast a vote against his or her party and is helping its opponents, though less than he or she would by turning out and voting for them. In this case, luring the loyalist back to the polls with a blandishment is in a sense changing his or her vote. In this case – not an unusual one, according to our findings – even pure turnout buying inflicts a loss of autonomy on the voter. And it weakens the accountability function of elections.

The third potentially harmful effect of pure turnout buying is not on individual voters – or not on them alone – but on the polity as a whole: it potentially biases the outcome of elections. Even in instances in which parties pay would-be abstainers among their constituents who are simply put off by the cost of participation, the outcome of the election will be biased by the resources the parties have available to spend, which may be unequally distributed across parties or between incumbents and challengers.

It is also important to ask, why do we – and why do political theorists – consider broad voter participation to be so important for democracy? And does participation elicited by material inducements warrant the same central place in democratic theory?

Participation is often valued on consequentialist grounds. In one argument, people and groups who participate influence the actions of government, and categories of people should not be excluded from influencing their governments. Although the influence of individual voters on policy is negligible, in democracies the influence of groups who vote at high rates is considerable. Participation is also deemed to have beneficial consequences for the participant: it is educative, edifying, enlarging.[16] There are many nonconsequentialist grounds on which political theorists value participation.

Participation under payment is unlikely to have the same effects or meanings. Votes wield influence when they aggregate into mandates or into accountability as contingent renewal. There are reasons to doubt that purchased votes are part of these sums. Regarding the intrinsic benefits of participation for

---

[15] Nichter 2008, Dunning and Stokes 2008.
[16] See, e.g., Pateman 1970, Verba et al. 1978.

the voter, there is little systematic information available about the effects of voting on people whose participation is elicited by a private material inducement. However, one hint comes from studies – discussed in Chapter 1 – that use unobtrusive measures to gauge the prevalence of vote selling. The much higher rates of vote selling sometimes revealed by unobtrusive than by direct questions, among the same survey populations, imply that the practice is a source of embarrassment and shame. And Sunstein warned of the dangers of commodifying votes when people are paid to show up at the polls.[17]

Fused Turnout/Vote Buying

In contrast to pure turnout buying, here Party A dispenses a gift to a person and, as a result, he or she turns out to vote and votes for Party A. Counterfactually, without the bribe from Party A, this person would (1) not have voted and (2) if he or she had voted, he or she would have cast his or her ballot for Party B.

This fused form is a sharper departure from democratic norms than is pure turnout buying. It carries all of the negative consequences of vote buying, undermining both autonomy and equality (see next section). It also carries the same harms that we just saw may go with turnout buying, such as a blunting of accountability and a biasing of election results.

Vote Buying

Our study shows that parties try to buy the votes of a range of citizens: swing voters whose indifference is overcome with a bag of food or a mattress; mild opponents, who are willing to stomach supporting a party they don't like in return for a payment; even, perhaps, loyalists who are temporarily disgruntled. In all these cases, by assumption, the payment changes the vote; otherwise we would not call it vote buying. In this way, vote buying is distinct from turnout and organization buying, where votes may not be changed. For this reason, vote buying is a clearer and more egregious encroachment on voter autonomy. What's more, it is the threat of a sanction – the withdrawal of a reward, or worse – if one defects that gives vote buying its teeth.[18] How coercive vote buying is undoubtedly varies from situation to situation. But it lends itself more to coercion than do non–broker-mediated strategies and hence is more autonomy encroaching than they are.

Vote buying also undercuts the public's interest in elections as instruments of representation. Votes that are purchased carry little information about the preferences of the person who sold them. Does the voter (or class of voters) approve or disapprove of the incumbent's performance? Does the voter favor extending social benefits, cutting taxes, forging closer ties to other countries? It's hard to say when what lies behind the voter's electoral decision is a bag of

[17] Sunstein 1994.
[18] See Stokes 2005, p. 295.

rice or corrugated roofing for his or her home. Likewise, democratic account-ability is undercut. Incumbents who purchase the votes of people who would otherwise vote against them, because they are unhappy with the incumbent's performance, escape the accountability mechanism.

Vote buying also creates classes of voters whose votes are valued differently. Political machines are unlikely to purchase every citizen's vote, but will favor more responsive citizens over less-responsive ones: the poor, the indifferent, the loyalist at risk of defection. Political parties can largely ignore the policy preferences of vote sellers. Because some citizens' interests will be considered whereas others are ignored – their votes secured not through public policy but through payments – vote buying undermines political equality.

Abstention Buying

Where does abstention buying fall in the hierarchy of departures from demo-cratic norms? Is it just as bad for people to be paid to turn out to vote as to be paid to stay home? If Party A pays Jane to turn out to vote, she is likely to be a Party A supporter. If Party A pays Jane to stay home, she is a Party B supporter. Whereas turnout buying may mean a party paying its own support-ers to overcome the costs of voting, and vote buying may mean paying a party supporter not to defect, abstention buying always means inducing someone not to vote for their preferred party. For this reason it is the clearest instance of voters being induced to act against their preferences, and hence it is a striking instance of encroachment on voter autonomy.

One intuition for why turnout buying is less harmful than abstention buying is that without perfect monitoring by brokers, there is always a chance that the person who sells his or her participation may escape detection and reassert his or her autonomy by voting as she would have, absent the blandishment. Or that the person will reassert his or her autonomy and vote his or her preferences even while expecting to be detected and hence anticipating a break with his or her broker. The equivalent action on the part of the abstention seller would be to sneak to the polls; but (non-)participation is usually more easily detected than vote choice, so the abstention seller is more constrained. And as long as she stays home, she has no chance of defecting in the privacy of the voting booth.

9.3 ARGUMENTS IN FAVOR OF NONPROGRAMMATIC DISTRIBUTION

9.3.1 Participation

There are several arguments marshalled in favor of markets for votes. One of them, which we have already discussed, is that it can boost political participa-tion (turnout buying). Indeed, turnout buying historically and still today stim-ulates participation among sectors that are the most likely to abstain, absent an incentive: the poor and marginalized. Yet we noted potential countervailing harms, such as a degrading of participation when it is purchased. What is the meaning of a vote, or of the act of turning out and casting it, when it is elicited as part of a conditional exchange? Surely it carries little information about the policy preferences or assessments of incumbent performance, and some theorists point to the further deleterious effects of in the commodification of the vote.

We turn now to two other purported consequences of a market for votes that theorists sometimes extol: redistribution and efficiency.

9.3.2 Redistribution

What should we make of the case for vote trafficking as a mechanism of redistribution? Office seekers purchase the votes of poor people. If reformers were to eliminate the market for votes, the argument goes, politics would become less redistributive. Relatedly, one might infer from the fact that political machines know their constituents well and can efficiently deliver benefits to them that the demise of machines leaves vulnerable populations underserviced and neglected.

Several studies underscore the progressive elements of clientelist social and political relations, in comparison with relations of utter dependence and intimidation that they are assumed to displace. Scott's classic studies of machine politics locate it at an intermediate stage of social development.[19] A prior stage is one in which subordinate actors follow the dictates of their superiors, treating them with deference and subservience. By contrast, the political machine has almost democratic features. At the stage of development in which machines supplant landlords and notables, erstwhile dependents become clients who must be paid for their political support. Scott writes:

Given its principal concern for retaining office, the machine was a responsive, informal context within which bargaining based on reciprocity relationships was facilitated. Leaders of the machine were rarely in a position to dictate because those who supported them did so on the basis of value received or anticipated. The machine for the most part accepted its electoral clients as they were and responded to their needs in a manner that would elicit their support. The pragmatic, opportunistic orientation of the machine made it a flexible institution that could accommodate new groups and leaders in highly dynamic situations.[20]

This depiction of the machine, with its intimate connections to clients and its fine-grained attentiveness to their needs, anticipates Dixit and Londregan's view of the relationship between core constituents and their machine. The machine's "greater understanding translates into greater efficiency in the allocation of

---

[19] Scott 1969.
[20] Scott 1969, p. 1144.

particularistic benefits: patronage dollars are spent more effectively, while taxes may impose less pain per dollar."[21]

For those concerned with redistribution, the key question is whether clientelism is more or less redistributive than its likely alternatives. Scott's comparison is between electoral bribery and an historical antecedent, in which political support was elicited from lowly social subordinates with no need to compensate them. Yet in the historical cases of Britain and the United States considered in the last chapter, the decline of clientelism anticipated the rise of welfare states, which undoubtedly offered distributive gains to the poor of greater magnitude and more efficiently deployed than the clientelist systems that came before them. Some have suggested, indeed, that clientelism creates incentives for political machines to keep their constituents in poverty.[22] At the very least, the incentives that they have to improve the material conditions of their constituents are weak.

9.3.3 Efficiency

Positive theorists sometimes extol markets for votes on the grounds that they increase efficiency. The basic intuition is this. Assume that some voters care intensely about an outcome about which other voters care little. If those who care intensely can buy the votes of those who care little, then allowing a market for votes produces decisions that are Pareto-superior to, for instance, simple majority rule without vote buying.[23] Early enthusiasts found that markets for votes not only increased social welfare but also solved problems of instability in collective decisions.[24]

The main real-world setting that these theorists have in mind is legislatures. Yet some extend the argument to public elections and mass electorates.[25] Coleman, for instance, thinks stability and efficiency-enhancing exchanges of votes are available to "city councils, legislatures, town meetings, or social groups," and extends the exchange mechanisms in theory to collective decisions made by large numbers of individuals.[26] If arguments in favor of vote buying are apt for public elections, then it would seem that we should return to public voting. If that suggestion seems ludicrous, it becomes important to identify differences between voting in legislatures and voting in public elections that

---

[21] Dixit and Londregan 1996, p. 1134.

[22] Balland and Robinson 2007.

[23] An allocation X is Pareto-superior to Y if it makes at least one agent better off without making any agent worse off, relative to Y.

[24] Social choice studies underscoring the benefits of vote buying included Buchanan and Tullock 1962, Coleman 1966, and Mueller 1973. Other theorists have been skeptical about the stability-inducing effects of markets for votes: see inter alia Park 1967, Ferejohn 1974, Schwartz 1977, 1981.

[25] Buchanan and Tullock 1962, Coleman 1966.

[26] Coleman 1966, p. 1111.

would vitiate the comparison. What's more, as Hasen notes, vote trading is legal in legislatures but illegal in public elections, and it is not always self-evident why.[27]

Arguments from log-rolling in legislatures to vote buying in electorates ignore key differences between the two settings. In logrolls, legislators agree to support a policy proposal that they otherwise would not support and about which they have weak preferences. A legislator would not be induced to vote in a way that went against his or her sincere and intense wishes, especially if his or her vote would be pivotal to the outcome. In many legislative settings, it is not irrational for legislators to make their voting decisions on the assumption of tied votes.

The contrast with voters in mass electorates could hardly be more stark. They may indeed be induced by direct payments to cast votes that run strongly counter to their sincere preferences, precisely because there will basically never be anything at stake, at least not in a narrow material sense, in their vote. Once a voting body grows to more than 100, the chances of an individual casting a pivotal vote is indistinguishable from zero.

For these reasons, vote sellers in mass electorates are in danger of losing autonomy in ways that logrolling legislators are not. As mentioned, a counter-argument might be that the vote seller's desired state of the world is to be better off by the amount of the minor side payment and to forgo the expressive value of casting his or her vote for a sincerely preferred candidate or party.[28] And if the vote seller cares intensely enough about expressing his or her support for a different party, or casting a protest vote against the party he or she generally sides with, he or she might forgo the side payment, or take it and hope that the defection remains opaque. Or perhaps the vote seller cares intensely about expressing his or her desire for elections to be autonomy preserving; again the vote seller might forgo the direct payment. But votes as expressions do not bring these states of the world into being, and hence those who might cast them will often succumb to the temptation to take direct payoffs, all the more so when they value every addition to their income very highly.

Any assessment of the efficiency-enhancing effects that might be achieved by allowing people to sell their votes also must take into account possible negative externalities. Elections have public benefits, such as revealing the electorate's sentiments on matters of collective importance (mandates) and holding incumbents accountable for their actions. We have seen that, in theory, allowing people to sell their votes undermines the mandate and accountability

---

[27] Hasen 2000. An exception, in which logrolling is illegal, is the state legislature of Wisconsin, though there have no prosecutions under that law. See Hasen p. 1339.

[28] We use the term "sincere vote" loosely; the same logic as laid out here would apply to voters who vote "strategically" for a less-preferred candidate, to avoid "wasting" their votes on losers, as in Cox 1997.

functions of elections. Therefore, markets for votes entail substantial negative externalities.[29]

Efficiency arguments for vote buying in mass electorates founder, then, on the dissimilarities between vote sellers in legislatures and among mass publics and the latter's likely loss of autonomy when votes are bought and sold, and on the negative externalities likely to be involved, in particular the social costs from the loss of mandate and accountability functions of public elections.

To conclude, arguments in favor of markets for votes are not compelling, whether on participation, redistributive, or efficiency grounds.

9.4 CONCLUSIONS

We began this study with a series of vexing puzzles. Why is it generally deemed justified for parties to appeal to voters' material self-interest through programs but not with payments? Why are apparently unresponsive loyalists often the beneficiaries of non-programmatic distribution? Why did vote buying disappear from some democracies where it was once widespread? We hope to have delved deeply into the topic and to have offered compelling explanations.

The core arguments of our study can be briefly summarized. Political distribution of valued material goods is at the core of much democratic politics. Political distribution can be perfectly legitimate and just. It is legitimate and just when public reason and deliberation establish the rules for who gets what and when these public rules are respected in practice. When the rules are hidden or inconsequential, as in what we call nonprogrammatic politics, the justice of distribution can never be assured.

Our study pivots around another key distinction between different kinds of non-programmatic distribution. This distinction is between distribution in which voters are held to account for their voting choices and distribution in which the parties make no effort to enforce compliance. This difference in strategies is intimately linked to a difference in organizational structure. Parties that attempt to make benefits conditional on electoral choices – those that practice clientelism – deploy large numbers of broker to meet the information, distribution, and enforcement requirements for holding vote sellers to account. Reflecting the intimate link between strategic choice and party organizational structure, we have used the terms "clientelism" and "machine politics" interchangeably.

Brokers solve some problems for party leaders but cause new ones. The leader–broker dynamic explains how clientelism works and also why leaders abandon it when conditions allow.

Machine politics remains widespread in many developing-world democracies. It is rare in wealthy democracies. But a transition away from the political

---

[29] See Karlan 1994 for further discussion of the collective benefits of elections and how these benefits are reduced by vote trafficking.

distribution of the party machine and to programmatic politics often remains incomplete, even in the advanced democracies. In the latter, as we have seen, everything from emergency aid to hurricane victims to recreational facilities may be doled out according to criteria that are kept apart from "public reason."

We conclude this study knowing that several crucial questions remain unanswered. The current trajectory of clientelism in today's developing democracies is one such question. When in Chapter 6 we plotted levels of vote buying in African and Latin American countries against their national gross domestic products, we saw that the levels of the vote buying were "too high" in several, including Mexico and Argentina. A rich literature is currently emerging that points toward the rise of a more thoroughly programmatic politics in several Latin American countries.[30] Our own surveys in Argentina, carried out over nearly a decade between 2001 and 2009, registered a small but steady decline in the percentages of citizens who said they had received campaign gifts. We leave it to future scholarship to judge whether these trends will last, how quickly and consistently parties and governments will make the shift, and whether our models and analyses help shed light on the transitions. The unfinished path traveled by wealthy democracies shows that the triumph of public reason over hidden agendas is unlikely to be quick and irreversible. The coexistence in Mexico of the antipoverty program *Progresa*, with its many safety checks against bias, and *La Efectiva*, with its promise of access to public resources for those who voted the right way, counsels similar caution.

A second set of unanswered questions focuses not on clientelism but on what we have called "partisan bias," in which the real criteria of distribution are hidden, but the allocation of benefits is not conditional on voters' actions. Some countries, even at high levels of income and after many decades of uninterrupted democracy, persist in partisan bias, whether in the form of nonconditional benefits to individuals or pork-barrel politics. Our comparisons of the abrupt demise of clientelism in Britain and its contrastingly slow decline in the United States is suggestive of reasons – related to the contrasting natures of the electorates and institutional settings – why partisan bias remains more prevalent in the United States than in the U.K. today. Our model in Chapter 7 is suggestive of factors that can help explain leaders' choice between unmediated but nonprogrammatic versus programmatic distribution. But a fuller analytical treatment, along with systematic empirical tests, remains a task for future scholarship.

The conceptual scheme with which we opened this study began with a distinction between different kinds of distributive politics. We end with a comment on what one might think about as a prior branch, one distinguishing distributive strategies from politics that is not about the material distribution at all. Is

---

[30] See, e.g., Cornelius 2004 and Magaloni 2006 on Mexico; Zucco 2012 and Fried 2012 on Brazil; and De la O 2012 for a comparison of several comparative cash transfer programs in the region.

there not an inherent tension between distributive politics per se and democracy? Some might regard even programmatic *distributive* politics as introducing a certain crassness in public life, an encouragement to materialism and egocentrism. Or, at best, materialist motivations for voters' choices are required by "political pluralism," which is "predicated on the expectation that voters will pursue their individual good through the political process;" but this is not democracy at its most uplifting.[31] Our view is different. A universal role of states is to redistribute from the wealthy to the poor, the young to the old; to use public resources to insure against risks of unemployment and illness; to invest in public goods that cannot be left to the market to provide; and, in myriad other ways, to intervene in protecting the material welfare of its citizens and residents. Although something is amiss if distributive matters are all that public debate is about, as long as the choices need to be made, public-sphere discussions of them are a sign of a vibrant democracy.

From the opposite vantage point, skeptics might doubt that public deliberations produce anything more than rhetorical window dressing in favor of the economic interests of the majority or of the privileged and powerful. Fairness tests for distributive justice will seem to these skeptics quixotic. And certainly democratic politics offers much – too much – evidence in their favor. But if their skepticism were always warranted, then we would not expect democratic politics ever to produce policies that help minorities or that protect against risks to which only the powerless and vulnerable are exposed.

[31] U.S. Supreme Court 1982.

Appendix A
Argentina Brokers' Survey

To gather fine-grained information about the preferences and behaviors of political brokers, we surveyed elected city councilors and non-elected activists who work for those councilors in the Argentine provinces of Córdoba, San Luis, and Misiones, as well as the Conurbano area of greater Buenos Aires.[1] In this book, we refer to both councilors and non-elected activists as "brokers." This is appropriate, as councilors may work as operatives for mayors or other politicians at higher levels of the political system, whereas many councilors also had worked as neighborhood operatives before rising to elected office. The non-elected activists we surveyed, meanwhile, work directly as political operatives for councilors. We therefore believe that both elected councilors and their non-elected operatives should be considered local brokers. Surveying them gives us important insights into their preferences and behaviors.

The major difficulty involved in surveying brokers involves how to generate a representative sample. Previous researchers working in Argentina, such as Auyero and Levitsky, have generated valuable insights into the political function and behaviors of brokers.[2] Yet it is difficult to know how results from these convenience samples may or may not extend to the many tens of thousands of political operatives who comprise the population of interest. Generating a probability sample of these operatives is challenging, however, because a ready-made sampling frame – that is, a list of brokers from which one could draw a random sample – does not exist.

As outlined in Chapter 4, our approach to this problem was two-fold. First, we drew a probability sample of councilors by randomly sampling municipalities from four Argentine provinces and then randomly sampling city councilors

---

[1] Our surveys were approved by the Yale Human Subjects Expedited Review Committee under 1RB Protocol #0906005355.
[2] Auyero 2001, Levitsky 2003.

in each of those municipalities. Once municipalities were sampled, it was straightforward to obtain a list of councilors and thus a sampling frame for councilors in each municipality. Second, our survey instrument then asked sampled councilors for a list of the non-elected activists who work for them. This generated, for each sampled councilor, a sampling frame of brokers, from which we could then sample at random.

As far as we know, our data provide the first large, representative sample of brokers in any country. The subjects of the survey bear some resemblance to those sampled for the European Political Party Middle Level Elites study,[3] but our samples operate at a lower level and come from much more bottom-heavy parties or machines. Possible bias from nonresponse or from the failure of councilors to provide complete lists of their non-elected brokers – discussed later – could compromise the strict probability sampling of non-elected brokers. The elected councilors' selection would not be thus compromised, however.[4] Another innovative aspect of our effort was that we asked some questions as survey experiments, meaning that we recruited our experimental subjects in an unusual but valuable way. The value of our approach is that we are confident that our results can be reliably projected to the population of councilors from which our sample was drawn, and our procedure also generates systematic and likely quite representative data on non-elected brokers – a difficult population to study systematically.

In this Appendix we discuss our survey instrument, including its embedded survey experiments; describe our sampling design, including our procedure for drawing a probability sample of city councilors and a semiprobability sample of the non-elected operatives who work for them; and discuss challenges in data analysis, such as the bootstrapping of standard errors, that arise from the complex sampling design. The survey instrument was written and administered in Spanish; it was piloted in July 2009, and interviews took place between 2009 and 2011. In all, our sampling design called for us to interview approximately 800 brokers. Interviews were conducted by the authors, by a team of research assistants in each of the four provinces, and by Edwin Camp of Yale University, who was instrumental in planning and implementing the survey. Mariela Szwarzberg and Luis Schiumerini also helped us to develop the survey instrument; the surveys were implemented by us and by the team of research assistants we thank in the acknowledgments.

A.1 SURVEY INSTRUMENT

Our survey instrument sought to elicit several types of information from brokers.[5] At the start of each interview, we asked a battery of questions about the

[3] See Reif, Cayrol, and Niedermayer 1980.
[4] We might then describe our procedure as having generated a probability sample of councilors and a semiprobability sample of non-elected brokers.
[5] The survey instrument is posted in its entirety at http://www.thaddunning.com/data/brokers, along with the replication files and other materials.

broker's personal history working in politics: the party or parties the broker had worked for and elective offices sought or obtained. We also asked several questions tapping individual brokers' attitudes toward risk. At the conclusion of each interview, several questions also sought information on brokers' age, education, income, and other occupations.

Next, we asked several questions about the numbers and party affiliations of other brokers and voters in the neighborhood where the broker works. We also asked about the quantity and origin of resources obtained by brokers from party leaders and other sources, perceptions of the extent and nature of rent seeking by brokers, and the nature of relationships between individual brokers and "their" voters, including the kind and quality of information voters have about individual voters' preferences and behaviors. Finally, we asked a series of questions posing hypothetical scenarios for brokers, for instance, asking them to evaluate the types of voters that would be targeted for benefits in each scenario, what voters would do if they stopped receiving benefits, or what brokers would do if party leaders deprived them of resources.

Several of these latter questions were asked in the form of survey experiments. Thus we used four different versions of our questionnaire, with the version assigned at random to particular respondents.[6] Several survey-experimental questions were identical on versions 1 and 3 and versions 2 and 4; thus, for these questions, approximately one-half of respondents were assigned to one version of the question and one-half of respondents to the other. The main rationale for asking these questions in the form of survey experiments was that we were concerned that two questions posed to the same respondent, in which aspects of the scenario presented to the respondent varied across the two questions, would not provide valid counterfactuals for each other. In particular, we were concerned that exposure to one version of the question would condition responses to a second question – making it impossible to separate the effects of the particular scenario being posed from the effects of exposure to a different scenario earlier in the survey. One obvious alternative would have been to ask each broker every question but to randomize the question order, so that we could evaluate empirically the possibility of contamination by earlier questions. For logistical and cost reasons, however, we opted to confine the survey to different versions of paper-based questionnaires.[7] Because most survey-experimental questions had only two versions, moreover, we projected

---

[6] In practice, we implemented this by sorting stacks of questionnaires and working through the stacks in each municipality. There were many more respondents in each municipality than versions of the questionnaire (see Tables A.3.1 and A.3.2), and this ordered rotation very likely ensures that the version administered is statistically independent of respondents' characteristics or potential responses.

[7] We considered the purchase and use of electronic PDAs that would allow us to randomize question order more seamlessly. However, we did not pursue this alternative for the present study, for various reasons.

that we would have sufficient statistical power for detecting substantial effects
of exposure to different versions of the questions.

A.2 SAMPLING DESIGN

We purposively chose four Argentine provinces or subprovinces from which
to sample brokers: Córdoba, Misiones, San Luis, and the Conurbano area of
greater Buenos Aires. These areas vary with respect to the competitiveness of
the party system, the strength of Peronist and Radical party organizations, and
other factors such as urbanization that may be related to the efficacy or character of clientelism. Thus our chosen provinces include a large province with
a substantial Radical Party presence (Córdoba), an example of monopolistic
clientelism in which a single Peronist-affiliated family has long been politically
dominant (the Rodrguez Saá family in San Luis), a rural northeastern province
dominated by a single regional party (the *Partido Renovador* in Misiones,
which combines an important Radical faction and an important Peronist faction),[8] and the highly urban area of greater Buenos Aires that has historically
provided an important base for the Peronist party (the Conurbano). The sample
therefore contains two relatively competitive provinces and two monopolistic
provinces.

The Conurbano of Buenos Aires, with its heavy concentration of poor urban
voters, is judged to be of such importance to understanding clientelism in
Argentina that fine-grained information about the role of brokers there was a
particular priority. Moreover, as Szwarcberg and others emphasized, around
60 percent of registered voters in the province of Buenos Aires and one-quarter
of Argentina's total population live in the 24 municipalities of the Conurbano –
giving this area important influence over national electoral outcomes.[9] Thus,
we chose not to sample municipalities from the entire province of Buenos Aires
but focused instead on the Conurbano area.

Because these provinces were chosen purposively, we can only project results
from our survey to the population of brokers in these provinces. Still, these four
provinces or subprovinces contain a substantial proportion of the Argentine
population – around 52 percent of all Argentines.[10] They also include highly
politically relevant areas such the Conurbano, which makes these areas of
substantial interest and importance. We now describe how our samples of
municipalities and brokers were selected in each of the provinces.

[8] Perhaps 95 percent of mayors in Misiones are from the *Partido Renovador*, and they are quite
dominant in the province. Edwin Camp, personal communication.

[9] Szwarcberg 2009.

[10] Rounded, 2010 census figures give the population numbers as follows: Córdoba, 3.3 million;
Misiones 1 million; San Luis, 432,000; Conurbano, 16 million. These figures total to 20.7
million, or 52 percent of the 40 million residents in Argentina. Source: INDEC.

A.2.1 Sampling Municipalities

Within provinces, our design involved a multistage cluster sample. The primary sampling units were municipalities (*municipios*).[11] Within each of the three provinces and one sub-province (the Conurbano in Buenos Aires province), we sampled municipalities at random by assigning each municipality a quasi-random number uniformly distributed on the [0, 1] interval and sorting the municipalities in order of these numbers. We then worked down the lists in each until we had reached the overall target number of interviews of 800. We don't know the population of brokers in each province so could not design a strict probability-proportionate-to-size sample, but we drew more brokers from larger, more populated areas likely to have more brokers, such as the Conurbano (257 out of 800 brokers) and Córdoba (179 out of 800 brokers).[12] Our sampling design called for a particular fraction of the councilors in each municipality, and of the brokers working for these councilors, to be surveyed. Because we lacked a sampling frame for non-elected brokers in advance of data collection, and thus did not know how many brokers would enter our sample from each municipality, we opted to take the approach of working down the lists in each province until the required number of interviewees had been surveyed.[13]

Table A.1 shows the municipalities in each province that were selected into our sample. In the Conurbano of greater Buenos Aires, we sampled 10 of 24 municipalities; in Córdoba, 10 out of 249; in San Luis, 9 out of 18; and in Misiones, 20 out of 75.[14] In the Conurbano and Córdoba, the samples were self-weighting, whereas in San Luis and Misiones, municipalities with larger populations were weighted more heavily and thus had a larger probability of selection.[15] In San Luis, we excluded extremely small villages called communes ("*comunas*") from the universe of primary sampling units. More municipalities appear in Misiones than in other provinces in Table A.1 because municipalities in that province are on average smaller and have fewer councilors – necessitating sampling in more municipalities to reach our intended size of the broker sample in the province. Thus considering the universe of brokers in the four provinces as a whole, brokers from Misiones may be overrepresented.

---

[11] *Municipios* are administrative units somewhat akin to counties in the United States that, however, have city councils.

[12] See Table A.2. However, we also wound up with a large sample of 170 brokers from Misiones. San Luis, at 102 brokers, is also our least populous province, as described in a previous note in this Appendix A.

[13] We worked roughly synchronously in the different provinces, though started slightly earlier in Buenos Aires and Córdoba.

[14] Our bootstrapped standard errors, discussed below, take account of our sampling from small finite populations, which is especially important in the Conurbano and San Luis.

[15] In Misiones and San Luis, we weighted municipalities by population size: we divided each municipality's population by the province's total population and multiplied this ratio by the realization of a quasi-random number distributed uniformly on [0,1]. We then sorted the list in descending order according to the product of the population size ratio and the random number.

TABLE A.1. *Sampled Municipalities by Province*

Buenos Aires (Conurbano)	Córdoba	
Almirante Brown	Arroyito	
Avellaneda	Córdoba Capital	
Ezeiza	General Cabrera	
Florencio Varela	Huanchillas	
General San Martín	Las Varas	
Ituzaingó	San Francisco del Chañar	
Lanús	Santa María de Punilla	
Malvinas Argentinas	Tio Pujio	
San Martín	Villa Carlos Paz	
Tigre	Villa Fontana	

San Luis	Misiones	
Juana Koslay	25 de Mayo	Garupá
Justo Daract	Apóstoles	Jardín America
La Toma	Bernardo de Irigoyen	Oberá
Villa de Merlo	Campo Grande	Posadas
Naschel	Campo Ramón	Puerto Esperzanza
Quines	Candelaria	Puerto Iguazú
San Francisco del M. de O.	Com. Andres Guacurari	San Antonio
San Luis	Dos de Mayo	San Ignacio
Villa Mercedes	El Soberbio	San Pedro
	El Dorado	San Vicente

A.2.2 Sampling Brokers

Our method for sampling city councilors was simple. Once we had sampled municipalities, we obtained lists of the elected members of the city council in each sampled municipality. We then selected at random one-half of the councilors on each list and requested in-person, face-to-face interviews with these selected councilors.

Without a readily available sampling frame for non-elected brokers, the procedure for drawing a probability sample from that population was less straightforward. Indeed, the absence of such a sampling frame is a major obstacle to characterizing this population and constitutes an important contribution of our research.

Our strategy was as follows. During the interview with each councilor, we asked:

How many brokers [*referentes*[16]] work for you? Please, think only of those that you know by name.

---

[16] We used the word"*referente*" for broker, which might also be translated as "activist" or "operative" and which is more neutral than the often-used but sometimes pejorative term "*puntero.*"

The interviewer recorded this number. Among those who answered this question, the mean number of brokers was 19, with a standard deviation of 23.[17] We found substantial heterogeneity in answers to this question across provinces – from 23 in Buenos Aires and 22 in Misiones to 13 in Córdoba and 12 in San Luis.

Then, at the end of the interview, the councilor was read the following statement:

We thank you very much for your participation. The success of this academic study depends on the collaboration of many people like you. Thus, just as we have asked leaders throughout the country, we desire your collaboration to choose some of your brokers to interview. To assure that we interview a representative group, it is necessary that the selection of these people be done at random. I would like to ask for your help to sample some of the brokers who work for you, using a simple procedure that we have used in the other cases. Would you accept to help me?

Councilors who accepted this request were then asked for the name and contact information of each of their brokers. In most municipalities, we then sampled one-third of the brokers on these lists at random and attempted to contact these brokers to request interviews.[18] Two exceptions arose. When the interviewed councilor only named one broker, we interviewed that broker with probability one; when the councilor named two brokers, we interviewed one of them with probability one-half.

In principle, this procedure produces a probability sample of the non-elected brokers who work with city council members in our selected provinces. However, there are at least two important concerns about the representativeness of our sample of non-elected brokers. One is that councilors may not faithfully report the number of brokers who work for them, in response to our initial question. For instance, they may tend to inflate the number of brokers who they say work with them and then be unable to name this number of brokers at the end of the interview, making it difficult to evaluate the true nonresponse rate in our attempts to survey brokers. Our interviewers were asked to record whether the number of brokers each councilor gave in response to the initial question matched the number of names he or she ultimately provided on the list. These two numbers matched in about 42 percent of the cases; however, in 58 percent of the interviews, the numbers differed. Moreover, as Table A.2 shows, we sampled non-elected brokers at an approximate rate of about 1.7 per councilor – that is, we interviewed 516 non-elected brokers and 284 elected councilors. This implies that councilors each provided us lists of approximately

---

[17] Including one extreme outlier – a councilor who reported working with 1,000 brokers – raises the mean to 23 and the standard deviation to 69.

[18] In the Conurbano of Buenos Aires, we sampled one-fifth of the brokers in every municipality except Malvinas Argentinas and Tigre. We did this because we wanted to sample a larger number of municipalities to avoid excessive clustering of respondents within municipalities; in the Conurbano, councilors often have many non-elected operatives, so with a smaller sampling fraction we could have met our rough provincial target for brokers with just a few sampled municipalities.

TABLE A.2. *Sampled Brokers Numbers of Councilors and Non-Elected Brokers by Province*

	Buenos Aires (Conurbano)	Córdoba	San Luis	Misiones	Totals
Councilors	99	57	89	55	300
Non-elected brokers (*referentes*)	158	122	105	115	500
Totals	257	179	102	170	800

$(1.7)(3) = 5.1$ brokers' names, on average – which is substantially below the mean number of 19 brokers reported by councilors in response to the initial non-specific question about the numbers of brokers who work with them. This proportion varied somewhat by province – from 1.7 in Buenos Aires (where we sampled only one-fifth of brokers from each list) – to 1.9 in Córdoba and San Luis and 1.6 in Misiones.[19]

Another related, perhaps even more germane concern is that councilors may selectively name brokers at the end of the interview, or forget to report brokers with whom they work less frequently or less well. This tendency is very difficult to analyze systematically. If the characteristics of brokers that lead them to be included or excluded from the lists are related to their answers to our questions, councilors' selective reporting would compromise representativeness and generate bias.[20]

These potential problems are much less serious for our survey of elected brokers (i.e., councilors). We therefore think it is correct to call our survey of councilors a probability sample. Our survey of non-elected brokers might be called a semiprobability sample: probability procedures were used to select brokers from the sampling frame we built using our interviews of elected councilors, but that frame itself could be flawed.

Tables A.3.1 and A.3.2 break down Table A.2 by municipality.

[19] In Buenos Aires, we sampled only one-fifth of the brokers for some municipalities. Also, some city council members simply did not provide lists, and we were not able to interview every broker that we selected. The relatively low proportion of brokers to city council members, relative to provinces like Córdoba or Misiones (see Table A.2), is due to the brokers not being included, either because they were not named or were not found. We experienced particular difficulty interviewing non-elected brokers in Ezeiza.

[20] Another source of bias would arise if some of the brokers we identify refused to be interviewed. As Tables A.3.1 and A.3.2 show, summing across all provinces, we successfully surveyed 300 of 336 randomly selected councilors, for a response rate of 89.3 percent. Among non-elected brokers in the province of Buenos Aires, the response rate was 66.7 percent. Unfortunately, because lists of brokers' names from which we sampled in other provinces were inadvertently discarded, we cannot readily calculate the true response rate for non-elected brokers in those provinces. Note that substitutions were not allowed for either councilors or non-elected brokers, i.e., if a selected broker was not found, we did not substitute another who had not initially been randomly selected. In a few municipalities in Córdoba and San Luis, an additional councilor was inadvertently interviewed, which is why the number of surveyed councilors is occasionally greater than the number of sampled councilors.

TABLE A.3.1. *Survey Completion Rates by Province and Municipality (Buenos Aires, Córdoba, and San Luis)*

Province Municipality	Sampled Councilors	Surveyed Councilors	Surveyed Non-Elected Brokers
Buenos Aires (Conurbano)	**105**	**99**	**158**
Almirante Brown	12	11	26
Avellaneda	13	13	17
Ezeiza	10	7	0
Florencio Varela	11	11	26
General San Martín	13	12	12
Ituzaingó	10	10	28
Lanús	12	11	12
Malvinas Argentinas	12	12	26
Tigre	12	12	11
Córdoba	**58**	**57**	**122**
Arroyito	4	5	9
Córdoba Capital	16	22	69
General Cabrera	4	4	14
Huanchillas	4	1	0
Las Varas	4	4	1
Lozada	4	0	0
San Francisco del Chañar	4	5	29
Santa María de Punilla	4	4	3
Tío Pujio	4	2	1
Villa Carlos Paz	6	7	9
Villa Fontana	4	3	1
San Luis	**62**	**55**	**115**
Buena Esperanza	3	0	0
Candelaria	2	2	3
Concaran	3	3	8
Juana Koslay	5	4	5
Justo Daract	5	7	15
La Toma	4	4	14
Lujan	2	2	2
Villa de Merlo	5	5	10
Naschel	3	3	4
Quines	4	4	3
San Francisco del M. de O.	3	3	3
San Luis	7	6	13
Santa Rosa de Conlara	3	3	17
Tilisarao	4	5	3
Unión	2	0	0
Villa Mercedes	7	4	15

TABLE A.3.2. _Survey Completion Rates by Municipality (Misiones)_

Province Municipality	Sampled Councilors	Surveyed Councilors	Surveyed Non-Elected Brokers
Misiones	111	89	105
25 de Mayo	3	3	12
9 de Julio	2	1	2
Apóstoles	3	3	6
Aristobulo del Valle	3	2	2
Bernardo de Irigoyen	3	3	1
Campo Grande	3	3	2
Campo Ramón	3	2	4
Campo Viera	2	2	1
Candelaria	3	2	5
Capiovi	2	2	0
Caraguatay	2	1	0
Cerro Azul	2	1	0
Colonia Alberdi	2	2	0
Colonia Aurora	2	0	0
Colonia Victoria	2	2	0
Com. Andres Guacurari	3	1	1
Concepción de la Sierra	2	2	1
Dos Arroyos	2	1	0
Dos de Mayo	3	3	0
El Alcazar	2	2	3
El Soberbio	4	4	5
Eldorado	4	2	5
Garupá	3	2	9
Guaraní	2	0	0
Itacaruaré	2	1	0
Jardín America	3	3	5
Leandro N. Alem	4	3	3
Los Helechos	2	2	0
Oberá	3	2	9
Posadas	7	5	15
Puerto Esperzanza	3	3	4
Puerto Iguazú	4	2	1
Puerto Rico	3	3	1
San Antonio	2	2	2
San Ignacio	3	3	1
San José	2	2	0
San Pedro	3	2	3
San Vicente	5	5	2

A.3 BOOTSTRAPPING STANDARD ERRORS

Our design for sampling brokers was complex, as noted in the previous sections. After selecting municipalities in each province at random, we randomly sampled one-half of the city councilors for interviews. The number of councilors on each municipalities is an increasing function of municipal population, and hence the number we interviewed was not uniform across the selected municipalities. We then sampled one-half of the elected councilors in each municipality. Finally, we sampled one-third of the non-elected brokers working with each councilor (the sampling fraction was one-fifth in the Conurbano – again, to reduce clustering of brokers within municipalities). The procedure thus produced a multistage cluster sample, in which councilors are clustered by municipality, and brokers are clustered by councilor. Recall that we sampled municipalities without replacement from the small finite population of municipalities in each of four provinces (Córdoba, San Luis, Misiones, and Buenos Aires).[21] Given that the number of brokers in the sample depends on the particular municipalities sampled (because municipalities have unequal numbers of councilors) and on the particular councilors sampled (because different councilors may have different numbers of brokers working with them), the survey sample size is itself a random variable.

Our sampling procedures call for caution when we use the sample to estimate parameters in the population of brokers. Cluster sampling may make variance formulas based on simple random sampling inappropriate. In addition, because we sampled without replacement from small populations, we cannot assume i.i.d. sampling.[22] Finally, when we use the mean of the sample to estimate population means, we may have some ratio-estimator bias – because both the numerator (e.g., the sum of responses in the sample) and denominator (the sample size) are random variables.

This is a good situation in which to use the bootstrap, which is a procedure for using computer simulations to investigate the properties of statistical estimators and to estimate standard errors.[23] We begin by briefly reviewing the theory of the bootstrap before turning to a description of our use of it to estimate standard errors as well as the extent of ratio-estimator bias. Although the bootstrap is most helpful when analytic variance formulas may not apply, or when we want to estimate the degree of bias in certain estimators, the procedure is most easily understood for simple random samples.

---

[21] As noted in connection with Table A.1, the sample is especially large relative to the population of municipalities in the Conurbano, where we sampled 10 of 28 municipalities, and San Luis, where we sampled 9 out of 18. In Córdoba, we sampled 10 out of 249 municipalities, and in Misiones, 20 out of 75.

[22] Our sample of municipalities in Buenos Aires is especially large, relative to the population of municipalities in the Conurbano.

[23] Important references on the bootstrap include Efron 1979, Bickel and Freedman 1981, 1984, and Chao and Lo 1985. A very clear introduction is in Freedman 2005.

Suppose that we have drawn a simple random sample of size n from some (large) population. The parameters of this original population – say, the mean μ or the variance σ^2 – are unknown. Of course, we know from statistical theory that the mean of the sample, denoted $\overline{X}$, is an unbiased estimator of μ, and we know the sampling variance of the mean is σ^2/n. Also, the sample variance $\hat{\sigma}^2$ is an unbiased estimator for σ^2.[24]

However, suppose we have forgotten statistical theory. We can use the bootstrap to assess the unbiasedness and variance of the estimator $\overline{X}$. The procedure is as follows.

- The empirical sample of size n becomes a new "bootstrap population." We know the true parameters of this population – for example, the mean $\overline{X}$ and the variance $\hat{\sigma}^2$.
- We use the computer to draw a sample of size n at random with replacement from this bootstrap population. This sample is the first "bootstrap replicate." Drawing with replacement simulates the process of simple random sampling from a large population.
- Then, we calculate the estimator of interest – say, the sample mean – for this first bootstrap replicate. Denote this estimator by $\overline{X}^{(1)}$.
- We repeat this procedure, say, 1,000 times. Thus we create 1,000 bootstrap replicates, with means $\overline{X}^{(1)}, \overline{X}^{(2)}, \ldots, \overline{X}^{(999)}, \overline{X}^{(1000)}$.[25]

The *bootstrap principle* says that the sampling distribution of each bootstrap estimator $\overline{X}^{(i)}$ approximates the sampling distribution of the original estimator $\overline{X}$ – because the process of drawing bootstrap replicates with replacement is akin to the simple random sampling that produced the original data. Thus for any bootstrap replicate i, the distribution of $\overline{X}^{(i)} - \overline{X}$ approximates the distribution of $\overline{X} - \mu$. Moreover, the 1,000 bootstrap replicates trace out the sampling distribution of $\overline{X}^{(i)}$. For simple random samples, the mean of the 1,000 bootstrap replicates should be about equal to the mean of the bootstrap population – because the mean is unbiased – and the standard deviation of the 1,000 bootstrap replicates approximates the true standard error $\sigma/\sqrt{n}$.

Although this example shows how the bootstrap works, we typically want to use the bootstrap in more complex settings, where estimators may not be unbiased or analytic formulas for their variances may be unavailable. The key to bootstrapping is to mimic the actual sampling design that produced the empirical sample, for this is what will allow us to estimate the true variance as well as any bias in estimators. For the Argentina brokers' survey, this means replicating the two-stage clustering and other features of the sampling design.

---

[24] For this to be true, we must form the sample variance by dividing the sum of squared deviations from $\overline{X}$ by $(n-1)$.

[25] There is no requirement that we draw 1,000 bootstrap replicates; sometimes, a smaller number may suffice, or a larger number may be required.

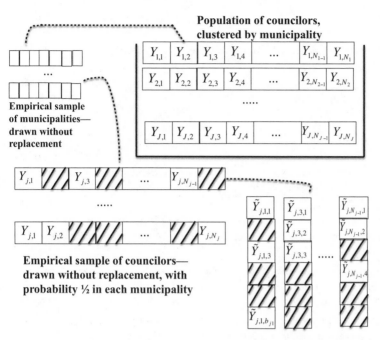

FIGURE A.1. Sampling Design: Argentina Brokers' Survey.

We now explain the use of the bootstrap in our setting.[26] First, we introduce the following notation. Each municipality $j = 1, \ldots, J$ in each of our four provinces has N_j councilors (recall that N_j varies as a function of municipal size). Next, index the responses for councilor i in municipality j by $Y_{j,i}$. Finally, each councilor in turn has b_{ij} non-elected brokers whose responses are indexed by $\tilde{Y}_{j,i,b_k}$, where j is the municipality, i is the councilor, and b_k is the kth non-elected broker or *referente* working for that councilor.

Then, we can depict the original sampling design as in Figure A.1. First, we draw n municipalities without replacement from the population of J municipalities, where $n < J$. Each sampled municipality j has N_j councilors. We then sample councilors at random from each of these municipalities. This is shown in Figure A.1 by crossing out with slashes those councilors in each municipality that are *not* sampled. Finally, for each selected councilor in each selected municipality, we select *referentes* – that is, non-elected brokers – at random.

---

[26] A Stata routine to implement the procedure described here was written by Joel Middleton and Edwin Camp.

In Figure A.1, we show the brokers for each of the councilors selected in the *first* municipality only, again crossing out with slashes those brokers that are not selected. Note that this sampling process takes place in each of the four provinces in our universe.

To bootstrap estimators such as the sample mean, we want to simulate this sampling design using the computer. We describe the procedure before discussing why it works.[27]

1. First, we copy each municipality in the empirical sample k times, where k is inverse of the sampling fraction; for instance, if there are 30 municipalities in the province or subprovince, and we sampled 15, then $k = 2$.[28] This creates a "bootstrap population" of municipalities, which has size $J * k$.[29]

2. Now, draw a random sample of size J *without replacement* from the bootstrap population of municipalities. Note that each of the J sampled municipalities has $\frac{N_j}{2}$ councilors.[30]

3. In each municipality in the empirical sample, copy each councilor once (because the sampling fraction is $\frac{1}{2}$ so $k = 2$); this creates a "bootstrap population" of N_j councilors for every municipality j.

4. Now, draw a random sample of $\frac{N_j}{2}$ councilors *without replacement* from the bootstrap population of councilors for every municipality j in each bootstrap replicate. Calculate and save the mean (or other estimator) of councilors' responses.

5. For each councilor in this bootstrap replicate, create a "bootstrap population" of *referentes* (non-elected brokers) as follows:
   • If a given councilor has 1 *referente* – in the original data – denote this sole *referente* as the bootstrap population of brokers for this councilor.
   • If a given councilor has 2 or more *referentes* – again in the original data – copy the responses for each *referente* three times (because the sampling fraction was one-third) to form the bootstrap population

6. Now for each sampled councilor, draw at random without replacement a number of *referentes* equal to the number of *referentes* originally sampled for this councilor.[31] Calculate and save the mean of brokers' responses in this bootstrap replicate.

7. Finally, repeat all these steps 1,000 times.

---

[27] The following procedure must be conducted separately for each province (or subprovince, in the case of the Conurbano of Buenos Aires).

[28] Recall that in Buenos Aires we only sample municipalities located in the Conurbano region of greater Buenos Aires.

[29] For now, assume k is an integer; we discuss the case when it is not later.

[30] Assume for now that N_j is even.

[31] For instance, if a councilor named 6 *referentes*, and we had originally sampled 2, we would copy responses for these two *referentes* three times to create a bootstrap population of size 6; then, we would draw twice at random without replacement from this bootstrap population.

Just as in the example of simple random sampling given above, the *bootstrap principle* here applies. That is, the distribution of any bootstrapped estimator, such as the mean of a bootstrap sample, should approximate the distribution of the original estimator. Thus, for any particular survey question, the standard deviation of the 1,000 replicates approximates the standard error. (These are calculated separately for councilors and non-elected brokers, as the sampling variances of the means should differ for these groups.) Also, if there is an appreciable difference between the mean of the empirical sample and the mean of the 1,000 bootstrap replicates, this suggests appreciable ratio-estimator bias.

Why does this procedure work? Consider first the problem raised by clustering: in our data, councilors are clustered within municipalities, and non-elected brokers (*referentes*) are clustered by councilor. The issue is that the responses of councilors in the same municipality, or of brokers working for the same councilor, may be less variable than responses of councilors and brokers in the universe as a whole; thus variance formulas that assume a simple random sample are inappropriate.[32] Our bootstrap procedure works because it preserves the clustered nature of the sampling process: councilors are sampled within municipal clusters, and brokers are sampled within clusters of councilors. If responses within clusters are much less variable than responses across clusters, the standard deviation of the 1,000 bootstrap replicates will be larger than for a simple random sample.

Next, consider the problem of sampling both municipalities, councilors, and non-elected brokers (*referentes*) without replacement. Our procedure creates several bootstrap populations:

- A population of municipalities of size $J * k$, by copying each sampled municipality k times
- J populations of councilors, each of size N_j, by copying the sampled councilors in each municipality 2 times
- $\frac{J * \sum_{j=1}^{J} N_j}{2}$ populations of non-elected brokers, one for each councilor.

Why do we do this copying, that is, why do we create a bootstrap population of municipalities of size $J * k$ by copying each municipality in the original sample k times? By creating a larger population of size (say) $J * k$ and drawing J municipalities without replacement, we mimic the procedure of sampling without replacement from a small finite population.[33] Importantly, copying each element the same number of times does not change the distribution of outcomes in the bootstrap populations; the moments (e.g., mean and variance) of the bootstrap populations should be the same as for the original empirical samples (and thus approximately equal to those of the true distribution).[34]

---

[32] In the survey literature, the ratio of the variance under clustered sampling to the variance from a simple random sample of equivalent size is known as the *design effect*; see Kish 1965.

[33] Bickel and Freedman 1984 and Chao and Lo 1985 discussed this strategy.

[34] Next some important wrinkles are discussed, however.

Finally, our bootstrap procedure also helps us estimate the bias that is due to the use of a ratio estimator (where random variables are in the numerator and denominator of the estimator). The reason is that for each bootstrap replicate, we can calculate a ratio estimator such as the sample mean – which is the sum of responses in the bootstrap replicate divided by the sample size, both of which are random variables due to our sampling design. The mean of the 1,000 replicates then tells us how far this ratio estimator is off, on average, from the true mean response in the population. If there is bias due to the fact that a nonlinear operation (i.e., division) is used to estimate the population parameter (the mean), this will be reflected naturally in the bootstrap estimates.

A.3.1 Bootstrapping Standard Errors for Treatment Effects

The discussion of bootstrapping thus far applies to the estimation of the variance of estimators of certain population parameters. For instance, suppose we want to know what percentage of brokers have never switched political parties. The mean percentage in our empirical sample estimates this quantity.[35] To attach a standard error to this estimate, however, we would want to conduct a bootstrap simulation, using observed responses to this particular question to form our bootstrap population. The standard deviation of this percentage across the 1,000 bootstrap replicates would estimate the standard error associated with the percentage.[36]

How should we estimate the standard errors for differences-of-means, as in treatment effects for our survey-experimental questions? Here, we are comparing responses of respondents exposed at random to different scenarios. One possibility is simply to calculate the usual standard error for treatment-effect estimators, for instance, as the square root of the sum of the variances in the treatment and control groups.[37] This procedure would produce estimate treatment effects for the sample (the so-called sample average treatment effect, or SATE). However, this procedure for estimating the standard error of treatment effects does not take into account the variability induced by the sampling design – it only takes into account the variability due to random assignment to different versions of our questionnaire, for the sample at hand.

---

[35] This is because our sampling design is "self-weighting" within provinces – we sample a fixed fraction of councilors and a fixed fraction of councilors' brokers in each municipality – so we do not need to adjust for the over- or under sampling of brokers from certain areas, at least within provinces.

[36] In principle, the bootstrap should be redone for each survey question, because the distribution of responses will vary across different questions; however, using one bootstrap estimate of the standard error for similar questions may suffice.

[37] See Freedman, Pisani, and Purves 2007, pp. A32–A34, n. 11) or Dunning 2012, Appendix 6.2, for discussion and justification of this procedure for estimating the standard error of treatment effects in experiments.

If we are interested in estimating the so-called population average treatment effect (PATE) – that is, the difference of means across any two treatment conditions, for the whole population of brokers from which we drew our sample – we must again account for the sampling design. We can use the bootstrap here as well. We simply add the following procedures to the steps in the bootstrap outlined previously.

- After step 4 in the description of the bootstrap above, divide the $\frac{N_j}{2}$ councilors sampled for the ith bootstrap replicate according to the version of the survey-experimental question to which they were assigned (i.e., whether they were assigned to one treatment condition or another). Now, sample $(\frac{N_j}{2})(\frac{1}{2})$ councilors at random *with replacement* from each group. Calculate the difference of mean outcomes in each group, and save this difference.
- After step 6, divide the non-elected brokers (*referentes*) sampled for each bootstrap replicate according to the version of the survey questionnaire to which they were assigned. Now, sample $(\frac{N_j}{2})(\frac{1}{2})$ councilors at random *with replacement* from each group. Calculate the difference of mean outcomes in each group, and save this difference.

Now, the standard deviation of the difference of means across the 1,000 bootstrap replicates estimates the standard error of the estimated PATE. This standard error is calculated separately for councilors and *referentes*, though results may certainly be combined. This procedure should give an accurate assessment of the uncertainty due to random assignment of brokers to different versions of the questionnaire – because analyzing experiments assuming sampling with replacement generates reasonable, though sometimes conservative, standard errors for treatment effects (Freedman, Pisani, and Purves 2007: A32–34, n. 11; Dunning 2012, Appendix 6.2) – while also taking into account the uncertainty introduced by the complex design for sampling brokers from the population.

Two further points may be made about the bootstrap procedure described in this section. First, notice that the sampling fraction k for municipalities may not be an integer, for example, in a province in which we sampled, say, 10 out of 25 municipalities (see step 1 earlier). In this case, we may use the approach described by Bickel and Freedman 1984 and Chao and Lo 1985. In the case of municipalities, let $J_1 < J * k < J_2$ be the two nearest integer multiples of $J * k$. The variance of the bootstrap mean is $F(J * k) = (1 - \frac{n}{J*k})(\frac{J*k(n-1)}{(J*k-1)})s^2$, where s^2 is the variance of responses in the bootstrap population. Now, because $F(\cdot)$ is increasing in its argument, there exists $\alpha \in (0, 1)$ such that

$$F(J * k) = (J_1) + (1 - \alpha)F(J_2). \tag{1}$$

Chao and Lo 1985 suggested randomizing between J_1 and J_2 with probability α and $1 - \alpha$, respectively, across the different bootstrap replicates.

Second, it is important to note that our procedure will understate sampling variability for brokers who are the only sampled broker from their councilor, because there will be no variance in responses in the bootstrap population. Thus, in cases in which the councilor in truth had two or three brokers, and we sampled one, our bootstrap procedure doesn't represent the sampling variability well. In addition, in cases in which we sampled two brokers in the empirical sample, the councilor may have had more or fewer than six brokers from which we sampled – that is, the true sampling fraction was not exactly one-third. In other words, the inverse of the sampling fraction for brokers may also not be an integer and may not be the same for all councilors. Our procedure thus provides only an approximation to the true sampling variance in these cases. Note, however, that the average number of brokers per councilor, at 5.1, was relatively large.

Appendix B
Argentina Voters' Surveys

This Appendix describes the sampling design and other aspects of the survey methodology for three different surveys we took of Argentine voters in the years 2001, 2003, and 2009.

B.1 2001 SURVEY

Our first surveys of Argentine voters took place in December 2001 and January 2002. We used multistage cluster sampling techniques, based on census tracts, to select a probability sample of 1,920 voters, in the provinces of Buenos Aires, Córdoba, and Misiones and including an oversample from the area of Mar del Plata in Buenos Aires province. There were 480 adults selected in each of the four areas, giving an overall margin of error of plus or minus 4.5 percent.

The survey allowed us to explore the strategies of clientelist parties indirectly, by revealing what kinds of voters these parties target and who among the voters are responsive to private rewards. Respondents were asked a variety of questions, for instance, whether they had received any goods from a political party during the election campaign that had taken place two months earlier, what kinds of goods they had received, whether respondents believed that receiving goods had influenced their vote, whether the person had turned to a locally important political actor for help during the past year, and whether, if the head of their household lost his or her job, the family would turn to a party operative for help (Job). See Stokes 2005 for further description of sampling design and survey questions.

B.2 2003 SURVEY

We also conducted an original survey in 2003 to explore various topics, including the relationship between income, risk aversion, and vote buying. We

279

instructed researchers to conduct face-to-face interviews with 500 randomly selected people age 18 and older in each of four Argentine provinces: Buenos Aires, Córdoba, Misiones, and San Luis, for a total of 2,000 interviews. The response rate was 97 percent, although this includes only direct refusals and may not include people whose houses were selected but were not at home. We again used multistage cluster sampling procedures, based on census tracts. The margin of error of the survey was plus or minus 6 percent. The analyses reported in the book mostly pool the surveys into a single dataset, but we check throughout, as reported, for variations in effects across the distinct regional samples. The interviews were conducted in August 2003.

B.3 2009 SURVEY

The 2009 Argentina survey was conducted in collaboration with Noam Lupu. The survey consisted of face-to-face interviews of 1,199 eligible voters in the Argentine provinces of Córdoba and Santa Fe (600 respondents per province) and was administered from August–October 2009 by the polling firm Consultores en Políticas Públicas.

Within each province, a two-stage clustered probability sample was generated based on the 2001 national census. Sixty *radios censales* (the smallest available geographic unit in the census) were selected as primary sampling units (PSUs), and 10 voters were sampled from each PSU. The PSUs with populations under 1,000 were excluded from the sampling frame. Choosing a random start point, investigators selected households using an interval sampling method (every fourth household) and used the birthday method (most recent birthday) to select adult respondents within each household. In case of refusals or failure to contact the selected adult after two attempts, households were replaced with the adjacent household. To administer the survey experiments described in the text, four different versions of the questionnaire were used in sequential order. The response rate for the survey was 19.3 percent, the cooperation rate was 30.7 percent, the refusal rate was 43.5 percent, and the contact rate was 62.9 percent. The margin of error assuming maximal variance (proportions of .5 on dichotomous questions) was 6.7 percent.

Appendix C
Venezuela Voters' Survey and the Maisanta Database

Our original data from Venezuela provide an important empirical referent discussed in the text. In this Appendix, we provide context and background on the electoral logic of social spending and clientelistic exchanges in contemporary Venezuela, describe the "Maisanta" database as well as our original survey data, and discuss several threats to valid inference in more detail than we do in the text.

C.1 EMPIRICAL CONTEXT: THE ELECTORAL LOGIC OF SOCIAL SPENDING IN VENEZUELA

C.1.1 The Recall Campaign of 2003–2004

Venezuelan politics in the contemporary period provides a particularly useful opportunity to study the electoral logic of social spending. First, the election of Hugo Chávez Frías in 1998 followed a period of party system decline and then of partisan realignment that had crystallized into a new set of political loyalties by around 2003. Second, beginning in late 2003, the government launched an intense electoral campaign against a recall referendum that threatened to remove Chávez from office in 2004. Third, also beginning in 2003, the incumbent government was endowed with a rapidly expanding budget (due to the oil price boom associated with the United States–led invasion of Iraq) that it used to create a range of targeted social programs. Finally, and perhaps most importantly from the social-scientific perspective, during the recall campaign, the Venezuelan government was able to exploit a remarkable source of individual-level data on political ideology and turnout propensity, which has also become widely publicly available in Venezuela. Together, these features make Venezuela a useful case for studying the relationship between ideology,

281

turnout, and distributive politics. In this section, we describe the empirical context, before turning to our data and analysis.

After a long political and economic crisis that followed a decline in government oil revenues during the 1980s and 1990s, and in the wake of the near-total collapse of electoral support for the two parties that had dominated Venezuelan politics for most of the democratic period after 1958, Hugo Chávez Frías was elected president in 1998. Electoral support for Chávez in 1998 came from a somewhat more diffuse group of voters in "class" terms than would be the case later in his presidency, and the new president was elected with a substantial mandate and very high initial approval ratings. However, continued low oil prices, together with the apparent inability to fulfill promises on public spending to relatively poor Venezuelans, implied substantially declining popularity rates for Chávez. The Venezuelan polity also became substantially polarized between pro-Chávez supporters and the political opposition, a polarization that crystallized in 2002 and 2003 – first with the failed coup attempt of April 2002, which was accompanied by violent confrontations in the streets of Caracas between pro- and anti-Chávez groups, and then in the nearly three-month general strike that was concentrated in the oil sector at the end of 2002 and beginning of 2003. Although managers and labor leaders in the state-owned oil company, along with other leaders of the strike, did not succeed in removing Chávez from power, the president's popularity was at an all-time low in the wake of the strike (see Figure C.1).

After the end of the strike, and given Chávez's low popularity at the time, the political opposition instead sought to take advantage of a clause in the new Venezuelan Constitution, approved by voters in 1999, that allowed the public to vote on a referendum to recall any elected official from office, once more than half of that official's term in office had transpired. The requirements were, first, that 20 percent of registered voters solicit a referendum by signing a petition, and, second, that a number greater than or equal to the number of voters who elected the official in the previous election vote to revoke the official's mandate (see Article 72, Constitución de la República Bolivariana de Venezuela).[1] Because Chávez had been re-elected as president in 2000, and given a six-year term for the presidency, the earliest possible date for a recall was the end of 2003 or beginning of 2004. In addition to the recall petition launched to recall Chávez from office, there was a petition drive intended to recall deputies from the opposition; however, although many voters signed recall petitions against opposition deputies, this referendum was not ultimately held, as the courts ruled that National Assembly elections were proximate enough that a recall was not warranted. The presidential recall was subject to some legal delays but was eventually held on August 15, 2004.

---

[1] An additional requirement was that at least 25 percent of registered voters had to vote in the recall referendum itself.

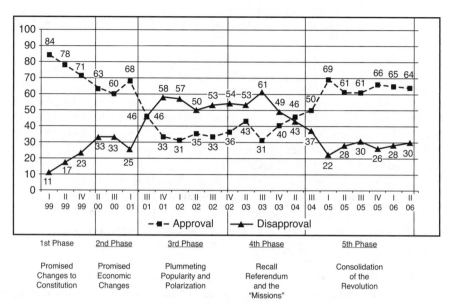

FIGURE C.1. Approval Ratings of Hugo Chávez (1999–2006). *Source*: KELLER y Asoc.: Estudios Nacionales de Opinión Pública, n = 1,200, 2nd quarter 2006.

At the time the recall referendum was launched, in early 2003, Chávez's approval had sunk to between 30 and 40 percent (Figure C.1); by the time the referendum was held on August 15, 2004, however, credible public opinion polls put Chávez's approval rating above 50 percent and his disapproval rating at around 35 percent. The "No" vote on the referendum (i.e., the vote to retain Chávez in office) then took nearly 60 percent of the vote.[2] After the recall, this president's popularity was clearly reinforced, with Chávez again taking around 60 percent of the vote in the presidential elections of December 2006, although in subsequent years he has sometimes faced fading public opinion ratings and additional electoral challenges. For present purposes, the key question centers

---

[2] Some members of the political opposition asserted (and continue to assert) that fraud took place in the recall elections of 2004, despite the fact that the results were certified by the Carter Center and other international observers after an audit of paper ballots in randomly selected voting centers. One allegation was that Chávez supporters on the National Electoral Council (CNE) knew the seed of the random-number generator in advance and thus could alter ballots in those voting centers not audited by election observers. Yet there is no credible claim that the audited voting centers were not themselves randomly selected, and the percentage of votes for the "No" in the audited sample were very close (and within the margin of sampling error) to the vote share reported by the CNE for the entire universe of voting centers. A simple extrapolation from the sample to the universe thus suggests that the argument for fraud is unconvincing. In addition, the "No" vote reported by the CNE closely tracked credibly public opinion polling in the days prior to the recall. For further discussion, see Carter Center 2004; for the view that the election involved fraud, see Hausmann and Rigobón 2004.

on explaining the recovery of the government's popularity between 2003 and 2004. What happened?

C.1.2 Targeted Social Spending Through the Missions

As other analysts have emphasized, at least part of the explanation for the Chávez government's restored popularity after 2003 is to be found in the establishment of the so-called "Missions," or social programs aimed at providing health care, adult literacy training, scholarships for high school degrees, subsidized food, and other goods and services to the Venezuelan population. Buoyed by positive developments in world oil markets beginning in spring 2003, as the United States–led coalition prepared to invade Iraq, and also by increased fiscal contributions by the oil parastatal PDVSA and international oil companies working in Venezuela, the fiscal coffers of the Venezuelan state swelled in 2003 and particularly in 2004 and 2005. Public spending nearly doubled in real terms between 2003 and 2006, rising from around Bs. 23 trillion in 2003 (measured in 2000 *bolívares*) to around 42 trillion in 2006 (MPD-SISOV 2005, 2006). Growth in social spending (on health care, education and other categories) was particularly marked, and the sharpest increases came after 2003; for instance, real social spending per capita as a whole rose more than 20 percent between 2003 and 2004. Real per capita spending on public education rose over 75 percent between 1998 and 2004, from 3.2 to 5.3 percent of GDP (Dunning 2008: 223–226). One important channel for this increased social spending was the so-called Missions.

The Missions comprise a panoply of social programs with differing aims and characters. Among the first important Missions was one called Barrio Adentro ("Neighborhood Within"), which was initially developed in collaboration with the office of the mayor of Caracas but was soon expanded nationwide by the central government; inter alia, this Mission puts Cuban doctors in the poorest Venezuelan neighborhoods as a means to provide primary and preventative care. The success of Barrio Adentro and other ventures apparently helped inspire the eventual proliferation of other Missions, from the network of subsidized supermarkets (Mission Mercal) to programs for adult literacy (Mission Robinson) and scholarships to finish high-school degrees (Mission Ribas). As previous analysts have emphasized, these programs differ along a range of dimensions. Some of the Missions, such as Mercal or Barrio Adentro, essentially provide local public goods (or at least goods that are broadly supplied and essentially non-excludable), whereas others provide benefits such as scholarships (Ribas and Robinson) that are highly targeted and highly excludable; we study the distribution of the benefits from the latter programs in the text.

We should be clear that we by no means assume at the outset that the Venezuelan Missions were intended to be used either for mobilization or persuasion of voters prior to, during, and after the recall referendum of 2004 – although the institutional detail we discuss later strongly suggests the plausibility that this was the case. Nor do we presume that clientelist quid pro quos are necessarily involved; indeed, as discussed in Chapter 1, it is useful to probe the logic of broker-mediated distribution even in the absence of clientelism. The various Missions vary in the class basis of their appeal, but they are generally programs that benefit poorer Venezuelans, and some of them are akin to means-tested programs.[3] The fact that poorer Venezuelans disproportionately received benefits under the Missions might suggest that the programs are "targeted" politically, given the natural constituency of the Chávez coalition among poor voters, yet this is obviously not evidence that benefits were allocated by the incumbent with electoral goals in mind; to put the point bluntly, a politician maximizing a social welfare function for relatively poor voters might conceivably choose a similar distribution of benefits. Our null hypothesis in the text is that political variables – such as the partisan affiliation of individual voters – do not explain receipt of benefits under the program, once we have controlled for income or its correlates; we will be interested in whether we can reject the null in favor of the alternative hypothesis that variables such as political affiliation (more to the point here, incumbent perception of individual affiliation or tendencies) help to predict program participation, once income and other variables are controlled. The data can therefore help us distinguish the extent to which political or electoral logics played a role and, of greater interest to us, which political or electoral logics played a role.

C.1.3 The Structure of the Maisanta Command

The central pillar of the incumbent government's campaign against the recall was the so-called "Maisanta Command" ("*Comando Maisanta*"). According to a government website, the "strategic objectives" of the Maisanta Command were as follows (the phrasing in Spanish is in the footnotes):

incorporate the base in the pursuit of votes; avoid [electoral] fraud; consolidate previous gains; attract indecisive sectors; neutralize the growth of the adversary; isolate the coup plotters; and incorporate the politically-excluded.[4]

Here we find a striking mix of apparent "loyal voter" and "swing voter" strategies.[5]

---

[3] The program with the broadest appeal is probably Mission Mercal, the chain of subsidized food stores, from which around 60 percent of Venezuelans report having benefited in public opinion surveys. Notwithstanding the breadth of benefits, the raison d'être of this Mission – the provision of cheap, subsidized food – suggests that they too will disproportionately benefit poorer voters.

[4] The original Spanish, in order of the bullet points, is as follows: "*incorporar a la base la búsqueda del voto; evitar el fraude; consolidar lo que se tiene; atraer el segmento indeciso; neutralizar el crecimiento del adversario; aislar a los golpistas; incorporar a los excluidos políticos.*" http://www.gobiernoenlinea.ve/miscelaneas/maisanta1.html. Accessed September 2009; this page appears no longer to be active as of December 2012.

[5] For instance, the intention to "incorporate the base in the pursuit of votes," "consolidate previous gains," and also "incorporate the politically-excluded" (in the context of a Venezuelan politics in which unregistered, disenfranchised voters would tend to be poor and would also tend to support

Indeed, qualitative detail on the structure and objectives of the Maisanta Command suggests the intent to use information on political loyalties recorded in Maisant to boost the incumbent's vote share in the recall campaign – and, perhaps, to guide the distribution of resources. The organizational structure of the "Comando Maisanta" or Maisanta Command reveals at least the potential for substantial political direction in the allocation of resources and benefits. At the top, the National Maisanta Command included as its commander-in-chief (Jefe del Comando) the president, Hugo Chávez Frías; its other members included such leaders of the Chavista coalition as Diosdado Cabello (in charge of Logistics and, at the time, candidate for governor of the state of Miranda); William Lara (Organization; also a deputy in the National Assembly); Jesse Chacón Escamillo (Communications Strategy; also the Minister of Communication and Information); William Izarra (Ideology; also the founder of MBR 200, the predecessor organization of Chávez's Movimiento Quinta República, MVR); and Haiman El Troudi (Secretary and at the time Chávez's chief-of-staff). It is especially striking that Rafael Ramírez, then the Minister of Energy and Mines (now called the Minister of Popular Power of Energy and Petroleum) was designated as the head of "Electoral Mobilization and Missions" for the National Maisanta Command. With the conclusion of the strike that had crippled the oil sector for nearly three months at the end of 2002 and beginning of 2003, the increasing assertion of government control over the state-owned oil company PDVSA, and the rise in world oil prices in the wake of the United States–led invasion of Iraq, oil began to play a much more direct role in financing public spending than it had in earlier years after the election of Chávez in 1998; PDVSA began to finance the various Missions in enormous amounts, both through direct transfers to the various Missions as well as through transfers to various funds at the national social and economic development bank (BANDES).[6] Important for our analysis that follows, the Ribas Mission (which provides scholarships to allow students to finish high school) was administered by PDVSA and the Ministry of Energy and Petroleum, rather than the Ministry of Education. As one Venezuelan television ad has put it, "Now oil has many

Chávez; see Ortega and Penfold 2008 on this point) seems clearly to point to core voter strategies. However, the desire to "attract indecisive sectors" and "isolate the coup plotters" (presumably by attracting elements of the moderate opposition) seems to illustrate classic "swing voter" logics.

[6] In 2004, for instance, PDVSA reports having transferred, inter alia, Bs. 916 billion (around US$486 million, at the official exchange rate for 2004) to the Misión Ribas, which funds secondary education; Bs. 197 billion (US$105 million) as of May 2005 to Misión Barrio Adentro (Mission Neighborhood Within), the primary health care Mission that sends Cuban doctors to Venezuela to serve as primary care physicians in poor neighborhoods; Bs. 179 billion (US$95 million) to the Misión Mercal, a subsidized supermarket chain; and other funds for a technical education mission (Misión Vuelvan Caras), for a mission that has registered previously unregistered voters (Misión Identidad), for a mission that provides assistance to indigenous communities (Misión Guaicaipuro), and for the construction of the Bolivarian University of Venezuela (UBV) as well as scholarships for students at the university. Other sources report PDVSA's total social expenditures in recent years at over US$7 billion per annum. See Dunning 2008, Chapter Four, for further discussion and sources.

Missions" (Dunning 2008). One such mission, given Minister Ramírez's role in the National Maisanta Command, was very plausibly electoral mobilization or persuasion.[7]

The distribution of resources and the flow of information was in turn organized through lower-level units that supervised local activists – brokers, in the terms of our book. Under the National Maisanta Command in the organizational hierarchy of the Maisanta project appear the State Maisanta Commands, the Municipal Maisanta Commands, and the Maisanta Command for Large Precincts (Parroquias).[8] According to the government, the objectives of these state, municipal, and neighborhood units were, inter alia, to "obtain, administer, and distribute resources and materials necessary to lend support to the Mission [i.e., the Mission Florentino or Maisanta]; install and operate the platform of technological assistance of the Mission [the Maisanta user interface]; design instruments; teach and instruct; gather and process information; periodically emit reports; evaluate and follow the Mission; [and] report to the National Maisanta Command the status of the Mission."[9] Then, under these national, state, municipal, and district commands in the organizational hierarchy of the Comanda Maisanta appear the units that are described by the government itself as the "most important link of the Maisanta Command, at the level of the voting center," that is, the so-called Units of Electoral Battle (Unidades de Batalla Electoral, UBE).[10] These units were to be organized geographically around the sites that are chosen throughout the country by the National Electoral Council (CNE) as voting centers.[11] According to the government, the UBEs would incorporate as their members elements of "all the Bolivarian factors (Missions, political parties, social movements, student and youth fronts, community organizations, etc.)" and would have a leadership that would be "democratically elected (allowing) the natural leadership of the community to prevail."[12]

According to the government, the UBEs would have the following functions; inter alia, they would:

coordinate the work of the electoral patrols [described below]; create an inventory of resources and possibilities available in the area of influence of each voting center; attend politically to the electoral base organized by the patrols; mobilize voters, particularly on the day of the referendum; implement networks of social intelligence with the goal of

[7] As a further example, PDVSA's financing of the Identity Mission, which helped new voters register for the first time, is particularly striking in light of Minister Ramírez's role in the Maisanta Command.

[8] See http://www.gobiernoenlinea.ve/miscelaneas/maisanta/maisanta6.html.

[9] Quoted from http://www.gobiernoenlinea.ve/miscelaneas/maisanta/maisanta6.html. Accessed September 2009.

[10] Quoted from http://www.gobiernoenlinea.ve/miscelaneas/maisanta/maisanta8.html. Accessed September 2009.

[11] These voting centers are often located at primary or secondary schools as well as other sites; there is substantial variance in the number of voters that may vote at any individual voting center.

[12] Ibid.

detecting illicit activities on the part of the opposition; apply the instruments of public opinion investigation (sondeos de opinión); implement measures to estimate the vote intention on the day of the elections; identify the Bolivarian electoral potential in the area of the voting center; establish the electoral map, through a census of the community and the information that is received through the structure of the Maisanta Command; identify voters who do not have ID numbers [*cédulas*], those who are not registered in the electoral registry, or those who need a change of address[13] and mobilize them [to apply for *cédulas*].[14]

Finally, much of the work of the UBEs on the ground would be carried out by electoral "patrols" (patrullas) comprised of approximately 10 people each. These patrols would "work with a list of voters supplied by the UBE and visit house-by-house the voters included in the [Maisanta] database, giving to each compatriot all information associated with the [recall] process... [and] identify vote intentions."[15] It is thus clear that, among the raisons dêtre of the Maisanta software, the intended users of the interface included brokers at the grassroots level, including members of the electoral patrols. In addition to the fact that electoral patrols were supposed to "visit house-by-house the voters included in the database," as just noted, a "read-me" text file that accompanies the Maisanta user interface explains that the software's function:

is to facilitate consultations by persons or groups of citizens of a voting center or any community. It serves as support for the mission and vision of the Battle of Santa Inés [i.e., the Maisanta Command]. The need to create this solution stems from different sources [including the need to] motivate electoral participation [and provide] technical support for the work of the patrols (UBEs).

Additional advantages supplied by the Maisanta software, according to the accompanying text document, include the ability it offers militants to "offer consultation services to the neighbors of your community" and the "low technical requirements" needed for its operation.

The organizational structure created by the Comando Maisanta was thus clearly intended to be used for voter mobilization and/or persuasion as well as for communication between local party militants and national leaders in the Chávez coalition. The question for analysis, though, is the extent to which the benefits of the Missions were allocated with electoral goals in mind – both during the recall campaign and, especially, in subsequent years – and whether and under what conditions they were used to "mobilize" loyal constituents or instead to "persuade" swing voters.[16] This is the question we have taken up in the text.

[13] I.e., voters whose addresses are outdated in the electoral registry.

[14] Quoted from http://www.gobiernoenlinea.ve/miscelaneas/maisanta/maisanta8.html. Accessed September 2009.

[15] Quoted from http://www.gobiernoenlinea.ve/miscelaneas/maisanta/maisanta9.html.

[16] Several recent papers have contributed to a small but growing recent literature on the electoral logic of social spending under the Venezuelan Missions; see Ortega and Penfold-Becerra 2006, Rosas and Hawkins 2008, and Penfold-Becerra 2006.

C.2 OUR DATA

In this section, we provide further detail on the Maisanta database and our Venezuela survey data analyzed in the text (see Chapters 2 and 4).

C.2.1 The Maisanta Database

Our first and principal source of data is the Maisanta database compiled by the Venezuelan government.[17] This database was based on the "Lista Tascón" compiled and published by a deputy in the Chávez coalition, Luís Tascón; the origins of the data appear somewhat unclear, although it has been alleged that the relevant data were sent by the president of the National Electoral Council (CNE) to President Chávez at the end of January or the beginning of February 2004.[18] More importantly for our purposes, the Lista Tascón may have also provided the initial basis for the construction of the much more extensive Maisanta database.[19] The Maisanta database and user interface eventually also became available to various groups of diverse political orientations and achieved wide public distribution in Venezuela.[20]

As discussed in the text (see Chapter 2), the Maisanta database represents a remarkable source of data on an incumbent's perceptions of individual voters' partisan leanings. The main aspect of the sophisticated software package is

---

[17] The full name for the database used by the Venezuelan government was the "Comando Maisanta, Batalla de Santa Inés" database. The "Batalla de Santa Inés" (Battle of Santa Ines) took place during the Federalist wars of the nineteenth century, when troops under the command of Ezequiel Zamora defeated one of the regional armies based in the western Andean region of Venezuela. According to the Venezuelan government's description, the electoral campaign so named would "guide revolutionary action oriented towards assuring electoral triumph in the national referendum of August 15, 2004, when the defeat of the national and foreign oligarchy by the sovereign people in the Battle of Santa Ines, masterfully directed by General Ezequiel Zamora, would be reenacted (in accordance with the collective imaginary of the Venezuelan people)." Quoted from http://www.gobiernoenlinea.ve/miscelaneas/maisanta1.html.

[18] One opposition blog presents a memo apparently signed by President Chávez and directed to the President of the National Electoral Council on January 30, 2004, which reads: "It is a pleasure to salute you in this opportunity whilst notifying you that I fully authorize Mr. Luis Tascón Gutierréz, ID No 9.239.964, to collect the certified copies of the forms utilized during the 2-A event, which took place between 11/28/03 and 12/1/03, whereby a group of citizens petitioned to activate a Recall Referendum on my mandate, as established in article 72 of the Bolivarian Republic of Venezuela." See http://www.vcrisis.com/index.php?content=letters/200509152101, accessed May 1, 2007.

[19] The link between the Lista Tascón and the Maisanta database is underscored by a text document, described in more detail later, that accompanies the Maisanta installation file and that is accessible through the Maisanta user interface; this document instructs users to look for updated versions of the software at www.luistascon.com, the website of Luis Tascón.

[20] After obtaining one version of the database from Francisco Rodríguez, then in the Economics Department at Wesleyan University, we subsequently purchased another copy on a CD-ROM from a street vendor in front of the National Assembly building in Caracas. The data are distributed in a series of Access files along with the user interface, which must be installed; the underlying files may be easily converted to standard statistical software packages.

a user interface that is readily searchable by people with relatively limited computing ability or knowledge; as we described earlier, one apparent purpose of this user interface was to facilitate the campaign work of party militants at the grassroots, neighborhood level. However, there are also additional records and databases that underlie the main user interface and that have also been useful to us in compiling data relevant to this inquiry.

The user interface constructed by the Chávez campaign is easily searchable either by ID number (*cédual* – the easiest and most accurate way to find individuals in the database) or by name (Figure 2.4 in the text). An individual hit using the Maisanta database reveals, in addition to the individuals cédula number, name, address, nationality,[21] and date of birth, the following records. First, a window in the upper-right hand portion of the screen indicates whether the individual signed the petition to establish the recall referendum against Chávez (an individual who did so is coded in the underlying Access database as an "opositor" or a member of the political opposition), did not sign any petition, or instead signed a petition to launch a recall referendum against certain opposition deputies in the National Assembly and other elected officials from the opposition (an individual who did so is coded as an "patriota" or "patriot"; we discuss these patriots or "contraopositores" later). Next, several boxes in the bottom-left of the screen give the following information: whether the individual is an "abstainer" or "abstencionista," whether the individual is deceased, whether the individual is a recipient of the Ribas Mission, and whether the individual is a participant in the Vuelvan Caras Mission.[22] Not displayed in the screen of Maisanta's user interface but available in the database's underlying files is another indicator, which we believe to report whether an individual participates in other Missions that existed at the time the Maisanta database was created.[23] Additional buttons on the interface give access to additional information. Perhaps most usefully, clicking on "Listar cédulas de mi Centro de Votación" gives the information on the screen for every voter who votes

---

[21] There are some foreign residents of Venezuela in Maisanta, perhaps because the Venezuelan Consitution gives adult foreigners who have lived in Venezuela for more than 10 years the right to vote in state, municipal and district (parroquia) elections; see Article 64 of the Constitución de la República Bolivariana de Venezuela, 1999. Another possibility is that Maisanta records as foreigners those individuals of foreign origin who have been naturalized as Venezuelan citizens under the terms of Article 33 of the Constitution and thus can vote in national (presidential and National Assembly) elections. We have not been able to confirm this topic; in our sample from the Maisanta database (discussed later), just under 1 percent of individuals are coded as foreigners (E for extranjeros rather than V for Venezolano).

[22] The Ribas Mission, as discussed elsewhere, is an educational program that provides scholarships for young adults and others wishing to complete their high school degrees (bachilleratos). The Vuelvan Caras Mission, since renamed Misión Che Guevara, is a program oriented toward inculcating socialist ideals.

[23] We have not been able to confirm the source of data for the three indicators of Mission participation included in Maisanta, but anecdotal evidence suggests that these were partly based on self-reports among people who registered for new cédulas under Misión Identidad; their reliability is suspect, and we do not analyze those data here.

TABLE C.1. *Variables in Maisanta*

Variable	Definition
Opposition	Signed a petition to launch a recall referendum against Chávez
"Patriot"	Signed a petition to launch a recall referendum against deputies of the opposition
Abstainer	Respondent is perceived as "abstainer" by Maisanta creators. Unclear how the government coded this; see text
Mission Ribas*	Participated in Ribas as of circa July 2004
Mission Vuelvan Caras*	Participated in Vuelvan Caras as of circa July 2004
Other Missions*	Participated in other Missions as of circa July 2004
Voting Center	Location of voting center, including access to individual and aggregate data on voting center

Other variables: name, address, bithdate, *cédula* number.
* Apparently based on self-reports.

at the current voters voting center; the software can therefore easily provide a snapshot of aggregate political tendencies in the voting center in question.

There are 12,394,109 individual records in the Maisanta database, which we believe to be the universe of registered voters eligible to vote in the referendum as of July 10, 2004, when the National Electoral Council closed the registration process for the August 15th referendum.[24] The important point about Maisanta is that it provides ex-ante measures of political ideology and turnout propensity: the indicators included in the database reflect the information set available to the government before it began its campaign against the recall referendum and as it rolled out the Mission social programs. Table C.1 describes the variables included in the Maisanta database that we use in our analysis.

C.2.2 Venezuela Voters' Survey

To gather data on benefit receipt, social program participation, and other variables, we administered a survey to a probability sample of 2,000 adults in

[24] This is difficult to assess with certainty, however, because the Maisanta database was apparently frequently updated between the time Chávez announced the formation of the Maisanta Command on June 6 and the close of voter registration on July 10, and we cannot be certain of the date our version of the Maisanta database was updated. The National Electoral Council (CNE) announced on the 15th of June, 2004, that 12,404,187 Venezuelan and foreign voters could particpate in the national referendum; however, July 10 was fixed as the final day on which voters could register and subsequently vote in the referendum on August 15, so additional voters likely came into the rolls and perhaps by this mechanisms into Maisanta after June 15, 2004. For all practical purposes, however, there can be little error from treating Maisanta as though it constitutes the universe of eligible voters at the time of the referendum. See the chronology at http://www.gobiernoenlinea.ve/miscelaneas/maisanta10.html.

the eight largest Venezuelan cities. The key to linking our survey questions to the Maisanta database was obtaining the unique personal identifier called the cédula. The cédula is a numerical identifier that is widely used in Venezuela not just for activities such as voting, paying taxes, and linking to social security records, but also for more mundane activities such as paying bills in restaurants; in terms of the frequency of use of the cédula in Venezuela and the level of privacy expectations associated with its disclosure, it is probably close to an individual telephone number in the United States, although as an instrument for linking data from multiple sources, it is more akin to a U.S. Social Security number.[25] We were able to obtain valid cédula numbers and merge them with the Maisanta database for about one-quarter of respondents; in the next section, we discuss threats to causal inference that might arise from missing data as well as other sources.

We focus in our analysis on receipt of benefits through participation in two targeted social programs, the Robinson Mission and the Ribas Mission. The former is an adult literacy program and the latter is a high-school equivalency program. Both provide scholarships to many of their participants; for example, payments under the Ribas Mission come in the form of "grants" (of Bs. 180,000 a month as of 2004, or about US$85 at official exchange rates) and "incentives" (of Bs. 200,000, or about US$94). Ribas and Robinson are only two of the Missions that provide benefits to Venezuelans, yet they best characterize the kind of benefits that may be targeted to swing voters or loyal constituents, following political criteria.

C.2.3 Threats to Causal Inference

When discussing inferences about the effects of voter ideology and turnout propensity on the likelihood of receiving a social benefit, it is useful to separate biases that may arise from survey nonresponse – in particular, our inability to match around three-quarters of the survey respondents to records in the Maisanta database – from other possible sources of bias, that is, those that could arise even with zero nonresponse. It turns out, however, that our attempts to confront these distinct issues will lead us to similar solutions.

First, the issue of nonresponse and missing data, always an issue with surveys, is especially important here: we only merged respondents' back to Maisanta using valid self-reported cédula numbers for about a quarter of the respondents. Table C.2 presents tests of covariate balance, across the 493 survey respondents whom we successfully matched to a record in the Maisanta dataset and the 1,508 respondents whom we could not match; in most of the latter cases, the respondent did not provide us with an accurate national identifier (cédula). In the jargon, this missing data is ignorable if it is statistically

---

[25] It is important to emphasize that the confidentiality of respondents' identity was maintained at every stage of our research, which was approved by Yale's Human Subjects' Committee.

TABLE C.2. *Covariate Balance Tests (Merged vs. Unmerged Respondents)*

Covariate	Merged Respondents	Unmerged Respondents	Difference of Means	p value
Age	49.2	44.1	5.1	0.00
	(0.7)	(0.4)	(0.8)	
Sex	38.3	39.0	−0.7	0.79
(% male)	(2.2)	(1.3)	(2.5)	
Household size	3.58	3.03	0.54	0.03
(adults over 18)	(0.20)	(0.13)	(0.26)	
Household income	5.97	6.50	−0.53	0.00
(ascending 1–12 scale)	(0.09)	(0.05)	(0.10)	
Household income pc	1.97	2.46	−0.49	0.00
(1–12 scale, normalized by household size)	(0.05)	(0.03)	(0.06)	
Education	4.6	5.1	−0.5	0.00
(ascending 1–11 scale)	(0.1)	(0.1)	(0.1)	
Self-identified social class	2.80	2.74	0.06	0.05
(ascending 1–4 scale)	(0.02)	(0.02)	(0.03)	
Works in public sector	24.2	15.8	−8.4	0.01
(% of employed workers)	(3.1)	(1.7)	(3.3)	
Oficialista	47.9	33.3	14.6	0.00
(% identifying with party in governing coalition)	(2.3)	(1.27)	(2.6)	
Oficialista2	76.4	70.6	5.8	0.07
(% identifying with party in governing coalition)	(1.8)	(1.8)	(3.1)	

The table compares the 493 survey respondents whom we successfully merged with Maisanta records to the 1,508 respondents whom we could not (in most cases due to respondents' failure to provide an accurate identifier or *cédula*). Oficialista and Oficialista2 are dummy variables equal to 1 for respondents who identify with any party that is part of the Chavez coalition; in the former, respondents who identify with no party are coded as zero, whereas in the latter, they are treated as missing. The *p* values are based on a two-tailed test; bolded entries are significant at the 0.05 level.

independent of income, political ideology, and other variables that may determine receipt of social benefits. This seems unlikely, however. Indeed, Table C.2 confirms that survey respondents who provided us with valid cédula numbers tend to be older, poorer, and less educated than those who refused, and they are also more likely to work in the public sector.

It is also true that people who provided valid identifiers also tended disproportionately to support the government (final two rows of Table C.2). However, this problem does not appear as egregious as we expected. We can investigate the relationship between government support and provision of the cédula in two ways. First, the final two rows of Table C.2 compare the reported party identification of our Maisanta-matched and unmatched surve respondents. (The first variable, *Oficialista*, is a dichotomous indicator equal to 1 for respondents who identify with any party in the Chávez coalition, where 0 includes those who identify with other parties or with no parties; in the second row, *Oficialista2* drops respondents who identify with no party). Note that these are ex-post measures of political ideology, because they reflect what respondents told us in 2008 about the political party with which they identify; we obviously cannot use Maisanta to measure the political ideologue of survey respondents we could not match to the Maisanta records. Although we find that those who identify with one of the parties in the government coalition are more likely to have provided a valid identifier, it matters whether we code the approximately 45 percent of respondents who reported no party identification as being nongovernment supporters (as in the Oficialista variable) or instead exclude them and only compare respondents who identify with a government party to respondents who identify with a party of the opposition (as in the Oficialista2 variable). With the former measurement strategy, the difference between the Maisanta-matched and unmatched respondents is substantively large (14.6 percentage points) and statistically significant; with the latter, the difference is smaller (5.8 percentage points) and statistically insignificant. This suggests that missing national ID data come disproportionately from those who do not identify with a government party but also do not identify with the opposition. In other words, opposition supporters do not appear to be substantially less likely than government supporters to provide their identifiers.

Table C.3, which provides a second way of investigating the relationship between government support and provision of the cédula, confirms this finding. Here, we compare the distribution of ex-ante political ideology (as recorded in Maisanta) among those survey respondents who we were able to merge to Maisanta with the distribution in the population, that is, all registered voters in the Maisanta database. Note that only registered voters who were at least 23 years old in 2008, when we took our survey, could conceivably be included in Maisanta's list of registered voters as of 2003–2004; our merged sample thus comprises a sample (with possibly nonrandom missing data) from this group of voters. As the table shows, 28.46 percent of merged respondents and 24.64 percent of the Maisanta population are opposition voters: thus the proportion of signers of the petition to recall Chávez is similar in our merged sample and in the Maisanta population. Howevere for loyal voters, we have 26.42 percent of merged respondents and just 12.35 percent of voters in the Maisanta population. The difference is made up by swing voters, who comprise 45.12 percent of merged respondents and 63.01 percent of the random sample of Maisanta. This table suggests the same story as Table C.2: opposition voters are not disproportionately likely to withhold their cédulas, but the proportion of loyal `·- ~~eater` in our sample of merged respondents than in the Maisanta `e` that respondents cannot manipulate the information about `leology` that is contained in Maisanta: if a greater propor- `ters` appear in our sample of matched respondents than in a

TABLE C.3. *Does Political Ideology Predict the Missing Data? (Merged Respondents vs. Maisanta Population)*

	Core Voter ("Patriota")	Swing Voter ("No Firmó")	Opposition Voter ("Opositor")	*Total*
Merged Respondents	26.42% (N = 130)	44.92% (N = 221)	28.46% (N = 140)	100.00% (N = 491)
Maisanta Population	12.35% (N = 1,530,673)	63.01% (N = 7,809,528)	24.64% (N = 3,053,908)	100.00% (N = 12,394,109)

The first row of the table shows the distribution of political ideology as recorded in Maisanta (for those cases we were able to merge with the Maisanta database, N = 492). The second row of the table shows the distribution of political ideology in the universe of registered voters included in the Maisanta database (N = 12,394,109). Percentages may not sum to 100% due to rounding.

representative sample from the Maisanta database, it is because some other category of voters is underreporting cédulas (and not because loyal voters are overreporting). The evidence therefore confirms that swing voters (those who did not sign either recall petition) are the ones doing the underreporting.[26] Nonetheless, the results in Tables C.2 and C.3 suggest that, in general, the missing data are not missing at random. In some of the analyses in the text, we condition on variables that predict the missing data, such as those in Table C.2, in the hope that the missing data will be ignorable conditional on covariates. Yet this provides one potential limitation on the validity of causal inferences drawn from our analysis of the Maisanta data – which is why we also present analyses using self-reported ideology, where these threats to inference from missing data do not arise (yet other limitations present themselves there).

A distinct set of threats to causal inferences arises not from missing data but from another sort of confounding: possible self-selection into Mission participation. For example, one obvious issue is that eligibility for adult education and other targeted social programs of the government – which often carry a financial reward for participants – depends in part on income and education levels. We therefore need to control for such variables – that is, we need to compare individuals with similar income and education levels and ask, for these individuals, how ex-ante political ideology and turnout propensity shape

[26] We have also compared the distribution of the Maisanta political ideology measures and turnout propensity in our sample of matched respondents and in a simple random sample of records from the Maisanta data base. (When doing cross-tabs of ideology and turnout propensity, it is useful to work with a random sample from Maisanta: the database is so large that substantial computing power is required to work with the full database). Our analysis here too suggests that the percentage of loyal voters is similar in the matched sample and in Maisanta population. However, in the sample of merged respondents, the marginal distribution of potential voters (absencionistas) is 23.78 percent, whereas it is 44.13 percent in the random sample of records. Thus merged respondents are less likely to be abstencionistas than voters in the random sample. Because Maisanta has missing data on perceived abstention for about one-third of the cases, in Table C.3 we look at political ideology without conditioning on abstention.

ex-post participation and benefit receipt. We do have substantial capacity to match on observed confounders that predict benefit receipt and may predict political ideology. For example, education may be an important confounder: after all, eligibility for participation in a high-school equivalency program such as Ribas depends on not having completed high school. Our ability to match on political ideology would be limited if opposition voters (those who signed against Chávez) could not be readily found along lower-education groups (or, conversely, if pro-Chávez signers from the opposition only came from upper education groups). (In the jargon, this would occur if the distribution of the political ideology variable by education level did not have common support.) However, supplementary analysis shows this is not the case: the distribution of ex-ante political ideology, as by signing of recall petitions, is substantially similar for those who have completed high school and those whose secondary education remains incomplete. Moreover, many of the variables that predict missingness (Table C.2) likely also predict political ideology, abstention, and social benefit receipt.

In Table 2.2 in the text, we therefore use matching and logistic regression to condition on variables such as gender, age, education, whether the respondent is a public-sector worker, and geographic place of residence. If a voter with a particular ex-ante political ideology or turnout propensity is, on average, substantially more likely to participate in a targeted social program than a voter with a different ideology or turnout profile – even though the voters share the same values on gender, age, education, occupation, or place-of-residence variables – we can have greater confidence that ideology and turnout propensity have a causal effect on benefit receipt. The size of some of the effects we report suggest that there is an electoral logic to social spending in Venezuela, as hidden confounders would have to be large to explain these effects. Nonetheless, a major concern here is the possibility of selection on unobservables; that is, unmeasured factors that are related to political loyalties and that cause receipt of benefits through Mission programs. The possibility of such unobserved confounders is one reason we do not push conditioning strategies very far in the text. Instead, we present our evidence from Venezuela as strongly suggestive of a loyal-voter logic to distribution, but not as conclusive or fully dispositive. Instead we turn to other research designs in different contexts that help to address some of the threats to valid causal inference discussed here.

Appendix D
India Voters' Survey

Our voters' survey in the Indian states of Karnataka, Bihar, and Rajasthan took place in the context of a study of the effect of caste-based quotas in local village councils (see Dunning 2010, Dunning and Nilekani 2012).[1] To select our study group of councils (called *gram panchayats*), we first purposively sampled six districts in Karnataka, which vary in terms of strength of different parties and locally dominant castes. We took advantage of the procedure by which quotas rotate across councils in different electoral terms to construct a regression-discontinuity (RD) design, in which the assignment to caste-based quotas was either truly randomized or as good a randomly assigned (see Dunning 2009). Using this RD design, we constructed a study group of 200 village council constituencies, 100 of which had their presidencies reserved for Scheduled Caste or Scheduled Tribe presidents in 2007 and 100 of which were unreserved or reserved for Backward Classes. Although council constituencies were selected according to the RD design, rather than by a probability sampling scheme, and although the six included districts were purposively sampled, means on a variety of covariates are quite similar in our selected councils and in a statewide dataset, suggesting that our sample may be quite representative of the state of Karnataka. Indeed, as the final column of Table Appendix D.1 shows, the data are consistent with a simple random sample from the underlying population of village councils.

We selected citizens at random, using an interval sampling method, in each of the 200 councils in our study group. Our sampling design called for a stratified random sample of 10 citizens drawn from the headquarter village of each council. Because we oversampled Scheduled Caste and Scheduled Tribe citizens by design, in some analyses we use sampling weights to recover parameter

---

[1] The surveys were approved by the Yale Human Subjects Expedited Review Committee under 1RB Protocols #0812004564 and #1106008688.

TABLE D.1. *Representativeness of the RD Study Group (Karnataka)*

	Average of Councils in Study Group (SD)	Average of Councils in Karnataka (SD)	Difference of Means (SE)
Population	5869.7	6132.1	−262.4
	(1912.03)	(2287.1)	(135.2)
Scheduled Caste population	1116.7	1129.7	−13.0
	(805.7)	(760.2)	(57.0)
Scheduled Tribe population	475.2	512.5	−37.3
	(506.5)	(715.8)	(35.8)
Number of literates	3196.1	3122.7	73.4
	(1133.4)	(1326.7)	(80.1)
Number of employed workers	2938.9	3005.9	−67.0
	(979.3)	(1092.5)	(69.2)
Number of councils	200	5760	

The unit of analysis is the village council; data are from the 2001 census. The first column gives the sample means and standard deviations (SD) for our Karnataka study group. The second column gives the population means and standard deviations, as measured by the census. The final column gives the difference between the first and second columns. The standard error (SE) in the final column is the standard deviation in the first column, divided by the square root of 200. Here, p values will give the probability of observing a sample mean as far in absolute value from the population mean as the observed value, if the N = 200 study group is a simple random sample from the population. * $p < 0.05$.

estimates that are valid for the population in our study group of councils. Citizens were asked a range of questions about benefit receipt and party affiliation and also participated in an experiment designed to assess the role of caste in shaping voting preferences. In each village, we also surveyed the council president, council secretary, and two council members. Fieldwork was undertaken in January–February 2009, over a year after the election of the council president in September 2007; the survey instruments and other materials are available online.[2]

---

[2] See http://www.thaddunning.com/research/all-research.

References

Abadie, A., D. Drukker, J. L. Herr, and G. W. Imbens. 2004. "Implementing matching estimators for average treatment effects in Stata." *Stata Journal* 4(3): 290–311.

Abernethy, Lloyd M. 1963. "Insurgency in Philadelphia, 1905." *Pennsylvania Magazine of History and Biography* 86: 7–20.

Abu El-Haj, Tabatha. 2011. "Changing the People: Legal Regulation and American Democracy." *New York University Law Review* 86(1): 1–68.

Acemoglu, Daron and James A. Robinson. 2006. *The Economic Origins of Dictatorship and Democracy*. Cambridge University Press.

Achen, Christopher H. 1992. "Social Psychology, Demographic Variables, and Linear Regression: Breaking the Iron Triangle in Voting Research." *Political Behavior* 14(3): 195–211.

Aidt, Toke S. and Peter S. Jensen. 2011. *From Open to Secret Ballot: Vote Buying and Modernization*. Unpublished typescript, University of Cambridge.

Albertus, Michael. 2010. "A Revolution for Whom? Measuring Political Bias in the Venezuelan Land Reform Using *Maisanta*." Department of Political Science, University of Chicago.

Aldrich, John. 1995. *Why Parties? The Origin and Transformation of Political Parties in America*. University of Chicago.

Alesina, Alberto, and Stephen E. Spear. 1988. "An Overlapping Generation Model of Electoral Competition." *Journal of Public Economics* 37(3): 359–379.

Alvarez, R. Michael 1997. *Information and Elections*. University of Michigan Press.

Ames, Barry. 2001. *The Deadlock of Democracy in Brazil*. University of Michigan Press.

Ansolabehere, Stephen, James M. Snyder, Jr., Aaron B. Strauss, and Michael M. Ting. 2005. "Voting Weights and Formateur Advantages in the Formation of Coalition Governments." *American Journal of Political Science* 49(3): 550–563.

Ansolobehere, Stephen, and James M. Snyder, Jr. 2006. "Party Control of State Government and the Distribution of Public Expenditures." *Scandinavian Journal of Economics* 108(4): 547–569.

Arulampalam, Wiji, Sugato Dasgupta, Amrita Dhillon, and Bhaskar Dutta. 2009. "Electoral goals and center-state transfers: A theoretical model and empirical evidence from India." *Journal of Development Economics* 88(1): 103–119.

Auyero Javier. 2001. *Poor People's Politics: Peronist Survival Networks and the Legacy of Evita*. Duke University Press.

Baland, Jean-Marie, and James A. Robinson. 2007. "How Does Vote Buying Shape the Economy?" In Frederic Charles Schaffer, ed., *Elections for Sale: The Causes and Consequences of Vote Buying*. Lynn Rienner.

Banfield, Edward, and James Q. Wilson. 1963. *City Politics*. Harvard University Press.

Banful, Afua Branoah. 2011. "Do Formula-Based Intergovernmental Transfer Mechanisms Eliminate Politically Motivated Targeting? Evidence from Ghana." *Journal of Development Economics* 96(2): 380–390.

Baron, David and John Ferejohn. 1989. "Bargaining in Legislatures." *American Political Science Review* 83: 1181–1206.

Barry, Brian. 1995. *Justice as Impartiality*. Clarendon Press.

Bensel, Richard F. 2004. *The American Ballot Box in the Mid-Nineteenth Century*. Cambridge University Press.

Berry, Christopher, R., Barry C. Burden, and William G. Howell. 2010. "The President and the Distribution of Federal Spending." *American Political Science Review* 104(4): 783–799.

Besley, Timothy, Rohini Pande, and Vijayendra Rao. 2008. "The Political Economy of the *Gram Panchayats* in South India." In Gopal K. Kadekodi, Ravi Kanbur, and Vijayendra Rao, eds., *Development in Karnataka: Challenges of Governance, Equity, and Empowerment*. Academic Foundation.

Bickel P. J, and Freedman, David A. 1981. "Some asymptotic theory for the bootstrap." *Annals of Statistics* 9: 1196–1217.

Bickel P. J, and Freedman, David A. 1984. "Asymptotic Normality and the Bootstrap in Stratified Sampling." *Annals of Statistics* 12(2): 470–482.

Bickers, Kenneth N. and Robert M. Stein. 2000. "The Congressional Pork Barrel in a Republican Era." *Journal of Politics* 62(4): 1070–1086.

Boix, Carles. 1998. *Political Parties, Growth, and Equality. Conservative and Social Democratic Strategies in the World Economy*. Cambridge University Press.

Breeding, Mary E. 2011. "The Micro-Politics of Vote Banks in Karnataka." *Economic & Political Weekly* XLVI(14): 71–77.

Bruhn, Kathleen. 1996. "Social Spending and Political Support: The Lessons of the National Solidarity Program in Mexico." *Comparative Politics* 28(2): 151–177.

Brusco, Valeria, Marcelo Nazareno, and Susan C. Stokes. 2004. "Vote Buying in Argentina." *Latin American Research Review* 35: 55–81.

Brusco, Valeria, Thad Dunning, Marcelo Nazareno, and Susan C. Stokes. 2007. "Poverty, Risk, and Clientelism." Paper prepared for delivery at the 2007 Annual Meeting of the American Political Science Association, August 30-September 2, 2007.

Buchanon, J.M. and Gordon Tullock. *The Calculus of Consent*. University of Michigan Press.

Buendía Laredo, Jorge. 2000. *Uncertainty and Voting Behavior in Transitions to Democracy*. Ph.D. dissertation, Department of Political Science, University of Chicago.

Burnham, Walter D. 1965. "The Changing Shape of the American Political Universe." *American Political Science Review* 54: 7–28.

Burnham, Walter D. 1974. "Theory and Voting Research: On Converse's 'Change in the American Electorate.'" *American Political Science Review* 68(3): 1002–1023.

Bussell, Jennifer. 2012. *Corruption and Reform in India: Public Services in the Digital Age.* Cambridge University Press.

Calvo, Ernesto and Maria Victoria Murillo. 2004. "Who Delivers? Partisan Clients in Argentine Electoral Market." *American Journal of Political Science* 48(4): 742–757.

Camp, Eddie. 2012. *Throwing a Wrench Into the Machine: The Costs of Brokers.* Unpublished doctoral dissertation, Yale University.

Camp, Edwin, Avinash Dixit, and Susan Stokes. *Prisoners of Strategy: Costly Ties and Distributive Politics.* Unpublished typescript, Yale University.

Campbell, Angus. 1960. "Surge and Decline: A Study of Electoral Change." *Public Opinion Quarterly* 24: 397–418.

Campbell, Angus, Philip E. Converse, Warren E. Miller, and Donald E. Stokes. *The American Voter.* Wiley.

Carey, John M. and Matthew Soberg Shurgart. 1995. "Incentives to Cultivate a Personal Vote: A Rank Ordering of Electoral Formulas." *Electoral Studies* 14(4): 417–439.

Caro, Robert A. 1974. *Power Broker: Robert Moses and the Fall of New York*, Knopf.

Carter Center. 2004. "Report on an Analysis of the Representativeness of the Second Audit Sample, and the Correlation between Petition Signers and the Yes Vote in the Aug. 15, 2004 Presidential Recall Referendum in Venezuela." Carter Center.

Case, Anne. 2001. "Election Goals and Income Redistribution: Recent Evidence from Albania." *European Economic Review* 45: 405–423.

Castells, Antoni, and Albert Solé-Ollé. 2005. "The Regional Allocation of Infrastructure Investment: The Role of Equity, Efficiency and Political Factors." *European Economic Review* 49: 1165–1205.

Chandra, Kanchan. 2004. *Why Ethnic Parties Succeed: Patronage and Ethnic Head Counts in India.* Cambridge University Press.

Chao, Min-Te and Shaw-Hwa Lo. 1985. "A Bootstrap Method for Finite Population." *Indian Journal of Statistics*, Series A, 47(3): 399–405.

Chattopadhyay, Raghabendra and Esther Duflo. 2004. "Impact of Reservation in Panchayati Raj: Evidence from a Nationwide Randomised Experiment." *Economic and Political Weekly* 39(9): 979–986.

Chen, Jowei. 2008. "Republican Vote Buying in the 2004 Presidential Election." Manuscript, Department of Political Science, Stanford University.

Chen, Jowei. 2009. "When Do Government Benefits Influence Voters' Behavior?" Unpublished manuscript, Department of Political Science, University of Michigan.

Chubb, Judith. 1981. "The Social Bases of an Urban Political Machine: The Case of Palermo." *Political Science Quarterly* 96(1): 107–125.

Chubb, Judith. 1982. *Patronage, Power, and Poverty in Southern Italy.* Cambridge University Press.

Collier, Ruth Berins. 1992. *The Contradictory Alliance: State-Labor Relations and Regime Change in Mexico.* University of California Press.

Collier, Ruth Berins, and Samuel Handlin, eds. 2009. *Reorganizing Popular Politics: Participation and the New Interest Regime in Latin America.* Pennsylvania State University Press.

Cole, Shawn. 2009. "Fixing Market Failures or Fixing Elections? Agricultural Credit in India." *American Economic Journal: Applied Economics* 1(1): 219–250.

Coleman, James S. 1966. "The Possibility of a Social Welfare Function." *American Economic Review* 56(5): 1105–1122.

Converse, Philip E. 1972. "Change in the American Electorate." In Angus Campbell and Philip E. Converse, eds., *The Human Meaning of Social Change*. Russell Sage Foundation, 263–337.

Coppedge, Michael. 1994. *Strong Parties and Lame Ducks: Presidential Partyarchy and Factionalism in Venezuela*. Stanford University Press.

Cornelius, Wayne A. 2004. "Mobilized Voting in the 2000 Elections: The Changing Efficacy of Vote Buying and Coercion in Mexican Electoral Politics." In Jorge I. Domínguez and Chappell H. Lawson, ed, *Mexico's Pivotal Democratic Elections: Candidates, Voters, and the Presidential Campaign of 2000*. Stanford University Press.

Corstange, Daniel. 2010. *Vote Buying under Competition and Monopsony: Evidence from a List Experiment in Lebanon*. Paper presented at 2010 Annual Conference of the American Political Science Association, Washington, D.C.

Cox, Gary. 1987. *The Efficient Secret: The Cabinet in the Development of Political Parties in Victorian England*. Cambridge University Press.

Cox, Gary. 1997. *Making Votes Count: Strategic Coordination and the World's Electoral Systems*. Cambridge University Press.

Cox, Gary W. 2009. "Swing Voters, Core Voters and Distributive Politics." In Ian Shapiro, Susan Stokes, Elisabeth Jean Wood, and Alexander S. Kirshner, eds., *Political Representation*. Cambridge University Press.

Cox, Gary W. and J. Morgan Kousser. 1981. "Turnout and Rural Corruption-New York as a Test Case." *American Journal of Political Science* 25: 646–663.

Cox, Gary W. and Mathew D. McCubbins. 1986. "Electoral Politics as a Redistributive Game." *Journal of Politics* 48(2): 370–389.

Craig, F.W.S., 1989. *British Electoral Facts 1832–1987*. Parliamentary Research Services.

Crampton, Erick. 2004. *Distributive Politics in a Strong Party System: Evidence from Canadian Job Grant Programs*. Presented at the Public Choice Society.

Dahlberg, Matz, and Eva Johansson. 2002. "On the Vote Purchasing Behavior of Incumbent Governments." *American Political Science Review* 96(1): 27–40.

Deacon, Robert and Perry Shapiro. 1975. "Private Preference for Collective Goods Revealed Through Voting on Referenda." *American Economic Review* 65(5): 943–955.

De la O, Ana. 2012. *The Silent Transformation of Social Assistance in Latin America*. Unpublished typescript, Yale University.

Denemark, David. 2000. "Partisan Pork-Barrel in Parliamentary Systems: Australian Constituency-Level Grants." *Journal of Politics* 62(3): 896–915.

De Luca, Miguel, Mark Jones and María Inés Tula. 2006. "Machine Politics and Party Primaries: The Uses and Consequences of Primaries within a Clientelist Political System." Paper prepared for the conference of the Mobilizing Democracy Group of the American Political Science Association, New York, January 2006.

Desposato, Scott. 2006. "How Informal Electoral Institutions Shape the Brazilian Legislative Arena." In Gretchen Helmke and Steven Levitsky, eds., *Informal Institutions and Democracy: Lessons from Latin America*. Johns Hopkins University Press.

Diaz-Cayeros, Alberto, Magaloni, Beatriz and Federico Estévez. *Strategies of Vote Buying: Democracy, Clientelism, and Poverty Relief in Mexico*. Forthcoming, Cambridge University Press.

Diener, Ed and Robert Biswas-Diener. 2002. "Will Money Increase Subjective Well-Being?" *Social Indicators Research* 57(2): 119–169.

Dixit, Avinash, and John Londregan. 1996. "The Determinants of Success of Special Interests in Redistributive Politics." *Journal of Politics* 58(4): 1132–1155.

Dorsett, Lyle W. 1977. *Franklin D. Roosevelt and the City Bosses*. Kennikat.

Downs, Anthony. 1957. *An Economic Theory of Democracy*. Harper.

Dunning, Thad. 2008. *Crude Democracy: Natural Resource Wealth and Political Regimes*. Cambridge University Press.

Dunning, Thad. 2010. "Do Quotas Promote Ethnic Solidarity? Field and Natural Experimental Evidence from India." Unpublished typescript, Yale University.

Dunning, Thad. 2012. *Natural Experiments in the Social Sciences: A Design-Based Approach*. Cambridge University Press.

Dunning, Thad and Janhavi Nilekani. 2013. "Ethnic Quotas and Political Mobilization: Caste, Parties, and Distribution in Indian Village Councils." *American Political Science Review* 107(1): 35–56.

Dunning, Thad, and Susan C. Stokes. 2007. *Clientelism as Mobilization and as Persuasion*. Unpublished typescript, Yale University.

Efron, B. 1979. "Bootstrap Methods: Another Look at the Jackknife." *Annals of Statistics* 1: 1–26.

Eggers, Andrew, and Arthur Spirling. 2011. *Electoral Corruption Trials in 19th Century Britain: Partisan Bias and Bipartisan Reform*. Unpublished typescript, Yale University and London School of Economics.

Erie, Steven P. 1988. *Rainbow's End: Irish Americans and the Dilemmas of Urban Machine Politics, 1840–1945*. University of California Press.

Faughnan, Brian M. and Elizabeth J. Zechmeister. 2011. "Vote Buying in the Americas." *Americas Barometer Insights* 57, Vanderbilt University.

Fiszbein, Ariel, and Norbert Schady. 2009. *Conditional Cash Transfers: Reducing Present and Future Poverty*. The World Bank.

Fenno, Richard F., Jr. *Home Style: House Members in their Districts*. Little, Brown.

Folke, Olle, Shigeo Hirano, and James M. Snyder, Jr. 2011. "Patronage and Elections in the U.S. States." *American Political Science Review* 105(3): 562–585.

Frederick, Brian. 2008. "Constituency Population and Representation in the U.S. House." *American Politics Research* 36(3): 358–381.

Freedman, David A. 2005. *Statistical Models: Theory and Practice*. Cambridge University Press.

Freedman, David A., Robert Pisani, and Roger Purves. 2007. *Statistics*, 4th Edition. Norton.

Gamson, William. 1961. "A Theory of Coalition Formation." *American Sociological Review* 26: 373–382.

Gans-Morse, Jordan, Sebastián Mazzuca, and Simeon Nichter. 2009. "Who Gets Bought? Vote Buying, Turnout Buying, and Other Strategies." Working paper 2009-0006, Weatherhead Center for International Affairs, Harvard University, April 2009.

Garrett, Geoffrey. 2001 "Globalization and Government Spending Around the World." *Studies in Comparative International Development* 35(4): 3–29.

Geddes, Barbara. 1991. "A Game Theoretic Model of Reform in Latin American Democracies." *American Political Science Review* 85(2): 371–392.

Geddes, Barbara. 1994. *Politician's Dilemma: Building State Capacity in Latin America.* University of California Press.

Gerber, Alan S., Gregory A. Huber, David Doherty, and Conor M. Dowling. 2013. "Is There a Secret Ballot? Ballot Secrecy Perceptions and Their Implications for Voting Behaviour." *British Journal of Political Science* 43(1): 77–102.

Gerber, Alan S., and Donald P. Green, 2000. "The Effects of Canvassing, Telephone Calls, and Direct Mail on Voter Turnout: A Field Experiment." *American Political Science Review* 94: 653–663.

Gibson, Edward L., and Ernesto Calvo. 2000. "Federalism and Low-Maintenance Constituencies: Territorial Dimensions of Economic Reform in Argentina." *Studies in Comparative International Development* 35(3): 32–55.

Golden, Miriam, and Lucio Picci. 2008. "Pork-Barrel Politics in Postwar Italy, 1953–94." *American Journal of Political Science* 52(2): 268–289.

Golden, Miriam, and Lucio Picci. 2011. "Redistribution and Reelection under Proportional Representation: The Postwar Italian Chamber of Deputies." Manuscript, Department of Political Science, UCLA, and Department of Economics, University of Bologna.

González-Ocantos, Ezequiel, Chad Kiewiet de Jonge, Carlos Meléndez, Javier Osorio, and David W. Nickerson. 2011. "Vote Buying and Social Desirability Bias: Experimental Evidence from Nicaragua." *American Journal of Political Science* 56(1): 202–217.

Gordin, Jorge P. 2006. "Intergovernmental Fiscal Relations, 'Argentine Style'." *Journal of Public Policy* 26(3): 255–277.

Green, Donald, Bradley Palmquist, and Eric Schickler. 2004. *Partisan Hearts and Minds: Political Parties and the Social Identities of Voters.* Yale University Press.

Greene, Kenneth F. 2007. *Why Dominant Parties Lose: Mexico's Democratization in Comparative Perspective.* Cambridge University Press.

Hanham, H.J. 1959. *Elections and Party Managements: Politics in the Time of Disraeli and Gladstone.* Harvester.

Harding, Robin. 2008. *Vote Buying Across Africa.* Unpublished manuscript, New York University.

Harrington, Joseph E. 1993. "The Impact of Reelection Pressures on the Fulfillment of Campaign Promises." *Games and Economic Behavior* 5(1): 71–97.

Hasen, Richard L. 2000. "Vote Buying." *California Law Review* 88(5): 1323–1371.

Hausmann, Ricardo and Roberto Rigobón. 2004. "In Search of the Black Swan: Analysis of the Statistical Evidence of Electoral Fraud in Venezuela." Manuscript, Harvard University and Massachusetts Institute of Technology.

Hawkins, Kurt. 2010. *Venezuela's Chavismo and Populism in Comparative Perspective.* Cambridge University Press.

Herron, Michael C. and Brett A. Theodus. 2004. "Government Redistribution in the Shadow of Legislative Elections: A Study of the Illinois Member Initiative Grants Program." *Legislative Studies Quarterly* 29(2): 287–311.

Hersh, Eitan D. and Brian F. Schaffner. 2011. *Campaign Voter Engagement Strategy in Competitive and Uncompetitive Elections.* Unpublished manuscript, Yale University.

Hibbs, Douglas A. 1987. *The Political Economy of Industrial Democracies.* Harvard University Press.

Hiskey, Jonathan. 1999. *Does Democracy Matter? Electoral Competition and Local Development in Mexico.* Doctoral dissertation, University of Pittsburgh.

Hirschman, Albert O. 1970. *Exit, Voice, and Loyalty.* Harvard.

Hoppen, Theodore K. 2000. *The Mid-Victorian Generation: 1846–1886.* Oxford University Press.

Horiuchi, Yusaku and Seungjoo Lee. 2008. "The Presidency, Regionalism, and Distributive Politics in South Korea." *Comparative Political Studies* 41(6): 861–882.

Hsieh, Chang-Tai, Edward Miguel, Daniel Ortega, and Francisco Rodríguez. 2011. "The Price of Political Opposition: Evidence from Venezuela's Maisanta." *American Economic Journal: Applied Economics* 3(2): 196–214.

Huber, John D. and Nolan McCarty. 2004. "Bureaucratic Capacity, Delegation, and Political Reform." *American Political Science Review* 98(3): 481–494.

Inglehart, Ronald. 2000. "Globalization and Post-Modern Values." *The Washington Quarterly* 23(1): 215–228.

James, Scott C. 2005. "Patronage Regimes and American Party Development from the 'Age of Jackson' to the Progressive Era." *British Journal of Political Science* 36: 39–60.

Jeansonne, Glen. 1977. *Leander Perez: Boss of the Delta.* LSU Press.

Jeffries, Julie. 2005. *People and Migration, The UK population: Past, Present and Future.* http://www.statistics.gov.uk/downloads.

Jenkins, Jefferey A. 2004. "Partisanship and Contested Election Cases in the House of Representatives, 1789–2002." *Studies in American Political Development* 18: 112–135.

Jenkins, Roy. 2002. *Gladstone: A Biography.* MacMillan.

Johansson, Eva. 2003. "Intergovernmental Grants as a Tactical Instrument: Empirical Evidence from Swedish Municipalities." *Journal of Public Economics* 87: 883–915.

John, Peter, and Hugh Ward. 2001. "Political Manipulation in a Majoritarian Democracy: Central Government Targeting of Public Funds to English Subnational Government, in Space and Across Time." *British Journal of Politics and International Relations* 3(3): 308–339.

John, Richard S. 1995. *Spreading the News: The American Postal System from Franklin to Morse.* Harvard University Press.

Kam, Christopher. 2009. *Partisanship, Enfranchisement, and the Political Economy of Electioneering in the United Kingdom, 1826–1906.* Unpublished typescript, University of British Columbia.

Karlan, Pamela. 1994. "Not by Virtue but by Money Won? Vote Trafficking and the Voting Rights Systems." *Virginia Law Review* 80: 1455–1475.

Keefer, Philip. 2007. "Clientelism, Credibility, and the Policy Choices of Young Democracies." *American Journal of Political Science* 51(4): 804–821.

Keefer, Philip and Razvan Vlaicu. 2008. "Democracy,Credibility, and Clientelism." *Journal of Law, Economics, and Organization* 24(2): 371–406.

Key, V.O., Jr. 1950. *Southern Politics in State and Nation.* Alfred A. Knopf.

Keyssar, Alexander. 2001. *The Right to Vote: The Contested History of Democracy in the United States.* Basic Books.

Khemani, Stuti. 2007. "Does Delegation of Fiscal Policy to an Independent Agency Make a Difference? Evidence from Intergovernmental Transfers in India." *Journal of Development Economics* 82(2): 464–484.

Kish, Leslie. 1965. *Survey Sampling.* Wiley.

Kleppner, Paul. 1982. *Who Voted? The Dynamics of Electoral Turnout, 1870–1980.* Praeger.

Klingeman, Hans-Dieter, Richard Hofferbert, and Ian Budge. 1994. *Parties, Policies, and Democracy.* Westview Press.

Knights, Mark. 1994. *Politics and Opinion in Crisis, 1678–1681.* Cambridge University Press.

Kitschelt, Herbert. 2011. *Linkage Strategies: A Descriptive Exploration.* Unpublished typescript, Duke University.

Kitschelt, Herbert. 2000. "Linkages between Citizens and Politicians in Democratic Polities." *Comparative Political Studies* 33(6–7): 845–879.

Kitschelt, Hubert and Steven I. Wilkinson. 2007. "Citizen-Politician Linkages: An Introduction." In *Patrons, Clients, and Policies: Patterns of Democratic Accountability and Political Competition.* Cambridge University Press.

Kuo, Didi, Jan Teorell, and Daniel Ziblatt. 2011. *Election Fraud and Contested Congressional Elections: An Analysis of the United States, 1840–1940.* Paper presented at the Annual Meeting of the American Political Science Association, Seattle, September 1–4.

Krishna, Anirudh. 2003. "What Is Happening to Caste? A View from Some North Indian Villages." *The Journal of Asian Studies* 62(4): 1171–1193.

Kwon, Kyeok Yong. 2005. "Targeting Public Spending in a New Democracy: Evidence from South Korea." *British Journal of Political Science* 35: 321–341.

Lawson, Chappell and Kenneth F. Greene. 2011. *Self-Enforcing Clientelism.* Unpublished typescript, MIT.

Lehoucq, Fabrice and Iván Molina. 2002. *Stuffing the Ballot Box: Fraud, Reform, and Democratization in Costa Rica.* Cambridge University Press.

Leip, Dave. 2005. *Atlas of U.S. Presidential Elections.* http://uselectionatlas.org.

Levitt, Steven D. and James M. Snyder, Jr. 1995. "Political Parties and the Distribution of Federal Outlays." *American Journal of Political Science* 39(4): 958–980.

Levitt, Steven D. and James M. Snyder, Jr. 1997. "The Impact of Federal Spending on House Election Outcomes." *Journal of Political Economy* 105(1): 30–53.

Levitsky, Steve. 2003. *Transforming Labor-Based Parties in Latin America: Argentine Peronism in Comparative Perspective.* Cambridge University Press.

Lindbeck, Assar and Jorgen W. Weibull. 1987. "Balanced-budget Redistribution as the Outcome of Political Competition." *Public Choice* 52: 273–297.

Lindert, Peter H. 2000. "Three Centuries of Inequality in Britain and America." In Anthony B. Atkinson and Francois Bourguignon, eds., *Handbook of Income Distribution.* Elseiver, 167–216.

Lindert, Peter H. 2004. *Growing Public: Social Spending and Economic Growth since the Eighteenth Century.* Cambridge University Press.

Lippert-Rasmussen, Kasper. 2011. "Vote Buying and Election Promises: Should Democrats Care About the Difference?" *The Journal of Political Philosophy* 19(2): 125–144.

Lipset, Seymour Martin. 1959. "Some Social Requisites of Democracy: Economic Development and Political Legitimacy." *American Political Science Review* 53(1): 69–105.

Lizzeri, Alessandro and Nicola Persico. 2004. "Why Did Elites Extend the Suffrage? Democracy and the Scope of Government, with an Application to Britain's 'Age of Reform'." *Quarterly Journal of Economics* 119(2): 707–765.

Lodola, Germán. 2005. "Protesta Popular y Redes Clientelares en Argentina: El Reparto Federal del Plan Trabajar." *Desarrollo Económico* 176(44): 515–536.

Magaloni, Beatriz. 2006. *Voting for Autocracy: Hegemonic Party Survival and its Demise in Mexico.* Cambridge University Press.

Magaloni, Beatriz, Alberto Diaz-Cayeros, and Federico Estévez. 2007. "Clientelism and Portfolio Diversification: A Model of Electoral Investment with Applications to Mexico." In Herbert Kitschelt and Steven Wilkinson, eds., *Patrons, Clients, and Policies: Patterns of Democratic Accountability and Political Competition.* Cambridge University Press.

Manin, Bernard. 1997. *Principles of Representative Government.* Cambridge University Press.

Manor, James. 2000. "Small-Time Political Fixers in India's States: 'Towel over Armpit.'" *Asian Survey* 40(5): 816–835.

Mansbridge, Jane. 2010. "The Place of Self-Interest and the Role of Power in Deliberative Democracy." *The Journal of Political Philosophy* 18(1): 64–100.

May, John D. 1973. "Opinion Structure of Political Parties: The Special Law of Curvilinear Disparity." *Political Studies* 21(2): 133–151.

Mayhew, David. 1986. *Placing Parties in American Politics: Organization, Electoral Settings, and Government Activity in the Twentieth Century.* Yale University Press.

McCormick, Richard L. 1981a. *From Realignment to Reform: Political Change in New York State, 1893–1910.* Cornell University Press.

McCormick, Richard L. 1981b. "The Discovery that Business Corrupts Politics: A reappraisal of the Origins of Progressivism." *The American Historical Review* 86(2): 247–274.

Medina, Luis Fernando, and Susan C. Stokes. 2007. "Monopoly and Monitoring: An Approach to Political Clientelism." In Herbert Kitschelt and Steven Wilkinson, eds., *Patrons, Clients, and Policies: Patterns of Democratic Accountability and Political Competition.* Cambridge University Press.

Milligan, Kevin, and Michael Smart. 2005. "Regional Grants as Pork Barrel Politics." *CESifo Working Paper* 1453.

Molinar, Juan and Jeffrey A. Weldon. 1994. "Electoral Determinants and Consequences of National Solidarity." In Wayne A. Cornelius, Ann L. Craig and Jonathan Fox eds., *Transforming State-Society Relations in Mexico: the National Solidarity Strategy.* Center for U.S.-Mexican Studies, University of California, San Diego, 123–141.

MPD-SISOV. 2005. "Sistema Integrado de Indicatores Sociales de Venezuela." Ministerio del Poder Popular para la Manificación y Desarrollo. Available at www.sivov.mpd.gov.ve, accessed April 18, 2008.

Mueller, Dennis C. 1973. "Constitutional Democracy and Social Welfare." *Quarterly Journal of Economics* 87(1): 60–80.

Mutch, Robert E. *Campaigns, Congress and Courts: The Making of Federal Campaign Finance Law.* Greenwood Publishing.

Nazareno, Marcelo, Valeria Brusco, and Susan Stokes. 2006. "Réditos y Peligros Electorales del Gasto Público en Argentina." *Desarrollo Económico* 46(181): 63–86.

Nichter, Simeon. 2008. "Vote Buying or Turnout Buying? Machine Politics and the Secret Ballot." *American Political Science Review.* 102(1): 19–31.

Oldenburg, Philip. 1987. "Middlemen in Third-World Corruption: Implications of an Indian Case." *World Politics* 39(4): 508–535.

Ortega, Daniel, and Michael Penfold-Becerra. 2008. "Does Clientelism Work? Electoral Returns of Excludable and Non-Excludable Goods in Chávez's Misiones Programs in Venezuela." Manuscript, Instituto de Estudios Superiores de Administración (IESA).

O'Gorman, Frank. 1989. *Voters, Patrons, and Parties: The Unreformed Electoral System of Hanoverian England, 1734–1832*. Clarendon Press.

O'Gorman, Frank. 2001. "Patronage and the Reform of the State in England, 1700–1860." In Simona Piattoni, ed. *Clientelism, Interests, and Democratic Representation: The European Experience in Historical and Comparative Perspective*. Cambridge University Press, 54–76.

O'Leary, Cornelius. 1962. *The Elimination of Corrupt Practices in British Elections, 1868–1911*. Oxford University Press.

Myerson, Roger. 1982. "Optimal Coordination Mechanisms in Generalized Principal-Agent Problems." *Journal of Mathematical Economics* 10: 67–81.

Orr, Graeme. 2006. "Suppressing Vote-Buying: the 'War' on Electoral Bribery from 1868." *Journal of Legal History* 27(3): 289–314.

Papakostas, Apostolis. 2001. "Why is there No Clientelism in Scandinavia?: A Comparison of the Swedish and Greek Sequences of Development." In Simona Piattoni, ed., *Clientelism, Interests, and Democratic Representation: The European Experience in Historical and Comparative Perspective*. Cambridge University Press.

Pateman, Carol. 1970. *Participation and Democratic Theory*. Cambridge University Press.

Peacey, Jason. 2004. *Politicians and Pamphleteers: Propaganda During the English Civil Wars and Interregnum*. Ashgate.

Persson, Torsten and Guido Tabellini. 2000. *Political Economics: Explaining Economic Policy*. MIT Press.

Pincus, Steven. 2006. "Rethinking the Public Sphere in Early Modern England." *Journal of British Studies* 45(2): 270–292.

Pitkin, Hanna F. 1967. *The Concept of Representation*. University of California Press.

Putnam, Robert with Robert Leonardi and Raffaela Y. Nonetti. 1993. *Making Democracy Work: Civic Traditions in Modern Italy*. Princeton University Press.

Rabin, Matthew. 2000. "Risk Aversion and Expected-utility Theory: A Calibration Theorem." *Econometrica* 68(5): 1281–1292.

Rawls, John. 1996. *Political Liberalism*. Columbia University Press.

Rawls, John. 1971. *A Theory of Justice*. Harvard University Press.

Reif, Karlheinz, Roland Cayrol, and Oskar Niedermayer. 1980. "National Political Parties' Middle Level Elites and European Integration." *European Journal of Political Research* 8(1): 91–112.

Remmer, Karen L. 2007. "The Political Economy of Patronage: Expenditure Patterns in the Argentine Provinces, 1983–2003." *Journal of Politics* 69(2): 363–377.

Reynolds, John F. 1988. *Testing Democracy: Electoral Behavior and Progressive Reform in New Jersey, 1880–1920*. University of North Carolina Press.

Reynolds, John F. and Richard L. McCormick. 1986. "Outlawing 'Treachery': Split Tickets and Ballot Laws in New York and New Jersey, 1880–1910." *The Journal of American History* 72(4): 835–858.

Riordan, William L. 1994[1905]. *Plunkitt of Tammany Hall: A Series of Very Plain Talks on Very Practical Politics*. Ed. by Terrence J. MacDonald. Bedford/St. Martins.

Rix, Kathryn. 2008. "The Elimination of Corrupt Practices in British Elections? Reassessing the Impact of the Corrupt Practices Act of 1883." *English Historical Review* 123(500): 65–97.

Rocca, Helen M. 1928. *Corrupt Practices Legislation*. League of Women Voters.

Rodden, Jonathan, and Marta Arretche. 2003. *Legislative Bargaining and Distributive Politics in Brazil: An Empirical Approach*. Unpublished typescript, MIT.

Rodden, Jonathan, and Steven Wilkinson. 2004. *The Shifting Political Economy of Redistribution in the Indian Federation*. Unpublished manuscript, MIT.

Rosas, Guillermo, and Kirk Hawkins. 2008. "Turncoats, True Believers, and Turnout: Machine Politics in the Absence of Vote Monitoring." Manuscript, Departments of Political Science, Washington University in St. Louis and Brigham Young University.

Rosenstone, Steven J. and John Mark Hansen. 1993. *Mobilization, Participation, and Democracy in America*. MacMillan.

Sabato, Larry J. and Glenn R. Simpson. 1996. *Dirty Little Secrets: The Persistence of Corruption in American Politics*. Random House.

Salmon, Philip J. 2003. "Electoral Reform and the Political Modernization of England, 1832." *Parliaments, Estates, and Representation* 23: 49–67.

Scanlon, Thomas. 1998. *What We Owe to Each Other*. Harvard University Press.

Schady, Norbert R. 2000. "The Political Economy of Expenditures by the Peruvian Social Fund (FONCODES), 1991–1995." *The American Political Science Review* 94(2): 289–304.

Scott, James C. 1969. "Corruption, Machine Politics, and Political Change." *American Political Science Review* 63(4): 1142–1158.

Seymour, Charles. 1970[1915]. *Electoral Reform in England and Wales: The Development and Operation of the Parliamentary Franchise*. David and Charles Reprints.

Shefter, Martin. 1977. "Party and Patronage: Germany, England, and Italy." *Politics and Society* 7(4): 403–451.

Sikes, Earl R. 1928. *State and Federal Corrupt-Practices Legislation*. Duke University Press.

Skowronek, Stephen. 1982. *Building a New American State: The Expansion of National Administrative Capacities, 1877–1920*. Cambridge University Press.

Smith, Alastair, and Bruce Bueno de Mesquita. 2011. "Contingent Prize Allocation and Pivotal Voting." *British Journal of Political Science* 42(2): 371–392.

Smith, Michael. 2004. "Parliamentary Reform and the Electorate." In Chris Williams, ed., *A Companion to 19th Century Britain*. Blackwells.

Srinivas, M. N. 1955. "The Social Structure of Life in a Mysore Village." In McKim Marriott (ed.), *Village India*. University of Chicago Press.

Stokes, Susan C. 2001. *Mandates and Democracy: Neoliberalism by Surprise in Latin America*. Cambridge University Press.

Stokes, Susan C. 2005. "Perverse Accountability: A Formal Model of Machine Politics with Evidence from Argentina." *American Political Science Review* 99(3): 315–326.

Sunstein, Cass R. 1994. "Incommensurability and Valuation in Law." *Michigan Law Review* 92: 779–849.

Szwarcberg, Mariela. 2009. *Making Local Democracy Work: Political Machines, Clientelism, and Social Networks in Argentina*. Doctoral dissertation, Political Science Department, University of Chicago.

Szwarcberg, Mariela. 2013. "The Microfoundations of Political Clientelism: Lessons from the Argentine Case." *Latin American Research Review* 48(2).

Tam, Waikeung. 2008. *Political Insecurity and Clientelist Politics: The Case of Singapore.* Unpublished typescript, University of Chicago.

Teorell, Jan. 2011. *Cleaning Up the Vote: The Case of Electoral Fraud in Sweden, 1719–1909.* Unpublished typescript, University of Lund.

Tomz, Michael and Robert P. Van Houweling. 2009. "The Electoral Implications of Candidate Ambiguity." *American Political Science Review* 103(1): 83–98.

Vaishnav, Milan, and Neelanjan Sircar. 2010. *The Politics of Pork: Building Schools and Rewarding Voters in Tamil Nadu, India.* Unpublished typescript, Columbia University.

Vallance, Edward. 2009. *A Radical History of Britain.* Little, Brown.

Varbero, Richard A. *Urbanization and Acculturation: Philadelphia's South Italians 1918–1932.* Ph.D. dissertation, Temple University.

Veiga, Linda Goncalves and Maria Manuel Pinho. 2007. "The Political Economy of Intergovernmental Grants: Evidence from a Maturing Democracy." *Public Choice* 133(3/4): 457–477.

Verba, Sidney, Norman Nie and Jae-on Kim. 1978. *Participation and Political Equality.* Cambridge University Press.

Wade, Robert. 1985. "The Market for Public Office: Why the Indian State is Not Better at Development." *World Development* 13(4): 467–497.

Wallis, John Joseph. 1987. "Employment, Politics, and Economic Recovery during the Great Depression." *Review of Economics and Statistics* 69(3): 516–520.

Wantchekon, Leonard. 2003. "Clientelism and Voting Behavior: Evidence from a Field Experiment in Benin." *World Politics* 55(3): 399–422.

Weisskopf, Michael. 1978. "Baltimore: Politics as Usual: Precinct Payouts Typify Election Windup." *Washington Post*, September 11.

Weitz-Shapiro, Rebecca. 2011. *Choosing Clientelism: Politics, Poverty, and Social Policy in Argentina.* Unpublished manuscript, Brown University.

Wilkinson, Steven I. 2007. "Explaining Changing Patterns of Party-Voter Linkages in India." In Herbert Kitschelt and Steven I. Wilkinson, eds., *Patrons, Clients or Policies: Patterns of Democratic Accountability and Competition.* Cambridge University Press.

Winkler, Adam. 2000. "Voters' Rights and Parties' Wrongs: Early Political Party Regulation in the State Courts, 1886–1915." *Columbia Law Review* 100(3): 873–900.

Woodall, Robert. 1974. "The Ballot Act of 1872." *History Today* 24(7): 464–471.

Worthington, Andrew C. and Brian E. Dollery. 1998. "The Political Determination of Intergovernmental Grants in Australia." *Public Choice* 94(3/4): 299–315.

Wright, Gavin. 1974. "The Political Economy of New Deal Spending: An Econometric Analysis." *Review of Economics and Statistics* 56(1): 30–38.

Ziegfeld, Adam. 2012. "Coalition Government and Party System Change: Explaining the Rise of Regional Political Parties in India." *Comparative Politics* 45(1): 69–87.

Zucco, Cesar. 2012. *When Pay Outs Pay Off: Conditional Cash Transfers and Vote Buying in Brazil, 2002–2010.* SSRN: http://ssrn.com/abstract=1753234.

Index

abstention buying, definition of, 14n, 135
  normative implications of, 254
accountability, 183, 246, 252–254, 257–258
Adams County, Ohio, 227
Afrobarometer surveys, 154, 161, 165
Aid to Families with Dependent Children
  (United States), 229, 230
Albania, 137
Albany (city of, United States), 232
Alfonsín, Raúl (Argentina), 37
aligned district, definition of, 133
anggota tim sukses (success team members,
  Indonesia), 19
Anti-Corrupt Practices Act. See Corrupt and
  Illegal Practices Act of 1883 (Britain)
Ashton-under-Lyne, (borough of, Britain),
  224
Australia, 5, 10, 136
Australian Ballot, see Ballot
autonomy, of voters, 13, 154, 226, 246–247,
  249, 252–254, 257–258
Ávila, Eruviel (Mexico), 4

ballot,
  secrecy of, 19, 35, 81, 101, 104, 181, 182n,
    183, 202, 225
  party-produced or ticket, in United States,
    239, 242
  Australian, definition of, 101, 103n, 183,
    220, 227, 251
  official (United States), 205
  reform, and decline of clientelism, 184,
    184–185, 205, 241

reform of, United States, 184n, 220, 227,
  232, 238, 242, 251
reform of, Britain, 220, 221, 223–226
Ballot Act of 1872 (Britain), 220, 222, 225
Baltimore (city of, United States), 230, 232
Bangalore (city of, India), 160
Benin, 17
Beverly (borough of, Britain), 208, 223n
Bihar (India), 52–53, 65, 297
Birmingham, (constituencies in, Britain),
  214
Bolivia, 156
Bologna (city of, Italy)
bootstrapping, 98, 262, 265n, 271–275. (See
  also Bootstrapped standard errors.)
Boston (city of, United States), 232, 234
Botswana, 156
Brazil, 19, 155
Bright, John, 226
brokers, as information providers, 19
  definition of, 75
  utility function of, 81
Bush, George W., 143

cabos electorais (vote brokers, Brazil), 19
caciques (vote brokers, Mexico), 19, 96n
Campaign Manifestos Project, 9n
Can you Forgive Her? See also Anthony
  Trollope, 208
Canada, 25, 137
Cárdenas, Cuauhtémoc, 145
certain voters, definition of, 66
Chartists, 225

311

Uruguay, 156–157
Uttar Pradesh, 119

Vare machine (Philadelphia, United States),
 228
vecteurs (vectors, Senegal), 19
vote buying, definition of, 14
 and normative democratic theory, 246–248,
 251, 253–254, 256, 256n, 257–258
vote selling, see Vote buying
vote trafficking, see Vote buying

voters, utility function, 33
Vuelvan Caras, 45, 45n

weakly opposed voters, definition of,
 36
Works Progress Administration (WPA), 142,
 228–229
World Bank, 153

York (city of, Britain), 217
Yrigoyen, Hipólito, 120